Ching Chong China Girl

From fruitshop to foreign correspondent

Helene Chung

ABC Books

Published by ABC Books for the
AUSTRALIAN BROADCASTING CORPORATION
GPO BOX 9994 Sydney NSW 2001

Copyright © Helene Chung

First published April 2008

All rights reserved. No part of this publication may be reproduced, stored in a retrieval system, or transmitted, in any form or by any means, electronic, mechanical, photocopying, recording or otherwise, without the prior written permission of the Australian Broadcasting Corporation.

National Library of Australia
Cataloguing in Publication entry

Chung Martin, Helene, 1945-
   Ching chong China girl
   ISBN: 9780733322914 (pbk.)
   Chung Martin, Helene, 1945-
   Chinese Australians--Biography.
   Ethnic attitudes--Australia.
   Foreign correspondents--Australia--Biography.
   Reporters and reporting--Australia--Biography.
070.433092

Cover and picture section by Darian Causby, Highway 51
Cover photographs courtesy of ABC, Greg Noakes and Chung Martin collection
Typeset in 11 on 16pt ACaslon by Kirby Jones
Printed in Australia by Griffin, South Australia

5 4 3 2 1

www.helenechung.com
Photographic credits
The author has made every effort to contact copyright holders. She and her publisher would be pleased to hear from any copyright holder to correct and/or insert any omission.
Map of Tasmania by Spencer Chung
Maps of Tasmanian–Chinese Homeland and East and Central China adapted from maps by Sophie Newman in *Shouting from China*

How sharper than a dragon's tooth it is
To have a thankless child!

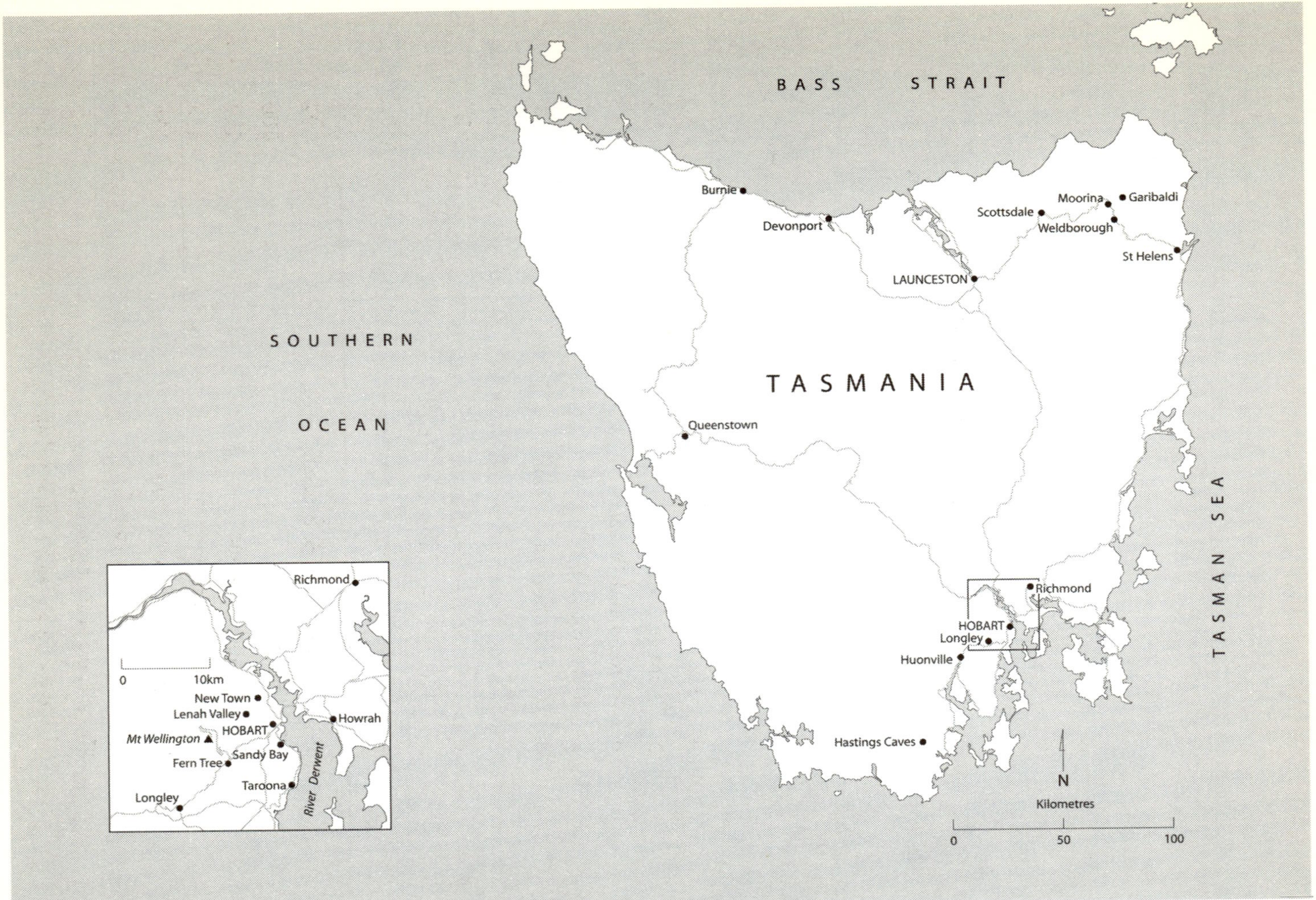

BASS STRAIT
SOUTHERN
OCEAN
TASMAN SEA
TASMANIA
Burnie
Devonport
LAUNCESTON
Scottsdale
Moorina
Garibaldi
Weldborough
St Helens
Queenstown
Richmond
HOBART
Longley
Huonville
Hastings Caves
N
Kilometres
0
50
100
0
10km
Richmond
New Town
Lenah Valley
HOBART
Howrah
Mt Wellington
Sandy Bay
Fern Tree
Taroona
River Derwent
Longley

Contents

1	Reunion: Saturday, 1 May 1993	1
2	One Town, Two Families	6
3	My Wicked Mother	17
4	The Chinese Wall	22
5	Foreign Devils	28
6	Parents and Partners	32
7	My Model Mother	39
8	Montagues and Capulets	46
9	Praying and Playing	53
10	What My Sister Might Say	61
11	The Red MG, Rex and Rajah	66
12	How Now Brown Cow	74
13	Longley	82
14	A-Smokin' 'n' A-Storkin'	92
15	Old Nick	100
16	Lambert Avenue	107
17	Tasmanian Tiger	118
18	Snow Route to Singapore	124
19	First Taste of Asia	137
20	Colonial Hong Kong	145
21	Bowing to Buckingham Palace	164

22	Shot on the Nile	182
23	Down Under Again	197
24	Sex, Race and White Australia	212
25	Bullet Train to China	218
26	Alien in the Motherland	230
27	Puzzling the Tin Trail	247
28	A Chinese Cupid's Arrow	265
29	The Mystery of the Red Envelope	270
30	Double Ninth	279
31	The Twelve Apostles	300
32	Jekyll and Hyde on Harley	310
33	Requiem: Saturday, 17 February 2001	315
	Epilogue	325

Acknowledgements	331
Sources	335
References	337
Quotations	341
Chinese names	342
Maps of Tasmanian–Chinese Homeland and East and Central China	344
The Henry and Chung families	346
Index	348

Author's Note

I use the term Australian Chinese because, like my predecessors and all my generation of Australian-born Chinese (ABC's), I grew up known as an Australian Chinese, a term that stresses my Chinese ethnicity over my Australian nationality. However, I support the term that is gaining ground, Chinese Australian: 670,000 Australians of Chinese ancestry now make up 3.4 per cent of the resident population, with Chinese the most spoken language after English in Australian homes, according to the 2006 census. The use of the term Chinese Australian recognises that I, like other Asian Australians, am equally Australian as are white, Anglo-Celtic Australians. This is especially so in the new Australia of former China diplomat, Labor Prime Minister Kevin Rudd. His election in November 2007 gave Australia – and the Western world – its first fluent Mandarin-speaking leader.

Warning: This book is not to be read by convent girls not wearing their gloves.

1

Reunion: Saturday, 1 May 1993

In 1945 two events occurred of which I recall nothing at all: my birth and the end of the Second World War. In 1993 occurred two events both of which I remember vividly: the death of my husband, John Martin, on 29 September and our last trip to Tasmania to celebrate the 125th anniversary of my former school.

On Saturday, 1 May 1993, a sea of tables and faces floated up to me as I stood, front centre stage, of Hobart's Wrest Point Convention Centre. I was one of five girls invited to share their memories on 'What St Mary's Means to Me'.

> Archbishop D'Arcy, Monsignor Green, sisters, principal, staff and old scholars.
>
> St Mary's College means to me the only school I know – a time when I formed so many attitudes, values and friendships I still retain.
>
> In this copy of the school magazine *Santa Maria*, 1950, my first year, is a photograph of St Mary's girls, including my sister, Lehene, who's also here tonight and me. The caption reads: 'Representatives of Various Countries'. Now I'm holding it up, so

you can all see it clearly, including you girls giggling down the back. Here, at either end of the front row, Lehene and I are standing, hands clasped in front of our pleated tunics, as representatives of China, our straight black hair curled by our mother for the occasion. The others in the photograph include four Polish girls, a Ukrainian, a Czech, several English pupils, a Scottish lass and a pretty little blue-eyed angel representing – it says here – 'Tasmania'. We all know our island state represents a separate country, distinct from the mainland of Australia.

Despite this photograph, China was unknown to me in 1950. Little did I realise that more than thirty years later, as a fourth-generation Tasmanian, I would represent Australia in China and spend three years there as Australian Broadcasting Corporation Peking correspondent – the first woman ever posted abroad by the ABC.

At school, despite the odd initial taunt of 'Ching Chong Chinaman' – which didn't last long – in those days of assimilation, when Anglo-Celtic Australia was the only norm, St Mary's gave Lehene and me a sense of belonging. We felt part of the school and of the larger society, long before multiculturalism was politicised.

School conjures up so many memories for me: Sally Lacy with her beautiful golden locks; the wonderful birthday parties of Gail Bennetto, Geraldine Jones and other girls of my class; Sister Rita, on frosty winter mornings with her cane, rapping the knuckles of my chilblained fingers when they stumbled onto the wrong notes of the piano; Julie Sales confiding how she wished she had black hair too so she wouldn't have to wash it; Anthony Dabrowski telling me the facts of life in Grade 2, before he was banished to the boys' school up on the hill.

School was also a time of some contradiction. Decades before the Australian vogue of the single parent, having a mother who was divorced, insisted on being called Miss Henry, was an artist's model and drove a red MG wasn't seen as helping me to heaven.

In the years before Vatican II, the teaching of theology was somewhat limited. I recall, for example, in Grade 3, Sister Malachy strapping the cat across the face in the playground because it may have been 'the devil in disguise'.

I'm also dubious about the benefit of learning to speak French with Sister Brendan's Irish accent.

But whatever the sisters, in keeping with many other teachers and schools in Tasmania at the time, may have lacked in formal qualifications, they more than compensated for by their dedication, their total commitment to all of us. For that I shall always be grateful.

I'm grateful for the discipline and high standards set by SMC. In this era of the faded, torn blue jeans and sneakers, I look back with pride on my neat green uniform, hat with badge, brown leather shoes and brown kid gloves.

But I'm especially grateful to St Mary's for its teaching of English grammar, its fostering of a love of English literature and its encouragement of the arts, particularly speech and drama. The part I played in the College team drama productions and in other school activities, was no doubt influential in my decision to work in the media. For surely broadcast journalism is a form of voice production.

As you may be aware, some Australian journalists have recently been exposed for either plagiarism – stealing the work of others, using it without attribution – or for reporting on subjects in which they have a vested interest.

Now, although I'm not trying to paint myself lily white – how could I? – the high ethical standards drummed into me at St Mary's are with me to this day. That means that even when tempted to tell a white lie, unfortunately, I can't. It's not that I fear eternal damnation. It's simply that I'm still afraid that, somehow, Mother Imelda just might find out.

When all five had spoken we followed each other down from the stage. Several Presentation convent nuns approached me. No longer shrouded in stiff starched white headdresses and clanging with heavy rosary beads tied at the waist of cumbersome layers of thick black cloth, they wore regular though loose-fitting costumes. They glowed with delight.

'Do you have a copy of your speech?' asked the lay principal Ann Stanfield.

I weaved my way through well wishers to rejoin my table where contemporaries of Lehene and mine continued the laughter and reminiscences. My mother, Dorothy, by now a respectable (no, never that!) widow called Mrs Greener, exuded her customary maternal pride.

John, always supportive, kissed me. 'Well done, darling.'

Only my sister showed less than total approval. Accusation flashed in her eyes. 'Did you have to mention the artist's model and the red MG?' Lehene whispered, reliving the pangs of childhood.

Three decades after I'd untied the knot of my school tie for the last time, I'd dared mention the unmentionable. Our mother, who so scandalised Hobart when we were growing up in the 1950s, was no longer shocking. What stigma was there to a broken home, even among Catholics in Hobart in 1993?

In 1972 when she was in her late twenties, Lehene had joined me in London. She stayed on, married an older, rather formal English businessman, David Goodenday, graduated from the Open University and London Polytechnic as a librarian and made London home. When she boarded the long flight to Australia for the school anniversary dinner, she was returning for only the third time. She wasn't abreast of the social changes that had transformed Down Under.

The embarrassment may never have entirely lifted from Lehene. Quiet, shy and supersensitive, she was composed of the finest porcelain with a glaze so delicate it easily scratched. She was fragile. As a child I bullied my big sister and she suffered in silence.

Perhaps, through my antics, I cultivated an outer skin, a show-off shield, to protect myself from racial taunts and the stain of my family.

During our last weeks together, in the bitter-sweet December before she died in London on New Year's Day 2001, Lehene surprised me.

'Miss Henry!' she mimicked softly through a gently mocking smile. 'Miss Henry! You know, now when I think about that, I realise the other girls must have thought we were illegitimate!'

2

One Town, Two Families

My grandfather – my mother's father – stepped foot on the Tasmanian tin fields in 1901, the year of Australia's birth as a nation and the year the White Australia policy was born. He left his impoverished village to find his fortune, but first he had to find his father, who had been gone for over a decade.

When the two came face to face, the youth understood. He realised why his mother had struggled for all of his sixteen years, unaided by remittances. Not a penny had his father ever sent home.

Like most of the Chinese around him, my great-grandfather had sought solace in opium. After a day's mining, when his thighs, his lower back and shoulders ached, it eased his body. In the harshness of the camp, in the lonely years without his wife and sons, it induced in him a sense of euphoria. He had been drawn to opium as a European to tobacco or beer. He had become an addict.

Grandfather, unlike his father, found no time to smoke. He neither planted the purplish-pink poppies grown around Weldborough, nor partook of their sap, but threw himself into work. During the glacial months of winter, when snow can carpet the island's northeast, he rose in the blackness of night to light fires beneath frozen water pipes. When the ice began to melt, he turned on the taps for the flow essential to alluvial mining.

The mine paid him 5 shillings a week and it took him two years to save enough for his father's passage back to Toishan to die. Only in the motherland can a Chinese spirit rest in peace.

After three years and with mining in decline, in 1904 Grandfather took to market gardening in Launceston. From street to street he hawked his vegetables, balancing baskets from a bamboo pole slung across his shoulders. Two years later he set south to Hobart and opened a laundry in Barrack Street, where he worked tirelessly at the boiler and starched and ironed the linen. Six years later he made the first of five return trips home.

Then, on 11 November 1918, after steaming back and forth for his third time, Grandfather docked in Sydney Harbour in the crush of Armistice Day. He brought with him his wife, Mary Lum Lee, and daughter Joyce, not two years old, who stepped from the gangplank onto their new alien land. They could hardly hear themselves for the blare of sirens and the pealing of bells. Martin Place jammed with foreign devils, clamouring, cheering and crying with relief and jubilation at the end of the First World War.

Grandfather made his fourth visit in 1923, with the addition of his sons Gordon and Lester, and, on this visit, not only went to Toishan County to visit his mother but also bought properties in the provincial capital, Canton.

Next year, in Hobart again, he established a new laundry that he combined with tobacco and fancy goods next door to Crisp & Gunn, the biggest timber yard, whose staff and customers flocked to him. Here, at 152 Elizabeth Street, my mother, Dorothy, was born.

The family moved across the road to 153 Elizabeth Street in 1927. At that time Grandfather incorporated tobacco and fancy goods with fruit and vegetables in a two-department store. He arranged one half with cauliflowers, pumpkins, parsnips, potatoes, pears, peaches and plums, the other half with Roger & Gallet soaps and perfumes, the aromas of which wafted around the store and mingled with the scent from bars of Cashmere Bouquet and Pears. Whiffs of tobacco merged with the leathery smell of purses and wallets. The counter displayed imported brushes and combs, pipes, cigarette lighters, shiny cufflinks and multibladed pocket knives. Sales in cigarettes and boxes of matches were brisk, as were, on Empire Day and Guy Fawkes, Chinese crackers.

Dorothy, by now in leg irons because she had rickets, followed her father about in the store or hovered at the entrance watching the goings-on up and down Elizabeth Street: businessmen in three-piece suits and Stetsons, ragamuffins with besmeared faces, housewives with their shopping baskets and tradesmen clippetty-clopping along in their horse and carts.

Within four years his success enabled him to ply the Pacific again, together with his wife and children, including baby Marie. Inquisitive five-year-old Dorothy strayed aboard the decks and wandered into a space where something gleamed a golden brown. When she got up close she could see her own face. Then her fingers touched a wide row of white, which tinkled and mesmerised her. She hoisted herself onto the stool and tapped away at the piano, determined to pester her father until, back in Hobart, he compromised and bought her a violin.

Meanwhile, in Toishan County, Grandfather at last realised his dream. He moved a short distance from *Loong Kai Lee* – Dragon Stream Village to *Loong Hen Lee* – Dragon Field Village – where he built a double-storey brick home. After three decades to and fro, he knelt in gratitude, worshipped at a shrine decorated with figurines and burnt incense to honour the ancestors. Beyond the shrine stretched the main room, furnished with a carved rosewood table and chairs. A flight of stairs opened onto a roof garden with views across the village and its rice paddies, sugar cane and buffaloes and into the distance where he might spy any bandits who dared advance towards Dragon Field.

His mother found fulfilment here. With tears in her eyes, she said, 'Now that I've seen what you've achieved, I'm ready to go and join your father.'

*

Grandfather pronounced his name Jin Jung – Jin (as in jingle) being his family name and Jung (as in jungle) his given name. In English he wrote his name as Gin Chung (and later Gen Chung). When he opened his first fruit store, the Toishanese name he had in mind sounded like Hen Lee, meaning Making a Profit. The signwriter, when asked to paint Hen Lee, misunderstood. He assumed Grandfather was like other Chinese who couldn't pronounce the letter 'R', so he painted 'Henry & Co.'.

Seeing the mistake, Grandfather chuckled. 'Henry is the name of your kings, English kings. Maybe this will bring me luck – the luck of kings. For a Chinese to have an English name is better for business. I will call myself Gen Chung Henry – Mr Henry of Henry & Co.'

In 1934, during the Depression, when Grandfather returned to Hobart from his final trip to Toishan, his cousin, who had taken over the Elizabeth Street shop, made no mention of handing it back to Grandfather. So he cast around and reopened Henry & Co. at 139 Liverpool Street. The Commercial Bank lent him £200, which he repaid within two years. With his reputation for regularly paying his bills on the 28th of the month, Grandfather didn't have to buy his initial stock: the suppliers offered to stock his shelves and gave him three months credit. 'We know we won't lose,' they said. 'Mr 28th of the month, we call you.'

Seven years later, as Grandfather lay near death, Archbishop Simonds, in his black soutane, purple sash and biretta, ascended the stairs of the shop that catered to the palace. 'I'm not going to let your father go to heaven without the badge of a soldier of Christ,' he told my Aunt Joyce, the oldest daughter and a fervent Catholic who had converted her younger brothers and sisters. With the sign of the cross, a sprinkling of holy water and application of sacred oil in the last rites, the archbishop saved Grandfather's soul.

On Wednesday, 5 February 1941, people crowded the streets as he was borne in procession from Liverpool Street, up the hill of Harrington Street and on to Cornelian Bay cemetery. The *Mercury* published his portrait and obituary:

> Mr. Gen Chung Henry, a leading member of the Chinese community in Hobart, died at the age of 56 years at Hobart on Monday ...
>
> A keen, energetic business man, Mr. Henry was well-known for his kindness and charity. He was president of the Tasmanian branch of the Kuo Min Tang (Chinese Nationalist Party) and gained complete mastery of the English language by diligence and perseverance.

Dorothy was fifteen and had just begun her second year of high school when her father died. She had left the nuns at St Columba's convent for the rough Elizabeth Street State School so as to enter Commercial High to learn bookkeeping and assist him in the business. Her father's death devastated Dorothy: he had meant everything to her.

Students at Elizabeth Street tormented her for being Chinese.

'Ching Chong Chinaman!' they jeered.

'Dirty yellow skin!' spat one girl.

After months of this, Dorothy stood up for herself. 'You call me names once more and you'll be sorry,' she dared her worst tormentor.

'Oh, will you Ching Chong? What'll you do Ching Chong?' goaded the much bigger girl.

'I'll use my martial arts. My black belt,' she fibbed.

The fight declared, a circle grew around the two until the whole school gathered to revel in the spectacle of Chink *versus* White Trash. Dorothy slugged a swift right into the chest of the bully.

'Oooh!' howled the mob, as she reeled. 'Get into her. Beat the slit eyes!'

Dorothy readied for the return. It didn't come. Bluff had won.

When hauled before a teacher, Dorothy defended herself. 'The dragon will awake and come to Australia.'

Afterwards, she was only called names behind her back.

*

Dorothy won those fights through the confidence engendered in her by her father. He had spoilt her, tried to make up for the abuse meted out to her by her mother. More traditional than her husband, she loved only her sons. 'You're only a girl. You should have been put in a bucket and drowned at birth!'

After her father's death, Joyce, Dorothy's big sister, who had especially suffered for being a girl, flew north to Brisbane. Joyce had run the shop, been on her feet day and night for years and now, at twenty-four, she was exhausted. As she had mothered her little sister, Dorothy now felt abandoned. She bought a brown leather suitcase and boarded a DC3 to Melbourne to stay with family friends, including her contemporary Mabel Wang. On one occasion, Dorothy suddenly woke with a scream in the dead of night and sat bolt upright in bed. Where am I? she wondered. Who am I? Then she fell back to sleep.

The worried family called the doctor but when he arrived, she felt less distraught. She knew she was Dorothy Henry.

Back in Hobart, she prepared for her mother's attacks. But she heard no voice raised, no questions asked. The silence was explained when Dorothy saw on the desk a letter to her big brother Gordon, now head of the family: 'In my opinion she should on no account be reprimanded or censured. She is suffering from severe neurosis and her recovery requires peace and quiet.'

In the following months, as Dorothy served full time in the shop, the law of life gradually asserted itself. Despite her feeling of irreparable loss, a sense of identity awakened in her. Imperceptibly, a new Dorothy emerged: bruised and incomplete without her father, but nonetheless an individual.

This new Dorothy was inveigled by family friend Teddy Chung Gon to doll up in a traditional body-clinging silk cheongsam with side slits and Mandarin collar. In Chung Gon's Pekin Gift Store, only a few doors from Henry & Co., she modelled for the camera.

'Miss China', the *Mercury* captioned its photograph. Standing and smiling with pleasure, Dorothy's hair is styled in a 1940s Victory Roll; her brows are shaped and her nails manicured. Her right hand, bedecked with jade bangle and ring, rests against her hip, while her left hand is draped above her head and held against a carved, bedragonned Chinese screen:

> MISS CHINA OF 1942 is personified by this attractive study of Hobart's Dorothy Henry. Dorothy is busily working for Allies Day on July 31, which will be marked by a big fair in the Hobart Town Hall. The stalls will carry the colours of China, Russia, Free France and Greece and a highlight of the carnival will be national costumes worn by helpers. Dorothy will play her part in this picturesque Chinese afternoon frock. The appeal gives us a wonderful chance to help those whose countries and homes have been desecrated by the enemy and I know we shall all do our best to ensure that it is a tremendous success.

Dorothy Henry was to win the heart of the brooding yet charming Charles Chung.

Hobart's other leading Chinese family lived only two blocks from Henry & Co. Chung Shing Loong, my paternal grandfather, also Anglicised his name. Born destitute into Sunwei County, he built his fortune in Tasmania and New Zealand as Willi Chung Sing. He ran a large market garden in suburban Hobart but lived over his retail store, Ah Ham & Co., on the corner of Collins and Harrington Streets. On a return trip to China he summoned his youngest son, 11-year-old Pak Koon, to join him and his brothers in Hobart. He sent the boy to St Virgil's College where he became known simply as Charles Chung, the pronunciation having changed from the original Joong to the more Western Chung (rhyming with hung).

By the 1940s Charles had met and become friends with two other young men about town, Gordon and Lester Henry. Within a year of their father's death, the Henrys introduced their kid sister to Charles. Immaculate in crisp shirt and well-cut suit, he courted her with bouquets and sweet words. Five years older and worldlier than

Dorothy, he asked her out to dance and hired a Chevrolet so they could wind down to Kingston and promenade on the beach.

A family photograph shows Charles with sun shining from his eyes, his hair Brylcreemed into shape and his arm swept around the shoulders of his 17-year-old sweetheart. Slightly apart from the couple, Gordon stands to camera right, a silk kerchief flowing from the pocket of his sportscoat, his cheeks dimpled in approval. While the two men gaze into the distance, Dorothy is obviously flattered: in flared skirt and buttoned jacket, a velvet bow crowning her head, she beams directly to lens. No one else is in sight. A wave is about to break on the pristine sands.

'You'd make a fine couple,' prompted Charles's father. 'I could set you up in a new shop. You run it and I'll join you for the evening meal.'

The pair married and were lavished by a set of Stuart crystal glasses and bowls, a gift from Willi Chung Sing. He insisted to his daughter-in-law, 'You must have this carved camphorwood chest.'

Dorothy and Charles established W. Chung Sing & Co. at 99 Liverpool Street, a block east of Dorothy's family's shop. Working long hours, they built up their clientele and attracted some already impressed by Dorothy at Henry & Co.

At the outbreak of spring, on 2 September 1943, Dorothy felt the pangs of labour and rushed to St Stephen's Private Hospital in Davey Street. The two midwives who ran the clinic immediately injected her with drugs, to which Dorothy proved hypersensitive: the medication she received at 10 that morning bombed her out until 6 that night.

'Mrs Chung, you have a beautiful baby daughter,' Dorothy heard as she awoke, still groggy, to receive a little bundle. Lehene had struggled into the world unaided except for a pair of forceps, which dented the sides of her forehead. The little bundle couldn't open her eyes; she was too weak to suck. Six days passed before she could take to the breast. She never showed the normal strength of a baby. My sister's frailty was to persist for life.

Sister Taylor, one of the midwives who delivered Lehene, was a keen photographer, who captured her at the keyboard when she was one year old. The sheer delight expressed in that portrait would develop into an abiding love of the piano.

For her second birth, sixteen months later, Dorothy received minimum medication. On 20 January 1945, shortly before the Allied victory in Europe, around 7.30 in the morning, a nurse at the new Calvary Hospital handed her another bundle. I began sucking within seconds. From that first gulp I would have a healthy appetite and by five months assume the size of a sumo wrestler.

'There's just a slight blue mark on her bottom, Mrs Chung, but nothing to worry about.' The nurse sounded anxious. 'It'll be gone in a day or two.'

'Of course,' soothed Dorothy. She knew it wasn't a bruise. She expected an inky blue mark on my bottom just as there'd been on my sister's. The Mongolian spot, as it's called after the Mongol Emperor Kublai Khan who ruled China in the thirteenth century, is found on most new-born Chinese and fades within months. According to legend, the blotch shows the infant has been eased out of the womb by a kick from the heavenly spirit.

Grandfather suggested a Chinese name for my sister: the sounds Lay-hern, meaning Something Special or Something Beautiful. Dorothy, being Australian-born, Anglicised the name. She kept the first sound, Lay, but changed the second sound to heen. She spelt the name L-e-h-e-n-e: Lehene – pronounced Lay-Heen (similar to Raylene but with equal emphasis on each syllable).

I was christened Helene without accents but pronounced in an Anglicised French style – He-Lane. So Lehene and I began our lives with names that few people – and hardly anyone in Hobart – could pronounce.

Dorothy's marriage transformed relations with her mother. On Lehene's birth our grandmother – Ah Hool, as we called her in Toishanese – stopped two-and-a-half years of crying over the loss of her husband. Maternal grandmother competed with paternal grandfather to indulge their new grandchild – even though she was a girl.

Meanwhile, our parents found themselves all too frequently on a short fuse with each other. Dorothy retraced her steps to her own mother six times before deciding to leave Charles permanently. She could take no more of his inexplicable mood swings and days of sullen silence.

One Sunday night, when seated in front of a fresh chicken salad she'd prepared, he suddenly upended the table. Lettuce leaves, grated carrot, celery sticks, tomatoes, chicken legs – everything scattered all over the floor.

'Why'd you do that?' she protested.

Without a word, he felled her with a punch to the chest.

She staggered to her feet, then hit back. After the brawl, she lifted me from my cradle, took Lehene by the hand and walked out.

Both grandparents tried to rescue the marriage. Ah Hool pleaded with Dorothy. 'Our families are friends. From neighbouring counties. I'll buy you your own home if you make it up.'

Charles too beseeched her. But Dorothy stood resolute. 'You've hit me once, you'll do it again. That's the end.'

A photograph, signed 'Charles', shows two infants sitting at Seven Mile Beach. Taller by half a head, Lehene, in a check skirt and woollen jumper, has a protective left arm around her little sister in a romper suit. Their bare feet crunch the sand. What are they thinking?

How long is this going to take? When can we get up and play? What's going on between Mummy and Daddy?

A light breeze ruffles their hair. The sky is overcast and thickening clouds threaten a storm.

In June 1946 the first Chinese divorce was splashed over the Tasmanian *Truth*. Women whispered as Dorothy approached. With bosoms puffed, they gaped at her from under the brims of their hats. Even those she had thought of as friends disappeared into shops, or scurried across the street, bringing Holdens and Hillmans screeching to a halt. She was beyond the pale. This was Hobart, not Hollywood.

At night at Henry & Co., in her big bed at the top of the stairs over the shop, Ah Hool lulled Lehene to sleep. She felt uncomfortable with Grandmother's bony arm under her neck but sensed the pleasure it gave Ah Hool, so just put up with it. Ah Hool believed the tot could do no wrong. If she picked up an egg in the shop and watched it splatter onto the floor, Ah Hool praised her: 'Oh, aren't you clever.'

Ah Hool indulged both of us with expensive clothes and other luxuries, even though she'd never allowed her own three daughters anything. After the divorce came through, she realised reconciliation was impossible. Declared our grandmother: 'The children will be brought up as Henrys. We don't need his money.'

When Lehene was four and I not yet three, Ah Hool was buried with her husband at Cornelian Bay. As the Civil War raged in China with relatives trying to flee, the family gave up the idea of disinterring Ah Goong's bones and sending them with Ah Hool's body back to Toishan.

Under the terms of Ah Hool's will, her three sons inherited Henry & Co. In the Chinese tradition, our mother and her sisters received nothing. As the years passed, Lehene and I never quite knew from where the money would come.

3

My Wicked Mother

I was crying at the bottom of the stairs. Convulsed in tears. I'd pleaded with my beautiful mother. I'd tugged at her, but lost. With a final kiss, she'd slipped out for a night, dressed in her soft fur coat and red crocodile handbag and high-heeled shoes. Left in the dim light, seated on the bottom step of the dark wooden staircase, I felt helpless. My body heaved with rage.

Uncle Lester picked me up and wrapped me in his arms.

'There, there,' he soothed, making his way across the rubber tiles that lined the floor of the shop. 'Naughty Mummy. Wicked Mummy. Going out again.'

He carried me past bunches of carrots, parsnips and rhubarb, lengths of celery and trays of Brownell, King Edward and Up-to-Date potatoes. Moving behind the cash register and glass cases gleaming with fruit, he fingered the chocolate shelves. He opened a bar of Cadbury's Dairy Milk, crinkling its silver wrapper. He popped a square of chocolate onto my tongue. Nestled against his grey dustcoat, with its familiar whiffs of Lucky Strike cigarettes, I calmed down.

Up the stairs he cradled me; the chocolate melted in my mouth and my sobbing slowed to intermittent gasps. He climbed the second flight of stairs outside Uncle Gordon's room. Landing outside his own room, he took me along the passage to my mother's room and tucked me in to sleep. When I awoke, I felt her smooth warmth, her back to me on the big bed, with one hand over her shoulder for me to hold while I cuddled against her skin.

Lehene had her own bed to bounce about on, a wooden bunk with a blue inner-spring mattress and two sliding drawers underneath that fitted in the narrow part of the L-shaped room at the base of Mama's bed.

That room at the top of the shop was the womb of my childhood. Happiness was encased in a blue floral cloth box with a hinged lid. I lifted and plunged the handle of a striped metal top, spinning out the fun. I pulled the cord attached to the neck of a wooden sausage dog, drawing it along on its low legs. I wound up a Hornby train and set it running along the track.

A shaft of northern light entered from a casement window. I watched Mama sitting in front of a round portable mirror, pencilling her eyebrows with minute black strokes. Putting on her make-up took forever. Yardley's lavender water lingered in the air.

In that room I first heard the wireless: the sound of classical music on the ABC. At the end of a piece Mama picked up a pen, seized an old envelope and wrote down what the announcer said, perhaps Bach, *Concerto in D Minor* or Chopin, 'Nocturne Op. 62'. I didn't like the sight of notes scattered about, so tidied them all up into a neat pile. In that room I listened to *Kindergarten of the Air* and later the *Children's Hour* with Uncle Mac and the Argonauts' Club.

When Mama took out her violin, tightened the bow and stood concentrating on Schubert's 'Serenade' propped up on the stand, Lehene and I had to creep around.

'Quiet please.'

Any more giggling risked a tap of the bow.

Blue-backed Pelican and orange Penguin paperbacks jammed wooden half-cases stamped TOMATOES. Faraway lands, magical kingdoms and mysterious castles arose from the pages of books. Shivers ran up our spines on the nights Mama read tales of the big bad Banksia men in *Snugglepot and Cuddlepie*. Two slim red volumes,

Stories from Chaucer and *Stories from Shakespeare*, intrigued Lehene and me. When I heard the one about two feuding families in the Italian city of Verona, I thought of the Montagues and the Capulets as the Henrys and the Chungs.

Mama's friends dropped by bringing books on art. I fancied the squiggly bright red and yellow shapes of Miro and Mama pinned prints of his work onto the wall. The grown ups lounged on the bed or squatted on the green linoleum, talking, laughing and sipping coffee from pottery mugs. Mama took out her tortoise-shell cigarette holder from its sleek black case and passed around a red and gold tin of Craven A. I imitated them with chocolate cigarettes from Moore's Variety up the street.

Uncle Gordon, head of the Henrys, never smoked and always looked important. Dressed in a suit, he ran the firm from his desk in the wholesale store. At the shop on Sunday nights, wearing a cardigan, he prepared the window display. He stacked Valencia oranges, firm King William pears and glossy Ladies in the Snow on individual racks he designed in the shape of pyramids. As I watched, he painted the label for packets of peanuts freshly roasted by Henry & Co.

From his room flowed his trained tenor voice. 'Some Enchanted Evening' he sang as he changed into slippers and picked up the *Saturday Evening Post*. When I bounded in, he smothered me with kisses and when I went to school I turned to him for pocket money. I was his favourite.

'Now Bo Co,' he rhymed a variation of my pet name, Wo Wo, 'you tell Uncle what you want it for.'

'An icy pole and some cobbers.'

'Well, don't spend it all at once,' he cautioned, fumbling for a shilling.

Lehene always got 2 shillings just by looking up at Uncle Lester.

Happy-go-lucky, he played the harmonica, won and lost on mah-jong, drove the Dodge fast and went rabbiting with a rifle. He whistled at work, carting crates of bananas to and from the cool shed at the store on the corner of Collins and Campbell Streets. He took Henry's delivery service to shops, schools, hotels, clubs and the archbishop's palace. Sometimes I climbed the hills of Hobart, sitting up in the truck next to him in his dustcoat. But Uncle also liked dressing up and every Tuesday evening he wore a suit to go with Uncle Gordon to their reserved seats at the Avalon picture theatre.

One morning I couldn't stand up. I tried to get out of bed in the room above the shop but fell back down. My legs kept collapsing.

Doctor Dorney loomed over me. 'Take a deep breath.'

The metal felt cold against my chest.

'That's a good girl. Now, once more.' Through his instrument, he listened again. 'Pneumonia, I'm afraid.'

'So what can you do?' Mama asked.

'It's serious but not to worry,' he assured her. 'A shot of penicillin will do the trick.' He fished a needle out of his Gladstone bag.

'She just put herself to bed last night. I didn't know she was ill until this morning.' Mama led the doctor out.

She soon tempted me with *jook* (or Chinese porridge, which is known as 'congee' in English). 'It'll do you good. Just made with fresh chicken.'

I sat up against the pillows, held the round porcelain Chinese bowl and sipped with its matching spoon. Chinese porridge, a delicious, hot and velvety, savoury rice dish, slipped down easily and I bounced back to health.

Pneumonia meant I missed my First Communion with the other six year olds. I had to go another Sunday, not to St Mary's Cathedral but to the chapel around the side of the sacristy. Excited, I got up early and put on my new white dress and veil. I made sure to fast because even a sip of water would have stopped me from receiving the small round host, the size of a penny, which represented the body and blood of Christ. I was led with Mama by nuns through the gloom of the convent corridors into the chapel. Surrounded by nuns flapping into pews in their long black habits and white bibs, I knelt down to the clickety-clack of rosary beads.

That was Mama's sole Mass during my childhood. She didn't go near church. She was a bad Catholic. She lived in mortal sin.

I was still in junior school when I learnt a few lines from *The Rime of the Ancient Mariner*:

Water, water, everywhere,
And all the boards did shrink;
Water, water, everywhere,
Nor any drop to drink.

Until then I'd never heard of an albatross, the beautiful bird of good omen that is slain by the ancient mariner, only for its spirit to become a burden and hence an ill omen to the ancient mariner and his crew. It made me think of Mama. Coleridge gave me a word for what I'd felt from an early age. My mother's guilt weighed like an albatross around my neck.

Uncle Gordon or Uncle Lester took Lehene and me to Mass.

One Sunday, as we parked outside St Joseph's Orphanage, Uncle Gordon pointed, 'That's where your father wanted to put you.'

I shuddered as the walls of the orphanage towered like a prison over me.

Clutching his hand, I hurried across the road, up to the corner and into St Joseph's. Stretching my right arm, I reached up with my fingers into the font and then made the sign of the cross with holy water.

'You'll have to pray for your mother so she can be saved,' urged Uncle Gordon.

Shepherded down the aisle of the stained-glassed sanctuary, I knelt with my sister and my uncle, my head bowed before the crucifix. I felt the shame of my mother's sins. I felt the burden of her soul.

4

The Chinese Wall

A sense of excitement suffused the air as Lehene and I watched, our eyes wider than the arms of the lounge suite on which we perched. Lights shone. Grown ups in double-breasted suits or cocktail frocks glided across the floor to the sounds of Glenn Miller and his orchestra, 'In the Mood'. In an interval between dancing Doris Griffiths played the piano, undulating as her soprano voice rang out: 'I Know Where I'm Going'. Then we heard the gramophone again. Silk-stockinged legs and high heels, interlocked limbs, flounces and frills waltzed to Perry Como's 'Till the End of Time'. Before we were packed off to bed, a local Ivor Novello character burst into his rendition of 'We'll gather lilacs in the spring again and walk together down an endless lane'.

Uncle Gordon and Uncle Lester held their dances on the other side – the other side of Henry & Co. – over the Reeds' bakery. They sold hot meat pies and pasties, flaky pastry, crusty tin loaves and fresh cream sponges. Their upper floors had been rented by the Wattle Tea Rooms, which served a three-course meal for 1 shilling.

After Grandfather's death the family renovated and expanded the living area of 139 Liverpool Street. Plumbers installed a green-tiled bathroom on the top floor where Lehene and I would one day sit entwined at either end in a steaming bath. Soaked in Lux suds and swinging from side to side, we would sing 'Row, row, row your boat, gently down the stream …'.

The Henrys extended their two upper floors over the Reeds' ground floor next door. The former tearooms transformed into a spacious lounge, a dining room and a kitchen, with more rooms above. A flight of stairs from the street led to the new eastern side that the family joined to the existing western side by knocking down part of an internal wall.

Dorothy experimented with the new Hotpoint electric stove. She grilled her first pork chop, roasted her first leg of lamb, baked an apple pie and made a batch of scones. The Kelvinator glistened and kept food cool and fresh.

With the new lounge Gordon and Lester began their weekly soirées for friends and associates – almost all foreign devils. Charles met Gordon when invited by Lester to one of their dances. By the time I was born the parties had become a tradition.

The arrival of Big Girl wrought change.

Big Girl wasn't her real name but that's how I thought of her. Big Girl was the wife of Mama's Big Brother Fon, the adopted son number one. He alone had been raised and schooled in China.

Before Grandmother first sailed for Australia, she had borne her first child – a bitter disappointment. 'I should've strangled you and thrown you in the river!' She cursed the infant. 'What use are you, a girl?' She ranted at baby Joyce.

Within days Grandfather had scouted the village and paid for 3-year-old Fon. Only a son could take care of parents in their old age. Only a son could worship the ancestors and continue the family line. A daughter would marry into someone else's family.

So Grandmother began motherhood with two babies. She always resented Joyce for being a girl.

Dorothy, like all the children except Joyce and Fon, had been born in Hobart. When she travelled from Tasmania with her family, Dorothy had just turned six by the time she met Fon in China. The eighteen year old comforted her when Gordon had upset her.

'Dorf, close your eyes and open your mouth,' Gordon enticed. 'I've got a surprise for you.'

Expecting a lolly, she played along and shut her eyes until she felt something hard and jagged on her tongue.' She pulled out a smelly old tooth. 'Yuck!' She tossed it away and broke into sobs. 'What a horrid trick.'

'Don't you worry,' soothed Fon. 'I'll buy you a whistle.'

In the Chinese tradition, Dorothy didn't call Fon by his name. She called him Ah Goo, meaning Big Brother Number One in Toishanese. When Fon married, his wife became Ngit Thlaw – Wife of Big Brother Number One; Dorothy called her Ah Thlaw.

A couple of years after that trip to China, Grandfather brought Fon out to work in Henry & Co. Fon's wife stayed in Dragon Field Village in charge of the new family home. It contained the valuables Grandmother had packed and taken back to Toishan from Tasmania and included a set of English china and a chest full of pure silver ornaments, rings, other jewellery and trinkets. All were hidden between the walls in readiness for Grandmother to enjoy her final years on native soil. But while Grandmother stayed in Australia, Fon's wife had to escape the Japanese, who bludgeoned, raped and pillaged their way from the north down to southern China, where they swept into Guangdong Province and Toishan County. They tore into Dragon Field Village, ransacked Grandfather's dream home and absconded with its treasure.

After Grandmother joined Grandfather in the afterlife in 1947, the family decided that Fon's wife should be reunited with him in Australia. She had not only experienced the Japanese invasion but was also still living in the turmoil of China's Civil War between the Nationalist government of Chiang Kai-shek and the Communists under Mao Zedong. On 1 October 1949 the Red Flag would be raised and Mao would launch his twenty-seven year reign of repression and bloodshed. Property owners such as the Henrys would not only have their assets seized, but also be particular targets for personal attack.

Such was the fate Fon's wife avoided when she landed in Hobart with her two teenage children and a maid in 1948.

By now Big Brother Fon had become affectionately known in English as Moonshine. Dorothy had named him after a character from the comic book *Wags*. Big Brother Moonshine was solidly built and, as his wife was sizeable, Wife of Big Brother became Big Girl.

When I was very small, Big Girl loomed very large, very Chinese and very frightening.

'Ah Wo Wo,' she gave my pet name a Chinese twist.

I cowered beneath the menacing glint of gold teeth. 'Ah Wo Wo' sounded Chinese off her tongue. And that was all I could understand. My smattering of Toishanese didn't extend to whatever else Big Girl said. Everything about her was weird. Just as I, chubby with cow's milk, Kraft cheddar and little lamb chops, smelt like a Tasmanian devil to her, Big Girl emitted mysterious and alien aromas to me.

Upstairs, where she lived on the other side, she tempted me with a dried Chinese plum. Wrapped in paper covered with Chinese squiggles, it looked like a lolly. The purplish lump tasted nothing like a Mintie. But I eagerly took the dried lychees she handed me. They were a Chinese delicacy. I descended the steep internal wooden stairs from her room with a pocketful, unable to resist cracking open the coarse, round, brown shell and letting its chewy flesh slip into my mouth.

Big Girl had enjoyed a rare privilege in Toishan. Under Chinese custom a wife moved into her husband's family home and could become a virtual slave to a tyrannical mother-in-law. When Grandmother returned to Australia, Big Girl resided in China and ruled the household, supported by three maids and remittances from Henry & Co. When she set forth from China with one maid – her so-called Little Sister, or Muoi Muoi – Grandmother had already died. So, after more than fourteen years' reign in Dragon Field Village, Big Girl alighted in Hobart to assume unto herself all the status and power of the first and only wife of son number one.

Big Girl's attempt to transfer village authority to Tasmania proved hazardous. Although older, Moonshine already recognised Gordon, with his grasp of English and Western business skills, as head of the family. Straight from Toishan, Big Girl couldn't be expected to conform. From her height she looked down upon her little sister-in-law Dorothy, divorced and with Lehene and me in tow. To Big Girl, Dorothy had no status at all.

'You don't belong here.' Big Girl shunted her out of the way. 'You belong with your husband. You should go back to him.'

Such a clash of cultures guaranteed territorial disputes. Can two women ever enjoy equal rights in a kitchen? In the late 1940s, Big Girl couldn't tolerate Dorothy, let alone her grilling baby lamb chops. Or occupying the Kelvinator with five pints of milk a day. Out clanged the bottles onto the floor, as Big Girl ejected them one by one. Lester was summoned to arbitrate.

After two years of hostilities the factions called a truce. In 1950 – the year I turned five and enrolled in grade 1A – Uncle Gordon and Uncle Lester bought out Moonshine's share of Henry & Co. They closed the opening that joined both sides of the property. A wall of solid bricks, floor-to-ceiling, blocked any crossing between east and west.

The gramophone wound down, the foxtrots and the waltzes ceased and spring brought no more lilacs.

During the cold war that ensued I rarely saw Moonshine, Big Girl, or the Little Nuck Nucks, the name we gave their Australian-born children after the sounds they made when learning to talk. Their Toishan-born older sister, Laraine, a decade my senior, is in the 1950 *Santa Maria* photograph, 'Representatives of Various Countries', taken during her year at St Mary's just as I began. Her departure left Lehene and me the only Chinese until the arrival of two much younger cousins just as I was about to leave.

Even during the thaw of the late 1950s, I wasn't sure how or whether I was related to the Henrys – Moonshine and Big Girl – who lived over and operated the Green Glen on Sandy Bay Road.

Not until I'd grown up would I come to appreciate Big Girl.

'Ah Dor-lor-thee.' She appeared at the front door.

'Ah Thlaw,' Mama welcomed her.

'Ah Wo Wo.' Her teeth glinted.

Only as an adult would I learn about the Great Wall of China that snakes around mountains and down into valley floors for some three thousand miles or more. Reduced to rubble or missing in regions, rebuilt and strengthened elsewhere, it dates back to the Emperor Qin. Formerly known as Chin, he vanquished the rulers of many rival kingdoms and unified their realms into an empire in 221 BC. China bears his name. The first emperor proved a ruthless tyrant who burnt the Confucian classics and buried scholars alive. He enslaved almost a million labourers – soldiers, peasants and prisoners – to link up existing walls, some already centuries old, in a gigantic engineering feat.

One of the Seven Wonders of the World – though not visible from the moon – the Great Wall was built as a defence against the Mongol hordes. Genghis Khan and his horsemen breached the fortifications. His grandson Kublai Khan conquered China and founded the capital of his vast Mongol empire on the site of Peking. He created a splendid palace and garden overlooking a beautiful lake.

Coleridge wrote, while intoxicated after two grains of opium, long before my great-grandfather became an addict:

In Xanadu did Kubla Khan
A stately pleasure-dome decree:
Where Alph, the sacred river, ran
Through caverns measureless to man
Down to a sunless sea.

When those words captivated me as a schoolgirl, I didn't imagine myself in China. But by the time I trod the site of the pleasure dome and roamed the ramparts of the Great Wall, both Henry factions had risen above Hobart's Chinese wall.

5

Foreign Devils

They were everywhere. In the shop, in the street, on the tram, wherever you looked, they were there. They ran the place. It was theirs. You couldn't escape them: *fangwei* – foreign devils. Everyone, except us Chinese, was a foreign devil.

Aunty Marie married a *fangwei*, a red-haired devil. Uncle Mervyn, with his waves of flame, was the family's first *fangwei*. He looked nothing like the real devil, Satan, with his leering eyes, his horns, his trailing tail and black pitchfork. The real devil could jab you with his pitchfork if you were tempted into mortal sin and died without confessing and you were plunged into the eternal fires of hell. Uncle Mervyn was different from the Tasmanian devil, too. With its black fur, piercing eyes, glowing pink ears, terrible temper and ghostly growl, it skulked about at night to feast on rotting flesh.

Except for his hair, Uncle Mervyn was hardly devilish at all. An ex-air force man, he once worked at the Green Gate on the corner opposite the shop. Uncle Mervyn used to mix frothy milk shakes and malted milks. He served mouth-watering peach melbas and hot waffles with strawberry jam and mountains of whipped cream. Now he worked at the store, opening and carrying boxes of fruit and vegetables for Henry & Co.'s wholesale trade.

'One day at the Green Gate,' he told me, 'I could see it raining outside the front door. It was bucketing down. Then I went out the back and the sun was shining. No rain at all.'

Impressed by this, I repeated it to Uncle Gordon. 'I know who was under the weather,' he tut-tutted.

Uncle Gordon and Uncle Lester didn't touch a drop. Even though a bottle of gin stood handy for cooking on the kitchen bench, no one drank. Mama said, 'If I so much as sip a glass of Moselle, my face turns scarlet.'

When I was growing up only foreign devils drank and Uncle Mervyn didn't mind his tipple.

He took me to his mother's place for my first Christmas with foreign devils. I rode on the pillion seat of his BSA 250, clinging onto him as we roared up Liverpool Street, turned left into Harrington, right into a lane and pulled up outside a stone cottage.

His mother had to be 100 years old. A tiny person, hunched over, with wizened skin and wisps of white hair, she had wrists as thin as pencils and bony fingers I feared would snap. She hobbled about like a little old lady in an Enid Blyton story book. But her frail figure belied her strength. With a dainty apron around her waist, she busied herself at the fire of the black cast-iron stove. Steam from a cauldron bubbling away on the top rose up the chimney.

The room would have been dark without electric light as curtains covered much of the window. In the corner a Christmas tree twinkled with little fairy lights while a Santa Claus cloth and napkins decorated the table – we never used a tablecloth or napkins at the shop. We all sat down, tied on our cardboard hats in blue, red, green, silver or gold and fingered the crackers laid out for each of us. I'd never seen such a magical setting.

'Come and help me, Merv,' called his mother.

I watched as they lifted out a huge calico bundle dripping from the boiling cauldron.

'You wait till you see this,' nudged Aunty Marie.

Suddenly, all went black. A flame leapt out of the blackness and crept across to the table. The flame died down, lights flickered on, glasses clinked and cheers rang through the cottage. I savoured the taste of that first pudding: sweet, moist, rich and tantalising. Then my teeth hit on something hard. I picked it out of my mouth and found a silver threepence. The pudding was made with threepenny and sixpenny pieces. I fancied that foreign devil fare.

For lunch on schooldays we ate plain foreign food. Lehene and I went home to the shop at midday. I envied the other girls who stayed at school and had more time to play. We faced knives and forks and our Bunnykins plates, set out on large new sheets of brown paper. Mama gave us each two grilled baby lamb cutlets – sometimes a single grilled pork chop with apple sauce for a change – half a grilled tomato and vegetables from the three baskets of the pressure cooker. This contraption frightened us. It made a deafening hiss and blew out steam like the funnel of a train.

'It's going to explode,' cried out Lehene.

Sometimes we took a school friend home and she always lapped up everything. But if we were having lunch and Uncle Gordon happened to reach the top of the stairs – where the kitchen was installed when the wall went up – things weren't so happy. 'Oh, lamb again,' he winced.

Raised on a southern Chinese diet, Uncle Gordon was repelled not so much by the smell of grilling, but by the smell of lamb itself. Unlike northern Chinese, southerners detest all sheep products. Although apt to boast, 'We eat anything that flies except an aeroplane and anything on four legs except a table,' they draw the line at lamb.

My grandparents never overcame this prejudice. Ah Hool found the odour of dairy food, especially ever so slightly rancid butter, as repugnant as the scent of lamb. She complained, 'The rancid smell oozes from their pores.'

Mama, as the second youngest, developed a taste for what her brothers shunned. She brought up Lehene and me with Western palates.

Grandmother's generation of Chinese saw New Gold Mountain as a land of opportunity but with no history, culture or cuisine. From time immemorial Chinese thought of their country as the Middle Kingdom, the self-sufficient centre of civilisation, surrounded by barbarians. As Ah Hool told her children: 'We Chinese were wearing silk when Europeans were still climbing up trees.'

Ah Hool was appalled by the idea of any of her offspring consorting with a foreign devil. When Lester regularly asked out Australian girls, Grandmother hurtled him down the aisle to an arranged Chinese bride.

When I was young I always heard the Chinese word *fangwei*. Even its pronunciation, fung-gweer, suggested queerness. Adults dropped it into an otherwise English conversation:

'So, who did she marry?'

'*Fangwei*. Tom Smith. His family was from Sydney.'

For my mother, uncles and aunts, *fangwei* had lost its literal meaning of 'foreign devil' and become synonymous with 'Australian', implying anyone of a non-Chinese, white ethnic background. They meant no offence when *fangwei* slipped from their lips. I never heard anything like 'She married a foreign devil'.

No, they only used foreign devil in jest and followed the words with a laugh. I knew that they knew we were the foreign devils Down Under.

What I couldn't know was that Lehene and I would both marry foreign devils: Lehene, a devil of an Englishman and I, a Tasmanian devil.

6

Parents and Partners

One day, when I was six, Uncle Gordon burst into Mama's room over the shop. The strains of 'Träumerei' ceased, the bow idle over the fiddle as Mama caught the spark from his face.

'Dorf,' he said, 'Charles is off. He's off to China.'

'Is he now?'

'Wants to get married again. Find a new wife.' Then, spotting me on the floor with my fingers in plasticine, chopping up baby lamb cutlets: 'Bo Co, your father's going home to China to bring you back a stepmother.'

'You're not getting any stepmother,' I heard my mother's voice. 'You're not getting any stepmother, not till I'm dead.'

As time passed I became aware of the new wife: if I happened by Charles Fruit Store in Bathurst Street (and later diagonally up and across the road from us), I caught a glimpse of Mollance and later of two little boys. Then, one overcast Saturday morning, Lehene and I readied ourselves upstairs and waited, rather nervous, downstairs in the shop. I was nine, Lehene ten or eleven, and we were about to go off with our father for the first time that I knew of. We were to help paint the house being built for his new family. I would have been less surprised and more at ease, had I been asked to curtsy and hand a bouquet to the queen.

In Liverpool Street, trams rattled by, customers popped in and out of the shop and the register rang repeatedly. Anxious, I kept glancing up from the Walt Disney comic I was reading.

'I thought you could give me a hand.' He closed the utility door.

We swept past Government House and the Domain where I had stood for an eternity with hordes of other children, waiting to wave our flags at the queen as she appeared on her fleeting royal tour. On the south side, we saw the regatta grounds where I had wandered licking fairy floss and paid to gawk at the fat woman on ice. Over the floating bridge we crossed the River Derwent. Two ferries plied its waters. In near silence we continued past off-white timber houses in Bellerive, where a mass of yachts bobbed by the shore. A plane soared overhead. Seated together in the front, Lehene and I exchanged a roll of our eyes. On we pressed to the new suburb of Howrah where bitumen turned to gravel, new homes rose from excavation sites and carports, paths, pergolas, fences, letter boxes, grass and shrubs replaced rubble. We stopped at a block of land in Tranmere Road.

'I'll get the paint.' Our father left us by a stack of weatherboards and strolled towards a shed at the far end.

'What are we meant to do?' I asked Lehene.

'Whatever we're told, I suppose.'

'I'd rather be riding my bike.' I saw myself pedalling around Constitution Dock and out on Elizabeth Street Pier.

'Well, we just have to do what we're told.'

He returned with a tin of pink primer. He shook it vigorously, stirred it with a stick and began to paint a plank. 'Here, Lehene, you can take over. And Helene, you can begin on this one.' He laid out another board and handed me a brush as though this were routine. Then he left us to our own devices.

'Daddy never talks,' said Lehene. 'At least he didn't when I lived with him at Ah Ham & Co.'

'Is that why you left?'

'No. Because he slapped me. I'd gone to visit you and Mummy. And when Daddy found out, he slapped me. So Mummy said I had to come home.'

I soon forgot the strangeness of the occasion and threw myself into the job. I loved sloshing about with paint. But we made meagre impact.

Our father never took us anywhere again; we didn't see his house until I was about sixteen.

One day, unbeknown to us, a little girl called Maple was fossicking about in a closet when a suitcase suddenly snapped open. She opened it further and discovered some fine linen, smooth sheets and thick towels, unlike anything she'd ever seen. Her fingers stumbled on a different texture: a card with a stout red Santa and crinkly white beard. Inside, from a child's hand, she read: 'Dear Daddy, Happy Christmas with love from Lehene.' A prickly feeling crept up her spine. She knew she was alone but turned her head, just to check. She picked up another card, for Father's Day, and read inside: 'Dear Daddy … Love Helene.' Bewildered, Maple shut the case. She left it exactly as she'd found it. She'd never heard of Lehene or Helene. Were the cards to her own father? He had never hinted of any other children. All she knew was that she had better not ask. She whispered her secret only to her big sister.

Not long after Lehene and I primed the weatherboards, I met my father's wife Mollance. She dropped into the shop to see Mama. Upstairs in the bedroom by the window Mama demonstrated the rudiments of makeup to Mollance. They began to talk women's business. I crept out as I heard them compare notes.

'I remember he used to –'

'What's more he –'

'No man's worth it.'

'I didn't know what to do when –'

'I wasn't having any more of that.'

'You're well out of it.'

I asked no questions; I had no interest in my father's affairs. Vague mention of a wife in China meant less to me than the story of Cinderella and her wicked stepmother. Like a Shetland pony dragging the cart of a draughthorse, I already felt overloaded with my mother's things and didn't want the strain of my father's.

My mother broke the Ten Commandments daily hammered into us in catechism class. Sister Lucy held up her finger, her face reddening as she instilled in us: 'What God has joined together, let no man put asunder.'

Braving it out, I kept quiet, praying that no one knew of my mother's divorce.

'Why do you have to call yourself Miss Henry?' I beseeched Mama.

'I can't bear to use your father's name. You should be called Henry too. I never want to be Mrs Anyone again.'

The only others called Miss were either young unmarried ladies or spinsters. From my Enid Blyton books, I imagined spinsters as shrivelled old women who lived with cats, wore bonnets, carried baskets and acted queer. I cringed as I fronted up to the counter at Vernon's delicatessen: 'My mother, Miss Henry, says please could she have a quarter of a pound of ham: the little pieces you give her from the end of the knuckle.'

I shuffled in my shoes and examined the parapet when Sister Lucy spoke to my mother, 'Now, Mrs Chung –' No nun could address any mother as Miss Anyone while my mother objected to being called Mrs Anyone, least of all Mrs Chung.

Then there were my mother's friends. First, Gordon Walters the artist with grey-green eyes and curly hair. He worked as a government clerk and had his own flat but stayed with us when Mama, Lehene and I lived at Uncle Gordon's new, unfurnished house before he moved there. Gordon sketched me in pencil when I was asleep. 'You wouldn't keep still enough when wide awake.'

Back at the shop, in strode a hulking Dutch blond, a French teacher who excelled at soccer. Suddenly, the mother who had dismissed all sport dragged me off on a Saturday afternoon to watch him bounce the ball off his head to cheering crowds. He introduced us to yoghurt when hardly anyone in Hobart had heard of it. Following his instructions, Mama poured tepid milk into a Pyrex dish, stirred in a culture, covered the dish, wrapped it in wads of newspaper, then a blanket and let it set on a bench heated by the hot water tank. I loved the thick creamy skin.

'*Mange*,' I uttered my first French, imitating '*Mange*, Marguerite,' he urged his daughter on a visit.

As she was younger than Lehene and me, we helped her to eat. '*Mange*, Marguerite.' We grew fluent.

Even after Uncle Gordon married and lived at Lenah Valley, he still presided over family meals at the shop. One evening I accidentally let the cat out of the bag.

'I had to wait so long to get into the bathroom this morning,' I complained to Mama. 'Alain took ages.'

'What?' Uncle Gordon scowled above his rice.

I felt the jab and saw my mother's daggers.

'You mean that fellow's been staying the night?'

As though he hadn't heard his brother, Uncle Lester, who had an eye for girls and no ear for interference in private affairs, reached with his chopsticks for breast of salted chicken. But his wife Eva, less than enamoured of her sister-in-law, put down her bowl. 'Yes,' she flung her voice across the table. 'And he be-um bring his little girl here too.'

While Mama glowered at Lehene and me – a lesson that 'children and fools speak true' – Uncle Gordon expressed his disapproval. 'Ooh,' the subject pained him. 'As if all that philosophy and Sartre and Krishnamurti weren't enough; now your mother has to learn French. So, what does she do? She falls for a Frenchman.'

I was eight when her new friend, artist Daryl Harrison, gave me an easel and showed me how to use oils. I squeezed the tubes onto a glass palate, used a knife to mix the colours and applied the paint with a brush, or squeezed directly and freely onto the page, imagining myself with a future as a great abstract artist. I sent a self-portrait to Phidias (the artist Jeffrey Smart), who inspired us in the ABC's Argonauts Club. Although I listened most afternoons to Uncle Mac exhort us to 'Row, row, Argonauts' by sending in contributions, I only made one contribution, my portrait, which didn't rate a mention. Unlike other Argonauts, I never rowed hard enough to win the points to join Jason in his search for the Golden Fleece.

One weekend, when an American warship had docked at Hobart, Daryl took his little brother, Rowland, Mama and me down to the wharf. We'd barely begun our inspection amid swarms of sightseers before Rowland disappeared from the deck into the engine room. I didn't see him again until after school next week. Wearing his grey St Virgil's uniform, he stopped me in Harrington Street. I checked over my shoulder for any goody-goody in sight. Talking to boys was against school rules, far worse than entering a milk bar or not wearing our hats. Talking to Rowland thrilled me with guilt.

'Do you play marbles?' His smile revealed perfect white teeth.

'Of course.' I thought of the glass balls I kept in a mustard-coloured suede pouch and rolled onto the lino.

'I bet you haven't seen one like this,' he challenged. From his pocket he produced a ball that dazzled me with its size.

'No, never.' I stared at the wavy white, blue and black hues glinting in the sun.

'I'll show you how to play.'

At the shop, in Mama's room, he explained. 'You don't have to fire from the floor; you can gauge your distance – your height from the floor – and then let it drop for a direct hit.' It fell, its target bowled over to the wall. 'A bull's eye.'

It amazed me.

'Here, you can keep these.' He fished two giant marbles from his pocket. 'You can practise until next time.'

While Rowland and I were exact contemporaries, Daryl was somewhat younger than Mama, a fact that hadn't escaped his parents.

'Dorf,' Uncle Gordon frowned over dinner. 'They're not happy. His – whatsisname's – mother phoned to say so. You're older than him.

"And, what's more," she said, "your sister's already had two other boyfriends." What was I to say? At least she didn't say anything about being Chinese.'

Daryl's parents soon packed him off to study in London, leaving Mama to remember him by his paintings, his navy leather-bound copy of *The Life of the Buddha* and his T-shirt tucked beneath her pillow.

With such minefields to negotiate as I grew up in the maternal camp, I had no wish to explore what other explosives lay planted across in the paternal camp.

7

My Model Mother

The strap fell across his white whiskers. The tabby screeched and ran for his life.

'How do you know he isn't the devil in disguise?' challenged Sister Malachy. Indeed. The cat had been publicly polishing his private parts.

Our Grade 3 was reciting the lives of the saints by learning them off by heart from strips of paper picked out of an old chocolate tin. We paced the courtyard, mouthing the words on each saint, trying to memorise as many lives as we could. I'd just finished St Cecilia, patron saint of church music. She made me think of Sister Cecilia who taught the big girls Latin; she also coached in basketball and wore her habit a bit short, even showing her black stockinged ankles when netting a goal.

I'd picked up St Catherine when I noticed the cat sitting out there, licking and polishing himself in the sun.

I was repeating to myself: 'St Catherine of Alexandria was an early Christian martyr. She was tortured on a spiked wheel. It broke and beheaded her. The Catherine wheel was named –' when we all stopped in our tracks.

'Whoosh!' I heard. Then, 'Yeeaow!'

Mad Sister Malachy we called her, but somewhere behind her pearl-white skin and starched exterior lay a heart. I liked her and knew from her manner and enquiries about my aunt that she liked me. She acted only for our own good, so we could go to heaven.

Other nuns were different.

I was nine and mortified. I could feel fifty pairs of eyes from row upon row of girls peering at me.

'Eyes to the front,' snapped Sister Lawrence to the swish of her strap through the air and the rattle of rosary beads against her heavy black folds. Whenever she patrolled the aisles of the class we Grade 4 girls shared with Grade 5 her strap was always handy. She was always ready to lash out in any direction for any misdemeanour.

'Sit up straight. How often do I have to tell you?'

I'd done nothing wrong this morning and neither of my hands was red or stinging. Yet my round chubby cheeks felt as if they were on fire. A wave of heat rolled down from under my black fringe, engulfed my ears and circled my neck, choked by the Windsor knot tying the collar of my fawn blouse. My mind whirled. I, who was always in trouble for talking in class, couldn't say a word. I sat glued to my seat in the second middle row, my eyes downcast. My wooden ruler, my pen with its new nib, my lined exercise book with its neat margin and 'A.M.D.G.' – 'For the greater glory of God' – in copperplate at the top, blurred into the grain of my sloping desk. Perhaps there were miracles after all. Perhaps I could vanish, become invisible, be swallowed up into the chimney, fall forgotten through the polished floor, or disintegrate into dust.

'Your mother's at tech,' Sister Lawrence had said, suddenly turning from squeaking chalk on the blackboard to point at me, 'so she can paint the Nativity scene.'

How could I possibly explain to Sister Lawrence, of all the nuns? She, who had a thin mean mouth, a taut face, a sharp tongue; the nun the girls called spiteful. Although she'd never picked on me unfairly, I knew Sister Lawrence didn't like me. Not even the goody-goodies could please her, despite all their novenas, their special devotions and prayers. Not even the boarders with their pasty freckled faces, fed on Holy Communion and stodge. Sister Lawrence didn't like anyone.

I glanced at the blackboard. Yes, they were still there: the two words Sister Lawrence had added to the list. I read: Cards, Carols, Crib, Enactment, Nativity Painting.

My mother *was* at Hobart Technical College. She went there each Tuesday and Thursday afternoon. But she could no more paint than I could. I loved squeezing the oils and watching them ooze with their smell from the tubes onto the page, or onto my glass palette where I mixed them before dabbing on colours with a knife or a brush. It was fun, playing around at home à la Jackson Pollock long before I knew his name. But a picture of the Virgin Mary clad modestly in her long flowing blue veil and Joseph in his dark brownish tones with the infant Jesus being born in a stable at Bethlehem? I could never paint that. Mama could never paint that. She was no draughtsman; she couldn't draw. She *was* drawn. She was an artist's model. That's what she was at tech. How could I explain that to Sister Lawrence? 'Full figure' it was called. Without any clothes. She modelled nude. As if it wasn't enough for Lehene and me to be the only Chinese, the only ones with divorced parents, our mother had to be a nude model.

'Modesty, girls,' I could hear Mother Imelda intone at school assembly, her eyes penetrating each of us from her raised position on the bench in the yard. The bronze bell in her hand hung silent as 500 pupils, all in pleated green tunics over regulation green bloomers elasticised over each thigh, stood to attention, lined up on asphalt in class rows.

'Always be modest – pure in thought and deed. Think of the Virgin Mary. Let her be your model. Be as pure as the Virgin Mary. Don't you let the devil tempt you with any impure thought. And girls, don't you tempt others through your own deeds. Now, you all know the rules.'

We all held our breath, sensing something was coming.

'Despite the rules,' the principal continued, 'on Monday morning one girl arrived wearing a pair of patent leather shoes. She knows who she was, wearing such shiny shoes.'

As a titter erupted and faces broke into smirks, Mother Imelda shook the bell. 'No sniggering please.'

In the avalanche of quiet I dared not blink an eye. I wasn't guilty. I wore no such shoes. They were vulgar. They could show your knickers and lead a boy to sinful thoughts.

The noon bell brought me back to Sister Lawrence's class. As it chimed throughout the school, chairs scraped floorboards and down tumbled aisles of knees for the angelus: 'Angelus domini –' The angel of the Lord had rescued me.

I whipped out of class, grabbed my straw hat from its peg in the sheltershed and scooted across the parapet, down the concrete stairs, around the side of the convent, through the spacious grounds of the garden with its manicured lawns, flowing fountain, ancient oaks, roses in bloom and pots of petunias, down the long path next to the trimmed green hedge, down the steps to the huge sandstone wall and, by now with my gloves on, passed into Harrington Street. I was off down the hill, home to lunch.

I made no mention of the Nativity to Mama – or to anyone else. All I wanted was to protect myself, to keep the shame of my secret from spreading at school. Why tell others and invite their scorn? I just kept my feelings all knotted up inside myself.

Even members of artistic families were scandalised by nude modelling. When Mama posed for the artists at Lady Franklin Museum, rumour had it the wife of the group president kept him at home to protect him from the sight of a naked woman.

Dorothy first modelled for her portrait as a teenager when still at school. Two promising young Hobart artists, Eileen Brooker and Oliffe Richmond, noticed her in the shop and asked if she would sit for them. 'We've never drawn a Chinese face. We'd really like the chance.'

Then, in her early twenties, after Lehene and I were born and Mama had divorced and had no prospects other than serving in a shop, she chose hairdressing. She hoped to open her own salon, to offer fine service and sell beautiful French perfumes. Although she didn't accomplish that, she made a start and that led to modelling. Too old to be apprenticed, she studied interstate for about eighteen months, leaving us in the care of Ah Hool and our uncles but making return visits to Hobart.

While enrolled in hairdressing in Sydney, she followed Eileen Brooker's advice: 'Pay the fees and support yourself through modelling.'

Mama passed her evenings at East Sydney Technical College, the Julian Ashton Art School, the Antonio Dattilo Rubbo Art School and other studios. She modelled for the classes of Desiderius Orban at the Quay, Francis Lymburner at Bellevue Hill and Thea Proctor in George Street. Friday nights she reserved for the Society of Realist Artists. Afterwards she wound up at the Arabian Coffee Lounge, a bohemian haunt in Kings Cross, with the up-and-coming artists Bernard Sahm, Bill Sewell, Charles Blackman and Gordon Walters, a New Zealander with whom she later lived. As they tossed about ideas on art, books and philosophy, she listened, wide-eyed. Although most of what they said flew above her head, she caught the drift and a little filtered through to Lehene and me.

In Melbourne she posed for the Victorian Artists' Society and for William Dargie's classes at the National Gallery Art School. One day as she stepped off the tram in St Kilda Road, another passenger stopped and introduced himself: 'Louis Kahan. I've just had an exhibition at Georges. Would you mind posing for me?'

Mama told me – I was too young to remember – that she took me along to the Hobart Tech. I amused myself between the easels and stools while she modelled for the life classes run by portraitist Jack Carington Smith or water colourists Rosamund McCulloch and Dorothy Stoner. Sometimes the students drew me too. And in late 2007 I was to be surprised when a complete stranger to me, Sue Briginshaw née Page, curator at St Helens History Room in northeast Tasmania, told me over the phone: 'I once painted your portrait. I was in Carington Smith's class.'

*

I most associate Mama's modelling with the time we lived at Uncle Gordon's new, pale blue brick house at 7 Edge Avenue, Lenah Valley. I remember the day snow blanketed Hobart for the first and only occasion in all my years there. I was six or seven when Lehene led me onto the tram to school, only to find it deserted.

'Good gracious, girls, go home.' The nuns waved us off as though we were chooks.

Back at Edge Avenue, we had the time of our lives building a snowman with the help of our next door neighbour, who did most of the work. My fingers iced inside my astrakhan gloves and it took ages to make the snowman grow, but every pat of white fluff counted until the snowman was almost double my height. I wanted him to last forever and felt sad as he melted down to sludge.

We went back to the shop before Uncle Gordon moved in with his beautiful Chinese bride whom he married in Jamaica. He had wall-to-wall carpet installed. 'Can you feel how spongy it is on your feet, Bo Co?' he said. 'Rubber. Rubber underneath.'

I'd never seen or felt anything like it. It was as magical as playing on the escalators in the Charles Davis hardware store. When we lived at Lenah Valley, we walked on bare floorboards and, except for the lounge suite, the bedroom suite and the piano, the house was unfurnished. We ate in the kitchen seated on orange boxes at a Formica table under the glare of an exposed bulb.

Once a week several artists arrived at the front door and were taken into the living room to draw Mama. Double glass doors connected the room with what would become the dining room but where I then slept. Sheets of newspaper covered these doors to prevent the living room light from disturbing me. One night I popped out of bed and peeped.

'Quick! Come and have a look!' I urged Lehene.

Through a tiny gap we could just make out Mama's tummy, somewhat twisted in our direction. We could see her navel. We had to move around to various angles to get her full figure. She stood in front of the unlit fireplace, her right elbow draped on the mantelpiece, her hand hanging down loose over the edge, her head turned slightly to the right, gazing into the wall, her lips not quite closed. A clean-shaven Stephen Walker, a future sculptor, worked furiously, shading in a section on his pad. Tas Fehlberg seemed intent on studying her feet, the right foot a fraction in front of the left. From his position in the far corner, Max Angus, the water colourist, sketched at a steady pace with a stick of charcoal.

It all looked very serious. For some time, Lehene and I remained quiet, then I glanced at Lehene and we burst out giggling. With our hands over our mouths, we dashed out of the room and into the main bedroom, set up for Uncle Gordon but being used by Lehene. We threw ourselves onto his big new bed, rolled onto our backs and laughed ourselves silly.

8

Montagues and Capulets

From Uncle Lester's room on the second floor over the shop, I looked down from sash windows to green trams trundling along Liverpool Street. Across the road, up from the Green Gate, Jackson's newsagency kept our weekly copy of *Chick's Own*, my favourite comic, filled with its black and yellow chicks, Timmy the Cat and pink Percy Pig.

The room was furnished with a four-piece mahogany suite. One of the drawers of the dresser held a round tin of sticky Rexona ointment that smelt of eucalyptus. We always rushed to this green goo to heal any sort of cut, scratch, burn or other ailment of the skin. Uncle Lester kept his Brylcreem on the glass top of the dresser. He stood in front of the winged mirror, slapped on the gel and combed his hair into shape with a wave on the left.

He shared his room with Aunty Eva. As the wife of Third Brother, she was Thlum Thlaw in Toishanese, so became known as Atum. Although kind to Lehene and me, Atum seemed less well disposed towards Mama.

Mama had worked for René Henri's salon in Melbourne and Hadley's in Hobart and sometimes cut, set or permed the hair of friends in her room. Whenever she wound someone's hair with strips of tissue paper around the thin wooden rollers, I smelt the perming solution. She also shampooed and set Atum's hair. She covered it all with a net, protected each of Atum's ears with a wad of cotton wool and settled her under the drone of the black Bakelite dryer where she couldn't hear you talk. When Mama brushed and combed Atum's hair, then sprayed it with lacquer, it gave Atum pleasure.

'Thank you Dor-wofy,' she said in her broken English, as Mama showed her her reflection in the mirror.

But the set didn't last long and, with its disappearance, the scowl on her face reappeared. As Uncle Lester's wife, Atum had charge over the girls in the shop and tried to hold purse strings over her pretty but penniless sister-in-law.

One afternoon, when I was sent to Pearce & Son, the butcher, to buy six baby lamb chops, instead of going to the refrigerator as he usually did, then sharpen his knife and cut and trim every chop, Mr Pearce just stood, his hands against the striped blue apron tied around the waist of his once-white coat.

'Now you tell Miss 'enry I can't give 'er anythin' today because Mrs 'enry has cut 'er off.'

I suddenly felt hemmed in by surrounding bodies, adult sneers stretching down nostrils. Through a passage of handbags, I vanished out the flyscreen.

That evening in the kitchen Mama wailed to Lester, 'We've been cut off again!'

'Oh,' he groaned, turning to Atum, 'Why'd you go and do that?'

Before she finished her shrill response, he snapped, 'Don't! Don't do that again!'

Strange odours wafted through the dark spooky storeroom behind a curtain off the kitchen. Cramming the shelves lay tins of herbs and tea, bottles of soy sauce and sweet Oriental wines, packets of dried shrimp, bean curd in strips and in sheets, mushrooms and other fungi, translucent vermicelli and black seaweed to cook in broth – something

I could never stomach. When drowned by liquid, the seaweed reminded me of clumps of matted hair. From hooks on the wall hung strings of dried pork or liver sausages made in Melbourne – very tasty when steamed over rice, thinly sliced and served with steamed salted duck eggs.

Before Uncle Gordon took his place at the head of the table, everyone was poised to eat. He crossed himself, closed his eyes, lowered his head, joined his hands upright in front of his chest and said grace: 'Bless us O Lord for these Thy gifts we are about to receive –'

He no sooner tasted the soup than his brows furrowed. 'Oh, too salty! Use a little less salt, Eva.'

Everyone else continued dipping their porcelain spoons into the large steaming bowls.

Uncle Gordon's chopsticks stretched out for a slice of pork. 'What's happened to the crackling? It should be crisper. And without quite so much fat.'

Almost every dish disappointed him. Even though Atum and Mama plied him with choice morsels, he complained in a low whine, finding this too hot, that too cold and every other dish his chopsticks touched either too sweet, a little sour, or in some other way not to his liking.

At the far end of the table Lehene and I warded off Mama's attention.

'You have this. It's good for you.' She popped stir-fried melon onto my rice.

'Not so much. Let me help myself.' I pulled my bowl away.

In the Chinese village manner, I used my chopsticks to shovel rice from my bowl into my mouth. I bit and sucked the flesh from servings of whole fresh fish or bite-size portions of chopped chicken, pork or pigeon and, with my chopsticks, placed any bones straight onto the table. I ate heartily. Lehene lingered, ladylike.

'Nay Nay, please eat up. Don't just pick at your food,' urged Mama.

*

As we grew older in our extended family, we couldn't escape the constant arguments, usually conducted over dinner.

'The children need new uniforms,' said Mama.

'They've got uniforms. What's wrong with what they've got?' Uncle Gordon was indignant.

'They've grown out of them. They have to have new ones. And shoes too.'

'What about their father? Why can't he pay for something for a change?'

'You know he won't pay a penny. We've been through all this before.'

Then, after a pause, 'I'll think about it.'

'You've been thinking about it,' Mama retorted as he made his escape. 'And they're back at school next week.'

Almost every bill caused a scene. We sat through scenes over school fees, books, ballet fees, art fees, music fees, drama fees and doctors and dentists too. The family argued in a mixture of English and Chinese that added a bizarre note to our feeling of distress. We couldn't repeat the Chinese but we understood every word. We listened, our eyes widening and our ears pricked for the explosive end – followed by silence. Then, not the tinkle of a teaspoon could be heard in that kitchen at the top of the stairs.

No one who saw Lehene or me could have guessed the drama played out over the shop. We were always well dressed but only after Mama had fought. When the going got tough, she entreated Lehene, 'Pet, you go and cry to Uncle Lester.'

As his favourite, she didn't need to cry. She just stood at his feet, shyly twisting her hair around her little finger. He drew up a cheque.

'We had the best of everything,' Lehene would reminisce as an adult, 'but what we had to go through to get it. No child should have to go through what we went through.'

Like circus monkeys put through hoops for their peanuts, we had to perform. As I wrote, at the age of nine, to Mama when she was away in Sydney:

9th June 1954

    139 Liverpool St.

    Hob. TAS.

    Dear Mummy,

    I got this bill on the sat-ur-day be-fore you left and I asked Un-call Lester and he said he will not pay for it and Daddy said the same.

    There is a letter for you from Uncall Gordon.

    Come back very soon.

    Love Wo Wo

    XXXXXXX

Twelve months on, bills still came.

    In 1955 I was flung down the steps of Hobart's new Richardson's Building into the jaws of the Golden Dragon. Long before the modern glass complex opened – with its novelty of the Manhattan, a cafe hissing and gurgling with Hobart's first cappuccino machine, an open carpark at the rear where drivers paid a uniformed attendant to park their cars and an underground cinema that screened newsreels on the hour – I had shared Uncle Gordon's excitement. After a trip to America he had surprised me with a packet of Spearmint chewing gum, individual flat strips wrapped in silver foil and nothing like the white-coated lumps we sold at the shop. He planned Tasmania's first supermarket. I spent the summer holidays helping him from morning to night: I filled and weighed bags of sugar, stamped prices on tins of Sunshine milk, packets of Cornflakes and Pears soap and stacked the goods on shelves separated by aisles, preparing for the revolution of customers serving themselves and passing through a checkout counter. I knew nothing about the new Chung venture, the Golden Dragon – Hobart's first Chinese restaurant.

    'Wait over there,' sniffed the imitation Oriental dolled in tight black and stilettos. 'Your father's busy.'

    I perched myself on the edge of the settee. The outline of a golden dragon swirled its tail across double doors. I took off my green felt winter hat, but dared not move. I stayed as stiff as the porcelain statues and miniature jade Buddhas locked behind glass. My gloved hand gripped a window envelope.

From behind the display counter, Miss Marshall answered the phone. I could hear her saccharine voice and see the swish of her straight, dyed black hair: 'No, you don't have to use chopsticks. All the tables are set with forks and spoons but if you want chopsticks, we can provide them.'

I began to fidget. My feet couldn't reach the floor. The garters holding up my socks tightened around the calves. I suffocated under the stares of curious diners, about to relax over chicken and almonds or sweet and sour, before heading next door to the Tatler newsreel theatre. How long would I have to sit there, at the entrance? I didn't belong to the basement of Richardson's building; I belonged to the ground floor up on Murray Street.

What could my father be doing, ensconced behind the door of his office, hidden by closed venetian blinds? I couldn't begin to imagine. I'd so rarely seen him. Once, he had suddenly appeared at the shop, a sheepish face at the top of the stairs. With hardly a word or a glance, he handed me a brand new tennis racket. I slipped it out of its red check sheath and examined the strings and the lettering – SPALDING. I undid the pouch and found two new balls.

'Thank you, Daddy,' was all I had managed.

The voice of the imitation Oriental abruptly brought me back to the Golden Dragon. 'Your father will see you now.'

I approached his door, knocked and entered.

Dressed in a dark tailored suit, he barely lifted his head. 'What you want?' He shifted uneasily in his chair, no trace of smile beneath the slicked black hair.

'The school fees,' I stammered, putting the envelope on his blotter. 'They haven't been paid for two terms.'

'Your mother send you?'

'Yes.'

'And how's Lehene?'

'Well, thank you, Daddy.'

He said no more. What more could I say, separated by the desk and linked to him only by the tick-tock of the clock? I preferred waiting in the corridor outside the school library for the strap from Mother Imelda. That was predictable: it cut, it burnt into the palms of my hands, but I knew when it would end. At school there were rules. Inside my father's office there were no rules.

9

Praying and Playing

'You're not even wearing a scapular,' Anne rebuked me.

I stared at the brown woollen tab, the size of two postage stamps, peeping out from under my cousin's singlet and hanging from a thread around her shoulders.

'If you don't wear a scapular you're not preserved from going to hell.'

I peered down at my own singlet. Perhaps the Holy Ghost had performed a miracle. No, I wasn't wearing a scapular. I wasn't preserved from hell. What could I do? It was too late now, just when we were undressing for bed. I would have to rely on the rosary we'd just said as we fingered our beads while kneeling on the rose-patterned carpet on the sitting room floor. Pulling the sheet and blankets around my neck, I gazed up at the ceiling in gloom. I would have to stay awake all night. But my eyelids kept closing. Turning towards the crucifix on the wall, I prayed once more: 'Dear God, please save me from hell. Please let me wake up in the morning.'

Despite its constant reminders of sin and guilt, I loved my cousins' house. Out the back a walnut tree opened like a huge umbrella, half its branches spread over Uncle Timmy's vegetable patch where scarlet runner beans curled their way up wooden spikes and baby marrows emerged from seed. Other branches grew out over the grass, in which a dirt path had been worn under the swing. That was my delight:

gripping the ropes, being pushed by my cousin Marie and swinging higher and higher.

I, alone of the four of us, climbed up the walnut tree, though not far. Even I was too scared to sit on a branch. Perhaps if I'd belonged to the Boy Scouts or even the Girl Guides I wouldn't have been such a sook. I could never be as brave as Georgina of the Famous Five. She was my hero. George would have climbed right to the top and built a cubby house there.

Because Lehene and I lived over the shop, our cousins' garden was the one we knew best. I'd played in Uncle Gordon's backyard when it was still rubble. That was where I discovered worms. I picked one up, dangled it between my fingers and then let it wriggle around, cold and slimy, in my hand. I poked about for another. The one I found was big and fat and it shocked me when it broke into two. I dashed inside, grabbed a knife, plucked out another juicy worm and chopped it in half. One section slithered off to the paling fence, the other to the rotary clothesline.

Uncle Timmy used a big knife to prepare chicken for the pot. In the far corner of his yard clucked black Australorps with beady eyes, white Leghorns with pink combs, Rhode Island Reds with orange-brown feathers and bright red combs. When I stayed at my cousins', I awoke to 'Cock-a-doodle-do'. At feeding time I helped mix food, pollard and water with a wooden spoon and unlatched the wire gate. I wasn't afraid. I didn't mind the chooks flapping about my feet, squawking as I entered the pen to collect eggs from straw on the shelf. Only later, after seeing *The Birds* by Alfred Hitchcock, would I dread feathers and cringe even if a swallow flew near.

Uncle Timmy never showed fear. A man of slight build and few words, he seized a hen and carried it out of the cage by its wings. Marie, Anne and I jumped about, watching the ritual. Lehene cowered by the rose bushes, trying to avoid the scene. With a single slit of the knife, Uncle Timmy had blood spurting from the neck straight into the bowl on the bench by the walnut tree.

'Inside,' he grunted and began to pluck and clean the chook.

I took the brimming bowl, carried it from the outer yard through the hedge to the inner yard. Holding it carefully so the blood wouldn't spill, I went down the grey stone path that divided the toilet, tool shed and laundry block from the square of grass. Then, up three steps and I reached the kitchen.

'Oh, that is a good girl, dear,' said Aunty Joyce, wringing her hands in front of her apron. 'I'll just add a little water and let it set.'

At lunch, while Lehene contented herself with a sliver of breast, I relished the chicken blood. After it had set into a wobbly jelly, it was slipped into hot broth just before being served. With chopsticks I dipped a segment into soy sauce, popped it into my mouth and polished it off with rice.

Aunty Joyce was better known for her afternoon teas. Anne stood on a box to whip the cream and let me lick the beater.

'Now you take this over to the brothers.' Aunty Joyce handed us each a platter with a cream sponge topped with passionfruit icing.

We crossed the road to the Redemptorist monastery where the monks, swishing in their black habits, were constantly blessed with cakes. Then we joined the adults in the sitting room, sipping tea from pink, blue and lemon pastel porcelain cups as dainty sandwich triangles disappeared and tiny silver forks grazed plates with vanishing slices of cream sponge.

A gilt-framed image of Christ, His Sacred Heart aflame, hung on the wall, guarding us. On the mantelpiece below stood the Infant Jesus of Prague, radiant in jewel-encrusted crown and heavy white robe embroidered with gold. On either side glowed a small red lamp. God suffused my aunt's house.

Aunty Joyce was the most religious person I knew, apart from Sister Malachy.

'I was first in the family to find Our Lord,' she told me when I was helping her in the laundry one weekend. A packet of Rinso stood on the window ledge. Laundry wasn't a chore to me; as we had no copper at the shop we sent our linen off to the Happy Wash.

'I was drawn to Christianity in my search for love.' Her hands gripped and turned the wringer handle. 'I found Christ's love. My mother didn't love me. Oh, I was such a disappointment to her. Her firstborn, a daughter. She didn't love us girls.' She shrugged, wiping her brow with her sleeve. 'She only loved her sons, especially Gordon. She couldn't do enough for him. She doted on him.'

Aunty Joyce, so strict about modesty that she always locked the bathroom door, didn't berate her little sister. Mama was allowed to sunbathe naked on the grass out the back. 'Shoo!' my aunt brushed my cousins, Lehene and me away. 'Aunty Dorothy's out there. Keep yourselves in the front.'

But once, when Mama stayed with Aunty Joyce and our cousins at 59 Cross Street, a nude portrait of her by Francis Lymburner went missing from her case.

'Aunty Joyce had a terrible life as a girl,' Mama explained as she opened a box of photographs from the camphorwood chest. 'That's why she spends so much time on her knees. Mum gave her hell. Gave me hell, too. Aunty Marie escaped. She was the baby. But Joyce and I got a tongue lashing every night.'

Grandmother, standing composed and elegant, her hands resting on the back of a bentwood chair in the photographer's studio, appealed to me. Her short straight hair has a fringe. She wears spectacles and a black cotton frock Mama said Ah Hool made herself from material Mama helped her buy from Mathers in Liverpool Street. It's buttoned at the front with red stitching on the corners of the collar. Ah Hool's ears are adorned with drop earrings – her red rubies. A jade bracelet is clasped on her left wrist and on her fingers are several rings, including her gold wedding ring and triple-diamond engagement ring. I couldn't imagine her uttering a harsh word.

Yet I heard my mother say, 'I still get nightmares. I hear Mum shouting at me: "You should never have been born!" Joyce learnt to offer everything up to God. She worked until late every night in the shop, until after the pictures closed.'

I saw my aunt when young, tired but busy serving people who'd poured out of the Strand and His Majesty's, down Liverpool Street and into the shop. They lined the counter, drinking bottles of orangeade or sarsaparilla, holding out a hand for change, ripping open a packet of peanuts, or savouring the sight of Joyce weighing half a pound of cherries.

'But she never got a kind word from Mum, only insults and cruel taunts,' my mother continued. 'I would have been lost without Joyce. We slept in the same bed until she went up to Brisbane, met Timothy and married him.'

Visions of Aunty Joyce flashed by: her kindness, her cream cakes and all the Enid Blyton books she gave me on my birthdays. I resolved never to do anything to upset her. I wanted the fun of her house to go on forever.

The fun began when we played swans because Marie and Anne had a piano, in the airy front room opposite the phone. With Mama at the keyboard, the four of us became immersed in the strains of Saint-Saëns. Lehene was best because of her swan-like neck. I tried to lengthen mine so it looked like hers. We let our bodies float between water lilies across the lake, our arms gliding as wings, until we gradually sank down to the waxed floor, soft and feathery like dying swans.

One day Uncle Timmy lugged in a cardboard box marked ELECTROLUX.

'See how it works,' said Marie.

'Yes, look.' Anne tore up bits of paper into tiny pieces that Marie sucked up with the howling metal tube.

'So now you don't have to sprinkle damp tea leaves over the carpet.' Lehene could hardly be heard over the din.

Our cousins were relieved of having to use a straw broom to sweep up the dust that clung to all the leaves. The Electrolux was the most exciting thing since my shilling ride on a Shetland pony across the Domain that came with the regatta but once a year.

Most fun came with riding my bike at my cousins' as there I could compete with them. On a summer's day Lehene, with *Fifth Formers of St Clare's* tucked under her arm, took the tram with Mama, while I rode all the way to New Town. First, I warmed up around the city. In a pair of yellow shorts I pedalled from the shop over to Battery Point, peering into boatsheds and passing clusters of Georgian cottages. I freewheeled down to Salamanca Place, with its grim stone warehouses and roamed along to the wharf where an ocean liner had docked; nets were spread out and fishing vessels, ferries and yachts were moored in the deep green of the Derwent. Seagulls scattered before my wheels. I tasted the salt air and caught the whiff of fish and chips in newspaper wafting up. From the wharf I headed towards North Hobart and struggled up Elizabeth Street, past Victorian mansions hidden behind cedars and pines, until I reached the Shell service station at Augusta Road. There I pumped up the tyres and collected Shell's free panels of blotting paper, enough to share with the others.

We all loved to race our bikes along the flat stretch of Cross Street. We dared each other to ride with no hands, with hands off the handle bar and feet off the pedals. I went a step further. I stood with both feet on the seat of my Malvern Star while grasping the handlebars, then, with only one foot while holding with both hands and finally, like an arabesque with my left foot on the seat, my right leg swung out behind me, with only my left hand on the handlebar.

'That's silly. Stop showing off,' Lehene reproached.

The others were inside playing Monopoly by the fire on the Saturday I found myself alone with the boy who did odd jobs at the monastery. I was about nine. I knew Gabriel from the times the brothers sent him on errands across the road. This day, while he was doing number one in the toilet out the back near the walnut tree, he let me hold his thing.

A strange sensation it was, standing next to him on concrete, the darkness pierced only by a dull light from the slot above the closed door. It felt nothing like the worms I'd found wriggling around in the ground. Holding his thing felt different. I held it only briefly between my thumb and index finger. Unlike the worms, there was nothing slimy. Unlike the worms, it felt warm, not cold. And unlike the worms, after holding it, I now had to cleanse not just my body but my soul.

Even though there was no Commandment – Thou shalt not hold a boy's thing – I knew I'd done wrong. Not even Mother Imelda had stood at assembly and proclaimed that. No. Yet I sensed it was forbidden. That was what tempted me. The forbidden gave me that fleeting thrill. But I'd given in to the devil. Worse, I'd led a younger person astray, a boy not near my age. Like Eve in the Garden of Eden, I was a bad influence. I would be damned with the fallen angels to burn in the fires of hell.

What if Aunty Joyce found out? I would be disgraced. That would be the end of the swing. The end of cream cakes. The end of Enid Blyton books. The end of racing my bike. Aunty Joyce would be disgraced. The monastery would be disgraced. The whole school would be disgraced. I would be expelled. Aunty Joyce would write a letter to the Pope and he would excommunicate me. I would be cut off from the Church and any chance of saving my immortal soul. While my aunt wrote the letter, I would be locked in the dark vacuum cleaner cupboard, with all the spiders, snakes, creepy-crawlies, ghosts and hobgoblins.

I had to get to confession.

'Bless me Father for I have sinned,' I whispered. 'My last confession was two weeks ago.'

'Bless you my child. And what do you wish to confess?' came the familiar voice from the other side of the grille in the wall of the wooden confessional.

'A sin of impurity,' I quaked. Oh, what if Father Rogers knew who I was under the brim of my hat in the dark? He, the tall, handsome, popular Irish priest with a magnificent singing voice. He, who appeared without warning in class, interrupting the lesson with cheer, much to our delight. How could I ever look him in the face again?

'By yourself, my child, or with another?'

I squirmed from knee to knee. 'With another, Father.'

'Then, for your penance say five Our Fathers and ten Hail Marys. Go in peace, my child, and sin no more.'

10

What My Sister Might Say

Helene always talks about her bike. It was mine. Uncle Lester gave it to me for my tenth birthday. 'Come downstairs and see what I've got for you.'

I didn't know what to expect; I hadn't asked for anything. But there it stood, in the shop: a sparkling blue-and-white Malvern Star, size 24. I was too nervous to ride it straight away. Helene and I had both learnt on Marie and Anne's bikes. That was out at Cross Street, level and hardly any cars. I wasn't sure about Liverpool Street and dodging all the traffic and trams. But Helene? Next Saturday she was up early and away for hours. I hardly saw it after that.

'You can have Mummy's bike,' she said.

It's true we had our mother's bike, all reconditioned and gleaming and not being used. She kept it as a treasure from her father. I did get around to riding it, but it was size 26. Besides, that's not the point. Helene took my bike. And later, when she got her own – a fancy black Raleigh with gears and every other contraption – she sold my bike. She was down at Taroona at the time and I was at Uncle Gordon's at Lenah Valley.

One day she just let drop, 'Oh, Shirley's got your bike.'

'What do you mean she's got my bike?'

'I sold it to her.'

'Why?'

'She wanted it.'

Shirley was another St Mary's girl, in the class between Helene and me. I didn't object to Shirley, but I did object to Helene selling my bike. She just said, 'Well, you never used it,' and stalked off.

Sold my Latin books, too. I kept them in perfect condition, the covers all wrapped in new brown paper and handed them down to her. She sold them and bought new ones. That's what she was like. She did just as she pleased.

When we lived at the shop and Uncle Lester moved down to Taroona, I moved into his room, which meant I had more space to play dolls. I loved dolls. I dressed one in delicate pink satin and white lace and walked her on her dainty buttoned shoes across the floor. Her blue eyes stared out at me and her eyelashes fluttered. I could even make her talk, though it did sound more like a squawk.

Helene wasn't interested in dolls. Hardly touched them. A tomboy. She had a yellow clip-on tie she wore at home – except when she put it on Teddy. She once scooted off on her red Cyclops to buy a chocolate pipe but came back without one.

'I reached the counter of Moore's Variety,' she said, 'and when I looked down I saw my tie. I was still wearing it, a boy's tie. I felt so silly I had to leave.'

There's a picture of her at a girl's birthday party. Everyone's done up in a frilly frock except Helene. She's standing there in her pigtails and the pair of new jodhpurs Mummy bought her in Sydney. Helene was going to be a policewoman. Or a tram driver. After she was old enough to go to America and have an operation to change into a boy. Uncle Gordon said they could do that there.

She seemed to like the black doll. She played with that – until its head broke off. I don't know how that happened. One of us must have dropped it. I'm sure we weren't fighting over it. There would have been no point. Helene would have won.

We did fight out at Calvary. That was a lot of fun. We were both in hospital having our tonsils out. The best part – even better than all the jelly and icecream – was pillow fighting. We were in a ward with another girl from school, Carmel, and she threw a pillow at Helene. After that, we were all jumping about on the beds, squealing, throwing pillows at each other. Then a nun walked in.

'Now, now. We can't have this. Feathers all over the place. Into bed. Straight away. All of you.'

People say that big sisters are bossy. So what happened to us? I remember when Joseph, a distant relation or clan member or something, who didn't speak much English, left to start his own shop and Helene moved into his room. It was poky with only a bed against one wall. She raced downstairs to the back of the shop where the empty fruit cases were stacked, came back with a fresh orange case, stood it on its side, covered it with a towel and had a bedside table. Trouble was she could now lay out her guns: cap guns and water pistol. I was in my room, kneeling by the bed and dressing my doll, when she suddenly appeared in her cowboy suit, squirted me, laughed and ran off. Happened all the time.

When I was in Grade 5 and in charge of breakfast, Helene couldn't wait to get to school. In winter she dashed off without anything. Sometimes she didn't even drink the milk I heated and mixed with Aktavite and glucose in our Bunnykins mugs. Not that we had much for breakfast. We were supposed to have Weet-Bix. Except on Saturdays, when Mummy cooked us a thin eye fillet – which we always called 'fillet eye' – in butter, with an egg and half a grilled tomato. Helene wolfed hers down but I never ate much. Except for sponge fingers. I could always eat them. I was even taken to the doctor to see what was wrong with me.

'You don't like milk, do you?' Dr Millar said.

I must have shaken my head.

'Then you don't have to drink it.'

I wanted to tell him I didn't mind milk. I much preferred milk to the Lane's emulsion – a bit like cod liver oil – we had to have. But the words wouldn't come out. Helene and I got through five pints a day between us. Mummy said it was good for us. Said her mother didn't give her any milk at all. She was weaned on rice water. That's why she had rickets and had to wear leg irons for years when she was little. So we had to have milk five times a day.

'I don't think there's a problem,' I heard the doctor say. 'Just leave a few raisins about. If she's hungry, she'll eat them.' I felt his eyes on me again. 'And what do you want to do when you grow up?'

'I don't know.'

And that was it. 'That'll be three guineas, Mrs Chung.'

I never really knew what I wanted. Helene? When she was eight she disappeared downstairs, picked out a case, used the tomahawk to prise off any nails sticking out and split the boards into kindling. Then she carted the bundle in newspaper up the hill to school. When I went later it was still frosty. I trudged up Harrington Street with my Globite case, seeing my breath rise in clouds in front of my face, feeling my chilblains itch inside my gloves and my toes frozen and swollen in my shoes.

'I want to have the fire lit before Miss Kuhn arrives,' she said. It was the same right through winter. She would do anything to please Miss Kuhn. And lighting matches made Helene feel grown up. My class was just along the parapet from Grade 3 and once I glimpsed her fire roaring under the mantelpiece beneath Our Lady. The fire in our room hadn't even been set.

Miss Kuhn stood out from the Presentation sisters. She tried to blend in by wearing black. She wore a tight black skirt with a zip up the front. We'd never seen such a thing. Only men had openings at the front and they were buttoned up, not zipped. Helene idolised her and she encouraged Helene in art. Miss Kuhn asked her for some of her paintings to show to someone (though I don't think she ever did). She even asked Helene to demonstrate in class. Helene carried her easel, palette, knife and tubes of oils up to school and painted an abstract, there, with everyone looking on. That would have terrified me.

The funny thing is, I had a painting published. Not Helene. In a book of children's self-portraits from around the world. The first is a fuzzy round face of a 4-year-old New Zealand girl, the last, a 15-year-old Mexican with his butterfly collection. I'm the second: against a yellow background, my short black hair sits straight across my forehead and a red blob is on either cheek. I've painted myself in a long-sleeved blue jumper over a flared blue and yellow check skirt. Underneath the portrait is printed: '6 Jahre, LEHENE CHUNG, China'.

That's one thing Helene can't take from me.

11

The Red MG, Rex and Rajah

The red MG TF1500 glimmered in the showroom window.

'I have to have it,' said Mama.

Six months old and the only one of its type in Tasmania, it cost £800. Uncle Lester wrote out a cheque and Mama paid him back £10 a week.

'I need it for practical reasons,' she explained. 'I can't carry all the food and parcels home on the tram. They won't fit into a string bag.'

My mother wasn't practical or patriotic enough to buy a Holden. She didn't even have a licence, so Rex drove at first but soon had to relinquish the wheel.

Rex Walden, a New Zealand radio announcer with a rich, golden voice, had met Mama in Sydney. He flew down to Hobart and in 1955 he and Mama rented an unremarkable red brick house at 26 Seymour Street, New Town. After a long stint with Melbourne's 3AW and fresh from Sydney's 2UE, Rex began work at 7HT, one of Hobart's two commercial radio stations. He developed quite a following, especially on his late night music shift when he played classical recordings, not only conventional commercial fare. Rex also freelanced for the ABC as a regular voice in schools broadcasts and radio dramas, which drew a large audience in that pre- and, from 1956, early television age.

A binge drinker, Rex used to hit the bottle, then he'd have a long dry spell and swear he'd never touch another drop, never, at least until his next bottle of Johnnie Walker Black Label. Once, in the creepiness of night, we fled to Uncle Lester's at Taroona.

At about the time we acquired the MG, Hobart introduced Australia's first parking meters. Shapely meter maids patrolled the blocks as I slotted in a threepenny piece for fifteen minutes or sixpence for half an hour.

Although a woman could saunter the streets, collecting coins and fishing for fines, she rarely sat in a driver's seat. Certainly no one in Hobart except Mama navigated an open-air sportscar. Something of a beauty at thirty, with her jet black hair and Chinese features, she stood a petite 5 feet. Rex, handsome, powerfully built and 6 feet tall, in his tailored tweed vest and jacket, grey flannels and brown suede shoes exuded the air of an English aristocrat. When they stepped out of the red MG they weren't easy to miss. Then one and later two, German shepherds occupied the bench behind the bucket seats.

No longer living at the shop, Lehene and I stayed at school at midday. Mama developed a habit of buying our lunch from a coffee shop in Criterion Street. She left the sandwiches and cream cake – 'too much cream', Lehene complained – in each of our school lockers, together with an orange she peeled so that the skin remained loosely coiled around the fruit. One touch freed the orange.

On Fridays, Catholics shunned meat under pain of mortal sin. We offered this small sacrifice in recompense for Christ's own sacrifice of dying on the Cross for our salvation.

'And remember, girls,' warned Sister Lucy with her Irish lilt, 'make sure your mother buys only Vegemite, not Marmite. Remember: V for Vegemite and vegetables, M for Marmite and meat. They may look the same. They may even taste the same. But Marmite contains an extract of meat.'

The wily devil was trying to confuse us. One Friday, sitting with my class on a bench in the sheltershed, our hats hanging on pegs above our heads, I became stricken by conscience. Was the dark brown paste between the bread in my hand and partly in my mouth, meat or vegetable? Might I slip on the parapet steps after lunch, crack my head and plunge to hell?

It was safer to reserve Fridays for fish. Soon Lehene and I were taking orders for others in our classes: eight lots of a shilling's worth of fish and chips, five lots of a shilling's worth of potato cakes and chips and four lots of scallops and chips. These parcels, all wrapped in newspaper, couldn't be left to go soggy in our lockers. Delivery time was critical: ideally, just before 12.30 when girls began pouring down the stairs and scrambling at the tuckshop window. But sometimes the queues for pies, pasties, cream buns and orangeade had already formed before the red MG nosed into the school grounds from the side entrance in Brisbane Street. Mama parked between the tuckshop and our locker room, in full view of the girls and any nun or visiting mother who strayed in the vicinity.

This caused Lehene such angst that she was to carry it through life. The MG set us, yet again, apart from our peers.

I suspected only one other girl may have been from a broken home, a subject I dared not broach with her. I was sure no one else had heard the word 'co-respondent'. Rex said co-respondent – a person cited as a third party in a divorce – conjured up an image of some bounder resplendent in a pair of two-toned shoes.

'There's no such thing as divorce,' Sister Lucy insisted. 'The Church doesn't recognise divorce.'

'But what if a man and a woman do get divorced, Sister, and the woman remarries?'

'In the eyes of the Church she can't remarry. She's still married to her husband.'

'But Sister, what if she does remarry, in the Registry Office?' the bold girl persisted.

'Marriage outside the Church is no marriage. Without the sanctity of marriage, she lives in a state of sin at the peril of her immortal soul.

And without the sanctity of marriage she's condemned to the eternal fires of hell.'

I tried not to quiver in my seat. I wasn't asking any questions. I wasn't drawing attention to myself. Not on this subject. I just wanted to blend in. We all knew the answers anyway; they were repeated year after year. I didn't need any more catechism lessons to know my mother was condemned to hell. The image of Mama engulfed in flames terrified me. I had to push it from my mind. I couldn't save her. She had to save herself. She had to exercise her own free will. I could only hope she would relent before she died, confess her sins and receive the last sacrament. Meanwhile, I had to save myself from the other girls in class.

Most of them would never have guessed Mama was divorced, but many of their parents must have known. Although the mothers of our friends were cordial and a few even warm towards her, some showed less than Christian courtesy. When she alighted from the red MG and crossed their paths, they tossed their heads. They raised their brows and averted their gaze. They couldn't disgrace themselves by speaking to a fallen woman.

Our house was opposite a vacant block where I trudged up the slope of a dirt path to the tram. From over the side of a paling fence floated the pitiable whining of a dog, Rajah, a German shepherd who spent most of his time chained up outside his master's house. One day, when let off the leash, he ceased to whine and sat contentedly outside our front gate. Mama gave him water to drink. On another occasion Rajah followed her to the telephone booth at the end of the street. Once he padded behind her over to Aunty Joyce's house, waited with ears pricked during afternoon tea and tracked Mama home.

'Is this your dog?' she eventually asked the owner.

''e's not bothering you is 'e?'

'No. Not at all. I was just wondering if you'd mind if he stayed with me sometimes.'

'As far as I'm concerned you can 'ave 'im.'

After Rajah joined the household, Uncle Lester and Atum, who had adopted Michael, a little Chinese boy from Melbourne, decided to buy a dog and asked Mama to help. On the advice of a vet, she went to Wayville Kennels at Moonah to see Mrs Badcock, an immense woman who roared with infectious laughter. She bred the best German shepherds and always won prizes at the Royal Hobart Show.

'Hello duck,' she greeted Mama. 'You should have one of my new litter. This pup's got the best head and coat. Moira she's called. You take her along to your brother.'

Uncle Lester hadn't bargained on the responsibility of rearing, bathing, brushing, walking and training a German shepherd. So Moira became ours.

About this time I came home from Saturday art class determined to have a cat. 'Only if it's Persian,' ruled Mama.

Although eighteen months passed before the slightest sign of Sooty's Persian pedigree appeared, I loved his shiny black fluffy coat and soft white paws. He slept on my bed, almost pushing me out, so close to me did he curl.

Within a few years Mama, Lehene and I would be squashed into the MG on our way to live in the countryside at Longley where we would have enough pets to open a zoo: two German shepherds, Moira and Marcia, at either end of the settee with the pedigreed Suffolk sheep, Corby, ensconced between; two cats, Sooty and a tabby named Mandy; Nicole the magpie who spent mornings pattering about indoors; and the geese permitted onto the verandah as far as the front door. Not to mention the goldfish from our years at the shop.

The MG met its fate on Easter Saturday 1961 while we were based at Longley. I was sixteen and in my first year of matriculation.

Mama and I had just left the Theatre Royal after seeing a performance of *I am a Camera*, an adaptation of Christopher Isherwood's *Berlin Stories* that would become best known as the film *Cabaret*, my introduction to the titillating night life of 1930s Berlin and the rise of Nazism. It was after 10 o'clock and I nestled in the passenger seat while Mama drove towards Taroona where I was staying with Uncle Lester.

I felt snug in my low-slung leather seat, comfortable in the dimness of the cabin. I was aware but taking no notice of the smooth Sandy Bay Road, the street lamps and shadows as we curved through the shopping centre and the two-way traffic on the wide straight stretch before us. Suddenly, I was blinded by lights. I tensed with fear as the glare advanced directly towards me, beaming down through the windscreen and then swallowing me in a blaze of white. Perhaps I shot skywards. Then spun in the air. After the blaze of white I knew nothing until I realised I was sprawled out on the road, my left cheek and ear hard against bitumen.

'You all right, Miss?' The flash of a torch dazzled me.

I squinted, trying to get my bearings.

'Here, let me help you up. Just take my hand,' coaxed the policemen.

Still dazed, I struggled to my feet. I was facing town, the opposite direction to our destination. In the darkness I heard voices over a low rumble that turned out to be hundreds of apples, pouring out of their crates and rolling everywhere; they surrounded me. Some had rolled up against the gutter on the other side of the street.

'Your mother's all right, Miss. It was a ten-ton truck loaded with apples.'

I have an image of Mama standing in the darkness talking to officials. They had rushed to the scene of the crash, right outside the police station. I felt helpless but calm, too stunned to be frightened. I was grateful to the policeman who led me into the station. I can't remember how we got home.

The MG was a wreck: the passenger side was smashed in, the left front wheel ripped off and the left side of the windscreen broken. Glass and metal littered the road. The crash had caused the MG to spin around twice and it too ended up facing town.

Even though I wasn't wearing a seatbelt – Hobart hadn't heard of such a thing – I had only superficial injuries to my face and neck and what would prove to be long-lasting whiplash. A photograph of the crumpled MG shows how lucky I was to escape. The car was a write-off, but, as it turned out, the accident had one positive effect: I had to have a thorough medical examination.

'You're in shock,' said the doctor. 'You need complete rest in hospital.'

At St Helen's Hospital in Macquarie Street I mentioned the stomach aches that had forced me to leave class and sit huddled forward on the shelf of my locker. A GP had told me I was nervous and needed to relax through regular soaking in a hot bath. My new GP took a different approach. He brought a specialist to hospital, who tapped my tummy twice, then declared, 'It's coming out tomorrow.'

Next morning he removed a cyst from my left ovary.

'It was rather big,' he explained. 'About the size of a telephone,' referring to the old black telephone with a rotary dial. 'No wonder you were in pain. And it had hairs and teeth.'

'Hairs and teeth! What does that mean?'

'Well, we don't really know. But such a growth isn't uncommon. The only theory I can offer is that you may have begun as a twin in the womb, gradually become stronger than the other twin and absorbed it.'

'A twin!'

'Yes. And you should know that having only one ovary makes no difference to having children. You only need one ovary.' Then, about to leave: 'Oh, incidentally, the pathology department of the Royal Hobart Hospital would like to keep your cyst as a specimen.'

Although the theory of twins remained theoretical, whenever the subject of my telephone arose, Lehene groaned, 'Oh, not two of you! I couldn't bear it!'

Decades later, when in Devonport in northern Tasmania to cross Bass Strait by ferry, I spotted a red MG a little ahead in the queue of vehicles. I caught sight of its classic, low-slung dashboard, its familiar canvas roof and wire wheels.

I popped out of my car to take a closer look. I sidled up to a magnificently maintained vehicle and leant down to peer through the window. 'Not bad,' I complimented the owner.

'No, it's not in bad nick. Did it up myself. A wreck when I bought it.'

'How long have you had it?'

'Oh, about thirty years. Bought it from some lady at, at –' he struggled to remember.

'Longley?' I prompted.

'That's it, Longley. A Chinese lady.'

'She was my mother. That was our MG.'

12

How Now Brown Cow

A Tasmanian winter. My fingers and toes itched, swollen with chilblains. The red glow of the bar radiator in Mother Dymphna's music room thawed not a bone in my body. On the piano stool I sat, fingers fumbling for black and ivory. Perhaps if I'd had the ample form of Mother Dymphna by my side, her beam would have imbued me with warmth. Perhaps if she had taught me, as she had Lehene, I too would have been in harmony with Chopin's études and Beethoven's sonatas. Instead, on that cold frosty morning and all year round, I had Sister Rita. Poor Sister Rita, malformed and permanently twisted over to one side. Sister Rita for whom I felt sorry. Sister Rita who'd forsaken the world to give me a chance. I should have been grateful. She'd helped me through my preliminary, through Grades 1 and 2. Now she rapped my knuckles for Grade 3 of the Australian Music Examinations Board.

Her cane hit hard. It hit with a bitter, sour note. It hit my stumbling fingers once too often and didn't improve my playing. I hated the piano. I hated the lessons. I hated having to stay on after school to practise because we had no piano at home.

'You'll be sorry,' warned Mama. 'You'll be sorry if you give it up.'

She was right. Even before I had left school, I felt a twinge of regret. I had a set of 78 rpm records about a boy called Peter who hates the piano. One day he finds himself meeting all the instruments of the orchestra and wonders where the piano is. It's skulking in the background, upset by his behaviour. Peter feels sorry and apologises. The piano and he become friends for life. When I was sixteen, I dropped that set of records. They crashed onto the polished floorboards at Uncle Lester's house. I stood in disbelief at the sight of each disc cracked and broken in half. I felt a terrible sense of loss. I bent down and picked up the pieces, wishing I could put them together again. Like Peter, I too would one day have to make peace with the piano.

My revolt, at thirteen, over the keyboard was partly spurred by my passion for the spoken word. I wanted to spend more time and take private lessons in speech and drama.

I fell in love with the theatre at the age of seven. Mama arrived at school, knocked on the door to Grade 2, asked if I could be absented and whisked me off to a matinée of *A Midsummer Night's Dream*. Seated on the smooth red velvet of the Theatre Royal, I was enchanted by the fairy wood. Figures floated about draped in gossamer garments while a mischievous Puck tricked some coarse yokel named Bottom into having an ass's head.

My stage debut was at the Playhouse, pirouetting as a pupil of Jean Carver. She taught us ballet each week at St Mary's where we clumped about in pink ballet shoes in the assembly room. Lehene and I also went to her Saturday morning class. From the shop we turned the corner to hike up Murray Street into a barn-like space above the Boy Scouts' shop. I stood, or wobbled, on my toes, held onto the bar and moved through positions one to five. In the 1954–55 edition of *Santa Maria* is a photograph of me dressed in a sleek black costume as a pussycat with pointed ears, an attendant to the fairy queen. Centre stage, the gifted Julie Sales adopts her regal pose.

One day, when I was about nine and staying with Uncle Gordon at Lenah Valley, the red telephone in the hallway rang.

'Would you like to play Jack in *Jack and the Beanstalk*?' asked Miss Carver.

'Oh, yes.' I leapt at the chance.

I tingled with the thought of playing Jack. I pictured myself climbing up the magic beanstalk into fairyland, creeping into the castle that was rightly mine, catching the hen that laid the golden eggs and seizing the gold-stringed harp. I too would tread the boards of make believe at the Theatre Royal.

'Now, let me introduce you all. This is Ric Marshall,' Miss Carver announced, turning to a beefy ruby-cheeked man. 'He's new to Hobart and our producer. He's also playing the principal role of Dame Beeznees. If you're good, he's promised to give you youngsters a gold bracelet with your own name engraved on it.' A murmur of enthusiasm rose among us.

'And I'd like you all to meet Jack,' she continued. I puffed myself up, only to see a tall, lithe young lady more than twice my age nodding to us children grouped on the floor. 'And you, Helene, will play the part of Jack in the prologue.'

My heart stopped. I'd been misled, cheated by an adult. Just like the wicked giant, I came toppling down to earth. I swallowed and tried to smile.

'It won't take you long to learn your lines.'

It didn't. My role as Jack consisted of sitting in a boy's dressing gown at the foot of a grey-haired woman in front of the red velvet curtain. I opened the pantomime with the words, 'Grandma, please tell me the story of *Jack and the Beanstalk*.'

Claire Mitchell, the most popular teacher at school, could never mislead me. She captivated me the moment she walked through the door from the junior parapet to us Grade 4s. With her charisma, charm, elegance and energy, Mrs Mitchell held every girl's attention. She made the Wednesday art of speech (or arda speich) class pure pleasure: from the world of mime in which we tried to mimic the magic of Marcel Marceau, to the technicalities of phonetics. Everything Mrs Mitchell stood for – from the recitation of poetry to the production of plays – epitomised fun. Mrs Mitchell nurtured in me the notion of work as play.

Our history lessons began with William the Conqueror and the Battle of Hastings in 1066. We saw Tasmania as a little part of England, salted with white skins of Anglo-Celtic origin and lightly peppered, by the 1950s, with New Australians from Continental Europe. The island's Aborigines had been exterminated, according to our textbooks. At every event and at every film, we all rose from our seats for the anthem, *God Save the Queen*.

Strine was not only discouraged, but also condemned by the nuns. Haitch (or hightch) was a hanging offence. Long before elitism became a dirty word, Mrs Mitchell cajoled us into educated Australian – not Austra-yan – speech. We were gunned down for any gunnas: 'We gunna do this,' and got for any goddas: 'We godda do that.' We pounced on Peter Piper and picked his peck of pickled peppers. We were judged by our manners, the shine on our shoes and the sound of our vowels: 'How now brown cow' and 'The rain in Spain stays mainly in the plain.'

My hands ran down the lustrous bronze satin of the toga I wore in my first performance produced by Mrs Mitchell. Set in Pompeii against the backdrop of Mount Vesuvius, *The Sleeping Fires* was my first play at the Playhouse. I had a minor role as a child of about nine or ten. I snatched a wreath, put it on my head and proclaimed myself the divine emperor, only to be mocked by the other children. I felt strange yet elated to see my name in a review in the *Mercury*.

We all relished rehearsals on Saturday afternoons at Mrs Mitchell's house, Strathleigh, on the waterfront in a meandering garden at Claremont, not far from Cadbury's chocolate factory. She introduced us to iced coffee, made with chilled milk, a dollop of icecream and topped with whipped cream. I floated on clouds.

Like other girls, I competed in the Hobart Eisteddfod and, after taking private lessons, prepared for the AMEB speech and drama exams too. We memorised each piece, be it verse by Blake or Belloc, an excerpt from Shakespeare, Shaw or Anouilh, a passage from *The Pickwick Papers*, or old Jolyon's death scene from *The Forsyte Saga*. We also learnt Australian works, including Douglas Stewart's *The Fire on the Snow*, Mary Gilmore's 'Old Henry Parkes' and John Shaw Neilson's 'Stony Town'.

Although my memory mostly served me well at school, it once failed me dismally. In 1959 St Mary's began an annual interhouse talent quest. The sisters asked me to coach our College house team in choral speaking, to direct and act in plays and to participate in the prose and poetry sections. One year, when my turn came to recite a poem, I walked on stage at St Peter's Hall, looked out through the shadows onto rows of expectant faces of parents, the table of adjudicators with their papers and pens and I froze. I stood in the spotlight, unable to utter a word. The harder I tried, the more I was struck dumb. In cutting silence, I made an exit. After all the other contestants had had their turns, I fronted on stage again. When I finished, I felt relieved by the applause. Fear of drying up – being frozen in public – was to dog me. I would find myself unable to ad lib and would freeze.

Like Claire Mitchell at school, Rex had a strong influence on me at home. He borrowed records from Radio 7HT and encouraged me to borrow more from the Tasmanian State Library. I listened, rapt, to the voices of Richard Burton or Sir Laurence Olivier reading poetry or a story such as *The Strange Case of Dr Jekyll and Mr Hyde*. My favourite was the ringing tone of Dylan Thomas reading his own 'Poem in October: It was my thirtieth year to heaven'.

Rex arranged my first entry into an ABC premises – simply to play. His friend Ellis Blain, also an announcer, worked for the ABC and asked me over after school to play with his daughter Virginia. Ellis had recently begun living with his new, younger partner, reporter Anne Deveson, in an ABC-owned cottage opposite St David's Park, a stone's throw from the ABC building where I would later be launched into journalism. Virginia, a shy, retiring sort of girl, destined to become an academic in English literature, reminded me of Lehene.

As an adult, I began to notice Anne Deveson's name being mentioned as a documentary filmmaker, social commentator and author of a book on her son's schizophrenia, *Tell Me I'm Here*. After I heard her speak on resilience at the 2003 Melbourne Writers' Festival, I found myself milling right by her side.

'Thanks for your talk,' I said. 'I remember you and Ellis Blain in Hobart.'

'I was a scarlet woman; no one would talk to me.'

'Well, my mother, Dorothy Henry, was living with Rex Walden.'

'They were the only ones who would talk to me.'

Rex also arranged my first formal contact with the ABC: a drama audition in the musty brown interior of the old radio building facing the GPO in Elizabeth Street. Not long afterwards I played a tiny part – something like Third Eagle, with about ten lines – in a schools broadcast, a drama designed to complement the school curriculum in a subject such as history, geography or English. I was thirteen, in my second year of senior school and scheduled for two hours rehearsal and recording. Wild with excitement, when class finished at 4 o'clock I charged to studio 717. Because everyone else – all the adult professional actors – towered over me as we stood reading our scripts, producer Robert Cubbage gave me a footstool so I too could reach the microphone. Regrettably, no Shirley Temple of the air, I only had one or two other roles after that. But I did have the thrill of my very first cheque – £1 8s 4d.

When I was seventeen, Rex rewrote my speech, Our Giants of Sport, and coached me for the 1962 Youth Speaks for Tasmania title. 'Not so much Claire Mitchell,' he urged. 'Just let it sound natural.'

Apart from a visit to Aunty Joyce in Brisbane when a babe in my mother's arms, I'd never been off the island and rarely far from Hobart. In the year that newspaper magnate Sir Frank Packer contested the America's Cup with his yacht *Gretel* – Australia's first challenge – I recalled the tea manufacturer Sir Thomas Lipton's five unsuccessful challenges that made him a symbol of international sportsmanship. His efforts transformed the contest from one of foul play to one of fair play. Rex's efforts transformed my speech into one that took me beyond southern Tasmania for the first time. I travelled the 120 miles to the finals in Launceston, where Rex's work paid off: I won the competition and received the prize, a Kriesler transistor radio. In its black Bakelite case, it was only the size of a hardback.

'CAREER IN RADIO?' asks the caption of an undated yellowed clipping from the *Mercury*: 'Three St Mary's College students were taken on a conducted tour of Radio Station 7HO by its administrative executive (Mr. Keith Graham) yesterday.'

The photograph shows us examining a tape recorder. We are rugged up, one girl wearing gloves while I'm holding an umbrella. Despite that clipping, I didn't know what to do when I left school. For as long as I could remember, Mama had insisted, 'Whatever you do, you must be independent, not end up like me, only fit to work in a shop, having to ask for money.'

What could I do? I liked debating and toured the law school, only to hear that half the students drop out. I dropped out on the spot. I toyed with the idea of applying to the relatively new National Institute of Dramatic Art – NIDA, but the notion of a St Mary's girl studying in Sydney was as fantastic as flying to Rome for an audience with the Pope.

Rex suggested I enrol at the Australian National University in Canberra and learn Chinese. 'You're Chinese and it would be good if you could speak Chinese. You could join Radio Australia and broadcast on the Chinese service.'

That astounded me. The complications of living on the mainland and finding funds were beyond my comprehension. As to learning Chinese, I couldn't have been less receptive had he suggested Icelandic.

Rex's suggestion revived my early, often painful, childhood memories of Chinese. I remembered giggling with Lehene and my cousins at big family gatherings when all the grown ups jabbered away in Toishanese. The ancient market gardener with his long wispy beard frightened me in Chinese. Moonshine and Big Girl babbled in Chinese. Jack Ah Foo the laundryman spooked me in Chinese.

I remembered being jeered at for being Chinese. 'Ching Chong Chinaman', other little girls laughed at me on the top playground.

Even though I yelled back, 'White trash.' It hurt.

I withered with embarrassment when Mama suddenly broke into Chinese in front of my friends (usually to say something she didn't want them to understand). I wanted to die. Anyone heard speaking a language other than English aroused suspicion: people gaped as though watching freaks on show under the circus tent.

I couldn't help my Chinese face. Everyone asked, 'Where do you come from?' At least I could forestall the slowly enunciated, 'Do you speak English?' by opening my mouth. I had to assimilate. Being Chinese made me peculiar enough. Why learn to speak Chinese?

'That's crazy,' I told Rex. 'Learning Chinese is the last thing I want to do.'

13

Longley

In 1950s Hobart barely a soul whispered *ménage à trois*, not even beyond the thick sandstone walls of the convent. I can't remember when I first heard the term: certainly never from blushing Sister Brendan with whom we wrestled with irregular French verbs. But about the time I practised *la plume de ma tante*, I confronted what I dared not put into words. Even with having a mother living in sin I'd managed to keep up appearances, but now I faced the spectacle of *les deux hommes de ma mère*.

I'd never heard of Longley, a hamlet of about fifty folk 12 miles south of Hobart, until the day we drove down there to live. Rex must have been drinking again. Then, in autumn 1958, Mama squeezed Lehene and me into the MG and climbed to the crisp air of Fern Tree, high on the slope of the 4000-foot, snow-capped Mount Wellington. From here we descended the narrow Huon Road with its frightening hairpin bends, so sharp that any second we could have plunged over the cliff into the valley of our deaths: into the valley forest of eucalypts, wattles, blue gums, man ferns, dogwood and musk. We twisted towards the Huon Valley, famous for its apples. Twenty minutes from town, we turned in behind a thick hawthorn hedge. Gravel crunched on the semicircular drive. We pulled up by the verandah of a cream weatherboard house with a green hipped roof.

An ascetic, lanky figure with silken fair hair approached, smiling. He opened Mama's door. 'Welcome to Hawthorn Dene, Dorothy.'

'These are my two girls, Leslie. Lehene and Helene.'

'Delighted. I've been so looking forward to meeting you both. Let me show you through the house. Then we'll have tea down at the cottage.'

We entered through French doors and I looked around. Sets of oblong, scalloped-edged tables and matching chairs in blondwood lined the rectangular room.

'This is the main tearoom; it hasn't been used for years,' Leslie explained, edging towards the fireplace at the far end. 'Almost everything, including this model galleon on the mantelpiece and all the brass fittings, were here when we bought the place. They're a couple of my pastels.'

I took in the tranquil scenes of boats, blue waters and distant hills framed on the wall.

Leslie moved towards an archway at the other end and parted a curtain. 'Another tearoom through here,' he motioned to circular cedar tables and a window opening onto green pastures and huge pines. 'You may decide to use this as a bedroom, Dorothy.'

Without the sound of lightly clinking china, the purr of pouring tea and the hubbub I associated with tearooms, they felt cold and lifeless. 'I've never been in empty tearooms before.'

Lehene's scowl said, 'There's no need for you to say anything.'

'They used to be packed with tourists,' said Leslie. 'Pioneer buses parked in the driveway, coming and going to Huonville.'

'It must have been marvellous,' enthused Mama.

I thought of my jaunt with Uncle Gordon to inspect the orchards and packing sheds of Huonville. The export of red and golden delicious, Cox's orange pippins, gravensteins and Granny Smiths kept the island afloat. I'd watched apples being picked, graded, carefully wrapped in squares of white, pink or pale green tissue paper and packed into wooden cases. Before the isle enjoyed the comfort of soft Kleenex tissue, foreign devils used rolls of hard shiny paper in the smallest room in the house. Many simply tore up sheets of the *Mercury* and clipped the pieces onto a hook in the wall. We never did that. While at the shop we recycled apple-wrapping tissue.

'We've never stopped here,' I said, trailing Leslie through a curtained opening opposite the front door.

'This is the kitchen where we had our own scone chef,' he continued as I surveyed a blackened old-fashioned wood oven filling one wall; a cream and green double electric oven stood against an adjacent wall. I tried to imagine delicious hot scones, which I spread with butter rolled into pats; then I spooned on home-made raspberry jam and added a dollop of cream.

'We had our own dairy cows producing fresh butter and cream daily.'

'Oh, I would love to have seen it then,' said Mama.

'Hmm.' I was confused. I loved Devonshire tea, but neglected Hawthorn Dene as our home? We retreated to the living room with its tired carpet square. I peered into a cream, plaster-panelled room with slat windows that let the wind whistle through in winter and myriad minute insects fly through in summer, not knowing it would be my bedroom, on and off, for the next eight years.

Leslie had met Mama in the early 1950s at an art exhibition he organised in Hobart as Tasmania's founding director of Adult Education. Sydney artist Desiderius Orban featured in the exhibition. Mama had modelled for Orban and he introduced them.

By the time I encountered Leslie, he had recently been widowed by his second wife, Margaret Edmunds, and scratched a living from ABC radio: writing scripts for schools broadcasts, presenting news commentaries and reviews and occasionally acting in radio drama. He lived with his son, Guy, whom he called Pot, surrounded by records of an extraordinary life. Born in Cape Town during the Boer War – his father was paymaster during the siege of Mafeking – Captain Herbert Leslie Greener had been educated in England, trained at Sandhurst and served in India. He voyaged to New Zealand and studied art, eloped with artist Rhona Haszard who became his first wife, starved as a painter in Paris, taught French at Alexandria, where Rhona accidentally fell from a window to her death, after which Leslie immersed himself as an archaeological artist in Luxor, Egypt. The outbreak of the Second World War saw him in Sydney as a journalist with the weekly pictorial, *Pix*. He enlisted in the Australian Imperial Force, was an intelligence officer in the Eighth Army, captured at the surrender of Singapore and imprisoned in Changi.

Amid his library of books and publications, titles written by Leslie ranged from autobiography and the Second World War to science fiction, Egyptology and sculpture. Egyptian tapestries and Leslie's own watercolours adorned his sump-oiled cottage, tucked among foliage by the bridge over the North West Bay River.

A glorious field of lupins, billowing in hues of yellow, magenta, white, blue and red, separated the cottage from the house Mama at first rented on the 25-acre property. This proved no ordinary landlord–tenant relationship and the path trodden through the lupins soon linked two parts of one household.

'We're just about ready to eat,' signalled Mama, her cue for me to stand at the back door and beat a round brass gong to summon Leslie and Pot to dinner.

We ate in the kitchen where Mama had a new off-white automatic oven installed so her roast chicken or lamb could begin cooking were she still shopping or winding down the Huon Road in the laden MG.

Before Leslie took his place, he bent down on one knee and gazed up at Mama.

'Daw Fi, please will you marry me.'

'No,' she laughed gently. 'You know I don't believe in marriage.'

'Don't you girls think she should marry me?' he appealed to Lehene and me.

'No,' I bellowed over Lehene's bowed silence. 'You're too old!'

At fifty-eight (twenty-five years older than Mama), he looked, to my 13-year-old eyes, as ancient as the pharaohs with whom he had buried himself. Twelve-year-old Pot sat mute in his grey Friends'

School jumper, busy with knife and fork, shovelling in mouthfuls of mashed potatoes and freshly podded baby green peas. He shut out the scene created by the pa he fondly called the Old Man.

From time to time Mama and Leslie displayed the Open sign on the road, welcomed guests into the front room and revived the spirit of Hawthorn Dene. But within eighteen months or so, Leslie sold all the tearoom paraphernalia – furniture, silverware, china, cutlery, knickknacks and linen – for a song.

'All right, it's yours,' he agreed to an enterprising bargain hunter.

Mornings began down at the cottage where aqua cups hung from hooks on the kitchen shelf. Leslie tried to tempt Lehene and me with the leaden porridge he ladled out to his son. Pot could mimic Henry Crun of *The Goons* and reeled their shows off pat. He climbed up a built-in ladder and slept on a bunk just below the ceiling, his bedroom crammed with *Biggles* and other adventure books. A car enthusiast, he assembled a scale Dinky town with almost every model of Dinky toy. Later, Leslie converted a section of the cottage into rooms for Lehene and me – alas, not with ceiling-high bunks – which we occupied for a period when he let the house.

We waited outside the cottage for the school bus. Pot, no matter what the weather – drenching rain, burning sun, hail or storm – always wore his jumper but never a blazer, a coat or his red school cap. With city-bred snobbery I loathed being lumped in with all the country bumpkins picked up for miles along the Huon Road. Although I related to the romantic poets and the Lake District, I felt little affinity with the harsh Australian bush. But I could never have guessed the repercussions that school bus would have on my life.

Our presence at Longley doomed Leslie's weekly literary sessions. A group, mostly women, cosied around the cottage fire for his appraisal of their writing. At the first gathering after we appeared, one lady sat, in her customary way, darning Leslie's socks.

When it came time for supper he suggested, 'Daw Fi, perhaps you could pour the tea.'

The change in routine chilled the atmosphere. Within days Leslie received a letter saying that, with Miss Henry's arrival, it would no longer be possible to hold the literary evenings.

Meanwhile, a force more potent than Daw Fi threatened to disrupt Hawthorn Dene. The University of Chicago suddenly invited Leslie to resume his prewar position as archaeological artist at the Oriental Institute in Luxor. His contract would begin in December 1958, in the northern winter, and end with the onset of Egypt's intolerable summer. This posed a dilemma: Mama didn't feel safe living isolated in the countryside without a man. The solution? Rex.

Rex by now rented a gentleman's residence, owned by a doctor. When we left Seymour Street we'd moved with him for a spell by the water at Flinders Esplanade in Taroona and were in our third rented house, on the steep intersection between Alt-na-craig and Auvergne Avenues in Lenah Valley when Mama whisked Lehene and me down to Longley.

Once, when newly ensconced behind the black iron gates of his double-storey edifice in Bay Road, New Town, Rex telephoned at midnight sounding desperate: 'I'm going to kill myself.'

Up we raced in the MG to find him charming and perfectly contented.

Rex's younger son, Peter, also lived at Bay Road. Like his brother Michael, Peter was tall, dark and half-Maori; he was a tad older than Lehene. Both boys had been enrolled at Mentone Grammar, Melbourne, and flown back to Tasmania for school holidays. They were fun. Michael played bongo drums, which he would still play a generation later, entertaining swaying crowds at Wrest Point. At Seymour Street Peter made me a billycart. A scar on my left knee forever reminds me of my inaugural pelt down nearby Pedder Street. By the time of Alt-na-craig, Peter had settled into Hobart's Savio College and he and Mama, or Doff, as he called her, had become almost as close as mother and son.

So Rex wound up at Longley. With Leslie due to leave for Egypt, it didn't seem odd; although when Leslie returned, I knew it was extremely odd, especially to others. Uncle Gordon shook his head, 'Your mother living with two men.'

Even though no other comment reached my ears, I felt them burning. Gossip must have circulated from the Longley pub and into the bars and coteries of Hobart, especially as Rex and Leslie were both well known, on and beyond the ABC. Back at Hawthorn Dene the *ménage à trois* caused no argument.

Despite my unease, I had to accept it as yet another aspect of our abnormality. I coped by ignoring it, just as I ignored the divorce and all the other unconventional aspects of my life. Not once did I raise it with Mama, Lehene or anyone else. Nor did I chew over issues and depress myself. Rumination wasn't my method. I played with the mixed hand dealt out to me while craving something I could declare and lay on the table, not keep hidden close to my chest.

Peter joined us and spruced up the former coachman's cottage by the workshop and disused dairy. Decades ahead of its time ours became a blended, multicultural family.

Although some classmates lunched with Lehene and me when we lived at the shop and friends came to our uncles' places, I felt ashamed of Longley and never asked anyone to visit. However, a few friends dropped in, as did cousins by the carload.

Hawthorn Dene offered pure air and private walks. Amid the scent of pines and with buttercups and bluebells underfoot, we wandered through poplars, into the untamed bush of stringybark, peppermint and magpies. I learnt to drive in an open paddock: revving up, changing gear and circling uninterrupted in Pot's blue baby Austin 10. Our water flowed from the stream bordering the premises and Leslie ran a pump to fill our tanks. In summer we picnicked on boulders in the creek. I passed hours at that creek, clambering over rocks and splashing about in a blue rubber dinghy.

With Rex and Leslie as father figures and mentors, Longley

offered intellectual riches too. Lehene and I went to art exhibitions Leslie opened in and around Hobart. We did without television – though I did watch Michael Charlton on the ABC at Uncle Gordon's and *I Love Lucy* at Uncle Lester's – until we started renting an AWA in my last school holidays. We were surrounded by books and magazines, from *National Geographic*, *Quadrant* and *Encounter*, to *Life*, *Time* and *Newsweek*.

Yet I didn't appreciate Longley. Too outside the norm, life at Hawthorn Dene was too bohemian for me. Sometimes I detested it. Despite my silence on the *ménage à trois*, I bristled at the way we lived. Moira and Marcia, our German shepherds, commandeered the living room's shabby green couch, sharing it occasionally with Corby, the Suffolk sheep.

'It's too old. Not worth sitting on, anyway,' Mama decreed.

Sooty, my cat of dubious Persian pedigree, curled himself up on the wicker chair, except when it was occupied by Rex devouring newsprint. All that remained was a footstool carved by Uncle Gordon, a couple of leather pouffes, camel saddles from Egypt or a kitchen chair.

To please Mama, Leslie knocked down a wall between the kitchen and the living room. He installed a slow combustion wood heater but couldn't afford to cover the chimney and build adjoining shelves or cupboards. The room always looked raw, unfinished.

Mama used a portable mirror to make up her face while seated by the living room window. Cosmetic jars, tubes, creams, brushes, hair rollers, pins, nets and sprays cluttered her corner table.

'Why do we have to see it all? No one else lives like this,' I railed.

Feeding the pets also caused friction. Although Sooty dated back to Seymour Street, an irresistible stray, a splendid grey tabby, wandered into Longley. We adopted him, had him neutered and named him Mandy (after English society call girl Mandy Rice-Davies of the Christine Keeler and John Profumo scandal, which Rex followed daily in the Melbourne *Herald*). Jealous of Mandy, Sooty had to be assured of his superior status – literally. He jumped onto his own blue Formica table to feast on freshly steamed and boned fish, slices of kidney or round steak, an assortment of dried food and a bowl of milk. Mandy tucked in beneath the table.

'Oh, this is ridiculous, all that space for a cat. Why can't Sooty eat on the floor?'

'He's not just a cat,' Mama snapped at me. 'He's Sooty.'

'Oh,' Lehene groaned, 'why can't we be normal?'

Worst of all was Longley's distance, far from Hobart and all my activities. Play rehearsals and parties meant overnight stays. When I left school at the end of 1962, I relied more on Mama as a chauffeur, only rarely taking the infrequent Pioneer bus. Lehene had already matriculated and now worked at the state library, Rex was still at 7HT and Leslie too had functions in town. Mama also helped Uncle Lester in his shop, Tutti Frutti in Lower Sandy Bay, in exchange for fruit and vegetables and my university bookshop account. She spent half her life behind the wheel, ferrying up and down the Huon Road.

After the MG crash in 1961, Mama persuaded Leslie to buy a Jaguar. He sacrificed his trusty Holden and put himself in hock for years. Although no Stirling Moss, Miss Henry adored cars and could name every component of her opalescent bronze Mark II.

'Open the bonnet and the engine's clean enough to eat off,' Pot remarked.

She kept the chassis, leather upholstery, carpet and walnut interior in mint condition and year after year came first in the Jaguar Car Club of Tasmania's *concours d'élégance*. Eventually, she withdrew from competition to give others a chance.

We made countless journeys in that Jaguar on that icy Huon Road.

'You're taking up all the space,' protested Lehene, wedged against me on the front passenger seat.

'No I'm not; I can hardly breathe.'

'You're pushing me out the door,' she flared as we wound around another bend.

'I've got the gears sticking into me.'

'Well, could you just give me an inch?' She gritted her teeth.

'You could have the whole damn seat if we didn't have to have two German shepherds sitting in the back.'

'As well as me,' chimed in Rex, ever so gentlemanly.

'Yes, Rex trampled to death by two enormous dogs,' I added. 'It's crazy. They should be left behind. What's the point of having German shepherds just to drive them around?'

'I'm not just driving them around,' corrected Mama, double declutching for the next hairpin bend. 'I'm driving you around and they like to be with me.'

'But German shepherds are guard dogs. They should be guarding Hawthorn Dene.' I could feel myself getting all knotted up.

'They fret if they're left behind. They like to be with me and I like to have them.'

'That's mad, isn't it Rex?'

'I'm sure Doff knows what she's doing.'

'No she doesn't. No one acts like that. Carting pets all over the place. Squashing us all up to buggery. It's crazy. Doesn't make sense.'

'Quiet!' shouted Mama. The road was barely visible through the frosted windscreen. 'If I hear one more word I'll go straight over this cliff.'

'Oh, why can't we be normal?' refrained Lehene.

14

A-smokin' 'n' A-storkin'

In 1956, television burst into Australian homes and the world fastened on Melbourne as host of the Olympic Games. Uncle Gordon and Uncle Lester each had a big boxed set installed in the lounge. At home we listened to the wireless, though not to the Games. We didn't subscribe to the *Mercury* but Rex always bought the *Herald*. He and Mama nattered on about the Orr case, in which the University of Tasmania professor of philosophy was sacked for allegedly seducing his student. Mama had sat in on Orr's classes at the university. Rex worried about the Suez crisis and Menzies' support for Britain and laughed at a cartoon of Mrs Khrushchev, depicted as a hessian bag weighing a ton. I was eleven and had other things on my mind.

In Grade 6 our teacher was Sister Canice. Sturdy-framed, she exerted missionary zeal in her exhortations to us to feed coins into the begging hand of a toy black boy made of metal, who lifted his hand to his mouth and swallowed the money, which was later collected to help the starving millions in Africa.

At morning recess we gathered between the toilet block and the laundry to smoke while someone kept a lookout. I almost choked to death on my first cigarette but, as others were smoking, I couldn't be left behind. I tried to puff but fought for breath. Between all the spluttering, I felt I was growing up. I sniggered at the sight of smoke rising from behind the nuns' voluminous bloomers, pegged on rows on clotheslines, hanging out to dry.

By my mid teens I still didn't enjoy smoking. It was nothing compared with the chocolate cigarettes and pipes I fancied when small. I persisted only for the thrills, the risk of breaking the rules and not being caught.

When Mama went with Leslie on his second season to Egypt, she left Lehene with Uncle Gordon and Aunty Monica and me with Uncle Lester and Aunty Eva. During the Christmas–New Year recess I lured girls from my class down to Taroona. To the smooth sounds of Glenn Miller or the gyrations of Elvis the Pelvis, we relaxed in the lounge room overlooking the garden, the rooftops and bush, and the expanse of the River Derwent. Sometimes we darted downstairs for a game of ping pong. Mostly, we whiled away the afternoon puffing through tins of Craven A and packets of Marlboro. I envied Lorraine Cooper, a future head prefect. An example to me, she sat with her legs crossed and nonchalantly blew smoke rings, exhaling the rest of the smoke through her nostrils.

From where Mama lived with Leslie at Chicago House in Luxor, across the Nile from the Valley of the Kings, she filled aerogrammes with advice. When Lehene sent samples of material for a new dress, Mama suggested the plain blue but in linen, not cotton. Her reply of 29 January 1960 makes clear that Lehene had boys in mind:

Putti Mouse

    As you are now 16, I think it is quite in order that you go to the Stork Club, especially if somebody's Mother is chaperoning. That should be part of every child's education to mingle with people of their own age in mixed company to learn how to speak about 'all', or 'nothing' as the case may be, but to be able to 'speak', without being self conscious to mingle with people & to acquire poise & confidence. This is a <u>very important</u> part of our education & which so many have not had the benefit of from sheer ignorance of their parents. I, definitely being one of those unfortunates … 99 per cent of girls marry. The important thing is to know how to keep a marriage sound & that is not a part of our education … But as you have only just turned 16 & are still at school, you should not (not) be going to the Stork Club more than once in two weeks … don't let that part of your life be more important than your school work.

The Stork Club, forbidden to St Mary's girls, could in no way be compared with one of our school dances. Held under glaring lights, usually in St Peter's Hall, school dances had nuns peeking from the top of the stairs beside the stage. Sister Lucy vetted our frocks for modesty in advance. I once sought exception because I wanted mine to surprise (or so an amused Sister Lucy would recall at a school reunion long after I'd forgotten the dress and her permission). Seated stiffly on our side of the hall, we dreaded being stuck there like wallflowers and prayed that some St Virgil's boy – preferably without pimples or sweaty palms – would ask us onto the floor so we could stumble through the Pride of Erin, a waltz, a barn dance or a tango. A photograph of Lehene shows her in butterfly-winged glasses, self-conscious beside a nervous future premier of Tasmania, Douglas Lowe.

Friday night at the Stork Club, dim and smoky in Clare Street, New Town, pulsated to the traditional jazz of Pearce Pickering's Ragtime Five. From fifteen I tootled there with Lehene and her school pals, with no chaperoning mother within coo-ee. The boys we twisted and jived with included a heart-throb footballer, Jeremy Thiessen, and his older friend Robert, who sported a white Austin Healey. The first time they asked Lehene and me out on Saturday night, we sat cooped behind the bucket seats. We drove down to Lower Sandy Bay and stopped opposite Beach House Hotel.

'Won't be a tick,' Jeremy said as he and Robert vanished.

We waited, puzzled, our ears pricked to rising voices, then shouting. Finally, the pair scrambled back, looking dishevelled.

'We just had a fight over who's taking in Lehene,' blurted Jeremy. 'I won.'

Poor Robert copped me.

From the Middle East Mama continued her little thoughts on a balanced life for young ladies:

> I would be pleased if you could go to your little girl friends' places & perhaps have a little after-noon tea with them, etc. This is good for you & better than learning how to add up sums all the time – it is part of your education, but a part which is rather neglected, since I was not in a position to invite little girls 'Home', as there was no 'Home', to invite them to. Aunty Monica has been a very good 'Mother' to you in many ways. She has given little luncheons for you and a few little girl friends – then in return – the little girls have had you at their homes …
>
> Isn't Aunty Monica a pet to make a skirt for you – I hope you let her know how pleased you were & did not forget to thank her … to show her that you appreciate these things, you must thank her always very nicely. (To show her that you are not taking these things for granted: also too – I have brought you up to behave like a LADY.) …
>
> I am rather miserable and depressed here – all the time. I wonder what you and Wo are doing, so many things are happening & me so far away … Ah, well, I guess I should never have left home. There's no place like home.
>
> Much Love for now. Mumma.

One long school holiday, when the weeks yawned endlessly into summer, Lehene suggested, 'Let's have a party.'

I remembered the lovely birthday party Lehene had been given by Aunty Monica, who had spared no trouble preparing all the cakes, pavlova, dainty sandwiches, coconut ice, fruit salad, soft drinks and cups of afternoon tea. Lehene wore a new aquamarine frock, designed and made for her by our dressmaker. I relived the spontaneous party we staged ourselves at Uncle Lester's house one night for boys and girls. There was a lot of pashing on the long settee that night. But this one?

'Where?' I asked.

'Let's try Daddy.'

'Daddy? Don't be mad.'

'Uncle Gordon says he's living by himself.'

'What do you mean?'

'His wife's left.'

'What about his children?'

'Don't know, but they're not there. Maybe with their mother in Melbourne.'

'Well, you sort it out. Not me.'

That Saturday evening we rolled up with our friends, stacks of 45s, platters of watermelon, pineapple and grapes, paper bags bulging with cherries, packets of cigarettes, bottles of beer and lemonade. Just as when we painted weatherboards when the house was being built, again we were left to our own devices. Our father stood observing for a while from the kitchen, which opened onto the living room, then he made himself scarce.

We had the run of the place. We turned the sound up high and switched the lights down low. We were set to rock around the clock, to shake, rattle and roll with Bill Haley and his Comets. We were gonna rock, gonna rock, around the clock that night, gyrate to Little Richard's 'Tutti Frutti' – 'Tutti frutti, aw rootie … a-wop-bop-a-loo-lop a-lop-bam-boo' – and twist again with Chubby Checker: 'Come on baby let's do the twist.'

Neither of us drank alcohol and Lehene didn't even puff, but all the boys drank and smoked, mostly Craven A. Although I couldn't inhale because nicotine tasted too bitter, I felt I had to light up, so I puffed at Menthol, which disguised the bitterness. About 3 in the morning, when everyone had left, we turned the lights on to confront a shamble of glasses and bottles everywhere, ashtrays overflowing and butts fouling the air.

'Let's clean up in the morning,' I said. We collapsed into bed.

I awoke to sunlight and wondered where I was. Remembering, I stretched out my hand. I had a watch from my father, negotiated by Mama, his second gift to me after the tennis racquet. It was 10 o'clock.

'Wake up.' I roused Lehene in the other bed.

As I leapt onto the floor, I was struck by silence: nothing but the chirruping of birds. I snuck my head out the door, my eyes reaching through to the living room. Everything had been miraculously restored. In the quietness I padded through the house but could find no sign of our father.

'It's all been done,' I said as Lehene emerged, putting on her glasses.

'He's cleaned it all?'

'Must have. Did you hear anything?'

'No, nothing.'

'The vacuum cleaner?'

'I slept right through.'

'Look,' I said, 'not a single cigarette butt. It's unbelievable.'

The house looked immaculate. The kitchen shimmered; the couch and armchairs were plumped up and their beige lace antimacassars all straightened.

Not until I was posted to China would I see antimacassars again. In the Great Hall of the People, I covered Deng Xiaoping's meeting with British Foreign Secretary Sir Geoffrey Howe, in Peking to negotiate the return of Hong Kong to the mainland. Deng, in his tailored grey wool Sun Yat-sen suit, nestled deep into his russet armchair; Howe leant forward towards the edge of his seat. A semicircle of officials flanked the two leaders. Strategically positioned around the floor, awaited white enamel spittoons. On the arms and backs of all the chairs lay lace antimacassars. The scene took me back to that morning after the party at my father's house.

'So where's Daddy?'

'Don't know. Disappeared,' I shrugged.

'He must be somewhere.' She started poking her nose into each room.

'Well, he's not outside and the car's gone,' I called from the front door.

'Isn't it funny?' She giggled.

'The mystery of the disappearing father,' I joked, making myself comfortable in a chair. Then, I sprang up. 'Maybe he's hiding.'

I opened a cupboard. In front of me hung a rack of white shirts – as if in a menswear store – each on its own hanger, neatly buttoned and all facing the same direction. It reminded me of my father in his white shirt and suit at the Golden Dragon when I quivered before him with the bill for school fees, of his lean, well-dressed figure quickening his step outside Bidencope's, tailors and outfitters in Murray Street, barely pausing to say hello to me.

Most astounding was my realisation that we shared a similar sense of order. From the earliest age, I had imposed order on myself. My tunic had to hang straight on the hanger, with the blazer above, my shoes polished and ready below. The books on my desk, in my case, in the shelf or by my bed had to face the same direction. As I grew older and had my own wardrobe, all hangers and their garments had to face left: blouses, dresses, slacks and coats coordinated and separated from the other. Was this obsession an unconscious attempt at symmetry in a life otherwise reeking of irregularity? Did I inherit this from my father?

His shirts made me think of my mother when angry with me: 'Take that smirk off your face. Take it off or I'll slap it off!'

'But you said that I –'

'Don't you answer me back,' she lashed out.

'I'm only saying that –'

'I'm your mother. And if I say black is white, black is white.' Then, after a moment's pause, she accused: 'You look just like your father.'

She may have been born in Australia but she held a traditional Chinese attitude towards parental authority. Unlike some children, even as juniors Lehene and I didn't have to ask permission for everything. When I wanted a Kit Kat, I helped myself from the shop. When I wanted to watch a magician, I took myself off to Fitzgerald's where a rake of a man cloaked in black popped three unshelled eggs, flour and milk into his top hat, held the hat while turning his body around it three times and produced a cake. He passed it about for us to eat; it tasted cold. But once Mama made up her mind that black was white, I couldn't argue. She was beyond reason. And I only made things worse by answering back. As I did so my face assumed an expression just like my father's. I could do nothing about it. Yet it was all my fault.

To this day my father's whereabouts that morning and his thoughts on the party and cleaning up remain unknown to me. Through no fault of mine, we've exchanged not a word on that subject and scarcely a word on any other.

15

Old Nick

In February 1963 I fronted up to St Mary's College, not in a green school uniform and lace-ups but in a white linen suit and high heels and wearing make-up and nail varnish. Instead of lugging a heavy school bag, I carried under my arm a slim tan leather briefcase.

'Good morning, Miss Chung,' the eight year olds sang in chorus, holding out their tunics and curtsying to their 18-year-old teacher.

Still unsure what I wanted to do after matriculation, I decided on part-time study and part-time teaching: I continued Australian Music Examination Board exams to complete my associate in speech and drama while working towards my licentiate. At the same time I assisted Claire Mitchell in her private classes and, on Mondays, Wednesdays and Fridays, taught poetry, prose and drama to Grades 3 to 6 at my old school.

'Australians won't want to learn how to speak English from a Chinese,' cautioned Uncle Gordon.

Yet they did. School pupils and adults clambered up the open metal stairs to see me at Mrs Mitchell's first floor studio in Burnett Street, North Hobart.

I also enrolled in a single subject, English literature, towards a bachelor of arts degree at the university. From my first day, a mature-age student of twenty-nine, with grey-green eyes, tall and handsome in brown tweed jacket, suede shoes and corduroys, caught my eye. He took a seat right up the front next to the window wall, a row or so in front of me.

Our professor was the distinguished poet James McAuley, whom I recognised from Sunday Mass. With hair swept back, a penetrating gaze and passion in his voice, McAuley introduced our class to Shakespeare's sonnet:

Let me not to the marriage of true minds
Admit impediments. Love is not love
Which alters when it alteration finds ...
Love's not Time's fool, though rosy lips and cheeks
Within his bending sickle's compass come;
Love alters not with his brief hours and weeks,
But bears it out even to the edge of doom.

Thirteen years later, John Martin and I would begin our marriage of true minds.

My purpose on campus wasn't so much to find a man, or to get a degree, but to join the Old Nick Company. The student theatre group named after London's Old Vic Theatre, Old Nick chose as its emblem a crooked Lucifer clutching a three-pronged fork.

'Whatever you do, girls, avoid the Old Nick Company,' Mother Imelda advised, raising the alarm and whetting my appetite. 'You don't find nice girls there, only bold girls. It has a bad name and could ruin your reputation. You could be led astray. Just stay with members of the Catholic Newman Society and you'll stay on the right track.'

I couldn't join fast enough.

In the 1963 uni revue, *Sin-Til-Eight* – 'It's a most engaging fate' – I was typecast as a Datsun Bluebird, like Madame Butterfly, in a blue kimono. Holding a fan, I flitted across the stage and away into the wings.

I also played a poet based on Gwen Harwood, famous for proving that editors didn't read her work. The *Bulletin* had published her poem in which the first letters of each line, when read down the page, howled: F-U-C-K A-L-L E-D-I-T-O-R-S. As a television panellist, commanding the stage in an off-white sheath from Old Nick's wardrobe, I gave an ardent rendition of a poem that included the phrase, 'the flashing fire of your thighs'.

Unbeknown to me, in the audience at the Theatre Royal sat Gwen Harwood, who bubbled over in a letter to be published decades later. In May 1963 she wrote to the Melbourne poet Vincent Buckley:

My dear Vin,

Bill and I went to the revue last night and were entertained by a marvellous take-off by the students of an ABC forum – 'Pokus Point' – with me and Vivian [Smith, poet] maliciously and wittily parodied. The character playing Vivian read a bird poem about blue tits (with the obvious jokes) and 'Nancy Horzbush', a literary housewife, recited a wild parody of me at my worst and told a frightful dream of eagles ripping and tearing small birds. 'I' was played by a very sexy Chinese girl with a splendid figure – Bill pointed out to me this morning that they could easily have played me as an old bag and that it was really most complimentary. Amazing to see oneself parodied; I was amazed and delighted.

Then, in February 1964 to Vivian Smith, amid comments on her daily life as a receptionist for the eye specialist Dr David Waterworth, who fitted me with contact lenses: 'Lovely Helene Chung who played "me" in the uni review was in the surgery this morning and we had an amusing talk. She said: "Have you written any poetry lately?"'

That year, when I switched to full-time uni, I auditioned for the revue, *Vote No*, fairly confident of touring Tasmania as Queen Elizabeth. I was rejected for the role. This hurt. It not only dented my pride but it also clipped my wings when I had hoped to fly free. Producer Brian King suddenly made me realise the limitations of my Chinese face, which I had tried to ignore. Just as no female in the sixties could perform as Julius Caesar, no Oriental could pass as one of the merry wives of Windsor. Although I would come to see the humour of my audition, at the time I didn't laugh.

Uncle Gordon, Tasmania's honorary Chinese consul, added to the conflict between my inner and outer selves when he took me to task: 'The Asian students complain you don't mix with them.'

He astonished me. The very few non-Westerners were Colombo Plan students, new to Tasmania and mostly enrolled in economics and commerce, including several beautiful Vietnamese girls dressed in distinctive long Asian silks, *ao dai*. I saw them as Asian and different from me. If we chanced upon each other, naturally I said hello, but it never occurred to me to seek out someone on the basis of race; I associated with those who shared my interests. Had there been another Asian in Old Nick, we could have grown close, drawn together not by on our ethnic origins but by the stage.

Like a banana, I deceived: my Asian body masked my Western soul. My yellow skin had to be peeled back before anyone could taste my white flesh.

Old Nick took me out of Tasmania to the mainland for only the second time. In August 1964, at nineteen, I experienced the excitement of an aeroplane flight, over Bass Strait and on to the incredible image of Melbourne unfurling forever below the wings. I felt very conscious of being a mere Tasmanian as I trod the cloisters and quadrangles of Melbourne University, host of the Intervarsity Drama Festival. But I held my nerve for my small part, A Girl, in an adaptation of George Orwell's prophetic *1984* before all the swaggering sophisticates on the mainland.

On the first morning at The Gatwick, our seedy hotel in St Kilda, I showered and dressed, then opened the front door onto Fitzroy Street, only to be repelled by the filth, the hobos, the dirty footpath and the grey polluted air. Insulated by Hobart's clear blue sky and pure air, I felt sullied, tempted to slam the door, rush back inside and shower again.

A photograph in the *Sun*, captioned 'There's drama in their visit', shows another St Mary's girl bold enough to defy Mother Imelda and join Old Nick. Judy St Leger and I are checking our script: before the jeans craze, she in woollen rollneck, pendant and kid gloves and I in a scallop-necked suit and pearls. Despite my initial shock, Melbourne was exhilarating: a fortnight's feast of drama, from the Greek classics to the kitchen sink. Our Old Nick technical director, Jamie Lewis, went on to devote his life to lighting the Melbourne Theatre Company.

My role as Mabel in James Broom Lynne's *The Trigon* caused controversy at the Newcastle Festival in 1965. Mabel, 'the first stranger to enter … the small world of a masochist and sadist', had been played by Prunella Scales in the London premiere of 1963 and the rerun of 1964. Our producer, the ABC's John Baldwin, hired by Old Nick, added dialogue to explain my appearance: 'Her mother was Chinese. But Mabel was born here in London. You'll like her. She's very English.' This insertion didn't slip by unnoticed. Afterwards, Baldwin's right to tamper with the text caused heated debate between the audience and the Old Nick team.

Next year I headed to Brisbane to act as Marie in Eugene Ionesco's *Exit the King*. Reaction there was hostile. Our producer, Amanda Howard, another bold St Mary's girl, would become known as Amanda Lohrey, author of the award-winning novel, *Camille's Bread*. On stage for audience feedback, I wanted to hide beneath the boards, not tread them, as speaker after speaker stood to hurl brickbats about our production and performance. In my report to Old Nick's annual general meeting, I ducked for cover, arguing our entry was 'probably uncriticisable, in that it had not attained a rehearsal standard at which judgement could be passed. It was simply unrehearsed'.

I began 1966 exuberant at a summer drama school in Armidale, high in the mountains of New South Wales, which inspired me to initiate a series of monthly lunch hour play readings in Hobart, performed in the student common room and at the state library, a venture the *Mercury* trumpeted as Hobart's 'only opportunity to see regular and challenging theatre'. I produced an act from *Waiting for Godot* that playwright Samuel Beckett says concerns 'the art of failure'.

According to the *Mercury*'s 'Pleiades', it attempts 'to elucidate the impossible, to define the nothingness which is ultimate reality'. I cast the North American-born postgraduate student and future Australian Democrats senator Norman Sanders as the tramp Vladimir. A decade later, in our professional lives, we would be challenged again, near naked on television.

Old Nick president Roger Hodgman was an innovative and tireless producer, destined to make his name overseas and return as artistic director of the Melbourne Theatre Company. In our student newspaper, *Togatus*, he heaped few bouquets on my direction of Edward Albee's *The American Dream* as a performed play reading: 'Miss Chung appeared to have seen the play as a series of lines rather than a unified whole. However, she will obviously go on to better things.'

In what the *Mercury* dubbed a 'photo-finish', our eight-member team went on to win the 1966 Hobart Drama Festival and I received the producer's trophy. For the role of Albee's Young Man I recruited the tall dimple-chinned law student Rowland Harrison, who had taught me how to play marbles.

Most fun that year was Aristophanes' romp *Lysistrata*, in which Greek women withhold sexual favours to prevent their men from waging war. We roped in Lehene as a Spartan hostage and Rex's son Peter as the Athenian ambassador. Rex's older son, Michael, and future Labor politician John White whooped it up as sexually deprived Spartan soldiers. Claire Mitchell's husband, Vic, editor of the *Saturday Evening Mercury*, ensured maximum coverage. 'BACCHANALIAN REVELLERS!' and 'Grecian robes and tights' headlined our alluring publicity shots around the stone monuments and squares of Georgian Hobart. Three years before Sydney staged the rock musical *Hair*, with the nude scenes that would become passé by the time I saw them in London in 1972, the newspaper reported: 'The University Old Nick Company ... have submitted the script to the police. Official approval for the production is being withheld, however, until the play has been seen in rehearsal.'

The *Saturday Evening Mercury* said of our director, architect Brian Hodgkinson, recently drafted from English repertory theatre: 'An imaginative producer, he is presenting *Lysistrata* in an exciting combination of semi-classical female attire of flowing, diaphanous robes with 20th century jeans, T-shirts, tights and leotards.'

Togatus damned us with no faint praise. Under 'The Travesty and the Authentic', it compared our amateur production with that of the professional Athens Drama Company, a highlight of the 1966 Adelaide Arts Festival. Guest reviewer, Tom (O'Bedlam) Burvill, literary editor of Sydney University's *Honi Soit*, lampooned:

> If Miss Helen [sic] Chung wants to be what the Sydney R.S.L. circuit calls an 'exotic dancer' she could go there. The ease with which she dons the manner of a hussy would there earn money.

The stage was fun but wasn't going to earn me a quid.

16

Lambert Avenue

While I was away with Old Nick, Rex, after years of drinking, suddenly died, peacefully, in his sleep at the age of forty-seven. According to the *Mercury*, 'One of Hobart's most prominent radio announcers … had a heart complaint for some time.' 'He'll be missed,' added the *Saturday Evening Mercury*. 'His deep resonant voice was loved by thousands and envied by many.'

Much later, when reminiscing on a chapel filled with the strains of Tchaikovsky's 'Chanson Triste', I mused to Lehene, 'Leslie's funeral was my first.'

'No, it wasn't,' she said, 'Rex's funeral was your first. In 1966. With "Love's Death" from *Tristan and Isolde*.'

'Was it? That's funny. I can't remember a thing.'

Why not? Rex was so important to me. Such an influence on my life. I remembered him at Seymour Street, waving his arms, conducting Wagner. I remembered him reading *The Phenomenon of Man* by Pierre Teilhard de Chardin and *Psychology of Sex* by Havelock Ellis. I pictured him at Longley preparing poached eggs on toast: 'Remember, always press the hot toast with your hand before you butter it.'

Only fossicking out my first pocket appointments diary – for 1966 – convinced me I attended Rex's funeral.

Monday 29 August: Arrive Sydney [from Brisbane Intervarsity Drama Festival]. Depart for Hobart 5 pm.
Wednesday 31 August: Funeral 3.15 pm – for Rex.

One reason for my blank in memory may be that Rex's death plunged us into crisis – deeper than the crisis of his death itself – a crisis over where to live, a crisis that consumed my energy on the eve of third term when I had to tackle final undergraduate exams after throwing myself into Old Nick and not studying all year. Within days of my return from Queensland, Leslie had to leave for Egypt again and Mama couldn't cope alone, in the countryside, at Longley.

By 1966 Lehene worked as a reference assistant at the state library and daydreamed away evening classes in librarianship at tech. But she preferred the nights she sashayed under lights on the catwalk as a fashion model. For two years she had rented a bright new flat. Located at the top of Lauremont Avenue, Sandy Bay, unit 5/2 had muted green wall-to-wall carpet and a balcony facing the harbour. After her flatmate moved interstate, I nabbed the vacant room. It suited me as it was only a few bus stops from university.

By coincidence, John, whom I then knew slightly – he mixed with the sober Literary Society, not the extroverted Old Nick – lived with his wife in a house around the corner in Lipscombe Avenue. He sometimes stopped in his grey Austin, leant over to open the door and offered me a lift. When he hosted an evening with Gwen Harwood, I took Mama and Lehene along to celebrate the poet I'd parodied in the uni revue.

Now, without Rex, we faced a dilemma. Where could Mama live? I raced around real estate agents and stumbled on 3 Lambert Avenue, Sandy Bay, a freshly built and hardly used house in a cul-de-sac with established chestnut trees opposite Wrest Point Hotel. Designed by local architect Frank Stary, the two-bedroom brick veneer appeared unusual from the street. A flat driveway led to the carport right at the panelled wooden front door, just outside the high bathroom windows facing the avenue. A spacious north-facing living area, with sun pouring in, lay hidden at the rear. What took my fancy was the so-called uninhabitable space above – a marvellous garret running the width of the house – and which I envisaged as my bedroom–study, filled with paintings and books. Sitting at my desk by the wide main window, I would be able to see footballers playing close by on Queenborough Oval and look north across pines, rooftops and the modern university campus (a ten-minute stroll away) towards brooding Mount Wellington. The garret also had windows east and west. On tiptoe, I could glimpse over Sandy Bay Road and Wrest Point to the River Derwent. Below, the main bedroom also faced north. Alas, the rather small second bedroom faced south.

'Lehene, I've found a place for Mama, but we should all move in.'
'What do you mean? I'm not moving. I'm happy here.'
'But it'll be much better there. It's silly not to be all together.'
'I don't want to move.'
'You could at least come and look at it.'
'What would my room be like?'
'You'll really have to come and see. Not the size of your bedroom here, but you'll really love the house.'

Lehene had mixed feelings but nonetheless gave up her independence and moved to Lambert Avenue.

When we were very small, we piled into Uncle Gordon's black Dodge and later his two-tone green Chevrolet with shiny chrome fins (which Mama called vulgar) for a drive to Kingston Beach. As we wound the bends of the narrow road at Taroona, my eyes searched for a double-storeyed, off-white house with a blue tiled roof, a doll's house. Straight out of a picture story book, it beckoned from a rise at the end of a sweeping poplar-lined driveway.

'That's it,' Mama pointed to our left as Uncle Gordon steadied the wheel. 'That's the house Ah Hool promised to buy if I went back to your father. And she promised a piano too.'

'Then why didn't you?'

'I couldn't. I couldn't live with him any more. He was too moody. He went for weeks without talking. Before we were married he couldn't do enough for me. Afterwards he was different. I never knew where I stood.'

The house always awaited me. Whenever Uncle Lester or Uncle Gordon drove us through Taroona, I saw the home that could have been ours. I peered out the window, impatient for the sight and kept it in my mind long after it had vanished from view. We had passed the landmark shot tower, while the prospect of a slippery slide, sandcastles, hot sausage rolls and butterfly cakes at afternoon tea at Kingston grew closer and closer; yet I still focused on the blue tiled house.

What would it be like? The perfect home, carpeted and properly furnished, with a bedroom each for Lehene and me, a piano inside and a swing hanging from a branch of a tree. I pictured the four of us seated around the table at meals with never a voice raised over money; our father happily paid the bills. We had our own car and Lehene and I took off for a Sunday spin like a normal happy family with our mother and our father seated in the front.

At the age of twenty-one, long after I yearned for that doll's house and all it promised, I lived for the first time with my mother and sister in a home I cherished and felt proud to call ours.

At first we couldn't afford to furnish and fit Lambert Avenue as it deserved, or to landscape the rubble of a backyard, but we made do. Even though Leslie was still paying off the Jaguar from his earnings in Egypt, he managed the rent. Lehene, a neat seamstress, set about making the curtains and we both pitched in towards expenses, Lehene from her salary and I from my Commonwealth Scholarship allowance. Mama continued to serve customers at Uncle Lester's Frutti Tutti, which kept us in fresh fruit and vegetables; however, the raw floorboards – in all but the living room with its attractive sheen – posed a problem.

A solution jumped out at me from the noticeboard at the students' union:

WANTED

Students' World
Recruits to train
Enrol families in Students' World
Long hours. Good rewards.
Phone 24436

In late November, after the exams, I turned up with six other students, all curious about *Students' World*. A flash-suited salesman from Melbourne, with slicked-back hair, scanned us up and down.

'Now, it's important to remember you're not selling encyclopaedias. You're enrolling families in *Students' World*. This set of books, together with the kits, brochures and maps we send whenever asked, will help students in all their projects right through school. We have a method to enrol families in *Students' World* and if you follow our method you'll succeed.'

As he spoke, he not once lost eye contact. He deepened his gaze and continued: 'You each have it within you to succeed.' Then, nodding his head, he concluded, 'I'm sure you'll all agree that your success will help all those you enrol to succeed.'

We found ourselves nodding in agreement. This was key to the method in which we were to be trained.

Work in previous long vacations had made me aware of the socioeconomic reality that youth from poorer, less educated suburbs are more likely to appear before court than those from richer, better educated suburbs. As a junior research assistant for Professor Peter Scott in the geography department, my ignorance of geography didn't matter. I had to compile lists of juvenile delinquents and note their offences, where they lived and other details. It became obvious that young offenders from the housing commission estate of Warrane far outnumbered those from affluent Taroona.

This flooded back to me on the first day after training, when our *Students' World* boss drove us over to the Eastern Shore and let us loose on different blocks of Warrane with our carry cases and spiels. In this burgeoning, treeless territory, almost identical small weatherboard houses lined the streets. It would have taken no time to count all the books that lined the walls.

I knocked on my first door. 'Hello,' I smiled to the young woman who answered. 'I'm sorry to trouble you. I'm Helene and I'd like to show you how you can help your children through school. You do have children I see,' I pattered on, pointing to the swing in the yard and the dolls seated on a window ledge.

'Oh yes, Raelene and Joanna.'

'Well, if you'd like to help Raelene and Joanna, Mrs … I'm sorry I didn't …'

'Sharman. Mrs Sharman.'

'Mrs Sharman, if you'd like to help your girls through school, in their homework and in their projects, could you spare a few minutes to let me show you how?'

Once through the door, I headed, as instructed, for the kitchen where mothers apparently feel more at ease than in the sitting room. From next to a set of cream canisters on the bench, a wireless blared out an advertisement: 'Lan Choo is your cuppa tea.'

'Do you think we could turn that down a bit, Mrs Sharman?'

'I'll switch it off,' she answered to script.

Seated on upholstered chrome chairs, we faced each other across the middle of the pink Laminex table. I opened a volume of *Students' World* in her direction, making sure she could clearly see each page as I flipped it over.

'This set of books, with its easy-to-read layout, maps and illustrations, covers the whole school curriculum. If your girls have projects on, for example, the North Pole, life in the Middle Ages, the discovery of Australia, or convicts in Van Diemen's Land, all they have to do is write to *Students' World*. Raelene and Joanna will get all the extra knowledge, maps and guides they need.'

I outlined the program, the payments to be made and reached the end of the spiel.

'So I'm sure you'll agree, Mrs Sharman,' I put it to her, my eyes fixed on her and my head nodding up and down, 'that *Students' World* will help Raelene and Joanna. So if you'd just like to sign ... ' I poised the pen, ready for her grasp.

I broke the Tasmanian record for a new recruit and the boss offered me a permanent job. Though tempted, I declined: my first decision against lucre. I'd just turned twenty-two and to be filthy rich wasn't my goal. Had I accepted, even for a year to earn quick cash, I might have been caught in a spiral alien to me. The constant childhood rows over the payment of bills had taught me that money is better than poverty – 'if only for financial reasons', as Woody Allen would put it. I sought a standard of material comfort but not at any cost.

After graduation in 1967, I still didn't know what I wanted to do. The mantra chanted by my contemporaries, 'We can always fall back on teaching', meant the word 'unemployment' fell outside our vocabulary. The question seemed not so much whether we could find jobs but what sort of jobs appealed. I thought an honours year would give me more time and options. As it happened, John and I found ourselves together in the six-member history honours class so got to know each other a little. We celebrated the end of the year with our partners at a black tie dinner at the Dutch Inn, where, to the strains of a string quartet, John and I danced our first dance.

He sent me a Christmas card satirising the driest part of our course, the Industrial Revolution, run by Professor Gordon Rimmer, an economic historian who specialised in working-class housing in Leeds. John's card depicted the Nativity against a background of cottages in the Holy City. He had inscribed the card, 'Working Class Houses in Bethlehem'.

Although I spurned the chance of a lucrative sales career at the bottom rung of business, I believed in *Students' World*; it would have helped me through school. Some of those youngsters must have done better because of it. Yet part of me realised we peddled to the poor, targeting those more likely to be swayed than the better-off, those who might question us more and already have resources such as *Encyclopaedia Britannica* on their shelves. Significantly, our boss never unleashed us with our spiels outside the posh houses behind leafy private gardens in the best of Sandy Bay.

One person to resist my spiel was Mother Imelda. Did she believe St Mary's library already had the information provided by *Students' World?* Or did I fail to enrol my old school because I didn't insist the principal relax over the kitchen table, inhaling the stale odour of cooked cabbage and surrounded by platters of bread and dripping to be gobbled up by boarders? Instead, we perched as stiff as pokers in the gloomy convent parlour where Mother Imelda, fingers interlocked, sat below an image of the Blessed Virgin Mary.

Even without religious imprimatur, my stint with *Students' World* bankrolled the carpet for Lambert Avenue.

The sky glowed an intense orange the morning the carpet layer got down on his hands and knees on the floor. On that Tuesday, 7 February 1967, as the hours passed, the air grew scorching hot. We kept the curtains drawn. The man, whistling away in the hallway and on the stairs, rolled out an all-wool bronze-coloured carpet with velvet finish. With a sharp blade, he trimmed off the edges. Then, without warning, he left for an early lunch and didn't return.

At mid afternoon Lehene appeared unexpectedly. 'Tasmania's going up in smoke,' she gasped. 'We were all told to leave early. Everyone's left the library.'

'What about Longley?' Mama panicked. 'Quick, the radio.'

It wouldn't work. Neither would the lights. We were cut off.

'Don't worry.' I rushed out into the hall, over a roll of carpet, up the stairs to the garret. I grabbed my Kriesler transistor radio from the side of the bed and dashed back downstairs. We glued ourselves to that small black speaker:

ABC News. The worst fires for years are burning today in southern Tasmania. From a dozen towns in southern Tasmania, police and fire brigades have sent out urgent calls for volunteers to help stave off flames threatening to destroy houses.

Three houses have been burnt down in the Longley area 12 miles south of Hobart ... Early this afternoon the big Huon orchard district was virtually cut off from the rest of Tasmania by bushfires which blocked the Channel and Huon Highways. The temperatures in Hobart late this morning soared to 102 degrees, the hottest February day in the city for forty years.

Armageddon had arrived. Ferocious winds had set suburbs ablaze. Flames lashed dangerously close to the heart of Hobart. Mama, Lehene and I were ensconced at Lambert Avenue and I felt tense but relieved. We had escaped the conflagration of Longley.

Dugald McLeod reported on the 7 o'clock news that evening:

Late this afternoon one hundred and fifty people were trapped at Fern Tree in the foothills of Mount Wellington and there's been no word of them since. Communications are chaotic. No one in the Hobart area can see more than a few hundred yards through the smoke. It's been twilight since early this afternoon. Traffic has been rushing about in disorder and the telephone system from time to time has been jammed. As well, there have been periodic blackouts. Even prisoners from Risdon Goal near Hobart have gone out as fire fighters.

'The whole lot's gone,' Pot blurted, a blackened wreck and still half blind from smoke when he staggered through the front door. He had been living at the cottage and the house had been rented to a young married couple who fled with their belongings at dawn; but Pot stayed.

'One second it was there, then nothing. It all went up, Doff, everything. I thought the whole world was on fire. Not a shred left of Hawthorn Dene. Nothing. I'm OK. I got out, but just with what I'm standing in.'

'And Corby? What about Corby? What's happened to him?' Mama fretted.

She stayed on tenterhooks for forty-eight hours before it was safe to drive to Longley, past besmirched ruins of homes, past seared remnants of cattle. There, amid the debris of Hawthorn Dene wandered our pet Suffolk sheep, his woollen coat singed and his legs burnt. Toppled chimneys lay among the charred remains. At the cottage, the cast iron stove, with the melted Pyrex lid of a frypan, like a Dali painting, on top; the aluminium part had been consumed by the heat. Pot's old Model A Ford utility was parked where the back door had been, its tray facing the door. He had hurtled off to try to save tools from the shed, only to be cut off by the burning hawthorn hedge between the road and the burning garage. He returned to find the cottage and the old Ford ablaze.

Pot and a local farmer lifted Corby onto a piece of roofing iron, hoisted him aboard a van and drove him up to Lambert Avenue to join the rest of our four-legged retinue. Corby hoofed about in his new suburban surrounds for a fortnight until Mama accepted the vet's advice and had him put to sleep.

I felt for Pot and the loss of everything he had known from childhood, including his prized model Dinky town. I felt for Leslie, away in Egypt and what Hawthorn Dene meant to him and his selfless efforts to create a home for us there. Fortunately, most of his papers had been moved to Lambert Avenue. Our hasty retreat from Longley meant that even I had left behind some non-essentials; however, my overwhelming reaction to the inferno was relief. Sixty people died. Fate had spared us. I felt guilty about not caring more for Longley. I felt guilty because we owed Lambert Avenue to Rex's death.

Like other victims of Black Tuesday, Leslie received government compensation for the razing of Hawthorn Dene. This he put towards the purchase of Lambert Avenue and Uncle Gordon, Uncle Lester and Moonshine met the difference. The house became ours. For thirty-three years, Lehene and I would plough in part of our earnings to help maintain and improve the place. No matter where I lived, I would think of it as home. It was a sad day, despite the winter sun, when I stood with Mama between the beautiful camellias she'd lovingly nurtured, while we watched the auctioneer, his hammer hovering, close the door on my student world.

17

Tasmanian Tiger

The habit of arming myself with a tape recorder began with a wild animal: not the ferocious Tasmanian devil but the much larger, though bashful, Tasmanian tiger. Unlike the devil, the wolf-headed tiger, with its distinctive dark brown stripes and stiff tail, is believed to be extinct. Early white settlers who tried to exterminate the indigenous inhabitants (whom they regarded as 'upright animals') also captured the native tiger. Although Aborigines survived – contrary to what we were taught at school – thylacines were hunted, poisoned and gunned to oblivion.

Seen as a threat to sheep, they attracted a government bounty of £1 per head. A hundred years after the *Lady Nelson* landed at Risdon Cove in 1803, tigers, which had roamed the island's woodlands and plains for thousands of years, no longer burnt bright in the forests of the night. They were reduced to an endangered species and, in 1936, the last known thylacine died in the Hobart zoo. Since then, no one has produced proof of the tiger's existence.

In October 1968 I was hunkered down in a pink-walled study, except when I escaped to the sandstone parliamentary library by the waterfront. I spent hours in research, poring over musty pages of *Hansard's Parliamentary Debates*, *Journals of the House of Commons* and *Journals of the House of Lords*. Feeling my eyes glaze over, I rose, shuffled to my feet and crossed Salamanca Place in hope of revival. What have I done, I wondered, spooning the froth from the cappuccino, to lumber myself with such a task? Why was I still a student at twenty-three? The other five in my honours class – all male – seemed to know what they wanted in life. Three had left for the mainland: two for Canberra, as trainees in foreign affairs and trade. John had been offered two posts in regional Victoria, one in Ballarat, one in Geelong as a lecturer in humanities at the Gordon Institute of Technology. He chose Geelong. Only one other student had, like me, opted for postgraduate research. But did I really want to stay at university because I couldn't think of anything else? Because study could take me overseas – to more study, at Oxford or Cambridge perhaps, or maybe an American campus – and then, who knows what sort of an interesting future?

'"*Punch* and Judaism",' a friend had quipped. 'That could be your MA.'

'What a brilliant idea.' I thanked him. 'What fun.'

I'd enjoyed perusing volumes of *Punch* in honours year. I quoted the satirical journal and included several of its cartoons, as well as Aubrey Beardsley drawings adapted by an architect friend Charles Calvert, between the black endpapers of my yellow-bound thesis, 'Oscar Wilde: Cloven Man of Sorrow'. Now I could examine *Punch* more thoroughly for its attitude to Jews and anti-Semitism. Ever since listening as a child with Lehene, rapt as Mama read to us at bedtime from the crimson-covered *Stories from Shakespeare*, I had been aware of Jews as outcasts:

> Shylock was the worst of all the Jews in Venice. Antonio hated him because he knew him to be bad. Often he had called Shylock names and treated him roughly, because he was so angry with him for doing such wicked, cruel things.

Years later, when I read *The Merchant of Venice* at school, I felt sympathy for Shylock. A repellent money lender prepared to knife 'a weight of carrion flesh' from a Gentile delayed in the repayment of three thousand ducats, Shylock also suffered as a target of abuse. Perhaps, as a Chinese Tasmanian who had never fitted the norm, I subconsciously identified with another outsider. Besides, a man who loved his daughter as Shylock did Jessica couldn't be entirely bad.

At university Dr Michael Roe, teaching the history of ideas, aroused my interest in the Jewish question. He introduced our class to Hannah Arendt's *The Origins of Totalitarianism*, with its focus on anti-Semitism. So, when mulling over topics for a master's degree, I could think of no better than '*Punch* and Judaism'.

Unfortunately, I went before my horse to market and discovered that *Punch* had insufficient material on Jews to sustain a 40 000 word thesis. On hearing this, departmental head Professor Rimmer put his foot down. In that era when history and English literature were as Jew and Gentile to each other and intermarriage frowned upon, he had been less than enthusiastic about my choice of literary wit Oscar Wilde for my history honours thesis: 'I live in terror of not being misunderstood.'

Now he straightjacketed me into history. Instead of having fun, I had to trudge through miles of dry parliamentary debates to ferret out rare morsels, tasty and kosher. I was grateful for a trip to Melbourne to trowel through other journals under the domed ceiling of the Victorian State Library, but a book of Jewish jokes from a bookshop over the road engrossed me more. I pressed on to complete my thesis, 'Parliament, Press and Prejudice: the "Jewish Question" in Britain 1890–1905', but owe more to Professor Rimmer for side-stepping me into journalism, for had I not found *Hansard* so tedious – I staggered under the weight of each volume and felt my eyes and throat itch with hay fever from thick dust – I'm unlikely to have caught an advertisement in the *Mercury* for a position at the ABC. I can't remember what the job was – other than offering release from *Hansard* – but I do remember the reply to my application:

'Dear Sir/Madam, I regret to inform you … unsuccessful.' I tossed the half-quarto sheet and its buff-coloured envelope into the waste paper basket, not knowing I would invite serial rejection over three decades. Not once would I successfully apply for a job.

When I mentioned the rejection to Leslie, he exclaimed. 'You should have told me. I'll call Arthur.'

As a regular writer of ABC radio scripts, commentaries and reviews, my stepfather didn't earn much money but he did earn the right to call the ABC state manager by his first name.

In no time I entered the sparkling modern television building, where the controversial George Davis mural of a mosaic-tiled fish filled with nude female forms faced Harrington Street and shocked passers-by. From the lobby, a secretary ushered me into Arthur Winter's office. Over tea he asked about my background and then picked up the phone. 'David, I have someone here you may be able to use. What say I send her over and you see what you think?'

In the dingy brown radio building, where I had acted in a few minor roles when still at school, David Wilson beamed with enthusiasm. A former Singapore correspondent, the Hobart supervisor of radio talks bent over his desk facing the GPO clock and flipped through the pages of the *Mercury*. After a wink at me, he ran a pin around the edge of an article, lifted it out and handed it over. A Sandy Bay butcher claimed to have sighted a Tasmanian tiger.

'This is the record button. And remember to loop the microphone cable close to the mike and don't wriggle it about or you'll get a lot of clicks.' He gave a quick demonstration. 'One, two, three, four. One two, three, four. Hold it steady and keep the sound level outside the red zone, though it should peak in there at times.' He made it sound easy for someone who'd never tried a tape machine.

'Here, two taxi vouchers,' he said, as we walked into the lift.

He hailed a Yellow Cab, loaded me down with the world's heaviest reel-to-reel recorder, a Nagra, and slammed the door. 'Good luck.'

The butcher wiped his hands on his bloody apron while I gripped the microphone. I fired questions about his alleged sighting of a tiger and he pumped out answers until I heard a strange flapping sound. The tape had run out and was whizzing about on a single spool.

Back at the studio I stood, amazed, as Wilson performed like a magician.

'Watch this,' he said.

With fingers flashing between two recorders, he dub-edited my disjointed fifteen-minute sprawl down to a neat ninety seconds.

'Now we'll relay it up the line to Sydney.'

I couldn't believe when I heard it next morning on the national radio program, *AM*. A new world opened up. Like a stray pup, I'd been tossed a ball by a stranger, caught it in my jaw and now, with tail wagging, I wanted to run with it. I'd gone to the ABC with no specific goal in mind, yet within twenty-four hours tiger luck had me addicted to the adrenalin of broadcast journalism. Like the stage, it combined the thrill of production and performance; unlike postgraduate research, it instantly gave a sense of success or failure.

Weeks after that accidental October debut I replied to another ABC advertisement, this one for talks trainees. In January 1969 I sat opposite Murray Gordon, an executive from the mainland on his round of candidates throughout Australia. The head of spoken word had reached Hobart.

'You're as good as some of the best boys.' He sounded surprised, then warned, 'But of course, you have to understand that, all things being equal, if we have to make a choice between a boy and a girl, we'd have to give preference to the boy because you're going to go and get married and all the training would be wasted.'

I nodded in agreement. Just as my mother should have been drowned at birth, perhaps I should have drowned any ambition.

Although rejected – with no girl appointed – I wasn't out the door. Hobart happened to have a vacancy for a reporter: talks officer grade 1.

'You could be slotted in until it's filled,' Wilson suggested.

As a trainee reject I suddenly found myself on the payroll acting at a level above a trainee – though paid at the inferior, female rate. So set a pattern in which I not once waltzed through Aunty's front door but always slipped in through the back.

Out of the blue the university shot me a curt letter reminding me of my scholarship and demanding to know my intentions. I faced a tough decision. While I wanted the fun of the ABC – some people acted in positions for years – I didn't want to squander the work so far on my master's. I'd had an offer from Cambridge to enrol for a postgraduate diploma. If I were to consider that, it would involve fees and the rigmarole of applications for funds. A higher degree couldn't hurt. Torn with regret, I gave up the full-time job to freelance three mornings a week, while dragging myself back to those dusty tomes. When they led me to the issue of immigration and racial stereotypes, I felt it worth the haul.

The Russian Jews of the 1890s fled from anti-Semitism in their tens of thousands to build new lives in the United States. Of those who were rejected as unfit for New York, many settled in the East End of London where hostile English workers accused them of taking jobs from locals, introducing disease and increasing poverty and crime. By the 1960s when I wrote my thesis the Jews had progressed to middle-class Golders Green and been replaced in the East End by West Indians and Pakistanis. Like the Jews and the Irish before them, the new arrivals fought against the same prejudiced views, the racial stereotypes levelled against my Chinese forebears in Australia. The same prejudice was to be directed against the Indo-Chinese refugees of the 1970s and the Middle Eastern asylum seekers of the 2000s.

Still, academia couldn't compete with the surge of blood, the feeling of intoxication, that came from chasing and snaring a tiger.

18

Snow Route to Singapore

A galaxy of media stars besieged the snooty South Australian capital for the 1970 Adelaide Arts Festival. There as a freelancer, I felt rather intimidated by all the name dropping, the clamour for interviews and the tizz over attire for the Government House garden party. Spellbound by the Royal Shakespeare Company's avant-garde production of *A Winter's Tale*, starring Judi Dench and with characters rigged out in furry orange outfits, I scored an interview with the director, Trevor Nunn.

While in Adelaide I met two Radio Australia staffers. One of them, Richard Brown, tipped me off. 'There's a job going in Melbourne.'

On the way back to Hobart, while waiting for my connection in Melbourne, I called RA from a public telephone booth. The ABC's overseas service had already broadcast some of my freelance work from Tasmania, including an interview with the first conqueror of Mount Everest, Sir Edmund Hillary.

'When can you start?' I was thrilled to hear.

'As soon as I fly home and pack a few things.'

In my three days at Lambert Avenue before moving to the mainland, the telephone rang with a most unexpected caller. I could barely put a face to the voice of cameraman Neil Davis. 'A long time, yes. But I'm on leave in Hobart, mainly to see my aunt. Would you be free for dinner?'

We'd only met once before, eleven years earlier, when I was fourteen.

On that freezing winter's day I stood outside St David's Park, my skin turning blue. I rubbed my kid and astrakhan-gloved hands and paced the spot in my brown leather lace-ups. How much longer did I have to wait for the school bus? What a nuisance it was living down at Longley.

Suddenly a van pulled up. A rangy blond leant over and opened the door. 'Can I give you a lift?' He smiled. 'You must be one of Dorothy's daughters. I'm Neil, Neil Davis. I know Rex from the film unit and I know Leslie too. I'll take you home to Longley.'

I hopped in with my heavy school case, relieved to be out of the cold.

'Which one are you?'

'Helene.' I took off my green felt hat and rested it on my tunic.

'I'm a cameraman,' the 25-year-old stranger told me as the van chugged up Davey Street towards the snow blanketing the sides of Mount Wellington. 'I shoot the film for Rex to voiceover. That's how I know about you and your sister.'

The higher we ascended the more patches of white thickened the edges of the road. By the time we reached Fern Tree, the tavern, the rooftops of houses and the branches of trees were veiled in snow. The windscreen wipers whirred; the bonnet disappeared under powder. Neil navigated through slush.

'I'm pulling over.'

Tyres squelching, he turned off the road, followed a path on the upper side of the mountain and stopped in a clearing in the bush. A fluffy mass of snow smothered the ground; the white-feathered limbs of trees looked like a Christmas card.

As flakes drifted down all about us he moved across and kissed me. Shocked, I drew back. I'd accepted Neil's lift just as I'd once as a child got into the van of the family electrician, who'd entertained me by pointing out the spider in its web in the top left hand corner of the windscreen.

'Takes care of all the blowflies,' the electrician had explained while I peered at the web, hypnotised by the daddy long legs.

'Sorry,' said Neil the instant I recoiled. 'Didn't mean to upset you.' He retreated to the driver's side. 'Just couldn't help myself. Don't worry. You're safe.' He held up his hands in jest of the gesture of surrender. 'Promise.'

In the snow of Mount Wellington, I stayed alert in the charged, chill cabin but didn't feel threatened. We waited a while and then resumed the treacherous, slippery wind around the hairpin bends down to Longley. By the time we turned into the gravel at Hawthorn Dene, Neil had won my trust. A rogue, he had an irresistible charm. Over a cup of tea by the fire with the family, I didn't mention the pause in Fern Tree. Why cause trouble?

When in 1970 I saw Neil again, he worked for the international news service, Visnews, which had its headquarters in London; he based himself in Singapore and roamed Asia, concentrating on the Indo-China War. For six years his stories had been aired around the world, including on the ABC, which was, along with the BBC and Reuters newsagency, a shareholder of Visnews.

I felt shy but excited when I found myself with this softly spoken, sophisticated man with his tall, athletic good looks though unusual, pointed chin. He appeared to me as partly big brother and adviser; however, at twenty-five and long out of my green school uniform, I didn't need to recall our first meeting to realise he saw me as no little sister.

'Remember when I drove you home in the snow?' he reminisced with amusement.

After that Sunday's scaloppine, we met twice in Melbourne the following week. He rolled up with a small, cylindrical Sony transistor radio. A precursor to the Walkman, it was only one-third the size of my Kriesler. Nothing like it could be found in Australia.

'You can pick them up like matchboxes in Singapore,' he shrugged off his generosity.

In talking with Neil, my dreams of overseas travel began to take shape and to include an Asian dimension I hadn't ever before considered, while London had beckoned ever since I threw dice over the Monopoly board and became familiar with its squares named after Piccadilly, Bond Street, Park Lane and Mayfair. Long before the advent of cheap package deals, the goal of many young Tasmanians went beyond crossing Bass Strait. These denizens of Little England boarded a P&O liner with the UK in their sights. Despite my Chinese origins and even though I'd studied and tutored in Asian history, it took the fair-haired son of a farmer to spur me to an Asian country on my first trip abroad.

Lehene had already established herself in Melbourne on the corner of Toorak and Canterbury Roads in Toorak Village, where she rented a large bedsitter: light and airy, with a Murphy bed, a bed that folded down from the wall. For a year she'd fielded queries from researchers, producers and presenters at the ABC reference library hidden in the maze of ABC buildings on the corner of Lonsdale and William Streets (the complex was to become the site of the County Court). She had enjoyed the work but felt terrorised by her supervisor and so applied for a position at Melbourne University's Baillieu Library, where she now enjoyed her work without feeling tense and afraid.

She was madly in love with John Lachal, an ABC religious affairs broadcaster, who had studied for seven of the fourteen years necessary to be ordained a Jesuit priest before he left the Church. Charming and handsome, with a sense of humour, he shared Lehene's passion for classical music, was a vocal opponent of the Vietnam War and an extrovert who could suddenly stand on a street corner to make a speech just to draw the attention of passers-by. Lehene welcomed a visit from me, but wasn't keen on my coming to live.

'I thought I'd got away from you.'

'Well, you can once I find my own place. Anything going here?'

I knocked on all the doors of the two-storey red brick block.

'I'm about to leave,' said the tenant next to Lehene.

So I too set myself up comfortably. I organised an extension of Lehene's phone through the wall to my flat, enabling a three-way conversation with Mama in Hobart. With the portable record player from Hobart, I listened to *Rite of Spring*, loud, late at night.

At 529 Lonsdale Street, across and down the road from where Lehene first worked, gentlemanly Peter Homfray presided over Radio Australia. He couldn't have been a better boss. Knowledgeable, fair and friendly, he inspired confidence, so much so that, decades later, a crowd of us former employees from the English, Indonesian, French, Mandarin, Cantonese, Thai, Vietnamese and Japanese services gathered around him to celebrate his eightieth birthday.

My Friday duties at RA included *Talking Point*, which I produced either from scratch (from my own research and interviews) or from an existing program that I adapted from the ABC's domestic service. In the latter case, on one tape I recorded an opening, in which I introduced the speakers, and an ending; on another, I compiled the opening, followed by the edited program itself and then the ending. I left this completed tape ready for the weekend announcer to play on air. Unfortunately, I once left the wrong tape in the studio. When the announcer played my tape, all listeners heard was something like: 'In this week's *Talking Point*, Professor Shinsuke Tanaguchi ... And that ends this week's *Talking Point* from Radio Australia.'

On Monday morning I swung through the front door of the office to discover my mistake the office talking point. Mortified, I mounted the stairs to the director's office.

'Mr Homfray, I'm terribly sorry. I didn't –'

'Don't worry, Helene.' He had a kind, paternal air. 'Just don't let it happen again.'

I did worry, but I never repeated that mistake.

*

Meanwhile, at the end of April, I received my first letter from Neil: 'Dearest Helene, I don't even know how to spell your name – is that right?'

He had just returned to Singapore after a few days in Bali where he hired a Yamaha motorbike and drove up into the mountains. This followed two days in Sydney with fellow Tasmanian, ABC broadcaster Tim Bowden, and two in Canberra with another Tasmanian and former ABC correspondent, Philip Koch. To a Eurocentric Tasmanian like me, Neil offered a fresh perspective:

> Seven years since I was in Canberra. Really quite beautiful now, but too antiseptic and orderly – just no charm for me. Afraid I'm too accustomed to dirty old Asia – which nevertheless is loaded with charm and interest.

Neil's Visnews aerogramme arrived just as Melbourne prepared to stage a massive antiwar demonstration. On 8 May 1970, 100 000 protesters marched through the city demanding an end to conscription and Australia's role in the deepening American conflict in Vietnam. Demonstrators also converged on the streets of Sydney, the other capital cities, most regional centres and many country towns throughout Australia.

Despite Leslie's influence on me and his passion over issues – from Tasmania's destruction of Lake Peddar to America's bombing of Cambodia – I remained essentially disengaged from politics. Absorbed in Old Nick activities, as a student I rarely followed the news or read newspapers, odd behaviour for a young reporter that would naturally change as I embarked on a career in current affairs.

Many years later, when reminiscing with John on our campus days, he asked, 'Do you remember when Philip Koch came and talked to students in the union building?'

I had no recollection.

John recalled that, in 1965, Philip Koch, then the ABC's Jakarta-based correspondent, gave a lunchtime talk in his home town and was asked for his assessment of Indonesia's future. 'He was very positive. Next day came the *coup d'état*. All hell broke loose.'

John also reminded me of his only visit to Lambert Avenue as a student. In 1967, our honours year, he dropped in to borrow or lend a book. That day, Leslie was preoccupied not so much with ancient Egypt as with ancient Cambodia, especially the architectural wonder of Angkor Wat. On his way from Luxor, he had recently stopped in Phnom Penh, gone northwest to Angkor, capital of the ancient Khmer kingdom, and toured the vast Buddhist temple, rapt in its heritage of Khmer and Hindu carvings. He showed John some rubbings and grew angry over the war in neighbouring Vietnam and its threat to Angkor and the Cambodian people.

By 1970 President Nixon and his national security adviser, Henry Kissinger, had drawn Cambodia into the war. Flying B-52s, the US carpet bombed eastern Cambodia, targeting the Khmer Rouge and the Viet Cong (or National Liberation Front), composed of South Vietnamese communist guerrillas who had sanctuaries over the border. Inevitably, the victims were Cambodian civilians.

Neil's letter focused on Cambodia:

Will probably go to south Viet-Nam first for a few days. There I'll be able to get a far more accurate idea of the positions of the North Vietnamese and Viet-Cong forces in Cambodia. With the worsening situation in Cambodia now it would be almost impossible to get any accurate fix from there. The Cambodians will have to have help quickly or they may collapse. My friends are still missing – seven of them now. The only report I heard over the last couple of days was that a Caucasian answering to Sean Flynn's description was crucified in a Cambodian village by the VC. Which may sound improbable at first, but improbable enough to be true. The only other thing I heard was that the Viet-Cong denied they were holding any newsmen – which in itself is ominous because it is known that at least several of them were captured by the VC.

Sean Flynn, actor and photojournalist, was the son of Tasmanian-born film star Errol Flynn.

After being unofficially (with South Vietnamese troops) and officially in and out of Cambodia, Neil wrote from the Saigon bureau in early June:

> I'm flying to Phnom Penh to stay (officially) for two weeks. Very difficult to cover from the Cambodian side. One has to take a risk and drive out into the countryside to get any sort of story – and in the areas where the Cambodian Army is theoretically in control, the Communists do in fact control the roads. Result being that, at last count, 25 correspondents were missing – either killed or captured. Only definite one is an old friend – a CBS correspondent – who was found in a shallow grave a few days ago. Still, only the good die young – I'm therefore safe.

And he had time for personal sentiments: 'Love to your Mother and Lehene. All the remainder (approx. 98%) goes to you. When are you coming to visit me? Take care, *je t'aime*, Neil.'

Neil made me feel special. And he was special for me too. Meanwhile, I continued to see various friends in Melbourne. From interstate, one man, twenty-two years my senior, a Scot with a Pommy accent and a reputation as a *roué*, a former cavalryman turned geographer who proposed at our first dinner and had pursued me since I was nineteen, still declared undying love. A combined father figure, mentor and seducer, he conducted a one-sided affair. With Neil I felt a buzz of mutual attraction.

Later in June, from Phnom Penh Neil wrote on Hotel Monorom's tissue thin paper and slipped the letter into an envelope that was later stamped in red, CENSURÉ. Reading his slanting blue ballpoint, I could feel the adrenalin pumping through his veins, high on success:

> Have been here this time about two weeks and have had my best run of stories yet. Somewhat difficult to operate when one leaves

Phnom Penh, but the results invariably worthwhile. Have had 3 Eurovision stories in the last week. Think you probably know Eurovision. Had one of my best-ever close combat coverages from a place called Kompong Speu [southwest of Phnom Penh] about 10 days ago. Unfortunately very little would be getting back to Australia.

Although Australians saw much of Neil's war footage, including from Cambodia, his more graphic pictures were censored Down Under to sanitise the nightly news for family viewing.

I didn't know about Eurovision, so Neil typed an explanation from Singapore:

Eurovision is the organisation by which all of Europe sees the top news stories simultaneously every night … depending on the 'newsworthiness' (!) and not on the need to fill a bulletin. Eurovision news can run 30 seconds or ten minutes – or not at all. So, at about 7p.m. – when all intelligent Europeans are drinking up big in the pubs, or making love – the less intelligent are sitting down before their TV sets to view the evening news. And, if all Eurovision participants have agreed, as the top news story (from Cambodia, say) tells of yet further advances by the Communist forces – up on their screen, simultaneously from London to Moscow and from Helsinki to Rome, comes the very latest action film of blood & guts from Cambodia – taken possibly the previous day. A lot of words to explain Eurovision. But it's prestigious – if that means anything!

When I read those letters in my Toorak bedsitter, did I pore over them? Mull over every word? Go to the atlas and follow the details of the Indo-China War? No, I read Neil's letters, delighted and flattered by his interest in me and carefully folded each one back into its envelope. Did I worry about Neil being injured? Not really: he exuded such confidence, such invincibility, such a sense of knowing how to handle every situation. Besides, we hardly knew each other.

We'd met only three times (apart from in the snow): once as part of a foursome with Neil's friend, former Singapore and Washington correspondent Peter Barnett and his future wife. On that occasion I experienced the novelty of an Indian restaurant. Asian cuisine, other than Cantonese, was little known in pre-multicultural Melbourne and non-existent in Hobart. That evening I had my first taste of spicy food beyond the mild curry I ate, with hesitation, at the home of Brian Hodgkinson, the Old Nick producer of *Lysistrata* who had been inducted in Indian cafes in England.

Neil invariably made reference to Peter, who was then Radio Australia's news editor. Neil's first Asian assignment had been in 1964, when he and Peter covered the confrontation between Malaysia and Indonesia under President Sukarno. The father of independence, Sukarno was known as Brother or *Bung* Karno:

> Poor old Bung Karno died – which saddened me, as I'm sure it did Peter. How is Peter? And his affairs? ... All the best to Peter and tell him not to be like Churchill with his cigar!

In mid July Neil went with other correspondents to the north of South Vietnam to cover a farewell ceremony at sea for some sixty North Vietnamese Army POWs. The freed communists set out in the fishing junks they'd been given to return to North Vietnam, but as soon as they were clear of the South Vietnamese Navy vessel, they showed their disdain of their former captors and threw all the South Vietnamese gifts and clothing they'd been given into the South China Sea. Neil applauded the northerners as 'ungrateful wretches' and called their behaviour 'bloody marvellous', adding 'We all cheered their spirit.'

By now I'd booked for London and decided to visit Neil on the way there. As I'd never ventured by air or sea out of Australia, I was anxious about landing in Singapore only to find him away. The day Neil returned to Saigon's Continental Palace Hotel he tried to reassure me:

Have been suffering a mild attack of malarial fever. Thought I remembered distinctly answering your letter of June 22 just before I went north – but now I don't think I did.

Most important, of course, is that you come to see me whenever you want. I will arrange to be around somewhere. Just don't think about that side of it. Maybe I will have to work hard outside Singapore – almost surely in fact – but please come. And if I judge you to be the honest girl I think you are, with no foolish hang-ups, then I want you – and expect you – to tell me how much money you would like to make it easy for you. Please, but please, tell me – I will be disappointed and feel you don't trust me as a friend otherwise. Money is nothing. You need it now – I have it now. Someday I may need your help. Tell me as soon as possible (in Aust $s) – $300, $500, $1000 – just say. And no 'most gratefuls', 'loans', 'repayment', re. re. re. re. You owe me nothing – and you will owe me nothing – ever. Have your injections – they will save you trouble and inconvenience later ...

Cambodia was the best run of top stories I've ever had.

A fortnight later, back in Singapore, he repeated his offer almost word for word, just in case the Saigon letter had gone astray:

Main reason I'm writing is that, in my last letter, I told you that you must tell me how much money you will need to stop all that stupid worrying period that people have when they are going somewhere ... Why I am asking now is that I would prefer to write the letter to my Credit Union in Australia before I leave Singapore again – which will be in about 10 days time. Mails are so unreliable from other near countries.

I had no such foolish hang-ups. When I started going on dates in the 1960s, a lady was meant to be so above money that waiters presented her with menus without the prices, it being vulgar to trouble her with the fact that lamb cost less than lobster. Equally, a

My mother, Dorothy, in the Pekin Gift Store, Hobart, as Miss China of 1942. (Courtesy of the *Mercury*)

Obituary of my maternal grandfather, Gen Chung Henry, who joined his father on the Tasmanian tin fields in 1901, the year of Australia's birth as a nation and the year the White Australia policy was born. 6 February 1941. (Courtesy of the *Mercury*)

My maternal grandmother, Mary Lum Lee (Mrs Henry or Ah Hool), c.1930. (Chung Martin collection)

Left: The sun shines for my parents-to-be, Charles (left) and Dorothy with her brother Gordon at Kingston Beach, 1942. (Chung Martin collection)

Above: I develop from a healthy baby. (Burgess Watt)

Above right: Turning into a sumo wrestler at five months. (Chung Martin collection)

At twelve months my sister, Lehene, develops an abiding love of the piano. (Courtesy of Sister Taylor)

Uncle Lester with his favourite, Lehene, c.1949. (Chung Martin collection)

Aunty Joyce, holding baby Frances, and my mother, Dorothy, at 59 Cross Street, 1954. (Chung Martin collection)

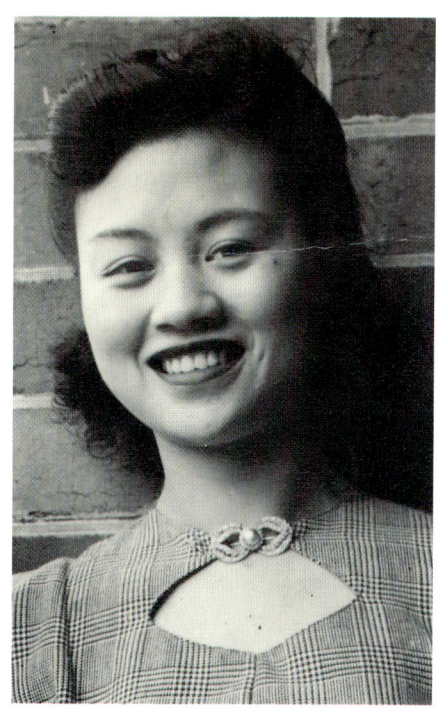

Aunty Marie, the first Henry to marry a foreign devil, c.1950. (Chung Martin collection)

Representatives of Various Countries in the St Mary's College magazine, *Santa Maria* 1950. Lehene (front right), me (front left) and (second row from top left) cousin Laraine represent China. When Laraine leaves that year, Lehene and I remain as the only Chinese among 500 girls for almost all our school years. (St Mary's College)

The prize of a Kriesler transistor radio. 8 October 1962. (Courtesy of the Launceston *Examiner*)

Rex Walden with Mrs Badcock's prize-winning German shepherd Wayville Alvon lapping up the attention, 1955. (Brian Curtis)

Snow blankets Hawthorn Dene in winter 1965. So Rex, Lehene (right) and I wait for the Pioneer bus, rather than have Mama risk driving on the treacherous Huon Road. (Leslie Greener)

The crumpled MG after its collision with a 10-ton apple truck, Easter 1961. (Brian Curtis)

Cast as a Datsun Bluebird in the 1963 uni revue, *Sin-Til-Eight*, I flit in a kimono across the stage in front of other players in the used car yard. (From left) Bill Dowd, Diane Bretherton, Greg Ferris, Regina Krutulyte, Geoff Millar, Claire Pentecost and Helen Willes. (Old Nick Company)

Another bold St Mary's girl Judy St Ledger with me in Melbourne for the Intervarsity Drama Festival. 24 August 1964. (Courtesy of *Herald Sun*)

Old Nick wins with *The American Dream*, 1 August 1966. (Front from left) Anne Spencer (Mrs Barker), Elizabeth Burnett (Mommy), me (producer) and Sylvia Hodgkinson (Grandma); (back from left) John Hensby (stage manager), Rowland Harrison (Young Man), John Craig (Daddy), and David Ryder-Turner (lighting). (Courtesy of the *Mercury*)

Sooty with Mama (*above left*) and Mandy with me (*above*) at Lambert Avenue in 1967, a year after we moved into our first home. (Maria Piscioneri)

She'll get things right

No wonder television researchers at the ABC don't mind checking their facts in the reference library.

Lovely Lehene Chung is there to help them.

Six months ago she came to the ABC from Tasmania — and says her only regret is leaving behind her pet alsation dog, Alexandra,

which she couldn't keep in her Toorak flat.

After work she likes to relax in a yoga position listening to Beethoven.

Lehene, an assistant in the ABC reference library, Melbourne, 22 January 1970.
(First Published *Newsday* © the *Age*. Reproduced with permission)

Hongkong Standard

Vol. XXII — No. 292 Saturday, October 23, 1971 40 Cents

Anne wants to shop, but there won't be time

PRINCESS Anne would like to spend at least one morning shopping in Hong kong but her official programme won't allow it.

In her first-ever radio interview — recorded recently in London with broadcaster Helene Chung — Anne said she would have liked a morning's shopping.

But the itinerary released a week ago by the Hongkong Government does not include this.

While it may be possible for the Princess to slip away undetected into London to shop, it would be impossible for her to do so here — where a much-photographed fair-haired woman stands out in a crowd — unless the trip was planned in advance with appropriate security measures.

In her radio interview, Princess Anne also said: "I hope to be able to see some of the things behind Hongkong a bit... if you see what I mean.

"The bits which possibly a lot of tourists avoid — and all the other things that people go there to see."

Hongkong people have also criticised the fact that Princess Anne (pictured left at the National Stud in Tehran) will spend time horse-riding in the New Territories — a thing she can do regularly at home.

But she will have no time to sail on a junk or visit a fortune teller, attractions unique to Hongkong.

Anne said she expected to see as much as she could of "a very crowded place" during her visit which begins on Tuesday.

But she added: "In most places, I think you are shown what they think they ought to show you, which isn't the same thing. But if it's your first visit its good enough.

"It would be very nice then to return, because you know exactly what you would like to see."

Listed

She will also see the work of the "Save The Children" Fund.

She listed some of the things she wants to do and see during her visit, in the interview broadcast over Radio Hongkong's English channel last night.

The programme can be heard again tomorrow at 9.15 am.

Princess Anne, who is president of the Fund, said the fund's organisers in the Colony need no special message "because they all know the value of their work."

She said they need encouragement more than anything else.

She assured the organisers that people all over the world were still with them and supported them in whatever they were doing.

Anne said that interest in the fund movement throughout the world could be promoted in different ways, mainly through the work of the people involved.

She explained it was the results of their work and the people they contacted that spread the right kind of publicity for them.

In Britain itself, she said, the fund movement was a success. This is reflected by the "amazing" amount of money collected, and the figures continue to go up.

She agreed there is an increasing awareness these days among young people about charity work and getting away from the "old-fashioned do-goodism," which she considered a "much more practical attitude."

The Princess will also visit the 14th/20th King's Hussars Hongkong, in her capacity as their Colonel-in-Chief.

Recalling a visit to the regiment in Germany when she was allowed to drive a Chieftan tank and seven armoured cars, Princess Anne said: "It's a marvellous experience driving around with 52 tons behind you".

While in Hongkong, Anne will try chopsticks. "Somebody taught me how to use them once. I dare say I have forgotten. But I gather that if one uses them just to shovel, then one does quite well."

Interviewer Helene Chung

A report on my radio interview in London, at Buckingham Palace, with HRH The Princess Anne before she flies to Hong Kong on her first unaccompanied visit abroad. 23 October 1971. (*Hongkong Standard*)

In Egypt with veiled heads at the Muslim Ibrahims' mud brick home, (from left) Lehene, Mr Ibrahim, me, Christian, Mama, Mrs Ibrahim and son, and Leslie, Luxor December 1972. (Chung Martin collection)

Not the day for horseriding around Egypt's biggest pyramids at Giza. An easy day in the sands of Egypt's oldest pyramids at Saqqara. (From right) Mama, Lehene and me outside Cairo, February 1973. (Leslie Greener)

lady was meant to be so oblivious to time that she was supposed not to wear a watch when escorted by a beau. He, being a gentleman, always paid the bill, the lady not having to encumber her dainty evening bag with a wallet. Besides, by 1970 I'd been spoilt for six years by my chivalrous older admirer. From the age of ten, when future butcher Bill Vermey, a boy who worked for Uncle Gordon in the store, took me to the Prince cinema and bought me a Choc Wedge, I'd never gone Dutch on a date.

Yet I had no need to accept Neil's offer. Even though my female wages were less than a male's, I'd saved enough for a Qantas Pacesetter fare to London, enough to tide me over for a while, plus an open Sitmar Line ticket from Southampton to Melbourne (although I would eventually return by air). My outgoing fare stipulated that I depart while still twenty-five and get to London within a year after two stopovers – one in Asia, another in Europe. I chose Singapore and Athens. I wanted to catch a performance of Aristophanes, traipse the Acropolis and tour Greece to see other temples, sculptures and mosaics that had enthralled me in classes on ancient civilisations.

Then a complication arose through Derek Davies, editor of the *Far Eastern Economic Review*. At the time I was assigned to interview him, I'd never heard of the authoritative Hong Kong-based weekly, but I quickly mugged up and had no problem in drawing out this stocky, bubbling well of information. Over dinner at Lazar's that evening, he drew me out on my plans.

'You should come to Hong Kong,' he suggested. 'You could work for my friend Tim Birch.'

Three weeks later an aerogramme 'On Her Majesty's Service' was winging its way to me from the controller of the English-language service of colonial Radio Hong Kong: 'I should be grateful if you would contact this office upon your arrival in Hong Kong so that we may arrange for an interview.'

In the interim I kept to my Singapore stopover, knowing I could arrange Singapore–Hong Kong–Singapore legs later. But what did Neil think?

Yes, Hong Kong should be okay for you to work. Quite a few girls get work in your line for Radio Hong Kong and I think with some other station there. Derek Davies is right in one way, wrong in another. You are certainly CLOSE to China in Hong Kong. But despite the fact that 99% of people there are Chinese it is still Hong Kong – a Crown Colony of Great Britain – and I loathe colonies, colonisation, etc. But if there is work, then of course it is worthwhile – as long as you don't fall into the trap of feeling Hong Kong represents China, or the Chinese – it is Hong Kong: beautiful, predictable, interesting, exciting in a way. I get a bit bored with Singapore – but it IS a country – the third China. Independent, progressive, fascist, socialist, arrogant, hard-working, also exciting in a different way – defying the world that expects (and even hopes) that they will go under – but, a country.

In mid September, fighting in Cambodia grew more intense, the battles more prolonged, as the government tried desperately to regain control of the countryside. Neil, about to fly back to Phnom Penh, wrote to allay my unease:

> Almost without doubt I'll be in S'pore to meet you. But if I'm not, have no fears – there will be somebody there with full instructions what to do. Just don't worry about that.

I knew I could depend on the bloke who picked me up at the bus stop to have me picked up from the plane.

19

First Taste of Asia

The air clung to me. In semi-darkness I disembarked from BA 723 at steamy Singapore. Bewildered in the crowd, I climbed aboard a strange, half-open bus. As it zigzagged, jolting passengers across the tarmac, exotic aromas engulfed me in a world of spices, pungent and sweet. Inside the terminus dark-skinned Malays and bearded turbaned Sikhs darted, clamouring in a jumble of tongues. They scurried about in seeming chaos, dumping suitcases that dripped with the sweat of multiple handlers. The calm of TAA and Ansett Airlines on the Apple Isle hadn't prepared me for the fever, the din, of the island republic.

On that sweltering Saturday, 31 October 1970, as the clock ticked towards midnight, peering faces glued themselves to the other side of the glass wall. There, a head above the crowd, stood Neil, waving. He picked up my two damp navy blue Globites, popped me into the passenger seat of his pearly grey Jaguar saloon and drove off past the orange glow of outdoor cafes into the sultry night. After the pleasure of my flight with lots of space (in a seat next to an emergency exit) and two extra seats in which to doze, relax and feast for ten hours, I could hardly believe the ease with which I glided into my first foreign experience.

Neil vacated the master bedroom for me. The most spacious bedroom I'd ever seen, it was fitted out with teak and cane furniture and a fan rotating almost silently from the high ceiling. When I arose next morning, Neil had already left for the office. In the dining room of his luxurious apartment, C4 at 7 Orange Grove Road, Ah Louey, the amah (maid) had set the table and laid out the *Straits Times*. In airconditioned comfort, began my addiction to a papaya for breakfast in the tropics.

I found it hard not to remove my own dishes, help in the kitchen and so forth but I was under strict instructions. 'Don't do anything or you'll offend Ah Louey. She takes pride in her work and is only too pleased to have you here as the place is deserted most of the time. I'm in Saigon, Phnom Penh or elsewhere nine or ten months of the year. Lending a hand is out of the question.'

That Sunday introduced me to Singapore's mixture of narrow old and wide new streets, huge death traps of tropical stormwater ditches, stately colonial architecture epitomised by Raffles Hotel, modern steel skyscrapers and crumbling wooden structures inhabited by Chinese merchants. Cranes testified to the construction boom, with apartment blocks and another forty hotels of international standard underway.

Traffic moved at an extraordinary pace, despite pedestrians wandering in all directions. I doubted I would ever dare cross one of those roads, trying to keep my balance on a raised ridge in the centre while trucks, cars, vans and motorcycles roared by on either side. Horns hooted non-stop, each hoot with its own meaning: 'I'm coming in any case, so watch out', or 'I see you, so go ahead', or 'Would you like a lift in my taxi?'

Even though I'd arrived fresh from the parks of Melbourne, I was struck by the greenery. Instant lawns sprang up overnight from rubble. From Mount Faber I could make out Indonesia to the south, Malaysia to the north and almost all of Singapore. I surveyed its tropical jungle, with Malay kampongs (villages) dotted between palms and giant ferns.

Accustomed to the relative uniformity of 1970 Anglo-Celtic Hobart and Melbourne, I was fascinated by the international atmosphere: the blend of European, Chinese, Malay and various Indian cultures, the clothes ranging from Western skirts to Chinese cheongsams, Malay sarongs and Indian saris, and the official languages: English, Malay, Mandarin and Tamil, as well as numerous Chinese, Indian and other dialects. In tourist spots English got me by with Singapore's attractive, beautifully dressed and well-educated Chinese, but in the city's Chinese sections, where vendors approached me, usually speaking Hokkien but sometimes Cantonese or the dialects of Hakka or Teochew – or several dialects all in a single sentence – I fell dumb and couldn't answer.

For hours I ambled, braving the tropical storms that suddenly crashed from the heavens. I felt sticky in the heat but the absence of flies made it bearable. No need for the Aussie salute to wave away blowies in Singapore. Rows of Chinese stores mesmerised me. They specialised in everything from firecrackers and gongs to beds and coffins. Peculiar smells emanated from walls packed with drawers of dried fungi and herbs and potions extracted from rare species said to prolong life and promote virility. I stared as scrawny carpenters in singlets hammered away at wooden coffins while women in loose black trousers laid massive paper wreaths against the walls of shops. Replicas of human beings, animals, houses, cars, furniture and clothes sat ready to be burnt amid incense and chanting at the funerals of rich Chinese. Around the corner snakes writhed in cages. Dead dogs hung from poles. I watched ducks being dipped into boiling water and then defeathered by machinery.

At a crocodile farm, reptiles huddled in a mass on top of each other in a corner of their pit, a dreadful sight. Still, I succumbed to a crocodile handbag with matching passport-size wallet and two crocodile claw key rings.

Eating outdoors around the clock was unfamiliar to me. Here, in the simplest of styles on mean wooden benches, Chinese devoured *lup cheong* (sausage) omelettes, fried noodles, steamed tripe or plates of cockleshells, alongside Malays with their sticks of satay and tasty sauces. Streets gave way entirely to food, including around the red-light district of Bugis Street late at night.

By 11 pm Bugis Street became a parade ground for prostitutes, many with tough, weather-beaten faces. Their mama sans, older, heavier and harder, busied themselves about the tables, checking that their girls were setting up a fair deal and that none were working for themselves on the sly. The transvestites sashayed onto the scene. Known as shims, these boys and men tricked up as females were slightly built. Their slender figures supported enormous breasts that bulged from their clothes and each mini exposed a pelvis.

In the dim light, seated onlookers ogled from tables chock a block with bottles of beer, cans of soft drinks and plates of fruit. Behind the throng, cooks stirred and tossed food in woks over flames, releasing aromas of oil, garlic, ginger and chilli into the air. It mingled with the odours of perspiration, the tang of ripe mangoes, papayas, custard apples, guavas and jackfruit, and the foul smell of Singapore's creamy-fleshed, surprisingly sweet fruit, durian.

Out to entice and entertain, the shims promenaded the aisles: their make-up overdone, they fluttered their incredibly long and obviously false eyelashes, the swagger of their hips extreme. With their long-nailed fingers, they brushed their flowing hair off their faces, caressed their wigs and posed – for a price – on the laps of tourists. Most shims derived their satisfaction just from being permitted to exhibit themselves, to be seen as women, though some were bought by acknowledged homosexuals or carted off by unsuspecting Americans. Long before sex change lost its sensationalism in the West, Bugis Street astounded me. I gaped, along with the audience of Europeans and Asians, visitors, sailors and soldiers, and locals of all colours, shapes, sizes and classes, a few drunk beyond redemption, staggering about bare-chested in tattered shorts.

As I sipped sugar cane juice, hawkers offered to sing a song for me, to sell me a laughing animal or a squeaking doll. Shoeshine boys wanted to polish my sandals. Cheeky little ragamuffins, boys from six to ten years old, milled through the street; they wagered Neil on noughts and crosses.

'Ten-to-one odds,' offered a crew-cut lad no higher than my waist. The boy was sure to win.

In a smart restaurant abundant with waiters and an equal abundance of bowing and scraping, I tasted my first Singapore–Chinese dish. Its spicy peppers set my tongue ablaze: chilli shot up my nostrils and swam around my head; tears streamed from both corners of my eyes. I felt as though I'd hit the ceiling. The island's ethnic mix, coupled with a tropical climate, created a fiery cuisine. After a few weeks I settled down and my Tasmanian tastebuds acclimatised.

Singapore enabled me to sample the delights of *dim sum* (touch the heart), a series of small delicacies, including pork, chicken, prawns, scallops, bean curd, yam, mushrooms and bean shoots, often wrapped in wafer thin pastry and steamed in bamboo baskets or deep fried. These delicious dumplings, the parcels of sticky rice encased in lotus leaves, the seasoned chicken feet, the baskets of octopus tentacles are usually followed by egg tarts, coconut squares, sago pudding, mango mousse, assorted jellies and other sweets. All are washed down with hot tea, or *cha*, and hence known collectively as *yum cha* (drink tea). Melbourne's Chinatown did not serve *yum cha* in 1970, although the Australian dim sim was a bastardised version of *dim sum*, just as the Chicko Roll was an Aussie bastardisation of the spring roll.

The image of Asian musicians on stage perhaps did most to break me from my insular Australian preconceptions. In the Hobart City Hall in 1963 I'd thrilled to Satchmo trumpeting 'When the Saints Go Marching In'. Louis Armstrong was the only non-white performer I'd seen before Singapore. Now, I stopped dancing in the middle of the nightclub floor to drink in the sight and sounds of a Philippine band. It dawned on me how odd I must have seemed as a student with Chinese features frolicking over the boards of the Playhouse and the Theatre Royal.

From beneath a façade of ethnic harmony, tension had seeped into Lee Kwan Yew's already highly regulated state. Only a year before, across the northern border in Malaysia, antagonism between Chinese and Malays had erupted into open conflict. The Chinese, who dominated business, tended to look down on Malays and Indians. Singaporean Chinese regaled me with how Malays were treated softly, given free schooling and allowed to maintain their wandering kampongs on valuable land. Through a Chinese executive I met an Indian, second in charge to the Chinese, whom I thought more interesting – and better looking – than his boss. The Chinese refrained from speaking of his underling by name, referring to him only as 'the Indian'.

On a flying visit to Kuala Lumpur with a Singaporean Chinese, ten years before the island upgraded to its modern Changi airport, my friend scoffed at Malaysia's impressive new airport: 'Look at all this empty space. Just for show. As if they'll ever need it.' His words would come back to me in 1998 when Kuala Lumpur's Petronas Twin Towers rose to be the world's tallest buildings, until overtaken by Taipei 101 in 2004.

Although I spent most of my two months in Singapore just imbibing the atmosphere, as everything leapt out at me as new, different and exciting, I also knuckled down to a little work. Shortly after my arrival I bought a Uher tape recorder, standard in the broadcast world, including the BBC, and not as expensive or heavy as the Nagra used by the ABC. Unlike the Nagra, the Uher enabled me to record and cut-edit tape on the one machine and so set me up as a freelancer.

When I bought the Uher, usually purchased by organisations rather than individuals, the sales manager, Mr Pang, asked, 'Why do you want it?'

My answer led him to take me on a tour of Radio Television Singapore, of the commercial channel Rediffusion, Nanyang University, the region's traditional centre of Chinese learning, and numerous other places. Mr Pang had either gone to school with or was a business or arts associate of all the directors who could smooth my way. He also took me to Tien Wah Press where Chinese girls assembled children's pop-up books for Hallmark. I left with a sample, *Astronauts on the Moon: The Story of the Apollo Moon Landings*. On opening the book, the rocket shoots into space and on successive pages tabs can be pulled to trigger Saturn 5 rising from the take-off pad, the movement of the lunar module, the landing of the astronauts, and Neil Armstrong and Buzz Aldrin's historic 1969 steps on the moon.

I sent my material – stories on an Indian swami, a British food technologist, a regional family planning seminar and a group of British marines who had just scaled Mount Menthosa in the Himalayas – back to Radio Australia via the Singapore bureau. Next door to Reuters, which also housed Visnews, the ABC's Asia headquarters at 15 Peck Hay Road sat in leafy tropical surrounds and looked more like a bungalow than an office.

I began with a report for the *Woman's Session* by interviewing Mrs Wallace, president of Maidenform, an American underwear corporation. Mrs Wallace, touring South-East Asia armed with the next season's bras and girdles, charmed me with her story of the first bra, made by her mother in 1922, for the launch of Maidenform. Her escort, Mr Rubenstein, who had stayed quietly in the background, then presented me with two pairs, one black, one white, of the new 1971 cling-all, no-feel, no-clip, soft and stretching bra and pants.

During my stay, Neil had flown in and out of Singapore on assignment to Phnom Penh and elsewhere. In November he covered the disastrous flooding caused by tidal waves in East Pakistan. He returned in early December, before heading off to Bangkok and back to the floods in Dacca. That tragedy would be followed by civil war, an exodus of Pakistani refugees into India and the birth of Bangladesh, one of the world's poorest nations.

I watched him pack meticulously, taking each shirt from its hanger, folding it and carefully fitting it into its own plastic bag. We wouldn't meet again for five years. By then he would be famous, as a womaniser and as a cameraman, especially as the intrepid Indo-China War correspondent, hailed for filming from the Vietnamese front line and for his image, on 30 April 1975, of the victorious Viet Cong tank, No. 843, with its red, blue and yellow flag, as it smashed through the front gates of Saigon's Independence Palace. 'Welcome to Saigon, comrade,' he would have rehearsed. 'I've been waiting for you.'

Before he left Singapore Neil cautioned me: 'Whatever you do, don't get trapped in Hong Kong. It's filled with Australians on their way to London. At some stage everyone drops in, so journalists based there think they're living at the centre of the universe. They're having such a good time they'll never leave. If you want experience, make sure you're on the plane to London.'

Hearing that from someone not keen on Europe but steeped in a love of Eastern cultures, I took note.

On Boxing Day I boarded American President Lines *Taylor* and settled myself into stateroom 10A. I was snoozing when the vessel sailed, just before dawn. As a cargo ship it carried only twelve first-class passengers and on this run had only nine: apart from me, four older American couples who called every vegetable from pumpkin to marrow, 'squash'. We took our meals with the gold-braided captain and officers: it was silver service all the way to Hong Kong. On that crossing of the South China Sea I gained my first impression of Americans as a group, to be followed by that of busloads of binocular-wielding, camera-draped Americans in Greece. Together they led me to regard Uncle Sam's citizens as courteous, well-bred and articulate.

Eight months later, in August 1971, I docked back in Singapore as one of 500 passengers on the *Taipooshan*: Chinese families, infants and the aged, children squealing with glee, widows and widowers refreshing their lives and young singles of all nationalities a-whoopee around the clock. Once again I had the fortune of my own cabin, which had two portholes and a bath. As I dined off china set on white damask, I gave no thought to my pioneering great-grandfather Gin, who made two sea voyages in the Pacific, his in the arduous conditions of turn-of-the-century steerage. I partied with the young set, including a Swedish philosopher, an American schoolteacher, an English miss on daddy's Diners Card and the First Mate, oblivious to how the labour of my forebears had lightened my load.

For the first and only time in my life I got sunburnt: I had fallen asleep reading *The Odyssey* while lying by the pool when we were crossing the equator. From Singapore I flew to Athens, where I traipsed through ancient ruins with my entire face peeling, a blackened wreck.

20

Colonial Hong Kong

Less than three days out of Australia and I feel the gods have been too kind to me. There must surely be some sorry jolts ahead. Life cannot always be as easy as this.

So I wrote home from the hothouse that is Singapore on Tuesday, 3 November 1970. When I docked in the brisk winter of Hong Kong on New Year's Eve, only in my wildest fantasies could I have imagined my luck would last.

Ferries crammed with commuters plied the harbour, hydrofoils swirled to and from Macao, tugboats churned their engines; freighters were being loaded and unloaded, liners that cruised the globe were being berthed; junks, graceful with ribbed sails and sampans fitted out as floating cafes sailed by.

To the harbour's north lay Kowloon, the bustling shopping Mecca of the East with its blazing neon lights, huge department stores, block after block of camera and electrical shops, alleys filled with tourists and touts, the jarring sounds of American pop music wrestling with Cantonese, and trestles covered with watches, bangles, penknives, cleavers, radios and torches, fake leather handbags and wallets, statues of Buddha, rolls of silk, plastic scuffs, bamboo mats, T-shirts, pots, pans, buckets and basins, and every conceivable trinket to tickle the fancy or the fanny.

To the harbour's south sat sedate Central, Hong Kong Island's pinstriped business zone. Bankers, stockbrokers, executives, clerks, hoteliers, traders and government officials strode with purpose, donned in dark tailored suits, expensive coats and silk scarves, their furled umbrellas hooked over their arms. Elegant in stilettos, women with round or almond eyes ascended escalators in glass plazas brandishing the labels of Aquascutum, Pringle of Scotland, Ballantyne and Burberrys.

All around the waterfront luxury hotels and glass and steel skyscrapers glistened; they dwarfed the few remnants of a bygone era. Double-decker buses, armoured cars, motorcycles, clapped-out taxis, chauffeured Rolls Royces, delivery vans, forklifts, trams and rickshaws vied for space on the clogged roads. Clinging to the precipitous sides of the island, office blocks, houses and tier after tier of jostling high-priced apartment towers somehow managed to hold their footings. The funicular train, which climbed up the granite hill, promised a magnificent view from Victoria Peak.

As much as I'd revelled in Singapore, it bore no comparison with what I perceived as the beauty, the excitement and sophistication of the Fragrant Harbour. At twenty-five, Singapore, to me, was to Hong Kong the backwater Hobart became when I first experienced Melbourne. Like Melbourne after Hobart, Hong Kong I soon discovered could be filthy. Whereas Lew Kwan Yew's campaign to 'keep Singapore clean, green and pollution free' – including a S$500 fine for the slightest littering with a bus ticket, a cigarette butt, or by spitting – kept even the dingiest rundown areas of the republic spotless, parts of Hong Kong oozed with strewn fruit peelings, muck and spittle. Still, to a young Tasmanian Chinese barely out of the antipodes, Hong Kong with its 4 million people seemed to offer the best of East and West.

As my taxi crawled along jam-packed Nathan Road, Kowloon's golden mile and Hong Kong's busiest shopping strip, I gazed up at the multistorey buildings with their signs flashing in red, black, gold, green and blue – all the colours of neon. Advertisements on walls, windows and awnings bawled out in English and Chinese. I could hardly see the upper residential levels for the rows of bamboo poles hanging out of windows with pairs of trousers and pillow slips, nappies and sheets, singlets, socks and every other item of linen and clothing strung out on them to dry. Boeings swooped overhead, taking off and landing at Kai Tak, some flying so close that their wings almost clipped the laundry in the world's most densely populated district.

Off the far northern end of Nathan Road, I checked into YMCA International House at Waterloo Road, a bit of a comedown from my stateroom on the *President Taylor* and Neil's sumptuous quarters on Orange Grove Road. Neil had sought advice from his Hong Kong Visnews colleague John Tulloh (a future ABC international news editor) and he had recommended this modern Y as affordable, clean and safe. Room 1203 proved surprisingly spacious, plain, but with a private bathroom and phone. John was to befriend me throughout my stay but meanwhile, before I'd even unlocked my cases, I dialled a friend of a friend and introduced myself.

'You should join us tonight for New Year's Eve,' Brigid Snow suggested. 'You'll have a ball.' A government employee known for her ability to organise anything at the drop of a hat, Brigid lived up to her reputation. 'Frank will collect you.'

That blind date with a ginger-haired American insurance broker initiated me into expatriate life in the bastion of British colonialism. From Kowloon we crossed on the *Star Ferry* to Central. Yet again, I was mesmerised by the gaudy neon, giant lights painting the harbour; a mass of white lights from apartments drawing my eyes up to the island's misty Peak. Within two minutes' walk from the ferry, we entered the Mandarin to make a party of twenty-two. As I wrote on a Mandarin postcard to my mother:

> Rated as one of the 10 best hotels in the world, it gave me a glimpse of the sort of artificial remoteness that HK islanders, especially Europeans, acquire after some time living apart from

reality – in a complete dream world. Here, at the Captain's Bar and then a private party in a suite upstairs.

From the Mandarin we took a taxi to the Royal Hong Kong Yacht Club at Causeway Bay to take our places at a swank haw-hawing dinner dance. By midnight we'd progressed to Sutherland House on Chater Road, back in Central, where we popped corks for the New Year over supper at the Foreign Correspondents' Club; the view from the men's loo on the thirteenth floor appears in John Le Carré's *The Honourable Schoolboy*. At about 4 o'clock, still wide awake and invigorated though swaying on my sea legs, I was led off and ushered through the rococo exterior into the exclusive Hong Kong Club. As the sun rose on New Year's Day, 1971, waiters in black tie hovered, serving us bacon and eggs and toast with butter and marmalade.

On my first full day in the colony I collapsed into bed at the same time I should have been rising. I snuggled into the sheets, tempted to pinch myself. Had I really been stirring through the South China Sea less than twenty-four hours ago? Had I just sampled the good life Neil had warned could snare me in the British enclave? I'd had a fantastic start, but as my eyes closed and my body began to relax, I suddenly stiffened. I realised how naïve I'd been: I'd worn the wrong clothes. Too eager to slip into my new batik trouser suit from Kuala Lumpur, I'd given no thought to Western after-five attire. No wonder Frank, in his dinner suit, had examined but made no comment on my rig-out when we met. With my Oriental face, amid the conventional finery of that company, I must have looked as though I'd wandered off the set of a Hong Kong nightclub show.

Within a week I placed an advertisement in the *South China Morning Post*: 'AUSTRALIAN BORN Chinese girl, university graduate, broadcaster, seeks paying-guest accommodation with family.'

'Well, I'm not really a family but –' I heard the Australian accent. 'There are three of us – all girls. We all speak Mandarin. And there's a room to let.'

I took a ferry across the harbour. Then I picked up a taxi that wound up the steep and narrow road between pines, banyans, azaleas and candlenut trees to the cool of Victoria Peak, where European imperialists had created a refuge from the summer heat and the hawking and other habits of celestials. Excluded from its rarefied heights, Chinese didn't ascend, except as rickshaw carriers and servants, until after the Second World War. Sir Robert Ho Tung, the wealthy Eurasian comprador and leader of the Chinese community, became the first part-Chinese to settle on the Peak.

On that first ride I stopped at Mid-Levels, at 17 Babington Path, named after Thomas Babington Macaulay, war secretary during the Opium War in which China was forced to cede Hong Kong to Britain. I moved into my own room, which had a pleasant outlook, in a large apartment, tastefully but simply furnished, though without airconditioning, something I didn't miss until summer struck. My flatmates at number 1A, a Brisbane theology graduate, a Melbourne arts graduate and a petite French student from the Sorbonne, all spoke fluent Mandarin as they were studying or had studied the language full time at Hong Kong University. Joining their household began and ended my attempt to learn Chinese in Hong Kong.

My ethnic background may have caused an identity problem in Australia but it wasn't resolved by living among Chinese in Cantonese-speaking Hong Kong. It was compounded.

'No use trying to learn Cantonese,' I was tipped. 'You'll never be able to speak like the locals. You go into one of the stores and try Cantonese and they'll laugh at you. Sneer. Treat you like a country bumpkin. Better just to speak English. You'll get better service.'

In restaurants and shops I quickly learnt not to invite derision by attempting my smattering of Cantonese garbled with my recollection of childhood Toishanese.

'If you stick to English, they may even think you speak Mandarin,' friends advised. The Cantonese of Hong Kong, who considered themselves independent of mainland China, showed a grudging respect for the Mandarin speakers from the north.

Taking a taxi required a particular approach. I could give directions in Cantonese – *'Ba-bington Doa'* – but was stumped if asked for details. When I answered in English I received one of two reactions: seemingly offended, the driver slammed his foot on the accelerator and lurched ahead in fury, or, he broke into a broad grin, glanced at me through the rear vision mirror to sum me up and tried out his English, 'My cousin, he live in San Francisco, he no speak Chinese', which always prompted a fractured exchange on the overseas Chinese.

I enrolled in evening Mandarin classes at Hong Kong University, a short distance up the slope from Central. But with my stumbling efforts as a beginner, I couldn't communicate with my housemates, so we naturally fell into English. Besides, I had little incentive to spend hours in the language laboratory, tussling with a tongue I might never use. In the West few spoke Mandarin apart from specialists who had trained full time for years, usually for diplomatic or academic careers. Latin, still compulsory in many a country, had far more speakers. Mandarin was one of four official languages in Singapore, but, with that exception, Mandarin-speaking Orientals were scarce beyond mainland China and the coast of Taiwan.

The nineteenth-century Chinese, lured to Gold Mountain in California and New Gold Mountain in New South Wales and Victoria, mostly came from the south, predominantly from Guangdong Province. They spoke Cantonese or, like my ancestors from the Four Counties district of Guangdong, dialects of Cantonese, just as they ate Cantonese food, usually stir fried and always with rice, a fact that made the term 'Chinese' cuisine in the West synonymous with Cantonese. When I left Melbourne in 1970 I had eaten only Cantonese; Peking, Shanghai, Sichuan and other varieties were practically unknown Down Under.

Mandarin expanded in the West in the late 1980s, when China allowed its people in their thousands to study overseas, numbers that multiplied dramatically after the Tiananmen Square massacre. In June

1989 Prime Minister Hawke wept for the victims of Tiananmen and granted asylum to all Chinese students in Australia. In cities worldwide Chinese protested against their government and later sought political asylum, claiming they faced persecution if forced back to their homeland. The families of successful applicants followed their husbands, wives and children from China, so swelling the ranks of Mandarin speakers throughout the West.

In Hong Kong in 1971, I couldn't foresee the day when Mandarin would be so prevalent outside the mainland, the day when white-faced strangers in Australia would try out their Mandarin on me – '*Ni hao* (Hello)'.

Being young and abroad for the first time, I couldn't resist the whirl of discotheques, the Den and the Polaris Club, throbbing into the night and I soon abandoned the classroom, shortly after I'd mastered '*Wo bu hui shuo Zhongguo hua*' – 'I can't speak Chinese'.

Only days after stepping ashore, I taxied out of the crowds to the contemporary headquarters of Radio Hong Kong at the foothills of Kowloon. Tim Birch, a cheerful New Zealander and head of the English service, had written to me in Melbourne on the recommendation of Derek Davies, the Hong Kong-based editor of *Far Eastern Economic Review* whom I'd had the luck to interview. When we met, Tim took me downstairs to the staff club for drinks with the director, an Englishman named Donald Brooks, and other staff and then dropped me back at the Y in his Alpha Romeo before he went home to the Peak.

Hired as a reporter on the daily public affairs programs, *Topics AM* and *Topics PM*, I worked to an Australian producer, Warren Rooke, from a small office in Sutherland House, a few floors below the Foreign Correspondents' Club. Despite cramped conditions and equipment of a standard less than the ABC norm, I had no complaints. From Babington Path at Mid-Levels, I picked up a *pakpai*, or cheap, illegal taxi, to Central. Ten minutes later, I seated myself on a high stool alongside my colleagues at a bench by the plate glass window. We looked south from the ninth floor across Chater Road to the green of the pitch, the Hong Kong Cricket Club, the dome of the colonnaded Courts of Justice and Statue Square depleted of the Queen Victoria bronze, over to the vaults of the Chartered Bank, the Hong Kong and Shanghai Bank and the Bank of China, past the Hong Kong Hilton and up towards Victoria Peak.

I was immediately thrust into the role of assistant commentator in an extensive live broadcast of the opening of the assizes. This elaborate ceremony, which involved the judiciary, the churches, the military and others of the colonial cream, marked the beginning of the new legal year. Hong Kong's bewigged legal fraternity, robed in crimson and black wool with ermine collars, assembled in and around the Supreme Court. Amid interminable speeches, the chief justice raised his concern over the increasing criminal use of knives and called for those who possessed such offensive weapons in public to be caned. The chief bailiff, bearing aloft his mace, led the solemn procession of judges to inspect the guard of honour, formed by the 7th Duke of Edinburgh's Own Ghurkha Rifles, the fearless Nepalese mercenaries who were a remnant of the raj. All the women dressed up to kill. Afterwards, everyone got boozed.

I'd never been live on air before, let alone commentator of a highfalutin affair, and felt daunted by the prospect.

'How do you pronounce your name,' asked the principal commentator, Radio Hong Kong's deputy director Ian Kingsley.

'He-LANE as in lane and Chung as in hung.'

'My God!' He threw up his arms in horror. 'I can't possibly say that. They'll all think I'm ignorant. It'll have to be *Choong*.'

To preserve his reputation, I agreed. So *Choong* I became in Hong Kong, only to revert to the Tasmanian convention the moment I left.

One of my colleagues on *Topics* was an English reporter who'd accompanied her economist husband to Hong Kong. Lyn and I were paid more than our bilingual Hong Kong-born Chinese colleague, who spoke English and Cantonese and had an understanding of the local scene infinitely greater than ours. Yet Bill – as part of the overwhelming Chinese majority – received second-class treatment. Unlike us, he couldn't aspire to the status of our senior colleague, a Canadian employed on expatriate terms: a high, low-taxed salary, a spacious apartment, a live-in amah and every conceivable material comfort. With my Australian sense of egalitarianism, this discrepancy made me ill at ease. So too did the discrepancy in housing between the most well-to-do Europeans and the poorest Chinese. While the former pleasured themselves up on the Peak or other parts of the island, the latter huddled in shanties, hoping to survive the next typhoon. However, Hong Kong's wealthiest inhabitants were not Westerners but Chinese tycoons.

While I lived in Hong Kong, China loomed tantalisingly close. Although just across the border, it was out of bounds. I applied for a visitor's visa at the China International Travel Service, known to locals as the China Anti-Travel Service as it proscribed more travel than it permitted.

An unkempt blue Mao-suited cadre shuffled towards me. 'Why do you want to go to China? Is it to return to the motherland?'

'The motherland?' I queried the alien concept. My mother had spoken of 'going back to China' as a child with her family but I knew Tasmania as home. 'I'm Chinese. My family comes from China. And I'd like to visit. But I don't know about returning to the motherland,' I admitted, with all the honesty inculcated in my convent years.

'But you do want to return to the motherland?' he prodded.

I reviewed my position. 'Yes.'

Although prepared – indeed, hoping – until the last moment, to change my Hong Kong–Athens–London schedule and sacrifice a Greek temple or two for the Imperial Palace, I realised I had slim chance of a visa. I was an Australian national and Canberra didn't recognise Peking, I looked Chinese but couldn't speak the language and I worked for British government-controlled Radio Hong Kong. Yet I wasn't refused a visa. Instead, on my regular trips to enquire, a cadre at the travel service repeated, as if by rote, 'The good word has not come from Peking.'

Curiosity carried me to the edge of the bamboo curtain. On a train from Hong Kong, I rolled through congested Kowloon and entered the lightly populated and largely rural expanse of the New Territories, where urban concrete and steel gave way to farms and fishing streams. Rows of traditional village dwellings with curved roofs remained. A peasant waded through the paddy field ploughing with the aid of a buffalo. Hakka women protected their faces from the sun with wide-brimmed straw hats that dripped with fringes. At the border post of Lowu, where British colonial administration gave way to Chinese, I had to disembark. I stood on the platform, the guard blew his whistle and I watched as other passengers whooshed by on their way to Canton.

I splashed by jetfoil to Portuguese Macao, 'a weed from Catholic Europe ... between some yellow mountains and a sea', as Auden and Isherwood described the colony. I trod the drab streets lined with Western architecture in sad repair and saw full bottles of Mateus Rosé heaped on the footpath next to rubbish. To Tasmanians in the 1960s Mateus Rosé had been an exotic expensive beverage. Now, bottles of it lay strewn before me and seemed to be worth less than the bottles of milk that were left at the front doors of houses in Hobart. I wandered past mounds of stinking garbage and a plague of beggars, refugees from China. Seized with pity and revulsion by their outstretched hands – some devoid of fingers – their ribs bursting through their flesh, their supplicant eyes or empty sockets, I fled inside to the tasteless opulence of the hotel-casino Lisboa, which boasted the largest chandelier in the world. Outside again, I mounted the steps to the baroque ruins of St Paul's Church and gazed across the frontier into the motherland.

As a child in Hobart I had gazed through the windows of the Pekin Gift Store, where Mama had been fitted and photographed as Miss China of 1942. Despite my mixed feelings about being Chinese, China held a fascination for me and the Pekin Gift Store was my magic window into that faraway land. I used to peer through the glass at its display of lacquered screens, embroidered cloths and full-length models – strangely, with very white faces – wearing silk cheongsams or heavy-sleeved kimonos. One model held a bamboo fan painted with riverboats twisting through misty mountains. On the window shelves lay cloisonné ornaments with a deep blue background and patterns of delicate pink and white blossoms threaded with gold. Jade rings sat inside the lining of red velvet boxes. Mesmerised, I ventured beyond the window display into the shop, wondering what it would be like inside China itself.

Now, from my bird's eye viewpoint on Macao, I spied armed sentries on patrol, yet still all I could do was merely wonder what lay beyond the magic of the Pekin Gift Store. What did my mother mean by 'going back to China'? What was this country of my forebears?

While I sought my passage for the vaguest of reasons, President Nixon, with an eye to re-election, secretly negotiated his passage to Red China through Henry Kissinger, his gravel-voiced envoy, who manoeuvred a rapprochement with the Communists. In April 1971 Peking astounded the world when it invited an American table tennis team, then competing in an international tournament in Japan, to play in China. This 'ping-pong diplomacy' led to the first semi-official visitors from the land of the free in decades.

Hong Kong, as the gateway to China, received a series of historic missions en route to the People's Republic. First over the line, in late June, was Canadian Industry Minister Jean-Luc Pépin and his press corps. At the beginning of July Australian Opposition leader Gough Whitlam advanced with his entourage. I interviewed the journalist representing the *Australian*, Tasmanian Kenneth Randall, and longed to be, like him, aboard Whitlam's train from Kowloon to Canton. The next contingent to China I covered was that of Canadian Opposition leader Robert Stanfield. I watched, awed and envious, as each of these delegations descended on the British Crown Colony and then disappeared into the mysterious beyond.

Meanwhile, four days after Whitlam met Prime Minister Zhou Enlai in the Great Hall of the People on 5 July, Kissinger secretly flew into Peking. Six months later, in February 1972, Nixon strode the

Great Wall of China and gave his assessment: 'This is a great wall.' He had hardly arrived at his guesthouse and was about to hop under the shower, when abruptly summoned to meet Chairman Mao. By then, London had summoned me and by the time Whitlam won government and switched recognition from Taipei to Peking in December 1972, I was physically and psychologically removed from the Far East.

Most of my work in Hong Kong was non-political. Unlike the ABC, Radio Hong Kong as a government department couldn't criticise the administration or engage in controversy, which made *Topics* rather tame. Further, being young and female, I tended to be assigned the lighter, less meaty stories anyway: the ready-to-wear fashion show and Miss Swinging Hot Pants Hong Kong 1971. None of this froth bothered me, it added to the fun. More than half my assignments were tarted-up public relations campaigns with handouts and freebies. In one journalist kit I received, at an Australian Trade promotion, I was surprised but pleased to find a boomerang. Reporting on speeches at the regular Rotary and Lions Club luncheons held at the top hotels – the Peninsula, the Mandarin and the Hilton – was no hardship. In seven months I downed enough cocktails, lunches and dinners in posh bars and ballrooms to last a lifetime. By the time the French consul-general's wife pronounced 'I now launch Chanel No 19', smashed a super-sized bottle of the perfume against the bow of the Hilton's *Wan Fu* and invited us all on deck for a sample and a champagne cruise lunch, I felt in danger of growing blasé.

'Press work in HK must be the most social on earth!' I sighed to Lehene.

> Often a job takes much longer than warranted because press conferences 'waste' time through the unlimited flow of cocktails. They almost literally 'butter up' the press here … Must leave HK soon, too enjoyable – the soul!

Hong Kong gave me a chance to savour other aspects of Chinese life, including the Lunar New Year.

> The Chinese New Year falls on a different date each year, depending on the lunar aspect, i.e. the position of the moon. This year – the Year of the Pig – was ushered in on Wednesday 27th January. So, 3 public holidays from Wednesday through to Friday …
>
> Many of the Chinese take the opportunity to visit relatives in China itself and even at the moment several thousands are going in daily, though of course the movement is now tapering off as the Festival comes to its end. The families have peach blossom trees in their homes – the bigger and richer the better – and the way in which they begin to flower and bloom is supposed to indicate the family's fortune for the year. Homes are decorated with tinsel and other 'western-style' ornamentation, though various plants and flowers are the order, especially a type of jonquil and some orange trees. All the homes have a superfluity of fruit, both fresh and preserved – the most delicious tiny, whole preserved oranges, mandarins, apricots etc and long strips of coconut and serve all manner of food to the innumerable guests – mainly relatives who visit through the period.
>
> For most Europeans the 'holiday' means several days of actual kitchen work – god forbid, as amahs take their traditional few days off (most usually have at least one day off each week too). They leave their 'masters' armed with their double pay, usually to visit relatives and friends. In fact, the whole season is a double pay period, i.e. paying out, as far as the Europeans are concerned. They must pay their staff double, give 'red packets' [of money] to children and the unmarried and are often burdened by doubled fares in taxis and hotels. But the Hilton this year offered a special concession to such 'poor' Europeans who thus took 3-4 days 'off' and stayed in luxury at special rates! (Much better than facing your own kitchen) …
>
> One day in the year sees the streets of HK relatively clean, as the Chinese parade in their newly-bought clothes, each taking the

> first step into the new year with brand new shoes. Debts are resolved before midnight, though can be re-borrowed five minutes later!

During the New Year festivities I was shown about by a geographer from Hong Kong University, a Scotsman who prized his collection of Mao badges as much as his drawer full of souvenired airline spoons.

> Charles took me around the flower market – quite enormous and bustling, at Causeway Bay on Tuesday evening – Chinese N Y Eve. Here he bought me a peach blossom tree, whose red buds are gradually indicating my fortune for the year, as well as a green 'blow-up' dragon. Quite like a fair, but much more crowded and jostling. On N Y's Day, went to Mr Lui's home for the traditional nonsense – where I exchanged a jar of Chinese ginger for several little 'red packets' from his family.

Mr Lui, a friend of Uncle Gordon, owned the popular Mocambo restaurant in the heart of Central. At lunchtime an army of waitresses pushed trolleys stacked high with steaming bamboo baskets, weaving the woven pagodas between tables that swarmed with Chinese clattering over *dim sum*. The restaurant softened to a nightclub after dark.

> The next day travelled round the island with Charles, visiting friends at Stanley – a rather 'to-do' area on the South coast – with the usual food of the season and another presentation of Ying Tong ginger. The other days were spent mainly seeing people, having a marvellous time: lunch with the English 'sugar-man' (that's his business I mean) and a French travel agent, trips to the New Territories – where you can still see parts of 'old China' – including walled villages, moats, the Hakka folk with the traditional and distinctive garb and of course many different types of splendid dinners.

One meal – taken in a far from splendid setting – had a lasting impression.

'You must try Peking Duck and toffee apples,' Chinese friends insisted. 'We'll go to the American Restaurant.'

I fancied roast duck. But toffee apples? I remembered the school fair, the sensation of my teeth cracking the coating of a Lady in the Snow, an apple, stuck on a stick. Why have that? And the American Restaurant? It made no sense.

We approached seedy Wanchai with its girlie bars: Playboy, Playgirl, Crazy Horse and Suzie Wong. Jumping with jukeboxes, these magnets drew GIs from Vietnam who were on the prowl. We went through the door into a cheap cafe with bright lights and the clank and clang of crockery and chopsticks against Laminex and took our seats. The others ordered beer while I sat on juice.

A whole duck with beautifully glazed skin appeared. I watched as it was sliced, only to discover it had extremely little flesh. Each slice consisted almost entirely of fine crisp skin – free from oil – with the merest sliver of soft, succulent flesh from the breast attached, so creating the exquisite combination of crisp, male yin and soft, female yang. Most of the meat was to be served with vegetables or made into delicacies and the bones simmered for soup. Using chopsticks, the waiter placed a slice on a small, wafer-thin pancake on each of our plates. With a spoon he sprinkled finely chopped spring onions onto the skin and then added a touch of plum sauce.

'Copy us,' said the others, rolling up their pancakes, their eyes on me.

With my fingers, I rolled my pancake into a packet. I took a bite. Delectable, especially for a lover of pork crackling.

I would later be surprised by the thick duck-breast flesh served with the skin of Peking Duck Down Under, adjusted to cater for the tastes of foreign devils.

'You'll like the deep-fried seaweed, too,' I was assured.

Seaweed? Tangled, blackish-brown rubbery strands littering the sands and boulders of Kingston Beach came to mind. Did I want that?

Deep fried? What turned up was a mass of shredded, dark green vegetable, crisp and crunchy, sweet and irresistible.

I couldn't wait for the toffee apples. Mystifying me, the waiter put a bowl of cold water with swirling ice in the centre of the table. He returned with a plate laden with bite-size slices of apple, all golden with toffee. Swift with his chopsticks, he picked up a piece, dipped it into water and put it on my plate.

'The water's to stop the bits from sticking to each other,' one of our group explained. 'If you leave all the pieces together on the plate, the toffee will harden like concrete, hard enough to break your teeth and the plate.'

Serving us each in turn, the waiter distributed every segment. Toffee from the central plate and water bowl stretched over to each of our plates, forming a delicate circular web around the table.

These sensational toffee apples bore no relation to those of schooldays. In restaurants around the world I would sample Peking Duck and toffee apples, but none would ever be as mouth-watering as that Saturday night's at the American Restaurant in Wanchai.

When I mentioned 'the soul' to Lehene, I meant it. My body, unlike my soul, found more than adequate nourishment while work and play merged in a non-stop party, a hedonist's heaven.

I mixed with Caucasians and Chinese. I dressed up for the St David's Day ball with its leek-eating ritual and music by the Royal Welsh Fusiliers, held in the presence of His Excellency the Governor at the Peninsula Hotel. I wended my way through cobwebs and exposed cables in the formerly Walled City of Kowloon, a foetid no man's land, a grotesque den of drugs and iniquity outside both British and Chinese rule, repelled yet fascinated by the sight of illegal dentists drilling into patients' mouths while advertising sets of teeth in glass jars on the window ledges. I dined alfresco by night at the Peak, learning how to manage a mango in polite society (by slicing the two halves from either side of the stone, criss-crossing the flesh with a knife, bending open each half to sit like an igloo on a plate and consuming each segment with a knife and fork). I boarded a double-decker bus and passed through a squalid part of town while – in the spirit of things and because Mother Imelda wasn't around – spitting lychee pips out of the window just for fun. I gadded about with a Cantonese police administrator, an American-educated British zoologist researching the sex life of snakes and a Canadian correspondent covering Ottawa's deputations to Peking. He proposed to me in the lift ascending the Mandarin Hotel. Life wasn't dull.

However, as I replied as a 26-year-old (in my circuitous, tautological manner) to my 48-year-old Australian suitor, who had pressed me to talk about myself:

> My object in life is to enjoy living and at the same time to maybe make myself a perhaps worthwhile individual; to make the most of all opportunities, so long as they don't 'hurt' others; and if possible to even 'help' others if the occasion arises. So the people I've been meeting have been and are primarily good company – good or otherwise – and that's all. If perchance I meet someone who happens to eventually mean more, then I'll think about it. But till then, let the winds blow me where they will …

Despite what Hong Kong offered, by and by I wished the winds to blow me away. The territory began to stifle me. Had I been a serious student of Chinese language and culture, a China watcher, I may have felt differently, become more in tune with the colony as a place to live rather than merely to party. I took to the New Territories and trekked up four hundred steps to the Temple of Ten Thousand Buddhas. I escaped to outlying islands. I yielded to dips by summer's moon in Middle Bay. But the longer my stay, the greater my sense of claustrophobia; the sheer energy and density of Hong Kong pressed in on me.

Most of all, I missed Western culture – theatre and the arts. I loved the novelty of seeing a Cantonese opera, I enjoyed a recital by two young pianists and a performance by the Hong Kong Singers of *Die*

Fledermaus. I awarded first prize to a show in international waters, the beautifully choreographed Crazy Horse striptease on the SS *Macao*. Still I itched for the theatre – a provocative play – and was less than enthusiastic about most of the films released:

> At last CROMWELL, which has only just hit the Hongkong screen and will probably not last very long, as the locals usually prefer blood and guts – thus the huge success of WATERLOO and TORA TORA TORA – such as you see in the great abominations produced by the local Shaw brothers, or their rivals – the Cathay organization – who specialise in epics of the One Armed Swordsman, or The Heroic Ones – fantastic, impossible spectaculars, with a cast of thousands, men flying and leaping over enormous walls, swords going in all directions and stars with such superhuman capacities that James Bond would retire palely defeated.

Long after its founding on the opium trade in 1842, the British outpost still reeked of commercial values. Only money mattered, so much so that an Englishman defined a Hong Kong queer as a man who liked women more than money. While the city catered for my material needs, it offered little of Western artistic or cultural stimulus. I feared that the longer I lingered, the more I risked the loss of my soul.

I heeded Neil's warning not to be trapped in Hong Kong and turned down the tempting offer of an expatriate staff contract with Radio Hong Kong. In August 1971, at the height of a sweltering summer, I left Hong Kong and headed via Singapore to Europe. I'd already booked for Aristophanes on my first night in Athens and Euripides on my last before London.

At Queens Pier, as I stood on the deck of the *Taipooshan*, I gripped the railing, my eyes fixed on my over-packed navy Globite that was being hoisted up into the air and over the water. My suitcase, which had been in perfect condition, had been so strained that it had come apart. Its locks had given way. I wished I'd sent more by sea, in the other case or the two black lacquer chests I'd bought in Hong Kong. I held my breath, afraid the brine would claim the lot. But as the metal arm gripping the case swung towards me, I could see the strap was still holding my luggage tight. I'd secured everything and nothing fell out. I sighed with relief. I'd lost neither my worldly possessions – nor my soul – to the Fragrant Harbour.

21

Bowing to Buckingham Palace

I fled from my flat into the foyer with its marble table holding Her Majesty's mail, ran up the red-carpeted steps, out the front door onto Campden Hill Road, hurried by the Windsor Castle where patrons indulged in their morning tipple, hastened down Kensington Place and along Kensington Church Street, past the windows filled with antiques, past the health food shop, past the dry cleaners, past the cobbler and into the Notting Hill Gate tube. Within minutes of putting down the phone, I'd jumped onto the Circle Line just before the carriage doors closed. I spotted an empty space and flopped down, blanking out the faces opposite, all of them lost in their own Friday fatigue, woes and joy. I took a deep breath. Oh, what a mess.

Three days earlier, I'd tucked onto the end of an aerogramme to Mama:

A job for OUTLOOK yesterday and one for DATELINE LONDON today, both programmes for the BBC World Service. And tomorrow I could make radio recording history in a rather mild way, when I interview Princess Anne at Buckingham Palace.

My diary entry for Wednesday, 6 October 1971 has only this: '4 pm B.P. Princess Anne'. Now, thirty hours later, I'd been thrown into panic.

'Get them back!' Ronald Boxall had fumed. 'You had no right to distribute those tapes. That interview belongs to Radio Hong Kong. Get those tapes back and make those cuts!'

Shaken beneath my façade of independent liberated female, I acted as the obedient convent girl I really was: I did exactly as I was told.

Despite my flaking face, burnt by the equatorial sun and further darkened by the Grecian sun, I'd disembarked at Heathrow exhilarated. For my generation of Tasmanians, students stuck at the end of the earth during London's swinging sixties, London embodied the Holy Grail, the centre of culture and the arts. There to greet me was a smiling, tall, frail, fatherly figure with tousled silvery hair. I recognised Bertram Willmore immediately. I knew my stepfather's friend from the kindness in the letters he'd written to me. Over two hours lingering at bus stops and lumbering along in two red buses that Sunday, he pointed out the sights from the airport, through central London, to the red-brick outskirts beyond the Monopoly board, down the Fulham Road until we reached Wandsworth SW 18. Bertram installed me in a newly decorated room in his home and daily picked me blackberries for breakfast and roses for my dresser.

'Now that my face has stopped peeling, my cough gone and my effects arrived and delivered from Hong Kong, I shall set about ringing people and meeting them,' I relayed to Mama, Leslie and Lehene.

> I am quite happy and contented here. It is lovely to see a garden again and buildings no more than about 4–5 storeys – Hong Kong is all 20 storeys high – what is more, the sun does shine in England (even though I thought I'd never want to see it again and was looking forward to chilblains).
>
> From here, Irish situation terribly serious and it seems to be getting near civil war every moment. A degree of industrial trouble

– workers striking because one man accused of working too hard and producing more than his share; train fares about to increase once more; little old women bemoaning the fate of the lost currency system and being utterly confused by new pence; universal scruff that you'd see in any city of the world inhabiting Piccadilly Circus – all jeans and falling-to-pieces leather; fashions so diverse that it's essential to choose 'your' style before you embark – if you want 'the pieces to fit'; a city where you can buy magazines the day/month of issue and actually hear topics discussed when events occur; where you're confronted with a 'choice' of theatre of almost every conceivable sort; and where – unlike bustling Hong Kong – you can even catch a bus and be given time not only to get on but pay your fare and alight. Despite all the dreadful things I've heard about London, I like it, I enjoy it and I can see myself here for a while. As for dirt, it's immaculate after Hong Kong and in fact is cleaner than Melbourne!

I'd landed with no illusions about prospects in London. Expatriates in Hong Kong had warned that almost everyone in England was out of work – one wag claimed they'd been working towards that for centuries. I was prepared to join the ranks of the unemployed, to live off my savings till they ran out, to wash dishes if necessary. But of course I hoped to pay my way with my Uher tape recorder and had plans to get started.

ABC Hobart had agreed to a series of six 15-minute interviews with young Tasmanians in London, 'Got No Hang-ups'. My subjects included the younger son of a former Tasmanian attorney-general, a boy I had met at my first school dance and who now lived in London.

'Let's meet at Hard Rock,' Paul White suggested over the phone. 'It's a hamburger place.'

He obviously sensed my shock at the thought of a Greasy Joe's like the caravan selling Hobart's only available tucker after late night rehearsals stretched into the wee hours.

'It's not what you think,' he added.

When I turned up at the trendy American joint just down from Park Lane, Paul wasn't exactly as I had thought of him. The ex-St Virgil's boy, brother of John White who acted in Old Nick's *Lysistrata*, was dressed in a full-length fur coat.

Radio Hong Kong had commissioned a series with former colonial dignitaries, 'Where Are They?', all of whose names were prefaced by 'Sir'.

Radio Australia had arranged for me to send freelance offerings on the arts and other subjects not covered by ABC staff correspondents. I was to despatch these reports through the ABC London bureau, which occupied a Regency terrace at 54 Portland Place, parallel to Harley Street and around the corner from the BBC's domestic service in the art deco Broadcasting House, just up from Oxford Circus.

Bertram, a former *Daily Telegraph* journalist during the Spanish Civil War, who by the time I met him had been an editor in the BBC's external service for more years than I had lived, circulated my CV among his colleagues in the labyrinth of Bush House, situated next to Australia House between Aldwych and The Strand. I entered its neoclassical portico, rode in one of the bank of lifts and found myself initiated into radio in London as a guest on the African service. At a time when the 'heart-shaped island of allure', as Tasmania House in London once dubbed the state, was barely known beyond the land of Oz – whose own cartographers regularly left it off the map – the producers in the African service considered my Tasmanian (not my Chinese) origins to be of such interest to listeners in a continent that embraced Tanzania as to interview me for two whole minutes and thirty-three seconds.

Had Wandsworth been better served by transport, I could have stayed spoilt at Bertram's indefinitely, even during his absences in his flights to his lady friend in Ireland, but from my first two commissions for the BBC I knew that to survive in the precarious world of a freelancer I had to be in central London, by an Underground station that enabled me to flit in any direction with my Uher at any time: to vegetarian diners and the chef at Good Gracious in Kensington (where I enjoyed a most appetising three-course meal), or to Christie's at St James's to report on the auction of a Bleriot monoplane, one of the world's only two known examples of the type XI in airworthy condition and in almost every way similar to the craft Louis Bleriot flew from Calais to Dover in 1909. It meant I had to navigate not only the crowded escalators in the bowels of London's Underground, but also the network of British Rail to get from Charing Cross to a charming village in Kent for an interview on drug addiction for Radio Hong Kong. For Britain's Central Office of Information broadcasting service I had to hire a car and be driven to Black Park in Buckinghamshire in order to ask John Cleese about *Monty Python's Big Red Book*, labelled VERY URGENT. Unlike Mao's *Little Red Book*, the *Big Red Book* was blue and inside it I found attached a special offer: FREE GAS COOKER GIVEN AWAY WITH EVERY OTHER COPY OF THIS BOOK*. Printed below was *See other copy.

To succeed in the fiercely competitive freelance market called for persistence. I needed a minimum of one interview a day to cover costs and when a producer rejected my idea, although dispirited, I had to plough on, phone the next producer and maybe the next. No point wallowing in misery after each rejection, I told myself. Just find a taker, a single commission. I liked to have a week booked in advance but even when I couldn't see more than a day or so ahead, not once did I think of looking for that free gas cooker.

In my search for a pad I inspected, among others, a dirty dump over a food stall on the King's Road for 13 guineas a week and a dim, nasty little room in a house in a row of neglected buildings off the Brompton Road for £15 a week. The ABC secretary then received £25 weekly. I know this because correspondents Peter Ivanoff, Malcolm Downing and John Sexton offered me the job for three weeks while the incumbent holidayed in Spain. Her replacement had just walked out because of problems with her boyfriend. John Sexton joked that if I couldn't type, he'd do it.

I realised that any dwelling worth considering would cost £25 a week, beyond my means. The BBC paid £7.75 for an interview I edited down to about 3 minutes 30 seconds, the Central Office of Information £8.50 and the British Forces Broadcasting Service £8.40 per item. All of them reimbursed transport costs and paid more for complex work.

Outside London, in cosy thatched-roofed pubs and cobbled lanes, I learnt how deluded I'd been on the Apple Isle: Tasmania, for all its pleasures, had nothing remotely resembling a village in the sceptred isle, but having lived in the hamlet of Longley now aided me in London. One evening I found myself inspecting a rather run-down bedsitter off Cromwell Road, South Kensington, with seven other flat-seekers. From the line-up emerged a suntanned bloke with blond hair, blue eyes and an accent that gave him away.

'You were on the school bus,' Geoff Watchorn grinned. 'Do you remember me from the Huon?'

'You went to Hutchins.' I recalled the striped black, gold and purple tie.

'Why don't we find a two-bedroom flat to share? We'd get much better value.'

From Huonville, Geoffrey had travelled via Sydney to Fiji, the United States and through Europe, working in sales, construction and industrial contracts. In London he sold cars and trucks for Britain's largest car sales, rental and servicing firm.

Next day we looked at four places, the most expensive and least suitable for £33. The last one, a basement flat on Campden Hill Road by the Notting Hill tube with three lines in all directions, proved best. Its front door opened onto a black and white-tiled entrance with a passage to the left, then a door to the left and another door straight ahead. This door led onto the bathroom where an ebony female bust reigned aloof on her pedestal. The door to the left opened onto a well-appointed bedroom, which I would take. The passageway had a telephone installed on a cabinet and connected to a second bedroom, which Geoff would take; and a furnished living room, including pottery lamps, a magnificent old wind-up gramophone, a set of antique brass scales and a marvellous urn. Tucked off the living room, the electric kitchen had been fitted out from Habitat. Freshly painted and carpeted, the flat came with central heating and hot water that were covered in the rent. We seized it for £29 a week, which fell to £28 with brand new beds when Geoff signed a twelve-month lease.

Sharing with Geoff worked well because, apart from the school bus, we had little in common. We each disclosed our habit of sleeping *au naturel* and preference for going to the bathroom unrobed, so we did, each passing the other nude without a thought. We hired a weekly cleaner, *jolie* Mademoiselle Chantel, and lived separately under a shared roof in far greater comfort than either of us could afford alone.

'Yes, Geoff would frighten off the burglars,' I rattled off to Lehene:

He's a typical, boasting, happy-go-lucky Australian male with an obvious Australian accent, but he dresses well, looks good and will be pleasant enough to flat with …

He's replaced his two beds with one large double-bed for 'entertainment' which seems to be rather frequent – while I have only one in here – to give me space for my recording equipment and desk. It comes with the place, simply a chest of drawers in which the top drawer pulls out into a table. But the spare bed is in the living room.

We rarely saw each other as Geoff was out all day and I out to dinner, films and theatre most nights. In almost a year's sharing we had just one meal together at the flat, when I roasted a free-range chicken for Bertram and his adult son, one of only two times that I cooked for visitors. Geoff often put on roasts for his birds. 'Better than taking them out. Closer to the bed.'

The flat design increased our independence, with Geoff's room at the far side where his queue of English gels tested the springs. 'They need a good Aussie service,' he smirked.

And, on one occasion, 'I got so pissed last night I almost made love to that black sheila by the bath.'

*

Campden Hill Road had been home for less than a week when I zipped up my new brown suede trouser suit with leather trim that cost me £100 at Simpson of Piccadilly (the model for the department store in the sitcom *Are You Being Served* and later taken over by Waterstone's, the bookstore chain). I tightened the brown leather belt with its heavy brass buckle around my waist, not caring that my mother would have told me to dress in a ladylike manner, in the camel cashmere skirt suit I had tailored in Hong Kong. But I asked no one's advice. The era of Emma Peel – the leather cat-suited, karate-kicking, gun-wielding television spy whose name was taken from Man Appeal or M. Appeal and is played by Diana Rigg in *The Avengers* – persisted in 1971. At least I left my black leather gear and knee-high, lace-up, high-heel boots in the wardrobe: I wanted to wear my latest rig-out.

I checked the battery of my Uher, heaved the machine into its leather case and draped it over my right shoulder, weighed down my left side with a satchel and set off on the tube to interview Princess Anne at Buckingham Palace.

The idea for this interview sprang from my initial meeting, a fortnight after my arrival, with information officer Ronald Boxall at the Hong Kong Government Office to toss about possibilities for Radio Hong Kong.

'If you know of anything, please let me know.'

'Well, there is something …' He paused. Then, measuring his words, 'and if it came off it would be a scoop.'

'What is it?' I leant forward.

'Princess Anne is off to Hong Kong at the end of next month and she's never been on radio. She's been on TV, the *Blue Peter* show, a BBC children's program, when she was visiting Africa. But never on radio.'

'Now's the time. I'll interview her.'

'It's not as easy as that,' he cautioned. 'She's refused every request from radio. The BBC has tried.'

'Well, let's see.'

'It occurs to me,' he deliberated, 'that a case could be made because this will be the first unaccompanied visit abroad by Her Royal

Highness. She's going to Hong Kong in her capacity as Colonel-in-Chief of the 14th/20th King's Hussars and as president of the Save the Children Fund. But she's never been overseas by herself before.'

I'd never heard of the King's Hussars but that didn't matter. I could find out.

'So if you wish,' Ron Boxall continued, 'I could put it to Bill Heseltine, the press secretary at Buckingham Palace. He's an Australian.'

Over following days I boned up on Anne. I pored through her file in the BBC clippings library at Broadcasting House. I learnt that protocol demanded that she be referred to as 'Her Royal Highness, The Princess Anne'. Born on 15 August 1950, she was a Leo – generous and warm-hearted. The first daughter of a British monarch to be enrolled in a public school, from thirteen she boarded at the all-girls Benenden in Kent. She won a cycling award in 1967, had her driving test the next year and received a Rover for her eighteenth birthday. (I would later hear she had an ovarian cyst removed, but maybe not the size of my telephone.)

Unfortunately, I couldn't just jot down a few memos for myself in a 4p W H Smith spiral notebook, turn up, have a brief chat and switch on the mike. Nor could I suss out the princess by a preliminary natter on the phone. No, royalty imposed firm procedures. I had to submit to the palace an advance list of proposed questions. As I sat tapping on the Royal portable that I'd bought in Hong Kong, I feared officials would restrict me to a dull ten minutes on the reasons for her visit. Obviously, I had to draw her out on both her charity and regimental roles, but I believed that listeners would also like an informal portrait, a fifteen to thirty minute interview on how Anne, as a 21 year old, thought and felt: What did she expect of Hong Kong? What did she think of Chinese food? How did she handle chopsticks? What sort of clothes did she like? How did she go about shopping? What were her ambitions as an equestrian? And among other areas I hoped to tease out were her views on two contentious issues of the day – the women's liberation movement and health foods.

Australia's famous Presentation convent girl, Germaine Greer, had long since flown from the strictures of Star of the Sea College in Gardenvale, Melbourne, for the freedom of Footlights and the Marlowe Society and the rigours of critical thought for a doctorate at Cambridge, with its cloisters and Bridge of Sighs. She was lecturing in English at Warwick University when, in 1970, her first book, *The Female Eunuch*, revolutionised women around the world. At the time I hit London *The Female Eunuch* had recently hit the shops. It sold from every shelf. It fell from every lip. I wrote enthusiastically to Lehene:

> If you haven't done so, do urge you to read it ... Very extreme in some instances and should be disregarded there, but very good summary of current thought on whole question of sex and the conventional roles of man and woman. The beginning may at first seem a little heavy and foreboding, well then skip that till later. The body of the work extremely readable.

Had Princess Anne read this subversive book? If so, how did she react? Did she regard herself as a liberated woman? Did her position limit her freedom? How liberated was her mother? How fettered were her female subjects? Did Anne have a responsibility to act as a role model to raise the barriers against her generation of young women? I didn't pose any such specific question but I did put on my list: women's liberation movement.

So-called health foods were also taking off in 1971. Under the influence of my mother's French teacher and lover my lifelong habit of daily yoghurt started at the age of eight. But in 1950s Hobart yoghurt was as exotic as chicken's blood in broth, one consumed by wogs, the other by Chinks. Bread consisted of white or brown tin loaves – the latter misleadingly labelled wholemeal – until the Domino delicatessen and cafe opened in the mid 1950s and introduced Hungarian goulash, German apple strudel and a Continental loaf crusted with poppy seeds. Mouths curled with disgust at the rumour that New Australians on the mainland ate black bread and blood sausage. By the late 1960s yoghurt had become better known Down Under. In Melbourne and Sydney it had spread from delicatessens to the burgeoning health food stores, but still raised more eyebrows than organic foods would thirty years later.

When I reached London various health food outlets including the pioneering Cranks (just off swinging Carnaby Street) sold all sorts of yoghurt, bread loaves as weighty as whales, mixtures of dried cereals, fruit and nuts they called muesli, free-range eggs, sea salt crystals and beverages such as dandelion tea. I was into all of it (while not eschewing Chinese chow or mainstream European fare) and I also practised yoga. Yoghurt had large enough an appeal for competing brands to be stacked in the refrigerated aisles of supermarkets such as Sainsbury. Naturally keen to know Princess Anne's attitude to this, I added to my list for the palace: health foods.

The princess granted the interview and made no objections to the subjects proposed. At 3.45 on the Wednesday, Ron Boxall and I advanced towards Buck House from The Mall. We rounded the statue of Victoria, august in her flowing robes, and passed through the huge iron gates, I conscious of my gnat-like status. Pressing on across the forecourt dotted with guards wearing busbies and red dress coats, we were admitted into the palace. Excited though not overwhelmed, I still felt more than the usual nervousness I feel before recording an interview.

The press secretary showed Boxall into a waiting room, then ushered me into a cage lift; as we ascended I peered through the bars down to the expanse of the ground floor. We landed in a hallway the size of a ballroom out of *Emma* or *Vanity Fair*. I almost expected musicians to strike up and Elizabeth Bennett or Becky Sharp in hooped finery to appear. Instead, I met The Princess Anne. I have an image of being introduced in the hallway but surely that's wrong. It must have been in the reception room to the left. I remember the grand piano – or maybe it was a baby grand. I also remember how simple and unaffected Anne seemed. Neither dressed up nor noticeably made up and coiffured, in her pale blue sweater, silk scarf and slacks she could have been an ordinary girl I happened to drop in upon unannounced.

'How do you do, Your Royal Highness.' We smiled and shook hands. Thereafter I addressed her as 'Ma'am'.

The Melbourne *Herald* titled my account of the meeting as 'She put Anne on tape':

> Princess Anne settled into the corner of the sofa, while I chose an armchair diagonally opposite, so as to hold the microphone still between us and avoid 'clicks'.
>
> As I fiddled with the machine on the low coffee table, testing for levels before recording, we chatted away almost oblivious of the press secretary, seated some yards away in his dual role as censor and guardian.
>
> About the magnificent view she enjoys from the windows of her second floor suite, of the splendid wrought iron gates, keeping back the throng of tourists and English, who patiently wait to catch a glimpse of royalty, of the imposing Queen Victoria Memorial and the calm majestic avenue of trees that line the approach to Buckingham Palace.
>
> We touched, like two laughing girls, on Christmas shopping, the mechanics of chopsticks, London traffic which she warns must be 'treated with respect' and Hong Kong …
>
> At all times I found her response quick, lively, natural and friendly, though on some issues, for obvious reasons, rather non-committal.
>
> To represent Britain in the next Olympics as a rider would be the ultimate in sport, but also very hard work.
>
> She's excited (though without losing poise or dignity) about Hong Kong and hopes not only to explore the shops, but also the less tourist visited areas of the crowded city.
>
> She does regard herself as 'easy to feed' and has no particular quirks with food.

As for theatre, the Princess prefers to be entertained, rather than make too much effort.

I put it to her that, as the daughter of the Queen and as fourth in succession to the throne, her every movement receives enormous publicity: does this infringe upon her private life?

She doesn't seem to think so, for while those avaricious journalists may think they know certain things, there's always something to keep to yourself.

One Tasmanian journalist whipped back to Campden Hill Road, not wishing to keep things to herself. She listened to the interview. It almost filled a 5-inch, fifteen-minute tape (the idea of a thirty-minute interview had been ruled out). It required hardly any editing, just a little tightening here and there.

Seated at my desk in front of the Uher, I marked two sections of the brown reel-to-reel tape with a waxy white pencil, a chinagraph, and fitted one marked section into the horizontal groove of the plastic editing plate permanently attached to the Uher. I picked up a sharp, one-sided razor blade and cut the tape down the slanting vertical cross groove and next, I cut the other marked section. Having thrown the unwanted tape into the bin, I then spliced the tape together again with a special adhesive tape the exact width of the recording tape. So I proceeded, fine tuning the interview to exactly thirteen minutes thirty seconds, allowing time for an announcer to introduce and close the program in a fifteen-minute radio slot.

Using a connecting lead, I copied the interview onto a Sony cassette recorder, bought in Hong Kong just for this sort of transfer. And, finally, from the Sony I recorded several copies of the interview onto reel-to-reel tape on the Uher.

It remained only for me to type out suggested introductions for different radio stations: Radio Hong Kong, ABC, BBC and CBC in Canada. Because, as a freelancer, I had to stretch my work as far as possible, I also sent to Radio Australia, on a pay-if-used basis, my extended interview for Radio Hong Kong on drug rehabilitation.

Similarly with that three-minute interview, commissioned by BBC, on the value of yoga to LSD drop-outs. Sometimes I tailor-cut different versions of the original interview for different audiences.

On the day after my interview with Princess Anne, a Thursday, I headed by tube to the West End to deliver the tapes, including a copy for the palace, which, like the list of questions, departed from routine. I felt rather chuffed: with several commissions for next week, things were working out. I also had an interesting weekend ahead – my first trip to the seaside resort of Brighton. I was booked on Friday's twilight train with an Irish political journalist covering the Labour Party conference, held one year after Harold Wilson's defeat by Conservative Edward Heath. Sunday would see us in Birmingham for an anti-internment rally to be addressed by Ireland's fiery young Bernadette Devlin.

Meanwhile, I enjoyed Thursday night's dinner. An English columnist I met on an assignment had invited me to her home off the King's Road in Chelsea. She and her husband introduced me to their skiing friend, a visiting Swiss-French engineer in a black velvet suit and violet turtle neck. Speaking with a Marseilles (rather than a sexy Parisian) accent, his boyish face beamed at me throughout the meal while the smell of his Gauloise cigarettes imbued the room.

Not for a moment did it cross my mind that Christian Christeller would introduce me to the Left Bank of Paris and, as my lover, lead me to the Latin Quarter where, in 1968, rioting students pelted police with stones, to the vast La Coupole with its muralled pillars, mirrors and *bombe Norvégienne*, to St Germain des Prés with its killer boutiques, that we would tour in his red Fiat sportscar around England and into Wales, home of my favourite Dylan Thomas, that we would wander through picturesque villages in the south of France and down onto the Riviera, or that Christian and I would fly to Egypt and on to a Kenyan game reserve, where we would confine ourselves inside the car as monkeys clambered aboard and their urine gushed down the windows.

That Thursday night, back at Campden Hill Road, I slipped between the black sheets under my leopard-patterned doona and closed my eyes, my head still soaring.

Next morning I was brought down to earth when, as they say off-air, the shit hit the fan: 'Get them back!' Ronald Boxall lost his British cool. 'You had no right to distribute those tapes. That interview belongs to Radio Hong Kong,' he thundered down the line; I imagined his thumping fist. 'Get those tapes back and make those cuts!'

I suddenly relived the sting of Mother Imelda's strap. At twenty-six, with my tail between my legs, I retrieved the tapes. Then, seated at my Uher with a Gem blade in my hand, I cut out two minutes and thirty seconds, including this:

> *HC* Do you think that in the extremes of the movement of women's lib these days, do you think that in these extremes women can lose their sense of femininity?
> *HRH* Well I think if you take anything to an extreme, which some people might do, they appear to the public eye so to speak – I mean this is the impression they're putting over, they may not have done – but the impression they give I think is often a little severe.
> *HC* Do you think the idea of women's lib is a good idea?
> *HRH* I don't know. I think the circumstances differ so much that you can't judge whether in fact it is a good thing or not unless you're the person involved or you can be particularly put out by it I think.

And this:

> *HC* Do you go in for odd things, Ma'am, like yoga?
> *HRH* No. No, I dare say. No. If I thought about it long enough I might try it. But no, I don't think I have the strength of mind to keep it up.

Although permitted to keep the first question and answer in the following exchange, the remainder was trashed:

HC There's a great emphasis these days on health, health foods and diet. What special foods do you like?

HRH I'm not a sort of health food addict. I don't think I'm particularly fussy. I like practically anything. I don't have any passionate likes or dislikes. So I'm quite easy to feed I think.

HC Do you eat breakfast, Ma'am?

HRH Oh yes. I couldn't do without that I don't think.

HC What sort of breakfast do you like?

HRH Well it could be described as an English breakfast, I presume. But in fact I don't eat all that much but breakfast is definitely important.

HC Marmalade?

HRH Not often, no.

HC Do you like —?

HRH Usually cooked, but that's all.

HC What about yoghurt?

HRH No.

HC This comes into the category of health foods.

HRH Comes into the category of health foods. No, I don't like that.

Then, after some banter about how she liked what passed for Chinese food in Britain and how she had once been shown how to use chopsticks, this, which was also cut:

HC How do you relax Ma'am, get away from your formal duties?

HRH I think I probably come up here and sit in a chair for about as long as I can. I don't read that much but one invariably finds something to do. And with a small brother, I'm invariably involved in something.

The palace offered no explanation, but it seemed Princess Anne's views on women's liberation, yoga, marmalade and yoghurt were judged too hot to handle. Perhaps officials feared braless women would barricade Buckingham Palace, or a wholesale exit from yoga classes, or a plunge in yoghurt sales as a result of royal disapproval. Maybe her words even threatened the institution of marmalade.

I wrote home:

> The Princess Anne interview was nothing startling. A great deal of censorship as you can imagine. So much so that she hardly says anything. Royalty must never offend any small group, such as health food addicts or yogis.

Radio Hong Kong ran the interview on Friday, 22 October and repeated it on Sunday. After I read the newspaper reaction, I become more upbeat. Saturday's *Hongkong Standard* splashed the news on its front page: 'Anne wants to shop, but there won't be time', as did the *South China Morning Post*: 'Chopsticks may pose a problem for Anne'. The broadcast also made page 2 of London's *Daily Express*: 'Quote: I think I'm fairly staid by fashion standards'.

When the BBC home service aired a segment on Sunday's *The World this Weekend*, it generated Monday headlines. Two seized on Anne's dress sense, the *Guardian* reporting, 'Princess admits: I'm staid' and the *Daily Telegraph*, 'THE "STAID" PRINCESS EXPLAINS'. The *Times*, on its front page, took a more staid approach: 'Royal view of defect in visits by royalty'. All this meant that when I called producers in London to suggest ideas for stories, they knew of the antipodean at the other end of the phone.

Monday's *South China Morning Post* had a short item, 'Helene seeks fame in London'. Recalling my work for *Topics* in Hong Kong, it said: 'Helene is now in England, seeking fame and fortune ...' Well, for the record, that scoop grossed me £10.50 from Radio Hong Kong, £20.00 from the *Herald* and £14.35 from the ABC (for which I waited six months): a total of £44.85 – less than the £50 minimum I needed to survive a week.

Still, I survived London and I loved it.

*

Fast forward to 1993 and Camillagate: the publication of an alleged mobile phone conversation between the older of Princess Anne's brothers, Prince Charles, and his then mistress, Camilla Parker Bowles, each expressing longing for the other.

According to a transcript, purportedly scanned without permission from the *Irish Times* and posted on the web, Charles sighs, 'Oh, God. I'll just live inside your trousers or something. It would be much easier.'

> *Camilla* (laughs) What are you going to turn into, a pair of knickers? (both laugh) Oh, you're going to come back as a pair of knickers.
> *Charles* Or, God forbid, a Tampax. Just my luck! (laughs)
> *Camilla* You are a complete idiot! (laughs) Oh what a wonderful idea!
> *Charles* My luck to be chucked down a lavatory and go on and on forever swirling round on the top, never going down!

From the distance of Melbourne I followed the scandal, shocked and amused. Amused by the lovers' playfulness, their sense of fun, but shocked because, if authentic, it seemed too intimate to be revealed. Irrespective of the moral question of canoodling between the married heir to the throne with another man's wife, I saw no public benefit in leaking such unsourced salacious detail.

Back in 1971, when ordered to edit my interview, not for a second did I hesitate. It didn't occur to me to try to flog the off-cuts and even if I had, the quality press would have turned their backs. Then, different standards applied, different ethics. In the future nothing would be sacrosanct – nothing out of bounds. I could open up on my own no-longer shocking childhood and my ever so tame brush with royalty.

Despite Lord Northcliffe's dictum – 'News is what someone, somewhere, doesn't want printed: all the rest is advertising' – I would never regret my kowtow, my bow, to Buckingham Palace.

22

Shot on the Nile

'What we really need is hard news.' The ABC's London editor looked serious. 'We don't have a stringer in Egypt.'

This unnerved me. I'd asked Neville Petersen about feature stories. But hard news? I wasn't sure how to begin.

'Just contact Reuters when you get to Cairo. We'll arrange for Granville Watts to let you see the wire and use the telex. I'm sure the BBC bloke will help too.'

My Egyptian adventure, initially conceived as a family reunion, turned into my first shot at reporting politics.

Towards the end of spring 1972 Lehene landed in London bearing a broken heart: John Lachal had felt the need to 'shake his shoes', as he put it. She joined me and tried to begin anew, as a temp – a temporary secretary – for various firms. At the onset of autumn we moved from Geoff's and Campden Hill Road to rent a newly converted basement flat with its own courtyard at 48 Queen's Gate Gardens, near Gloucester Road tube and by the Natural History Museum and the Victoria and Albert. Like me, Lehene grew to enjoy life in London but we couldn't resist the chance to join Mama and Leslie in Egypt. So we advertised in the *Times*, subleased our flat to rock band Jethro Tull's guitarist Martin Barre, packed up and, at the beginning of

December, flew to the Middle East on United Arab Airlines tickets that cost us £100 each and routed us London–Paris–Cairo–Nairobi–Cairo–Rome–London. (We didn't ask for Nairobi but Egypt Air threw it in, so we took the extra leg.) We stayed with Christian (and his Gauloise) in Paris for a while, then, the three of us took off together. We touched down in Cairo for the first time.

After so long in Britain, with its ordered squares and queues of patient beings, I'd forgotten how bewildered I felt that first night on Singapore's tarmac and the fear I felt trying to dodge Singapore's traffic, so was unprepared for the high-decibel chaos of Cairo airport and the excitement of hurtling along in a Cairo cab. On a worn-out seat free of its footings, we bumped about in the back of the cab while the left door routinely swung open as we went around bends; Christian hung on for dear life. Our driver plunged his foot to the floor, determined to overtake not only all donkey carts, but also buses crammed with casts of extras clinging on outside.

Within thirty-six hours we left the capital with Mama and Leslie for Luxor, a town in southern Egypt of some thirty thousand Muslims and Copts on the site of ancient Thebes. Over three decades Leslie had clocked up at least seven full years as an archaeological artist in Egypt, mostly for the Oriental Institute of Chicago, living with colleagues and their spouses at Chicago House in Luxor. They worked there only in winter, which they referred to as 'the season', Luxor's summer being unbearably hot for Europeans. We enjoyed the winter warmth in the south, not expecting that year's exceptional cold in the north. Leslie's lanky figure had become so familiar that everywhere we went locals, in their flowing galibiyas and white keffiyehs, greeted him with, 'Ah, Mr Greener'. They chatted away, puffing endlessly on cigarettes; some invited us to their mud brick homes, while lads looked on awaiting their chance of baksheesh.

By 1972, Leslie no longer worked in Luxor copying historical inscriptions and carvings or figuring out missing parts of faded paintings of god-kings. He worked in Cairo for the University of Pennsylvania on the Akhenaten Temple Project, the first attempt to reassemble a temple block by block using a computer – the 'world's largest jigsaw puzzle'.

The pharaoh Akhenaten, usually depicted as misshapen, with elongated limbs and a protruding stomach, married the serene beauty Nefertiti. The world's first monotheist, King Akhenaten revolutionised Egypt. He abandoned the plethora of old gods to worship solely the sun god, Aten, and established a new capital in his honour, Akhetaten (Tell el Armarna), midway between Cairo and Luxor. After the pharaoh died, his successor, Horemheb, tried to erase Akhenaten's legacy by destroying his works, including his noble Aten Temple in Thebes. Horemheb used many of its stone blocks as filling in three pylons at Karnak; some blocks were believed to be buried in the columns of Luxor Temple.

We booked into the New Winter Palace, close to this temple and its rivalries of yore. Not far away, through gaggles of giggling boys pestering with outstretched palms, sprawled the magnificent temple complex of Karnak, where we were treated to an experimental *son et lumière* presentation, twentieth-century methods to enhance understanding of structures created thousands of years before. Lehene and I had never stayed in such a place as the New Winter Palace: modern yet infused with ancient history through association with the adjoining Old Winter Palace. Former guests of this luxurious establishment included the British Egyptologist Howard Carter, who shook the world in 1922 when he discovered the tomb of Tutankhamen.

On my first morning at the hotel, I awoke dreamy and contented under the Egyptian cotton sheet. Christian was standing at the window, looking out through palm trees onto the River Nile. Suddenly, the door opened.

'Darling –' I heard my mother's voice.

Even before the door clicked shut with, 'Oh, I'm sorry', Christian had shot back to bed and pulled the sheet up to his brows. He lay flat on his back, his naked body trembling.

I began to laugh, though it took him a while to see the joke. That was Mama's only such breach with an adult daughter.

From the Winter Palace we watched the sun sink, burnishing the sky across the Nile and over the Valley of the Kings. I would never see a more brilliant sunset.

'Wouldn't it be wonderful if we could go on a cruise,' Lehene wished as lavish expeditions plied the river with deep-pocketed tourists. For us, such a venture was beyond question. The closest we got was dining with one of the cruise leaders, an English academic and associate of Leslie's. She made me want to save up to sail with her.

Christian, Lehene and I set off in the cool of early morning for the Valley of the Kings. With hired bicycles, we crossed the Nile by felucca, wheeled our bikes through sand, then cycled on the West Bank; not a soul in sight for over an hour.

We stopped at the Colossi of Memnon, two gigantic seated stone figures, remnants of a temple built by Amenhotep III, father of Amenhotep IV, the heretic pharaoh who changed his name to Akhenaten in homage of the sun disc, Aten. I'd first seen images of the colossi at uni. Now, standing beneath their hulking forms under the open sky, I felt awe: the scale of craftsmanship diminished me to insignificance. Gazing up at the damaged legs and ravaged, near featureless faces, I recalled from schooldays a verse by Shelley:

'My name is Ozymandias, king of kings:
  Look on my works, ye Mighty and despair!'
  Nothing beside remains.

Pushing on in the sun, we came to the side of a mountain where the terrace temple of Queen Hatshepsut was under reconstruction. An extraordinary woman in life, in death she suffered the indignity of having her face and inscriptions excised by her jealous half-brother, Tuthmosis III, who married her and reigned as co-regent. Almost all families are plagued by tensions, I mused, just as most regions are plagued by struggles for power and territory.

We left our roadsters to clamber over to the other side of the mountain. As my swollen feet slipped and slid over the rocks and my thighs ached with a numbing intensity, I realised the madness of our trek. Yet we forged on up the slope, compelled by our recent experience of London all a-rage with Tutmania.

Five years after its debut in Paris, the world's first blockbuster exhibition, *Treasures of Tutankhamen*, drew queues of Londoners, some of whom, in the chill of spring 1972, bedded down overnight on the footpath for blocks to catch opening day at the British Museum. In a city that offered free admission to galleries and museums, the fabulous gold mask, the gold-plated carved wood throne, the gold and lapis lazuli pendant and other treasures of Tutankhamen cost each visitor £1. Queues had lessened by the time Lehene and I paced through the display with Mama and Leslie.

The effort to scale our Everest proved worthwhile: such a sense of wonder to stand on the summit, silent, and view the valleys of the necropolis sweeping out as far as eye could see. Exhausted by the time we descended into the Valley of the Kings, I lay stretched out on the ground at the entrance to King Tut's tomb and slept for an hour.

When I awoke, my interest in burial chambers was revived. In musty gloom we explored the dugout of the famous boy king, possibly the son of Akhenaten, or maybe of his brother. I tried to imagine the tension, the excitement, the relief and the vindication Howard Carter felt after years of digging and scratching, defying all the doubters, when he finally peeked through a hole into the inner chamber to be dazzled by 'wonderful things'. To my surprise, I found Tut's tomb the least spectacular in the valley, perhaps because it had been emptied of its treasure, although, as the most intact when discovered, this repository dating back to the fourteenth century BC had yielded the jewels of Egypt. Small compared with others, but easily accessible through a single flight of steps, Tut's cave made me wonder what riches must have been plundered from the graves of rulers far more significant than the minor King Tutankhamen.

The most spectacular tomb lay in the Valley of the Queens, that of Nefetari, wife of Ramses II. One of the best preserved in Luxor, its delicate state – salts seeping from the mountain threatened ruin to its beautiful carvings – kept it closed to the general public, although we were privileged to visit. The colours, especially a deep sea blue, looked exactly the same as the blue reproduced on postcards of the tomb's interior. I would later learn that this blue was cobalt, bought from Middle Eastern countries by the Chinese for use on their chinaware before they discovered their own deposits.

After the ideal viewing conditions of the Tutankhamen exhibition in London, disappointment awaited at the Egyptian Museum in Cairo. I read in my guidebook that the museum, 'which contains a more comprehensive collection of Pharaonic art than any other museum in the world, should be visited at least twice'. Alas, I could barely distinguish the exhibits through the film of Saharan sand and the fly-blown glass. As I wrote to a friend:

> The Cairo museum contains some of the greatest treasures known to man, yet to visit the place is so sad. It sums up my feelings of almost all of Cairo. Everywhere one is faced with what was, with remnants of a great past, but everywhere one is met with disorder and deterioration. The Cairo museum for instance is so dust-infested that it's sometimes impossible to see the objects. And if one doesn't go in the early morning there's simply no chance of viewing a thing, as artificial lighting for the museum simply doesn't exist. Of course it's the war, this constant state which answers for all the country's problems.

In the Six Day War of 1967, Israel captured the Gaza Strip and the Sinai Peninsula. P&O liners no longer carried Australians from the Red Sea, where Moses once passed, along the Suez Canal to the Mediterranean and Europe because the canal was blocked to traffic. Only under United Nations military escort was I able to visit the zone, as part of a small diplomatic and press group. Bombed buildings stood derelict, roofless, windowless or lay in rubble. Baby date palms emerged from dry soil, the sun shone and a solitary seagull flew overhead. From the devastation I peered from behind barbed wire across the canal, where foreign vessels were still stranded, to the specks of Israeli soldiers occupying Sinai. They evoked the armed guards patrolling Red China I'd spied from the distance of Portuguese Macao.

A month after I inspected that peaceful war zone, Israeli phantom rockets blasted a Libyan Boeing 707 down onto Sinai. Ninety passengers and crew died. On Wednesday, 21 February 1973, over one hundred travellers had boarded at Benghazi airport bound for Cairo, only for the pilot to loose his way in poor weather conditions and stray over the enemy-held peninsula. At a packed news conference, I listened to the recording made in English by Egypt's control tower. Against the droning of his engine, the French pilot reported trouble with his instruments, the heading, which determines direction, and the compass. He added, 'We are being followed by four MiG fighters.'

At his mention of Russian craft a collective gasp rose from our midst. We calmed down when an official explained that a civilian pilot could not be expected to recognise different war planes or to identify them with accuracy; moreover, the pilot still believed himself to be in Egyptian-controlled airspace.

When he asked for a radar fix to determine his position, Cairo tower responded, 'We are trying to fix you by radar.'

The pilot repeated his problem with heading and compass. Then, his voice rising urgently, he uttered his final words: 'We are now shot! We are shot by fighters! We are shot by fighters!'

I froze on my seat. I'd never before encountered such real life drama, such real life death.

Bodies and mutilated remains of the ill-fated jet were flown to Egypt. As Benghazi prepared for a mass public funeral, Cairo too began mourning for some thirty Egyptian victims. Thousands poured into Tahrir (Liberation) Square to chant the Islamic last rites for two national heroes, television personalities Awad Mustafa and Salwa 'Mama' Hegazi. Waves of high-pitched wailing filled my ears as I taped those grieving Arab women.

'What a loss, what a loss,' black-robed female colleagues of Mrs

Hegazi lamented as they beat their faces and stretched out their arms. 'Our poor Salwa died so young.' Their cries spiralled to the heavens.

Nearby, students transformed the funeral into a political rally. 'War! War, Sadat,' they shouted. 'We want arms!'

The bereaved Mr Hegazi summed up the president's dilemma: 'We must revenge, take revenge for her! We want peace but we want our land.'

Covering this tragedy brought back my student days researching the Jews of the late nineteenth century: Jews fled Russian pogroms (organised persecutions) for sanctuary in America and England, in the absence of any sanctuary being available in their homelands. My research had made me want to go and live in Israel on a kibbutz (collective farm). Now, fate confronted me with a new reality: how the creation in 1948 of a Jewish homeland had displaced Palestinians. Israelis and Arabs both claimed rights to the land while both existed in dread. Neither enjoyed peace.

Nine months later, when I'd returned to Australia and was living in Sydney, I followed events as Egyptian troops crossed the Suez Canal on Yom Kippur – the Day of Atonement – the holiest day of the Jewish calendar, so launching with Syria the Yom Kippur War. Whereas that war was fought at a time when news travelled slowly and newsfilm underwent a long process before being screened, today's wars are fought in an era of high-tech, instant news. In 2006 television screens would horrify viewers with the carnage of Lebanon, images of dying or wounded civilians, victims of a war between Hezbollah guerrillas and Israeli forces. With so many wars in the Middle East over the past forty years, hatred, hostility, territorial campaigns and revenge in the ancient world would have taught the modern world nought except how to produce more deadly weapons.

In Cairo in 1973, for each report I filed – whether on the influence of Moscow on Cairo, the role of Black September terrorists in neighbouring Sudan, or the purge of local journalists for allegedly feeding the foreign press with falsehoods on Egypt – I had to seek the censor's purple stamp of approval. This meant I had to negotiate bags of sawdust walled up on the footpath, hold a candle as I stumbled my way up six flights of sawdust-strewn stairs and then sit, anxious, as the censor, aided by his own flickering candle, read my typed sheets of tissue-thin Egyptian writing paper. I waited for his verdict with the same nervousness I felt when waiting for Sister Lucy to approve my dress for the school dance. I always feared I would fall foul of the censor but not once did he refuse me his seal. Only after he had signed all three copies could I proceed to the broadcasting building by the Nile, where I then had to convince attendants that I had, indeed, booked a circuit. Eventually, admitted into the studio, I made repeated futile attempts at communication. It never ceased to surprise me when, at last, I made contact with ABC London.

There in Egypt I learnt the value of diplomatic briefings and sought information from the Australian Embassy, including on the importance of Australian wheat sales to Egypt and on Australia's participation in Cairo's International Trade Fair. I was disappointed to see Australia's pavilion almost dwarfed by the huge Soviet display, sheltered from the wind by neighbouring pavilions and overshadowed by the flags of other nations while the Blue Ensign hung limply. One experience I'll never forget is riding a horse through the Egyptian desert alongside second secretary Miles Kupa. As I rode, sand whipped my skin and the breeze tousled my hair as I gripped the reins, imagining myself Lawrence of Arabia, rounding the sphinx and the pyramids at sunset.

As foreseen by the ABC's London news editor, Neville Petersen, not only did Granville Watts of Reuters get me started in Egypt by giving me advice and invaluable support, but the BBC bloke also helped. Maurice Gent and his wife hosted a drinks party to introduce me around. Everyone befriended this Tasmanian novice: diplomats, seasoned correspondents and Egyptian journalists from their grand, twelve-storey *Al-Ahram* headquarters in Cairo's most up-to-date building, where everything, even the lifts, worked. That period of learning the ropes in a developing country and battling technical difficulties in Cairo trained me for Peking, where I was to work a decade later.

After our time in Luxor, Lehene, Christian and I made a detour to Nairobi. While in Kenya we visited a game reserve and relaxed by Lake Nakuru, home to a million pink flamingos whose reflections shimmer on the water. Then we raided Nairobi's Woolworths and flew with luxuries, such as international brands of soap and toothpaste (the Egyptian paste had earlier turned Mama's teeth black) and pantyhose (unavailable in Egypt) back to Cairo on Christmas Eve. When Leslie was assigned to the Akhenaten Temple Project, he had stayed by himself at Pension Newbury House, where he now booked for us all (though Christian departed for Paris on New Year's Day). By coincidence I found myself staying next door to Reuters, its office quartered in what once had glowed as Cairo's most prestigious building, Immobilia, but which had fallen into disrepair, the entrance and dark walls thick with years of dust and decay.

Although the pension had suited Leslie, an artist absorbed by his paintings in Egypt, former POW and man of simple tastes as he was, it didn't meet the expectations of his wife and two stepdaughters. 'The pension is not exactly what one would call ideal,' I understated the case. 'The hot water supply is hardly adequate. The "shower" to use a rather pretentious term is exactly as one ordinarily is just when turned off, immediately before the water ceases.' A month afterwards, we were installed at the Cleopatra Hotel where our balconies fronted Tahrir Square with its incessant honking of horns, in rooms that vibrated with the bellowing calls to prayer.

Unfortunately, Lehene had been unable to enjoy Cairo thoroughly. Constitutionally weak from birth, she couldn't withstand the conditions of that unusually bitter winter. Cairo almost cost her her life, as I wrote to friends in Australia:

It was quite impossible and we were all terribly ill with the flu. Lehene has not yet fully recovered from virus pneumonia and weeks of diarrhoea which completely debilitated her. Only last week did she recover sufficiently to walk more than a few steps …

The pension was really a nightmare. Everyone literally was affected by the flu and most freezing cold I've ever experienced, with no chance of ever getting warm, the proprietors were both bed-ridden, one servant died and all others either left of their own accord or were dismissed. We tried to help by slowly pottering round in the kitchen, but such appalling conditions you can't imagine: no hot water in the kitchen and only the occasional trickle in the bathroom.

When Lehene had gained enough strength, she flew back to London, to the home of David Goodenday, a businessman she had been seeing before we left for Egypt. Son of the founder of Kayser Bondor, the stockings, lingerie and bras company known in Australia simply as Kayser, David by now was the regional director for Europe, the Middle East and India of the Melbourne-based International Wool Secretariat.

Meanwhile, Lehene used every ounce of energy she had while, buoyed on either side by Mama and Leslie, she inched along the street to lunch. We often ate at the Cleopatra, where Mama produced handfuls of piastres to distribute to the numerous Nubian waiters who appeared, smiling, with palms already open, as we rose from table, and the galibiyaed attendants who crowded outside the lobby crying 'Baksheesh'. In fact, we sampled most of the main eateries in Cairo where Mama, reared on Cantonese food and lacking anything like my initiation in Singapore, tried in vain to avoid spices.

At the Hilton we indulged in the height of luxury when the waiter, balancing a silver tray on his upturned hand, asked, 'Would you care for coffee?'

'Yes, please.'

He lowered the tray, revealing a small round tin marked Nescafé, spooned a few grains into my cup and poured boiling water over it.

I liked traditional Egyptian coffee, sipped in cafes where the aroma of cumin wafted in the air and drunk until all that remained was layers of black mud. I needed it after a session haggling with vendors out to charm me with their leather pouffes and camel saddles, briefcases and brass trays while wizened men, seated at their water pipes, smoked hashish in the bazaar of Khan el-Khalili. But I couldn't take to black mud too often so a cup of Nescafé came as a welcome relief.

Among local dishes the *lait caillé*, or sour milk, became my daily yoghurt. I grew partial to shish kebabs and fancied *omali*, a nourishing sweet similar to muesli but served hot. Arab friends tempted me with their delicious spiced barbequed pigeons. Over time, however, just as I was to find in China, my palate craved ordinary, familiar but unobtainable tastes.

'Do you like cheese?' I asked an Egyptian employee of the United Nations Food and Agriculture Organisation; he screwed up his face in disgust.

Next time we met he handed me a tin. 'Danish,' he grinned.

It felt heavy. I examined it — about 5 inches in diameter and 4 inches deep — and realised I held a super-size tin of processed Cheddar. 'You can't give me this. It's aid.'

'Egyptians, they don't like it. They don't know what to do with it. Peasants think it soap and try to wash their clothes with it. "It's no good," they complain. "It won't lather."'

'I'll have it then,' I laughed.

The UN had more success with its efforts to save the ancient monuments of Philae, an island partially submerged for most of the year by the Aswan Dam. Only when the sluice gates opened for irrigation could the Pharaonic, Greco-Roman and Christian monuments be fully appreciated. When I heard that UNESCO delegates from fourteen nations planned to convene in Aswan in Upper Egypt to inspect Philae with Egyptian antiquity experts, I wanted to join the accompanying media. This led me to the Cairo office of a cultural bigwig who left me in no doubt of my press pass.

'Let me give you this,' he drawled, opening a narrow, pale green and gold box. He took out a plaster model of an obelisk and stood it on the large working table littered with documents and artefacts, then, he sat back against his chair, eyeing me for my response.

'Cleopatra's Needle. All covered with hieroglyphs. That's very kind of you, Dr Mokhtar.'

'Just a welcoming gesture,' he made light of it. 'I'd like to give you the complete set,' he added in his low, cultivated accent.

'I've seen this in London.'

'Yes, on the Thames, my dear.' He sipped his black mud, rose to pick up two smaller boxes from a shelf and resumed his seat. 'There's Sakhmet, the lion-headed Memphis goddess of war.' He revealed the replica and then, as he lifted the lid of the other box, 'And this beautiful scarab, Khepri, supporting the sun's disc.'

'Oh, I'm wearing a scarab. I bought it in Greece.' I tugged at the crimson medallion hanging from my black polo neck. 'This is very generous of you.'

'And there's more to come,' he edged closer to me, 'on each visit.'

As I edged away, his smile twisted into a leer. He lunged. I backed away, almost knocking over the chair as I tore around the table. He heaved after me. I don't know how many laps we made, but pausing, at the head of the table, I glimpsed his panting frame at the base, eyes bulging, a wolf open-mouthed in his lair of antiquities. How pathetic. How ridiculous.

The image of this incident remains frozen in my mind. I can't remember how I escaped, but I did and without having to endure the repulsive grasp of his paws. I didn't return for the rest of the set.

At the Cleopatra Hotel, I told Leslie how Dr Mokhtar had chased me in his office. The expression on Leslie's face warned: I want you to be careful. Take care. But as my stepfather, he wasn't going to tell me what to do.

I didn't tell Leslie – or anyone else – what happened later, 540 miles south of Cairo on the Philae expedition.

As part of an eighty-strong contingent, I sailed the Nile to examine the engineering feat designed to isolate Philae Island from the river by the construction of two massive steel-sheeted walls. UNESCO aimed to prevent further infiltration of water and transfer fifty-four thousand tons of sandstone blocks – some bearing inscriptions three thousand years old – to nearby Agilka Island.

Al Gomhuria of 28 March captures me against part of a temple covered with carvings peeping out of the river. A translation of the caption reads:

> A Journalist Recording 30 Films for History: An Australian journalist of Japanese origin was among the press crew which covered the meetings of the executive committee of UNESCO in Aswan. The journalist was very active. She recorded more than 30 films of the Philae monuments. She was also keen to record the antiquities to keep the recordings for history.

I took maybe six snaps.

We all stayed at the legendary Old Cataract Hotel, a Moorish construction featured in the film of Agatha Christie's *Death on the Nile*. Another *Al Gomhuria* photograph with a caption that makes the same mistake about my origins, shows me dancing, arms aswirl, surrounded by robed Nubians at the hotel:

> A Japanese Dance with Nubian Music: This Japanese journalist couldn't control herself while listening to the Nubian music during one of the parties at the Cataract Hotel in Aswan. She started dancing and was liked by everyone – those concerned with the culture and arts of UNESCO.

Among other records I still have of that week are the script of a report and my pocket appointments diary, which notes my room as 110, where I remember the mysterious sensation of sleeping beneath a mosquito net. It also lists the times of set lunches and dinners and the day I recorded an interview with Dr Mokhtar.

Yet no record exists of the white arc of Philae. As with so many of the ancient monuments, all that remains is a fragment, in this instance, a fragment of memory, fact reduced to a fragment, in retrospect I suppose because I found it so distasteful that I've suppressed it all these years.

I was walking as a member of the press corps on the right-hand side of a long hallway: it must have been under the high ceiling of the Old Cataract Hotel. We had a schedule to meet. It may have been to observe the UNESCO meeting to be held at 5 that Wednesday. I became aware of Dr Mokhtar hurrying up behind me. I wanted to give him the slip, so I slipped into an open doorway to my right, assuming he would continue down the hall to our destination.

Wrong.

Before I knew it, an off-white fluid shot like a bolt of lightning from behind me and hit the tiled wall. The off-white jet arced over the ceiling and spurted down the adjacent wall. Puzzled, then shocked by the realisation of what must have been streaming down the walls, I left, ignoring the arts functionary fumbling with his fly.

In a land of time immemorial, that shot on the Nile took no time.

23

Down Under Again

After almost three years abroad, I flew direct from a lush London summer to a dull grey Sydney winter. On 24 August 1973 I stood by the kerb in the city centre, taken aback. Where were the people? Where were the buildings? Where were the vehicles? Friday's late morning traffic barely moved. The roads seemed empty. The few cars crept along, even more slowly than I remembered traffic in Hobart. The scene resembled ants crawling on a dusty country track. After the pace, the colour, the variety and the intensity of my overseas experience, what was I doing here?

Still, it didn't take long before I discovered the delights and dynamism of Sydney, with its clean air, open skies and magnificent harbour. I discovered a new Australia, one quite different from the Australia I had left, an Australia transformed by Gough Whitlam, where I would learn new expressions, such as 'multiculturalism' and 'Women's Electoral Lobby', and witness a change in social attitude that would lead to the emergence of open same-sex relationships and the acceptance of single mothers. I was sorry I'd missed the excitement of Whitlam's election as prime minister and the euphoric early days of his new Labor government.

Among those who helped me to adjust was ABC reporter Paul Raffaele, even though he was busy adjusting himself to open the ABC

Peking bureau. Like Margaret Jones, who was appointed to open a bureau for the *Sydney Morning Herald* and the *Age*, Paul was a beneficiary of the new Whitlam government; one of Whitlam's first acts as Prime Minister had been to recognise the People's Republic of China and appoint the sinologist Dr Stephen FitzGerald to establish Australia's embassy in Peking. Although in Cairo I'd seen, for the first time, a performance of touring Chinese acrobats and marvelled at their extraordinary feats of balancing and juggling on chairs, bicycles and balls, I was at this stage so disengaged from China that today, more than three decades on, I can't recall whatever Paul told me of his expectations of China. I was not to tune into his story of Mao's Red Bandits until 1983 when he was based in Hong Kong and I, to my surprise, found myself following in his footsteps.

I first met Paul in Hobart in mid 1968 when, as a postgraduate student, I made my first and brief abortive attempt to learn Chinese, at an adult education evening class. Paul, a big shot reporter to me, was also there, down from Sydney. He was short and stocky, his head a mass of tumbled dark brown locks. One Thursday after class he took me to the ABC in Elizabeth Street and showed me his Nagra. 'This is the best recorder in the world,' he said. 'It costs over $1000. They use it to make movies. It's indestructible. Look.' He opened the window and, to my horror, dangled the machine by its strap over the footpath several floors below. 'I could drop it and it'd still work.' At that moment, I had no idea that within months, I too would use a Nagra, to net the Tasmanian tiger.

By the time we caught up in Sydney, Paul had married Cecilia, a softly-spoken woman of Chinese ancestry. Before he left for Peking in October, Paul worked as senior reporter on the *AM* and *PM* radio programs from one of the ABC's numerous sites around Sydney, this one a building on the south side of William Street, where I soon joined him on the *AM* and *PM* teams.

Traffic roared up and down the hill, trams trundled by; we were only blocks from the city centre. Outside the building, drunks and layabouts frequented the double stone stairway, which acted as a wall to William Street on the corner of Forbes Street and led to the Forbes Street studio that was a short distance up from the side of the office. In those days, before ABC radio public affairs had the facility for live interviews, we had to be nifty on our feet. From the office, as I tore down flights of stairs carrying the tape of an interview I'd just edited, I had to watch my step on what we called Chunder Crossing, before I dashed up to the studio and, breathless, handed the tape to the director, even as *AM* compere Robert Peach was already on air introducing the interview.

If I began a 5 o'clock morning shift or finished late at night, the ABC gave me a taxi voucher so I could be driven to or from the office. Otherwise, I footed the distance between William Street and my bedsitter, which was in a block that overlooked Beare Park on Elizabeth Bay and the harbour. The walk took about twelve minutes, unless I stopped to stare at the sights I passed in the seedy strip joints of King's Cross.

As commander-in-chief of public affairs, Russell Warner controlled us junior troops through constant fear and surprise shots of cajolery. If I dared tiptoe up to his giant figure, I steeled myself for the roar, 'What is it, girl?' He could soften into avuncular mode but I never knew when he would, or when he would turn to terror.

Warner railed at us from over the top of the stairwell, threatening with clenched fist a cheeky young trainee named Matt Peacock, who had dared answer back from the bottom of the stairs before darting out into William Street. I lacked the nerve.

As one of Warner's charges, hired as a temporary staffer, I grew itchy feet and edged my way towards television until the wise Robert Peach warned, 'Don't, don't go. Don't move to TV, not until you have permanency. Those television jobs are only temporary. Wait till you're permanent. Then you can have superannuation.'

'Super what?'

Within a year I had the temerity to apply for a position as a correspondent in London, which included coverage of the Middle

East. Flanked by executives, Warner, as chair of the assessment panel, sat behind his desk puffing clouds of smoke from his pipe.

He threw me a curly one: 'How would you, as a woman, manage if stranded in the desert in a ten-ton truck?'

Images of sand stretching evermore into the distance flashed through my mind, as did the gallantry I'd encountered in Egypt. 'I'd have a better chance than a man because I could ask men to shift the truck.'

It didn't land me the job.

Warner nonetheless gave me a great opportunity. When the seasoned correspondent Tim Bowden, friend and future biographer of Neil Davis, left the Sunday weekly *Correspondents Report* (partly due to undisguised antipathy between Warner and Bowden) for what he would develop into the ABC oral history unit, Warner trained and appointed me as compere of *Correspondents Report*. I felt honoured, as no female had yet fronted an ABC radio public affairs program. He even sanctioned a story about my new role, 'No visa for Peking, but a voice in public affairs', to run in the *ABC Radio Guide*. On the front cover is a picture of me against a map of the world looking serious, if not stern, with my shoulder-length hair newly cropped to urchin style hugging my face.

That haircut was the most expensive in my life. Foolishly, I was wearing a black ribbed cashmere jumper with a high rolled neck that zipped at the back. I undid the zip and pulled down the collar before the hairdresser secured a towel and a protective wrap around my neck, but he got carried away, let the wrap and towel fall onto the chair and kept snip snip snipping so that all the minute pieces fell down around my neck and onto the sweater. I didn't realise what was happening until too late. Because my hair is thick the next time I tried to wear the sweater it felt too prickly. I could never get the hair out; I had to throw that jumper away.

Meanwhile, I'd been made permanent and had also received an offer from TV. The position was sealed one evening in a Double Bay pub over a drink with a stranger, a senior representative of Tasmanian television. I wanted to be in Hobart, not only for the challenge of a different medium but also because lung cancer had stricken Leslie. Lehene now lived in London with her husband-to-be, David, and Mama needed me at home. As fate would have it, Leslie barely survived two months from the day I returned. He let himself go on 8 December 1974 after he'd written, in a wavering, spidery hand while propped up in bed, the closing words to his last manuscript, a fictional background to an earlier book he co-authored with Norman Laird, *Ross Bridge and the Sculpture of Daniel Herbert*. Leslie's final work, *Tea for a Stranger: A Novel of Convict Times in Van Diemen's Land*, was published posthumously.

When I left for Hobart, after just three weeks presenting *Correspondents Report*, I felt I'd let Warner down by leaving so soon and I apologised.

He bellowed the roof down. 'What do you mean, TV!' Then he tried to cajole: 'I've got big plans for you, girl. Big plans. You won't get anywhere on TV. Mark my words. But here, I'll make something of you.'

I was grateful for the chance but I had to go.

With raised fist, he yelled, 'Don't you darken my door again!'

This Day Tonight operated from the rear of the building where I'd once sipped tea with the manager, Arthur Winter. I arrived knowing nothing about television. In Sydney I'd awakened ministers in the Whitlam government to record their words for *AM*. I refused to accept their sleepy grunts of 'No comment' and kept pummelling until Frank Crean or Clyde Cameron spilt the beans over the radio waves. In Hobart I had to prove myself on screen.

One of my first interviewees was a hero of my schooldays, the poet Clive Sansom. A gentle and respected Hobart identity, Sansom was a friend of Leslie's who, as Tasmania's supervisor of speech education and a former London University examiner in spoken English, had developed material that I used in the classes I taught at St Mary's College in my first year out of school.

Now, a decade later, he had been awarded an Australia Council literary award to write his autobiography. I looked forward to meeting him again; that is, until I heard Brian Taylor, my executive producer, as he stood over my desk, shaking his fist as though beefing up a footy finals team.

'Get stuck into him, Chung,' he spurred me on. 'Why should the taxpayer foot the bill for what Clive Sansom writes? Who's interested in his life? Who would want to read about a poet?'

I was stunned. *TDT*'s clout came from its tough, aggressive interviewing, but was this how it worked? Putting the boot into everyone, not just politicians but artists and men of letters too? When Patrick White won the Nobel Prize for literature in late 1973, I'd taxied to his home at Sydney's Centennial Park and, with awe, held out my microphone to catch the jewels that slipped from his lips.

In a reflective tone and with a quaver in his voice, the novelist, who until then remained little known in his native land, told me that all sorts of people read him: 'Nothing to do with class or education. It's really a peculiar kind of mind. People who live intuitively rather than rationally.'

The *PM* radio producer, Clive Speed, raised neither voice nor fist with any injunction. He didn't order me to get stuck into White.

As I would discover, Hobart television public affairs had its own culture of success. The more we played devil's advocate, the more we provoked, the more protests from viewers, the more plaudits we won.

Usually a keen student, eager to learn, I followed the rules. I earned my stripes. Gentle Clive Sansom didn't know what had struck him. As we sat under the glare of lights, I attacked with the speed and ferocity of a pit bull terrier.

He turned white with fear. Telephones ran red hot and Taylor glowed, ecstatic. 'Good on you, Chung,' he congratulated me.

When I walked through the front door at home that night, the silence said it all. Leslie had telephoned Clive to apologise.

I would come to regret my obeisance to authority, instilled in me over thirteen years under the Presentation sisters.

In January 1975 the *Lake Illawarra*, a bulk carrier with a cargo of zinc concentrates, hit the Tasman Bridge linking Hobart with the Eastern

Shore. The disaster claimed the lives of seven crew members and five motorists. In one blow it crippled the state and offered a challenge. Commuters, forced to abandon their cars, once again crowded the decks of leisurely ferries. Long delays became part of life as crossing the Derwent meant queuing for a turn on the temporary, single-lane Bailey Bridge. To meet the deadline of a same-day television story – filmed and shown that night – my cameraman, sound recordist and I with all our gear often used four or five forms of transport: our blue ABC stationwagon, a helicopter, a light plane, a hire car or minivan and sometimes a boat. It wasn't all bad for the island economy.

On the same day the bridge collapsed, Norman Sanders, who'd acted in my production of *Waiting for Godot* in Old Nick, sailed on his sloop back into Hobart from North America. A former associate professor of geography at the University of California, he'd campaigned against the Santa Barbara oil spill and been so active in the environmental movement he felt burnt out and ready to retire in Tasmania. After *TDT* had exhausted every angle of the bridge disaster, I interviewed him on his trans-Pacific voyage. As the camera rolled, focusing on him, he forgot about retirement so that when the filming ceased he said to me. 'I rather like what you're doing. Do you think there'd be a job for me?'

As Norm was a keen yachtsman and my boss a lover of everything that sailed, he and Taylor hit it off. Next thing, Norm was a *TDT* reporter.

One morning, months later, when clouds shrouded Mount Wellington and we hunched over steaming mugs of hot coffee at 8.30, trying to warm our hands while nutting out that night's program, we faced a dearth of stories. Until associate producer Rory Sutton stirred things up: 'It's the centenary of the birth of Edgar Rice Burroughs, the creator of Tarzan.'

Tarzan, that super-human character, brought up by apes in the African jungle and who falls in love with Jane?

'Norm, you can be Tarzan.'

'Wow. Me Tarzan?' laughed Norm in his deep American accent.

'And you're Jane,' Sutton cast me, to my horror. 'Get your gear off, both of you and make it for tonight.'

'But I can't –'

'No buts.' He rapped his ruler on the desk.

'But it's unprofessional.'

'Listen,' he pointed his ruler, 'you're a reporter and your job is to carry out assignments as directed.'

Again compliant, I hopped into my secondhand white Fiat 850, nipped back to Lambert Avenue and fished out from the garret the set of leopard-patterned underwear I'd bought in Europe, never guessing I would wear it as Jane.

On the screen that night Norm and I hammed it up. Near naked, he swung from rope to rope in Hobart's adventure playground. Tall and bronzed in his swimming trunks, he puffed up his chest, extended his arms, clenched his fist and boomed, 'Me, Tarzan, you, Jane.'

Then he opened his mouth wide and howled like a wild animal to impress me.

'Hi, Tarzan,' I sounded sickly sweet American.

Stripped down to leopard-skin knickers and bra, the modicum of modestly I managed came from my high-heeled, brown suede boots that reached my thighs. In the film segment taken at the time, I'm shown reclining on a bench, gooey-eyed over Tarzan, until terrified by a spider, only to be rescued by hairy chest. Together, hand in hand, we spring through the jungle of eucalypts on the Queen's Domain, shivering on camera in the drizzle of 10° Celsius.

Years later, when Norm stood for a Senate seat in the ACT, a commercial channel phoned to ask if I had a copy of the film. I didn't but said, even if I did, I wouldn't hand it over. Norm's political opponents nonetheless included in their campaign close-up shots of the growling hairy-chested Tarzan.

Tasmania's *This Day Tonight* made anything possible.

I turned over my desk calendar to Friday, 23 April and glanced up at the blackboard. Rory Sutton had just chalked my initials against an interview to be recorded in the studio before *TDT* aired at 7.30: '4 pm – John Martin – HC'.

'That's not John Martin of Geelong, is it?' I asked, not believing it possible.

'Well, he is from the Gordon Institute of Technology in Geelong. Do you know him?'

'I knew a John Martin at uni who went off to Geelong. Haven't seen him since.' I smiled to myself, recalling his Christmas card in 1967 inscribed, 'Working Class Houses in Bethlehem'. In the intervening years since honours, John's name had cropped up only once, when I heard mention of his divorce in 1973. That had shocked me. I remembered him as a staunch Catholic in the Newman Society, which I'd left within months of joining.

'Anyway, the union's flown him over because of the plan to merge the TCAE with the university.'

As a lecturer in 1976, John taught the history of European intellectual thought, from the Middle Ages, through the Reformation, the Renaissance and the Enlightenment, to nineteenth-century Romanticism and the early twentieth century. He was popular with students, loved the work and had thrived on it for almost nine years. Now, at the onset of the amalgamation of tertiary institutions throughout Australia, the Gordon Institute was being restructured into the new Deakin University and John was fighting to retain his position. His principled stand on rights of tenure impressed the national leaders of the Federation of the Staff Associations of Australian Colleges of Advanced Education and they sent him to address colleagues at the Tasmanian College of Advanced Education. In Hobart John warned the staff of the risks they faced by absorption into the University of Tasmania.

The tall, trim man I'd admired as a student hadn't changed, other than to radiate more confidence and to have grown his sideburns long. Before me in the mirror, I watched his sculptured face with its bushy brown eyebrows as the make-up artist removed his foundation and blusher. He looked so handsome in his ginger-coloured corduroy suit and pull-on ankle-high boots. When he suggested dinner I didn't hesitate.

*

Across the table at Dirty Dick's I felt a nervous tension.

'Would you like a cigarette?' John flipped open a packet of Marlboro.

'No thanks. Gave it up when I left school.'

'Do you mind if I do?'

'No, not at all. Everyone's smoking.'

'I only have an occasional one.'

We both ordered an 8-ounce porterhouse steak – rare for me, medium for John; he drank wine, I, juice.

Slowly, through the evening, John confirmed my impression of him as a sensitive man. Not one to eat, drink and talk all at once without pause, he didn't launch headlong into an opinion on every topic and so, as he would put it, 'enrich others with the poverty of his own ignorance'. He had travelled only on holiday to New Zealand, England and Ireland but showed more insight into history and world affairs than I had grasped in three years abroad. I was drawn by his quiet elegance and wit, his understatement and his modesty. Compared with his inventive turns of phrase, I felt my comments superficial and clichéd.

We didn't disclose our personal lives, a sign that neither of us considered ourselves taken. Since arriving in Hobart, I'd been seeing a gentle, red-headed radiographer with a long beard. Outside his hospital hours, he acted as maitre d' at Mures Fish House, located in a white Georgian cottage a skip and a hop from the ABC. We'd become close friends but I saw no future with him. On a recent assignment to film the artist John Olsen, I'd met a lean, tanned arts administrator separated from his wife. He asked me out and we felt an intense rapport. We spent much of April together, including a rendezvous on the Friday of my interview with John. But legally, he was married so I still cast my eyes around.

Although I assumed John must have had some entanglement, he lived by himself. When we parted at the front door of Lambert

Avenue that Saturday night, I climbed the stairs to the garret convinced I'd botched any chance with him there may have been.

Four months later, in the frost of Hobart's winter, I picked up the phone, amazed to hear John's voice. Would I have dinner with him again?

'Where are you?'

'Geelong.'

A photograph of the evening captures me just as I blink. My long straight hair falls onto a flowing silk V-neck top over a polo neck. I'm obviously happy, but almost shy. John sits to my left, his smile self-conscious. His right arm hangs in the space between our chairs; his left hand is splayed on his lap. It's an image of two people feeling, if not awkward, not entirely at ease.

We were much more relaxed than in April. John had again booked a table at a restaurant in Battery Point, this time at Vader's Cellar, part of the Dutch Inn.

'Do you remember when we had our end-of-the year dinner upstairs?'

'You asked me to dance. You were wearing your penguin outfit.'

'You were the one who insisted we dress up. I've had that dinner suit since the fifties.'

'When I was still at school.'

'I'd left St Virgil's and gone over to Melbourne.'

'Before coming back to go to uni.'

'And giving Helene Chung a lift in my Austin.'

'So, what are you over here for now?'

'To see you.'

I didn't believe him but enjoyed his humour. 'Don't be silly.'

'I've taken ten days off just to see you.'

'You're sending me up.'

'I haven't got anything else arranged. Would you be free for a drive tomorrow?'

*

Just as I'd never sat down to draft a strategic plan for my professional life – and didn't know what I wanted to do until I chanced on the Tasmanian tiger – I'd never given serious thought to the qualities I sought in a man. I knew what I liked in those I met, just as I knew what I didn't. But no one quite measured up to that *je ne sais quoi* I desired. Perhaps my parents' unconventional behaviour made me cautious of commitment. Perhaps my childhood fear of rejection because of my Chinese face steeled me against rejection in love. I could brave out constant organisational rejection, but personal rejection would wound more deeply.

A few of the men who entered my life I wish I'd known better. Just as I understood when I was rejected as a talks trainee – 'All things being equal, if we have to make a choice between a boy and a girl, we'd have to give preference to the boy' – I recognised that a Western male might prefer a Western female. When a man didn't call again, I didn't pick up the phone. Rules had loosened since Jane Austin's era but not in essence.

Whatever the reason, that's how it was.

From the age of nineteen, when I was pursued by a much older man, each relationship in my life had been unequal. I'd been selfish, prepared to take but never to give.

Christian I ruthlessly abandoned without thought. After he departed Egypt on New Year's Day 1973 for work, we met again in Europe in summer. I agreed it would be fun to live with him in Paris and study French at the Sorbonne. Meanwhile, I accompanied him on his travels between France and Spain, winding down through the Pyrenees to Barcelona in his white, open-top Peugeot. He rented an apartment, not far from the Picasso Museum, as the base for his engineering project on an oil pipe from North Africa. We idled away nights and weekends in cafes and on the coast, exploring museums, castles and cathedrals. In Madrid we saw a bullfight with Franco in attendance. To please me, Christian motored on holiday through southern Spain to Portugal when, without warning and on an impulse, I bade him adieu by the shore at Lisbon. I had no reason other than I fancied fresh and even more exciting terrain.

I jetted off to another Frenchman. At a couscous party in Paris, Jacques had invited me to lunch and next day I found myself clinging to him on his motorbike as we cruised the Champs Elysées. Over lunch he pleaded with me to leave Christian for him but I refused. I went as planned to Spain with Christian. Now, Jacques awaited me at Orly with his Citroën and that night we feasted on *La Grande Bouffe*. *Ma grande erreur* became apparent and, within a fortnight, I'd fled. I refused to take Jacques' calls from Paris or to see him when he landed in London and stood, forlorn, wailing outside the door, disturbing Lehene and David's newly found domesticity. How could I explain to a lover that I thought his body was on the nose? Less cruel to thrust swift and clean than to linger, twisting the dagger into his heart.

Three years later, back in Tasmania, at thirty-one, I had never fallen in love.

On Sunday morning we settled into the Fiat and took off. With John behind the wheel, we drove up to Fern Tree where Neil had detoured in the snow, twisted down the bends and passed Longley where nothing remained of Hawthorn Dene, and pushed on south to the centre of the Huon. John had studied the collective history of the Huon district in the mid-nineteenth century for his honours thesis on John Donnellan Balfe, the Irishman who assisted the comptroller-general of convicts in Van Diemen's Land. From Huonville we bowled on to Geeveston, the Hartz Mountains rising lofty before us, and on to Dover for a lazy lunch. Back in the car, we kept going until we reached the spectacular Hastings Caves. There, among the crowd, in the dark and icy interior and the echoing drip, drip, drip of the limestone, I felt the soft skin of John's hand warming mine. Together we followed the flash of the tour guide's torch and tittered with the others at his joke: 'You only have to remember that the 'mites go up and the 'tites come down.'

On the long, winding journey home at sunset we realised we were in love. We had to pause by the roadside to let ourselves melt into each other's arms. I had never felt such hunger. Decorous ex-Catholics, we maintained our fast. Years later John, with a twinkle in his eye, would show me that he'd kept the two grey $1 admission tickets to the caves issued by the Tasmanian National Parks and Wildlife Service.

I became obsessed with John. Every fibre of my being tingled with John. I could concentrate on nothing but John. I felt he was integral to me and in everything I did, I felt as though I were floating in a dream, a state of bliss in which I realised I was dreaming and could awaken any second. I wanted the dream to continue, without ever awakening. Yet I knew that John was more than a dream, that he was real, that I was awake and the dream was true and would last.

As new lovers, we were oblivious of each other's shortcomings. Faults would not reveal themselves until later. In the spring of 1976, we thought each other flawless.

'You project too much onto me,' said John. 'I'm not all you imagine me to be.'

He thought he'd dashed his chances during our first dinner, just as I did. 'I didn't think you'd even consider me. Meeting you,' he said, 'makes me feel I've been reborn. You should call me "darling".'

An interview had sparked the marriage of true minds.

Ten days rushed past in a torrent. On a still-dark Monday morning we had the agony of parting. Wrapped in his trench coat to brace against the howling wind, John stepped onto the tarmac, threw a kiss from the top of the stairs and disappeared aboard his TAA flight. Then, from a window, he waved. Loving John gave me a reason for life, yet separation paralysed me and I could do nothing at all.

I endured an eternity until Friday week, 10 September. Although anxious to get to the airport that night, I also felt the studio was electrified. News had broken of the death in Peking on 9 September of the Great Helmsman, Mao Zedong, and the implications were being canvassed live on *This Day Tonight*. At 8 o'clock, as the credits rolled and I pictured John's plane touching down, I sped off, the first of many regular trips to and from airports, numbing hours fearing flight delays, airline strikes and false alarms lest something had happened to John.

*

I made my first trip to Geelong, an hour's drive west of Melbourne, where John rented a self-contained section of a rambling, two-storey, stuccoed stone mansion called Merchiston Hall. Number 2A Garden Street faced the Botanic Gardens and the park, where we collected pine cones for kindling. It was a minute's walk to the grassy slopes of Eastern Beach, where people sat in groups with their picnics spread out. We strolled down past swings and slides to promenade the boardwalk. John's kitchen contained bentwood chairs, freshly painted in primary colours, and a green and cream Kooka gas stove, but the rest of the nineteenth-century building, with its high ceilings, ornate cornices and cracks running through the off-white plaster walls, would have been improved by a costly restoration. With his sense of irony, he dubbed his rooms the Borgia Apartments, after Rodrigo Borgia, the profligate Pope Alexander VI.

By June 1977, after months of pulling every string in my bow, I managed to orchestrate a movement in the ABC. I fiddled for four weeks to *TDT* Sydney's tune and then scored Melbourne.

John's interest in architecture led us to a flat for sale in Newburn, 30 Queens Road, a four-storey block of twenty-four flats in off-form concrete, twelve minutes by car to the ABC's Ripponlea studios (which are close to the National Trust mansion, Ripponlea). Newburn, Australia's first design by the German functionalist architect Frederick Romberg, exemplifies the Bauhaus school of Walter Gropius. On the top floor, sun-drenched, private and quiet, we hardly heard the hum of traffic. From unit 23 we looked through the branches of an elm tree, with its resident possum, and a row of Lombardy poplars to the city skyline. With John I found the harmony and stability I'd craved from childhood.

We loved Newburn and would keep it until we were forced out by the jack-hammering destruction of stately Queens Road in the 1980s to make way for highrise. Before that civic battle with planners and developers, I would be embroiled in a professional battle with the ABC – a row over Chinese face.

24

Sex, Race and White Australia

In my first full year on the box in Victoria, my two big stories happened off-camera, the first while chasing the visiting American feminist and author Shere Hite.

Author of the groundbreaking work, *The Hite Report: A Nationwide Study on Female Sexuality*, Hite was my sole subject that Friday in April 1978. With a European duo, cameraman Wolfgang Beilharz and sound recordist Cornelius Lamers, I had no brief to interview Hite for *This Day Tonight*; rather my brief was to take 'a day on the road with ... ' approach and film the celebrity in various situations as she whizzed from one location to the next on her Melbourne publicity stint.

We began by filming her interview on Channel 0-10 (later Channel 10) at suburban Nunawading. When the interview was over, we hastened to repack our gear and tailed her car as it made a beeline towards Radio 3AW in the city. With Cornelius at the wheel and Wolfgang in the passenger seat, I sat in the back of the stationwagon, directly behind Wolfgang. All our heavy equipment lay loose either beside me on the rear seat or in metal boxes in the luggage compartment just behind. I concentrated on the story, listening through an earpiece, stopping and rewinding my cassette copy of

Hite's interview, jotting down the first and final words and approximate durations of grabs I might use. Suddenly, we crashed to a halt. A Datsun had hit us head-on.

More concerned with the effect on our report than on us, I picked up the speaker phone to executive producer John Vandenbeld: 'I'm sorry, John, but I don't think we'll make it tonight. We're stuck in the middle of the intersection of Middleborough Road and the Burwood Highway.'

Our blue Falcon was a write-off and all three of us injured in different ways. I suffered from whiplash, exacerbating the whiplash from my accident in the red MG, and bruising from the impact of the equipment falling against me. (As a result of this accident, the ABC installed a wire mesh blockade behind the rear seat of all its television vehicles and implemented a rule that equipment be carried behind the blockade to reduce the risk to staff.) During the few days off I took I was clicked into place by a chiropractor. Otherwise, I gave scant thought to the collision. I returned to the work I loved, with no notion that within a decade I would be diagnosed with prematurely advanced osteoarthritis that would cause chronic pain.

Of course, the accident aborted my Hite report. We spent the rest of that Friday in hospital and having medical checkups. The story had no chance of making it to air.

Precisely three months later, on Friday, 21 July, I found myself in another confrontation: this one designed to keep me off screen permanently. As part of a periodic program change, the ABC planned to replace *TDT*, currently at the prime time of 7.30, with *Nationwide* and slot it at the later time of 9 o'clock. Head of television public affairs Derek White flew down from Sydney to update Melbourne reporters.

I'd transferred from radio to television under White's predecessor Alan Martin; White inherited me along with the *TDT* theme tune and logo. We'd met in Hobart not long after his appointment, when the Tasmanian team took him to an Italian dinner after the show. Everyone enjoyed the restaurant (at the back of Moore's Variety where

I used to buy chocolate cigarettes) and I found him a likeable, slightly ocker character who reminded me of Barry Humphries' cultural attaché, Sir Les Patterson.

Now, like other Melbourne staff, I was scheduled for a personal meeting with White in the presence of Victoria's new executive producer, Damien Ryan. We were to discuss my role under the proposed 1979 format. Curious, I went into Ryan's office and closed the door. After a while I emerged, shaken. I'd been sacked.

So humiliated was I by the news that I couldn't tell anyone (this occurred before ABC sackings and restructuring became routine). I felt too ashamed to hold up my head. Deemed unworthy of television, I prepared to slink off to Radio Australia as decreed.

From early in life I'd learned to steel myself against rejection. What could a five year old say when told by a classmate, 'My mummy says I can't play with you because you're Chinese'?

At home that night I unburdened myself to John.

'That's outrageous. You can't let him get away with it. You've got to contact the union.'

But apart from speaking with John and phoning the Australian Journalists' Association, I kept my quiet.

Before breakfast the following Friday, I slipped down two flights of open stairs at the rear of Newburn to the milk bar, Mr Tubby's. I was after the *Age*. Imagine my horror when I saw, staring up at me from the counter, my own face on the front page of *Truth*. I bought a copy, wishing that no one could see me touch this muck-racking tabloid, but I was sure I could feel eyes bore into my back.

In a rectangular box at the top, centre right, 'Victoria's top-selling weekly paper' screeched: 'GIRL REPORTER COMPLAINS'. Below, to the right of the photograph, 'RACE ROW AT ABC – PAGE 3'.

Under the page 3 banner – 'THERE'S ALWAYS MORE NEWS IN YOUR TRUTH … THERE'S ALWAYS' – a well-upholstered brunette, nude except for make-up and nail polish and a revealing cloth tied around her loins and knotted to draw the eye down to her pubic folds – 'The loveliest girls are in your *Truth*, GORGEOUS DENISE!' – was the story.

MELBOURNE TRUTH, SATURDAY, JULY 29, 1978

THERE'S ALWAYS MORE NEWS IN YOUR TRUTH ... THERE'S ALWAYS

The loveliest girls are in your Truth

TDT GIRL CLAIMS ABC RACE SLUR

EXCLUSIVE REPORT BY ADRIAN TAME

A REPORTER on the ABC's This Day Tonight show claims an ABC official told her she has no future in television because of her Asian appearance.

Helene Chung, 33, also claims that a high-ranking official told her to stop wearing make-up because it accentuated her narrow eyes.

Miss Chung has complained to the Australian Journalists' Association about the racial nature of the statements.

Truth understands the statements were made to Miss Chung last week during a conversation with a senior ABC staff member.

An AJA spokesman told Truth: "I don't want to say too much about this until I have a chance to talk to Helene again.

ADVICE

"All I can say is she was referred to the AJA for discussion she had with someone at the ABC.

"We have given her certain advice, and she is about to act on that."

The spokesman said the alleged statements were racist and highly offensive.

He said one statement allegedly made to Miss Chung was that she had no future in the television industry because of her Chinese appearance.

The spokesman also said Miss Chung was alleging she had been told to stop wearing make-up which accentuated her eyes.

Miss Chung was born in Tasmania.

Early in her career with TDT, the ABC's current affairs program, Miss Chung reportedly received racist mail from a handful of viewers.

Miss Chung was unavailable for comment.

An ABC spokesman said: "We have absolutely no comment to make on this."

Television reporter complains to union

HELENE CHUNG...allegedly told she has no future in TV.

● ODD SPOT ★

Love tryst

A SEXY priest's illicit love session in a parked car was interrupted when a thief stripped him and his mistress of valuables.

Now the shamefaced priest may face obscenity charges in Naples and church punishment for breaking his chastity vows. — TRUTH SPECIAL.

GORGEOUS DENISE!

GORGEOUS model Denise Denny is very keen on dancing, cooking and boy friends — but not necessarily in that order.

Her other hobbies are badminton, table tennis and ice skating — and she once played for a show-business girls' football team as centre forward.

Denise speaks fluent French and has worked as a model and in films in Paris.

She is currently filming a comedy.

With Denise starring, we're sure it will be a big hit.

3 in 1 STEREO
AM/FM Stereo receiver with built in Cassette Recorder and Automatic turntable complete with dynamic 2 way speaker system.

RENT/BUY From **$2** WEEK

Metropolitan TV
234 Glenferrie Rd, Malvern. TEL: 509 7999

RENT BUY FOR INSTANT COLOUR TV DELIVERY

Ring 7 days a week 9 a.m. till 9 p.m.
PHONE 509 7999
Open all weekend

100% OF RENTAL PAYMENT CREDITED TO YOUR PURCHASE

From **$4** WEEK

Luxor — Rank
AWA — Thorn
Sharp
Nordmende
Lowie — General
HMV — GEC
and all German Brands. 18 years in the TV business.
We have the best Warranty and service plan. All servicing done by our own qualified service technicians.

METROPOLITAN TV
234 GLENFERRIE RD. MALVERN

Imagine my horror when I see, staring up at me from the counter of the milkbar on Friday, 19 July 1978, my own face on the front page of *Truth*!. Worse follows on page 3 of that 20 July edition.

The three of us, Lehene (right), Mama and me, together again for the first time in six years. London, Christmas 1979. (John Martin)

With John at Lambert Avenue on a farewell trip to Hobart before I fly to China as the new Peking correspondent. May 1983. (Dorothy Henry Greener)

At the Great Mosque, Xian, Imam Ma Liangji asks John, ABC interpreter Old Fan (in sunglasses) and me to watch a gong fu tournament marking the end of Ramadan, a scene John dubs 'Carry on Imam', July 1984. (Willi Phua)

Linked without roots between Mrs Chung senior and Mrs Chung junior and other members of this Chung family in this Dragon Field Village, all unrelated to me, after officials try to surprise me by unearthing my Chung roots. Toishan, June 1984. (Willi Phua)

On a newly-opened part of the Great Wall, after an hour's thigh-aching climb up steep granite stairs at Mutianyu outside Peking, April 1986. (Mark Hopkins)

Below: Weldborough, a hollow of 59 souls, the site of my Tasmanian roots, December 1987. (John Martin)

Above: Peter Burns and I inspect the Moorina Monument to Chinese spirits in northeast Tasmania, where the Gins/Henrys began life Down Under, December 1987. (John Martin)

Left: The Chung house in Sunwei City where my father, Charles, and his son Christopher were born is demolished in the 1990s. (Christopher Chung)

Below: My paternal grandfather, Willi Chung's memorial, including his wife's image, in an apartment on the site of the house he built in Sunwei City, September 2006. (Phillip Chung)

Lehene as bride, Mary Imlach as bridesmaid and me as the priest who's had a visit from the tooth fairy, c.1952. (Mary Hodgson collection)

Lehene at home in London, Spring 2000. (David Goodenday)

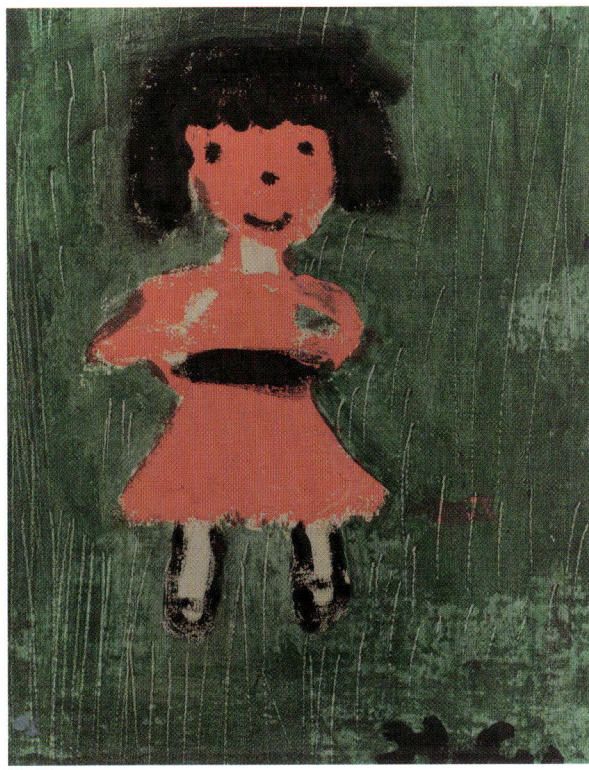

Above: John and me in the ABC Peking apartment, New Year's Eve, 1984. (Chung Martin collection)

Left: My self-portrait at eight years.

At the launch of *Lazy Man in China*, Asialink Melbourne, 29 September 2004. (Tom Gelai)

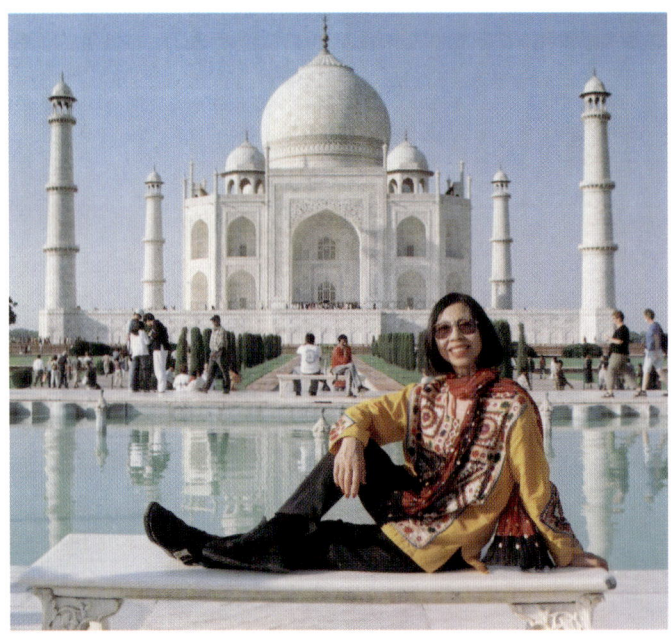

At the Taj Mahal – symbol of love and death – Agra, India, 4 October 2007. (R.L. Group)

'TDT GIRL CLAIMS ABC RACE SLUR' ran the headline, subheaded 'Television reporter complains to union', with another photograph of me. 'EXCLUSIVE REPORT BY ADRIAN TAME':

> A reporter on the ABC's *This Day Tonight* show claims an ABC official told her she has no future in television because of her Asian appearance.
>
> Helene Chung, 33, also claims that a high-ranking official told her to stop wearing make-up because it accentuated her narrow eyes.
>
> Miss Chung has complained to the Australian Journalists' Association about the racial nature of the statements.
>
> *Truth* understands the statements were made to Miss Chung last week during a conversation with a senior ABC staff member.
>
> An AJA spokesman told *Truth*: 'I don't want to say much about this until I have a chance to talk to Helene again.
>
> ADVICE 'All I can say is she has referred to the AJA a discussion she had with someone at the ABC.
>
> 'We have given her certain advice and she is about to act on that.'
>
> The spokesman said the alleged statements were racist and highly offensive.
>
> He said one statement allegedly made to Miss Chung was that she had no future in the television industry because of her Chinese appearance.
>
> The spokesman also said Miss Chung was alleging she had been told to stop wearing make-up which accentuated her eyes.
>
> Miss Chung was born in Tasmania.
>
> Early in her career with *TDT*, the ABC's current affairs program, Miss Chung reportedly received racist mail from a handful of viewers.
>
> Miss Chung was unavailable for comment.
>
> An ABC spokesman said: 'We have absolutely no comment to make on this.'

Just as my Chinese face precluded me from playing the Queen on stage, would it also preclude me from playing a reporter on television? We never learnt how the story made it to *Truth* but, as John said, it was spot on. Despite my silence the *Australian*, the *Age* and the *Sun* ran with it and I received a stream of letters of support.

It took the ABC six months to restore peace, while I soldiered on on television every night. Settlement would have been more drawn out had flamboyant Commissioner for Community Relations Al Grassby, advocate of multiculturalism, not rattled his sabre for me. In a letter to Talbot Duckmanton, general manager of the then Australian Broadcasting Commission dated 7 August, I put a question suggested by John: I asked 'whether or not the views expressed by Mr White are endorsed by Management and/or the Commission?' After trying to dodge the question, in a brief letter to Grassby (which Grassby photocopied for me) on 1 February 1979, the ABC titan finally declared:

> It is acknowledged that Miss Chung had cause to be concerned by the comments made to her by Mr. Derek White on 21 July 1978 and that in making these comments Mr White was not adhering to the Commission's policy.

The White plan to banish me disappeared.

Australian television in the late 1970s remained almost exclusively Anglo-Celtic in appearance. The ABC, in hiring me as the first non-white reporter, broke the barrier. However, in 1978 Channel 0–10 made me an attractive surprise offer to be co-newsreader. Although tempted, I turned it down. I believed in the ABC, its relative freedom from commercial pressure and conflicts of interest and I can't abide advertisements and the way they crash into programs. Moreover, 0–10 seemed to have had so many staff changes that I couldn't know when I might be next out the door. Deep down, too, I suppose, I recognised that I'm not a commercial type. I wouldn't rate. I felt in tune with the ABC.

The Special Broadcasting Service, SBS, with its multicultural mission and diversity of colour and accent, didn't open till October

1980 (only in Melbourne and Sydney). When it did, its newsreader was an Armenian-Greek-Australian, George Donikian. Another eight years passed before Indonesian-born, ethnic-Chinese Lee Lin Chin of Singapore presented the weekend news. And in the enlightened 1990s, when White took up his last ABC post – ironically, at the helm of Radio Australia and in charge of a multitude of so-called ethnics, including me – he was regarded as a fair boss.

When I interviewed reputed racist Bruce Ruxton, president of the Returned Services League and foe of Asian immigrants, he laid on the charm for me. In reply to my question on his tirade against those who 'should go back to where they came from', he leant over to me as the cameraman adjusted the lights and said, 'I don't mean you, dear. You're one of us.'

I stayed on *Nationwide* until mid 1983, when I took an unlikely route to the Middle Kingdom.

25

Bullet Train to China

The ABC chose me as Peking representative not because of my Chinese heritage, my fluency in Toishanese until the age of three, my ability to count from one to ten in Cantonese, or my mastery in Mandarin – *Wo bu hui shuo Zhongguo hua* (I can't speak Chinese). Nor was I selected because of my flirtation with Asian history or my single lecture on the comparison between Chinese and Japanese feudalism. My grounding in Hong Kong counted not. What propelled me to China was a flight to England and my fervour for Japan.

John and I first travelled overseas together in 1979 for a family reunion with Mama, Lehene and her husband, David. Two years later, during *Nationwide*'s long summer recess, John and I flew to Singapore (where our hotel rang with 'Jingle Bells'), Continental Europe (where ice impacted the streets) and on to London again. We wanted a white Christmas with Lehene, by now studying towards her arts degree at the Open University, and David, still a director of the International Wool Secretariat.

One day, alone with Lehene in the drawing room, with its view of the snow-covered garden extending onto the slope of Hampstead golf course, she said, 'Our mother has always been looking for a father figure. That's why she went for Leslie: he was twenty-five years older. She's never got over the death of her father.'

'I hadn't thought of it.' I poked at the fire.

'He spoilt her.'

'But she had a hard life as a child. Carting the chook food up Elizabeth Street in the morning and cleaning out the pen before school. After school nabbing a chook, carrying it home flapping in a hessian bag. Killing it for dinner. No time for homework. Working in the shop. Her mother screaming abuse at her –'

'Yes, yes. But she always got her own way with her father. He gave her a violin. A bike. Even took her to Melbourne on a business trip and bought her an expensive leather satchel.' Lehene put down the mohair vest she was knitting for me. 'Our father was no father to her: he was just another spoilt child. So she left him. And because we grew up without a father, we've both ended up with older men.'

'I haven't,' I objected. 'You have. David's old enough to be your father. A year older than Mama. But John's only eleven years older than me.'

'Still, he's older.'

The significance of the visit to London turned out to be an exhibition of an age infinitely older than either of our partners, the Great Japan Exhibition at the Royal Academy of Arts in Piccadilly.

Journey into Japan 1600–1868 depicted life and customs in the Edo era, when the country tried to isolate itself from the West. The period ended when Japan, forced at gunpoint to open to Western trade and influence, gave the capital Edo a new name, Tokyo, and began to transform itself through a policy of rapid industrialisation. The magnificent exhibition of traditional painted screens, beautiful sliding doors, suits of armour, elaborate Kabuki costumes and fine ceramics so engrossed me that it changed my life. I determined to visit the Land of the Rising Sun, a determination that took me to the Middle Kingdom of my ancestors.

At that stage I focused more on cultural than political aspects of matters Oriental. I went to any artistic event with a Chinese flavour and indulged in Chinese cuisine. I reported on the Vietnamese boatpeople as they washed ashore and increased the population of ethnic Chinese. Yet by 1982 my familiarity with Chinese and Indo-Chinese politics stretched to a single manila folder of newspaper clippings.

As for Japanese culture and politics, I didn't even keep a folder: something my visit to the Royal Academy changed. I set about informing myself and that year applied for an Australia–Japan Foundation journalist award, the only successful application of my career. It allowed me to study radio and television in Japan for a month, which I asked to extend by another month at my own expense. The ABC recorded news on film, a costly and time-consuming process: film had to be developed in a laboratory before being viewed. I wanted to explore the possibilities of Japan's electronic news gathering equipment – new lightweight cameras that enabled journalists to view their footage immediately, including on location, and edit and broadcast with minimum delay. This technology, called electronic news gathering (ENG), would become the industry norm.

I also applied for the position of ABC Tokyo representative. Tokyo was a one-person bureau, as was Peking, where the correspondent represented management as well as reported.

As part of my preparations I undertook an intensive Japanese language course at the Australian National University during my holidays in January 1983. John wrote to me:

> I hope you are treating your tutors with due respect – bowing whenever you see one … Goodness knows what awful punishments and privations they reserve for those who fail to cooperate fully with their masters. I wonder if already you have to stand for long hours in the sun during roll call.

In the fourth and final week of the course during an oppressive Canberra summer, I sat at the phone in my tutor Professor Crawcour's office to be interviewed for Tokyo. Over the line four ABC masters introduced themselves: federal news editor Bert Christie, Victorian news editor Tony Wells, acting radio public affairs head Brian Furlonger and controller Radio Australia Peter Barnett. Never before had I been so primed: I had soaked myself in trade statistics, Nakasone and his nation.

'What are the four main islands of Japan?' someone asked.

What a silly question. How could anyone apply for Tokyo and not know that? I reeled off 'Honshu, Hokkaido, Shikoku and Kyushu.'

Back in Melbourne when rumour reached me that a Sydney radio colleague had been chosen I was disappointed, naturally, but not surprised. I'd torn up so many of those green (or were they pinkish-red for 'no'?) rejection slips. After fifty years of existence the national broadcaster, unlike the national press, had still not posted a woman abroad. The only women the ABC employed overseas had taken themselves there. Pioneers such as British-born Patricia Penn in Hong Kong and Australian Diane Willman in war-torn Beirut made their names on air and I too had freelanced abroad, including from Cairo, for current affairs. But the ABC had never appointed a female foreign correspondent. So what was one more rejection slip?

I didn't know the successful Tokyo candidate, Peter Cave, but he was to befriend me in Japan, from where he went on to become one of the ABC's fastest firemen, with the ability to lob into any trouble spot – from Tiananmen Square to Fiji to the Wailing Wall to Baghdad – and file a story that was likely to win an award.

I consoled myself by thinking of my study tour: Tokyo, from there a ride on Japan's famous bullet train to the ancient capital of Kyoto, on to Nagasaki where, in the sixteenth century, Portuguese traders anchored, to Hiroshima of the infamous mushroom cloud of the first atomic bomb and Sendai in the northeast.

The language course altered my morning routine. Usually, I showered, did my yoga, ate breakfast prepared by John (freshly squeezed orange juice and yoghurt, tea or coffee and cereal or toast) while putting on my make-up and dressing, all the time tuned to ABC radio. Then I edged into the traffic on Queens Road and drove to Ripponlea, where

I was expected to have briefed myself on the overnight news and morning papers before *Nationwide*'s program meeting at 8.30. Now I added to that routine a half-hour session of listening to Japanese tapes through headphones before hopping into the car.

Just as I began to feel the course had paid off and I would arrive in Tokyo with some elementary Japanese I was put in a quandary. On Wednesday, 23 March 1983, my executive producer, Damien Ryan, popped his head into my cubby-hole office. 'They want to send you to Peking. Slap in an application! Quick!'

I wanted to go to Peking, of course, but not with the passion I felt for Tokyo. I'd dreamt about Japan for fifteen months; my head was bursting with Nipponese. Six weeks earlier, spotting a vacancy circulated by the ABC, I'd tossed my hat in the China ring. In the intervening period and now only three weeks before I was due in Japan, China had strayed from mind. My application had apparently strayed too under the administrative layers of the ABC, for here stood Ryan asking me to apply.

'But I've already put in an application.'

'Have you? Oh, I'll tell them.' He disappeared, muttering.

Next day Brian Furlonger phoned from Sydney. 'We fished out your application,' he chuckled. 'All we want is for you to record something on China. Anything you like. RA's a bit concerned you might sound too pukka, too British,' explained the Englishman in his distinctly English voice. 'They're afraid listeners might think they're tuned to the BBC instead of RA.'

The tape I made proved dinkum enough for Errol Hodge, RA's head of news and public affairs, to call within twenty-four hours. 'Helene, that was fine.' He rounded his vowels. 'Just what we want. If your speech hadn't been so fraightfully clipped till now, you would have been sent abroad years ago.'

Then why didn't he tell me?

I was never interviewed for Peking, but a week after Ryan first appeared at my door, I was given the nod. 'They want you in China as soon as possible,' he said, 'so you'd better organise yourself. But nothing's official. Don't breathe a word. If anything gets out before it's approved at the top, it might not go ahead.'

'But I'm flying to Japan in a fortnight.'

'Well, you can go, but not for two months. Go for one and get back quick.'

I didn't know whether to feel elated or dejected, exhilarated at being the first girl to play the boys' game or despondent at having to cut my kimono. I felt pressured, at an intersection, in a panic.

The secret also posed a dilemma for John. He had stayed with Deakin teaching Australian Studies for the first two years of the new university's life and then, having lost the battle to retain his position, transferred to the Victorian Education Department in Melbourne. At night, under the glow of green-shaded lamps at the state library, he trawled through a nineteenth-century American journal for his master's thesis, '*Arena*: Eternal Vanguard of Progress, 1889–1909'. By 1983 he was enjoying his role as a professional development officer, meeting and taking care of international teaching fellows, especially from Japan.

'What! China? I was prepared for Japan. Looking forward to it. An advanced country. But China!'

'It's a hardship post. But a chance. How can I say no?'

'Why can't they give you something decent? London. New York. Washington. Or better still,' his eyes danced, 'Brussels. Closer to Paris. I no more want to live in China than in Afghanistan.'

This was during the protracted Soviet occupation of Afghanistan, long before billionaire caveman Osama bin Laden made the headlines.

'I can't go if you don't come, at least for some of the time.'

'There's talk of a restructure next year. It won't be too good for me if I'm not around for that.'

'Please, darling. You'll probably find work there. You might even like it.'

After a silence, he came around. 'Oh well, if you're really set on going, I'll join you. I'll apply for leave.'

On 14 April, my mother's birthday, I stepped aboard Japan Airlines Flight 772, the cleanest of aircraft with the most ordered of passengers, bound for Tokyo. But as I buckled into the seat my head was spinning. I'd ditched my Japanese tapes and had with me another set, Mandarin, which only ensured that I touched down at Narita confused.

Meanwhile, John kept me posted:

I have just rung Damien for the third or fourth time. He has heard nothing official about China but quoted [national executive producer, *Nationwide*, Sydney] Ian Carroll as saying that there was absolutely no doubt that you had the posting but as yet there was nothing on paper.

When he wrote that aerogramme I'd left the capital and my role as visiting honorary male in Tokyo's broadcasting world, a world so overwhelmingly powered by men that it made the ABC seem matriarchal. I'd zoomed by bullet train to Kyoto, traipsed miles of temples amid throngs of Japanese under umbrellas in the pelting rain of the Golden Week holiday and had also brushed up with a maniac, as I told John from hilly Nagasaki:

The Kyoto incident occurred in mid-morning – Saturday, when three of us happened to be together, after being too late to visit the Imperial Palace. We walked – an American on the right, an Australian in the centre and me on the left – across a pedestrian crossing, when suddenly a complete stranger rushed up from behind and slapped the American on the face, then punched the Australian, before fleeing away. A watching policeman gave chase, but returned empty-handed. After going for 4½ hours with him to police stations, hospitals and a private clinic, we continued on our way. The authorities were most helpful and apologetic and we later learned there had been another attack on another foreign woman the same day. But all is well.

Mainichi Shimbun, *Yomiuri Shimbun* and *Kyoto Shimbun* each reported the assault and carried a photograph of Australian architect Josephine

Woolfrey, American student Lynn Meltzer and me. The English-language *Mainichi Shimbun* covered it next day. My Chinese face may have spared me the madman's fist as he, like the *Al Gomhuria* reporter, probably mistook me for Japanese. John had his own take on the society of endless bows:

> Clearly it does not pay in the long run to repress one's feelings under a veneer of politeness. I do hope you were none the worse for the experience.
>
> I must admit to being a little unhappy with the way things are at the moment. I can obtain no information from 'Nationwide' about the decision on China. Damien is always away sick and [associate producer] Julian [Lippi] is difficult to contact. Anyway I don't think they have heard themselves ...
>
> I have just tried to contact David Ransom and Tania [Nesbit from *Nationwide*] but neither is at home. It occurs to me that the delaying just might have something to do with obtaining security clearance and they are checking all your associations. Your [pro-Taipei] Uncle Gordon, as you have probably heard, is beside himself with annoyance at your going to Peking and has managed to worry your Mother about it. I think I have persuaded your Mother that his fears are groundless and that perhaps his motivations for berating her are somewhat complicated.

Only on the last stop of my tour, Sendai, did the sun shine. At Sendai I recalled my visit to the Japanese guard who had grown close to Leslie and featured in his wartime novel, *No Time to Look Back*. Seventeen years earlier, in an emotional reunion, Leslie too had been greeted at Hiroshima station by Jesuke Terai wearing his French wool cap:

> Leslie's former Changi prison camp captor ... is highly westernised and spent considerable time showing me his collection of European books – and videos (Greene/Shakespeare) and

playing American movies, Marilyn Monroe and Henry Fonda on his new video laser disc machine.

I am not concerned about ABC delay – it gives me more time ... Peter Cave got his papers 3 days before leaving for Tokyo.

Down Under again, I had less than three weeks in which to write my report, 'The Switched-on Country: Aspects of radio and television in Japan', finalise my affairs, farewell family and friends in Melbourne and Hobart and be briefed by diplomats and China specialists in Canberra. I was most fortunate to meet the Tasmanian-born Dr Stephen FitzGerald, who had the foresight to learn Mandarin long before it became fashionable and Whitlam appointed him as Australia's first ambassador to the People's Republic. As a China consultant in the 1980s, FitzGerald was to prove of immeasurable help to me during his visits to Peking; on that first meeting his advice extended beyond China's politics and foreign affairs to coping with the weather: 'The atmosphere in Peking is unbelievably dry. Even with humidifiers going you get electric shocks just by touching anything or shaking someone's hand. To preserve your skin, including the soles of your feet, soak in an oil bath.'

During a week spent in Sydney with administrative, financial, technical and program boffins, I won what I thought to be essential – approval for a six-week intensive language course at the University of Hong Kong, with its modern language laboratory and prized reputation for teaching Mandarin to people whose first language is English. Experts had warned against learning in Peking because, unlike Hong Kong, Taiwan and the West, it had no language laboratory or systematic training method for beginners.

As QF1 soared into the sky, I nestled myself in business class for the first time, took a deep breath and closed my eyes. In my ears rang the warning of a nervous news chief: 'There's a lot riding on your appointment.' I knew that if I failed or proved difficult, it would be a long time before the ABC risked another woman overseas.

*

My first test came on my Singapore stopover to meet Asia manager Peter Hollinshead. I would later be indebted to him for his support when he inspected the refurbished Peking bureau for 'the last shoot out at the OK corral'. He justified all our expenditure to the Sydney clerks whom he colourfully called 'the most gutless pack of ABC administrators it has been my misfortune to encounter'.

My misfortune was to have been so gutless at our first encounter. Surprised to learn of my full-time Mandarin course in Hong Kong, he picked up the phone, not to Sydney, but to Peking.

'So, Richard, what do you reckon?'

My heart sank as I sat listening to Hollinshead's side of his conversation with the outgoing correspondent. 'Peking Language Institute? … Recommended by the ambassador's wife? … Yeah, makes much more sense. Then you wouldn't have to stick around for another six weeks.'

It transpired that Richard Thwaites, fluent in Mandarin as a Melbourne University honours graduate in Chinese, after five years in Peking understandably had no desire to endure another oppressive summer, especially with only clapped-out airconditioners at his disposal.

'So, you heard that.' My new boss turned to me. 'Better to study in Peking, not Hong Kong. But you can still study full time. No need to report unless J. C. reappears.'

Mindful of what was riding on my appointment, I had little choice but to be carried along.

'Let's get to that fish-head curry.' He led me out into Singapore's sultry air.

After an absence of twelve years, I flew into Hong Kong praying for the good word from Peking. As I told John from the Lee Gardens Hotel in Causeway Bay:

> Hot and oppressively humid here – something you notice the moment you arrive and begin to walk off the plane – down the

metal shute – and each time you walk outside. Even inside this well-appointed and most comfortable hotel, there can be 'a smell of humidity'.

On Friday we were flying ahead of schedule but then our landing was delayed by what the captain called 'some showers'. They turned out to be the worst rainstorm for 17 years, resulting in 3 deaths and making hundreds homeless. People at the Peak were cut off from their gas supply, transport was halted and pedestrians at times waded thigh-high in water. Streams became torrential waterfalls. Classes were halted and other functions cancelled. Still – Hongkong business goes on and so did the Royal Ballet!

The top floor Chinese restaurant here is well worthwhile – certainly for *dim sum* – with a most interesting outlook on the Peak and parts of the harbour. There is no 'panoramic' view from the rooms, for the building's 22 floors are built-out by a 40-storey block in front. Hongkong is a mass of cranes and building sites that makes Queens and St Kilda Roads look like a quiet untouched rural scene. The buildings around Central and the Peak stand on top of each other, so much that you really shudder at the thought of an earthquake …

On the way from the airport, I stopped off in the rain at [the official New China] Xinhua newsagency (which also handles some visas) and left my passport and form/photographs there, in the hope that the 'good word' will arrive tomorrow.

The Peking language course proved to be as intense as a limp rag. It taught me much about China and socialist inefficiency but minimal Mandarin. Foreign diplomats laughed it off as a joke, the most fluent of them having studied full time in Hong Kong, Taiwan or elsewhere abroad for years. The course added flair to Mandarin already acquired systematically outside China and helped beginners with oodles of spare time to learn slowly in a Mandarin environment, but, compared with my Japanese language experience in Canberra, it was as a donkey to a jet plane. Marney Dunn, the ambassador's wife, afterwards agreed it was unsuited to my purpose: to learn the maximum spoken Chinese in minimum time. My account of the course so appalled Ken Myer, the new ABC chairman on a visit to Peking, he shot off a telex to Sydney: 'The same mistake must never be made again.'

Even though Jesus Christ didn't appear, I had no full-time Mandarin and news priorities ensured that I would never reach the stage I had in Japanese before I abandoned it. Still, the bullet train to China, with all the motherland's splendid horrors, cruel injustices and squalid beauty, set John and me on the adventure of our lives. To the foreign-devil mandarins who installed the Tasmanian tigress on the Dragon Throne, *arigato gozaimasu*.

26

Alien in the Motherland

At 7 o'clock on an already warm Wednesday morning at the end of June 1983, I stepped into a Russian Ilyushin for my first domestic flight on CAAC. I'd heard horror stories of the Civil Aviation Administration of China, notorious for its abysmal domestic safety record. But excitement overcame fear. During my first week in Peking for a handover with my predecessor, Richard Thwaites, I'd been welcomed to the imperial city in a round of farewell functions held for him by diplomats, journalists and Chinese foreign affairs officials. Now, flying south over the flat expanse of northern China, I was on my own.

The stewardess, wearing frilly pink, took me aback with a day-old copy of the *China Daily*, then amused me with a breakfast tray of icecream, a chocolate wafer, green tea and sticky, inedible lollies – inedible because the inedible-inked wrapper stuck to the sweets. I was on my way to Hong Kong to buy all the fixtures and fittings necessary to refurbish the bureau, which had deteriorated since Paul Raffaele opened it a decade earlier. Paul was succeeded by Warren Duncan and Thwaites.

A generation before capitalist techniques – socialism with Chinese characteristics – transformed a backward China into a world manufacturer whose 'Made in China' label would dominate the West, everything essential to a modern office and home had to be imported: from typewriters and recording tape to airconditioners and humidifiers, from washing machine and dryer to carpet and paint, from batteries to envelopes that could be sealed by the lick of the tongue, not only by a brush from a pot of glue, as well as personal items from clingwrap and cereals to cosmetics, tampons and pantyhose.

En route to Hong Kong I planned to stop at Nanking, capital of Jiangsu, Victoria's sister province; and Canton, capital of Guangdong, sister province of New South Wales. The ABC interpreter Old Fan, as I called him in the Chinese tradition (because he had a few years on me), had arranged my visit, and assured me that I would be met at every stage. I enjoyed my icecream, determined to enjoy the land of my forefathers.

The plane swooped in. Nanking was surrounded by hills, so different from Peking. Once inside the small functional airport, no matter how I peered around at individuals, I could spot no one with searchlights in his head. All the passengers had collected their luggage, the terminal had almost emptied and I began to question my faith in Fan, when a young man with a worried expression approached.

'Who are you looking for?'

'For someone to take me to Madame Fang Fei.'

'Then you're looking for me.' He sounded relieved. But the worried expression didn't lift. 'I'm looking for the Australian correspondent.'

'The Australian Broadcasting Commission correspondent,' I spelt it out. 'That's me.'

'But I'm looking for an Australian. And a man.'

'An Australian Chinese,' I laughed. 'An ABC, an Australian-born Chinese.'

'Lene Chung.'

'No, Helene Chung.'

'Oh, I'm sorry. I was told Lene Chung and I was expecting a man. An Aussie.'

Chen Junyuan had recently been interpreter for Nanking's Peking Opera during its six-week tour of Australia.

Together in the rear of our car, a decrepit blue Shanghai, we chatted easily about the opera, his experience in ABC studios and mutual acquaintances in the arts and the Chinese community Down Under.

'You must want to rest,' he suddenly proposed. 'Take a nap in a hotel room.'

'At 10 a.m.?'

'It's the custom.'

'Oh, no. Not for me. If there's time, I'd rather sort out my ticket. I'm going to Canton but can only go via Shanghai. Let's confirm my booking.' This had been impossible in Peking, as only the immediate next flight could be confirmed at any stage.

After coursing through avenues lined with overhanging plane trees, we passed into the gracious grounds of the former British Embassy. Nanking, which means southern capital (as distinct from Peking or northern capital) has served as the national capital at various times, including under the Ming in the fourteenth century and the Nationalist government of Chiang Kai-shek from 1928. With the threat of Japanese invasion at the end of 1937, Chiang retreated to Chungking (double celebration) and declared it China's capital. Then, following Chiang's defeat in the Civil War, in 1949 Mao Zedong restored Peking for the first time since 1928, as the capital.

In the former foreign compound, Chen led me past a clipped green hedge to the banqueting room of the Double Gate Hotel. A petite older woman with greying hair and a welcoming smile, Madame Fang Fei, rose to greet me. The product of a bygone missionary school, she asked in impeccable English, 'Would you like to toast sweet or strong?'

I glanced at the table laid out for a banquet and the two toasting glasses set for each of us. I hesitated and then chose. 'Sweet.'

A waiter poured the crimson liquid. I raised it to my lips but winced at the cloying sensation.

Mischievously, she pointed to another bottle. 'And now strong?'

The pallid dram barely wet my tongue before I recoiled from the acidity. Once again our glasses clinked. '*Ganbei!*' for Australian–Chinese friendship.

Those two toasts, one sickly sweet and the other bitterly strong, would come to represent the extremes of my experience in China.

During my sumptuous lunch as an honoured guest of Madame Fang Fei, vice-chair of the Association for Friendship with Foreign Countries, she emitted only positive vibes. As we discussed our two countries, friends in Australia and my plans for work in China, I felt genuine warmth and friendship.

After tearing myself away, I cooled my heels at the airport with a couple of hours to examine the dirty, overflowing ashtrays and the shabby, unattended airport shop. My delayed flight to Shanghai, on another Russian plane, gave me only minutes to connect to the Canton flight. Fortunately, Chen had phoned to tell his counterpart of my Chinese female appearance; as soon as I disembarked, two men whisked me away with only seconds to spare before take-off. I sat up the front, next to a Hong Kong businessman escorting several Scottish engineers employed to negotiate a project in the south.

When no one met me in Canton, the Scottish consultants suggested I go with them to the White Swan, the new showpiece 1000-room hotel on Shamian Island that offered the luxuries of airconditioning and a minibar to its rich overseas guests. I walked through its ostentatious foyer into a huge atrium that buzzed with tourists all ogling the lobby garden and its splashing waterfall crowned by a pagoda. I too stood and ogled until a bell boy called the lift. We rode to the twenty-fifth floor, where he ushered me into a cavernous room with king-size beds. Although by now weary and somewhat shaky around the knees, I was revived by the mesmerising view, a panorama of barges, outriggers, steamboats, motorboats, rowing boats, tugboats, jet boats, junks and hydrofoils, all flowing through the mouth of the Pearl River. As I looked down at the array of traffic, I mused on that accident of history that had lured Great-grandfather Gin all the way from Toishan to the bustle of Canton and on to New Gold Mountain.

Most of next morning I wasted on an antiquated telephone system, trying to contact Canton Foreign Affairs and the ABC Peking bureau.

Around noon, after making enquiries at a number of hotels, a Mr Wang phoned me.

'Why didn't we meet at the airport? Did you change your flight?'

Like Chen in Nanking, Wang had gone to the airport looking for a foreign male – not a Chinese-faced female. I resolved to stress to Old Fan the need to describe me as an Australian-Chinese woman.

Although I'd missed my morning appointments, I made it to lunch with two lively Foreign Affairs officials, Mr Ma and Mr Han. Briefed on news in their sister state, they raised the issue of New South Wales Premier Neville Wran's libel suit against the ABC. The television current affairs program *Four Corners* had reported an allegation that he tried to influence the magistracy over the committal of New South Wales Rugby League president Kevin Humphries, who was charged with misappropriation of funds. While Humphries would be convicted, nothing would be found or proven against Wran. After a Royal Commission and much legal wrangling, he eventually settled out of court.

'We don't have such laws in China,' said Ma. 'Imagine what would happen if Chinese tried to sue the Gang of Four', a reference to Mao Zedong's wife Jiang Qing and her three accomplices, judged to have been responsible for the turmoil of the Cultural Revolution. If all the victims of their ten-year reign of chaos successfully sought damages, the cost to China's treasury would be incalculable.

Between such speculation, as in Nanking, we toasted Australian–Chinese friendship. '*Ganbei!*'

Six months later, on leave from the Victorian Education Department, John had his passport stamped, confirming the good word from Peking. After a heavenly weekend together in Macao, we landed in subzero winter to an ironed-flat city spluttering with fireworks to welcome the New Year of the Rat. John found a job in the Australian Embassy aid section as part of a team of four, a New Zealander, a Tanzanian and a Texan, all women except him; he saw himself as 'both the token Australian and the token man'.

He liked his work and his colleagues at the embassy but his work there confined him to Peking, so in summer he switched to freelance journalism. As he put it in a letter to friends: 'I decided to resign so as to have time to see more of China and to do a little bit of writing too – not too much as I am rather lazy which is a disability like any other.'

The lazy man later had his own weekly column in Hong Kong's *South China Morning Post*.

Meanwhile, I found myself in Canton three more times – once en route to Hong Kong with John and twice to cover Australian politicians – before I ventured to my ancestral county of Toishan in June 1984. Sticky with perspiration, I stuck to the vinyl of a hot minivan that lurched from Canton along tatty roads. When we twice drove onto a ferry to cross tributaries of the muddy Pearl River, I managed to unpeel myself and stretch my legs in the open air. As we passed rice paddies, where peasants were bent over working, water swishing around their calves, I pictured Great-grandfather Gin approaching Canton 100 years earlier.

Born into a country wracked by poverty, hunger and rebellion and prey to imperialist powers, he seized the opportunity to earn riches abroad. Young and fit, he balanced across his shoulders a bamboo pole, weighed down at each end by a basket of essentials: his bamboo mat, a knife, chopsticks, spoons, bowls and cup and a change of clothes. With other recruits he set off in single file to ensure that no pole bumped into the other. Walking with a gait that lightened their loads, they jog-trotted out of Toishan, conical straw hats on their heads and long queues bumping against their backs. After several days, travelling by foot and by ferry, he finally made the 60 miles to Canton. The distance took me six hours.

I wondered what Great-grandfather made of his first sight of a foreign devil. Did he stop and stare? Did he wonder how such a long nose was possible, such angular features, so different from the soft, flattened features of the Cantonese? Did he shudder as he glimpsed the hairy back of a pink hand of some sea demon ensconced in a rickshaw? Did he squirm at the thought that the red-haired devil might have prickly hair all over his body?

Whereas Great-grandfather and his fellow villagers experienced the estuary of the Pearl River being herded like cattle to Hong Kong, I ferried in comfort from the economic showpiece of Shenzhen to another special economic zone, Zhuhai. I saw sailing junks, unchanged from his time, and modern motorised junks, sampans, oil rigs, fishing boats, houseboats, speedboats, dragon boats and dredgers. A brewing storm darkened the sky. The seats of the ferry were filthy and the air humid, but my cameraman and I were free to roam. I climbed upstairs to the captain, a Cantonese communist in grubby shorts and sweaty shirt. An electric fan whirred as Cantonese pop thumped out from British-controlled Radio Hong Kong.

'Please, help yourself,' he pointed to a plate of fresh plums. 'I insist.'

The sweetness filled my mouth. No offer of plums for Great-grandfather Gin.

I'd arrived in China not feeling Chinese but conscious of my Chinese heritage; however, my role as ABC correspondent almost obliterated any identity I may have felt with the motherland of my ancestors. I never felt more Australian – and less Chinese – than when living in China: I was an alien in the motherland.

As the representative of a foreign organisation and the holder of a foreign passport, naturally I was classified as a foreigner and, like John, was treated as a foreigner. We lived in an apartment on the twelfth floor of building eight in a foreign diplomatic compound – 8-12-2 Qi Jia Yuan – on an extension of Peking's main Avenue of Eternal Peace just along from the Forbidden City, the Great Hall of the People and Tiananmen Square. Armed guards stood at the gates, not so much to protect us, but to prevent the entry of unauthorised Chinese who could be contaminated by our Western notions of free speech and democracy. We were discouraged from making Chinese friends. While expulsion was the worst that could befall us for any infringement, a

Chinese deemed to have unnecessary contact with us invited increased surveillance and the risk of imprisonment.

John wrote to his mother, Marcia Laing, in Hobart:

> Foreigners have to remind themselves that this is not so much socialism as a Chinese preoccupation with secrecy. If a staff member works late a foreigner can authorise a driver to give him a lift home (and pay the driver overtime of course). The employer cannot drive him home as the employee's address is a state secret. When one day I was out of town at the Fragrant Hills Hotel (designed by I. M. Pei of [Melbourne's] Collins Place fame and now falling to bits after only one year) I found I had forgotten my phone number. At the hotel desk my request for a phone book caused great embarrassment. All telephone numbers are state secrets and there is no such thing as a directory. As I was Australian wanting an Australian number I was permitted to ring my Embassy and request my number from them. The clerk of course listened to my call to see that I did just that.

The interpreter, driver and cleaner were appointed by the Diplomatic Services Bureau, essentially as spies. We got on well – on as friendly terms as permitted by the system – but they kept tabs on John and me and our movements, monitored each other and reported to their masters.

Although China's apartheid system would be abolished by the turn of the century, in the 1980s it extended beyond housing, restaurants and hotels to a three-tier price system in which John and I were charged high foreigners' rates. Rates for everything from sitting on the camel to be photographed at the Great Wall to buying a train or airline ticket varied according to nationality and race: locals paid the least, overseas Chinese more and foreigners the most. If I thought I may at times have counted as an overseas Chinese – a *Huaqiao*, or Bridge of China – I was mistaken.

In December 1984 we joined a Foreign Affairs-sponsored journalists' tour of southeastern Fujian Province, Tasmania's sister state. Not so much a mountainous province as a province of mountains, Fujian occupies a narrow coastal strip along the Taiwan Strait that separates the People's Republic of China from the rival Republic of China on the island of Taiwan. As China's front line against Taiwan since the Communist victory of 1949, Fujian had devoted most of its resources to defence. Now it planned to put more effort into civil projects and improve living standards through foreign investment and tourism. Anti-aircraft guns protruded from the hillsides while MiG-16 fighters parked on the tarmac as we landed at the capital, Fuzhou.

Australian casuarinas – silky oaks – adorned the roads on which billboards proclaimed: FUJIAN AND TAIWAN ARE BROTHERS and WELCOME OVERSEAS CHINESE TO TAKE PART IN THE CONSTRUCTION OF THE MOTHERLAND. Keen to impress the foreign media, officials staged a press conference with zappy, pin-striped Deputy Governor Zhang Yi and accommodated us in large armchairs among potted chrysanthemums. As Zhang's statistics on Fujian's progress grew longer and more confusing – delivered through a shy young interpreter with poor English spoken in a broad cockney accent – I wriggled about, dying for a cup of tea. Tea was always served on these occasions but on this day had been replaced by bottles of Coca-Cola. A luxury in China, the distinctive bottles of brown fluid reflected Fujian's aspirations towards modernity. I can't bear Coke so had to go thirsty.

A statue of the Great Helmsman towered over Fuzhou's three-storey municipal headquarters. Mao's giant concrete right hand stretched out waving to the faithful in the square below, while his left hand, held behind his back, clutched a concrete cloth cap that rested against a heavy concrete greatcoat. Inside the town hall, where Mao's rear view dominated our meeting with the city fathers, Deputy Mayor Peng revealed a new policy towards overseas Chinese. Journalists with mouths full of fresh oranges, taken from piles on plates around the room, sat up when Peng announced that 'Fujian is implementing the policy of preferential half-price air tickets for overseas Chinese.'

'Who are overseas Chinese?' We clamoured to know.

'They are ethnic Chinese born overseas, including in South-East Asia, Australia and America.'

I took note. I'd always paid the top foreigners' rate and completed forms classifying me as a foreigner – until Fuzhou, where, like my ethnic Chinese colleague, Singaporean-born Mary Lee of the *Times* of London, I was given a form different from those distributed to John and the others.

'Because you and Miss Lee are overseas Chinese,' an official explained.

Next day, after we toured a Buddhist temple high on Drum Mountain, a tourism spokesman briefing us confirmed: 'We will not overcharge visiting ethnic Chinese.'

Mirth rippled through the crowd of correspondents.

From Fuzhou we took a bus down the coast, along a highway planted with Australian trees: casuarinas, eucalypts, acacias and other varieties seeded from Down Under. Our driver sounded his two discordant horns most of the way, scattering villagers and cyclists in his path and slowing down only for pigs. At our final destination, Amoy, a fascinating port city opened to the West during the Opium Wars and developed largely through overseas Chinese funds, we booked into the Overseas Chinese Hotel.

When time came to fly back to Peking, Mary and I put the new policy to the test. We tried to buy the special half-price fares for overseas Chinese.

'Your passport shows you're Australian,' barked the travel officer. 'And you're Singaporean,' he glared at Mary.

'Who are overseas Chinese?' I asked.

'Chinese citizens who are overseas,' came the surprise answer. Almost no Chinese could afford or was allowed to travel abroad except on a government-sponsored scheme. The rush of Chinese students abroad was yet to come while Chinese tourists didn't exist.

'Well, who are the twenty million overseas Chinese you want to invest in the motherland?'

'They are foreign overseas Chinese,' the cadre invented an entirely new category.

I was furious, if bemused by the verbal gymnastics.

Just after Mary and I forked out the full foreigners' price, one of our Chinese hosts asked Mary, whose parents had been born in Fujian, 'Have you been to your home village like the other overseas Chinese?'

'But I'm not an overseas Chinese.'

In Guangdong, my ancestral province, I was charged as a foreigner but feted as an overseas Chinese. When, at meal times, I found myself paying for tables filled with feasting officials I didn't know, I didn't demur; I accepted it as part of the cost of an assignment in China. I encountered none of the bureaucratic obfuscation that daily plagued me in Peking and met no extortionists such as those I encountered in Xian, home of the entombed warriors and site of the oldest extant mosque in China. As John recalled in a letter to friends:

> We were there last Thursday through to Sunday. Helene was doing some filming there with an A.B.C. cameraman brought in from Singapore. A difficult exercise as Singapore is not too keen on China and China is not too keen on either Singapore or cameramen.
>
> The filming was a mixed success. We spent a day filming (I was cameraman's rouseabout) the breaking of the fast of Ramadan at the Great Mosque. The Chinese authorities being rather keen to show what religious freedom there was in China. We even had two meals with the Imam there. One of these at his house in the suburbs. This Imam, while quite a pleasant bloke, was clearly a bit of a government stooge. He kept telling us how the revolution was the best thing since baked kebabs. Allah and Mohammed didn't rate a mention.
>
> Helene was pretty keen to film the entombed warriors even though – in my opinion – they've been done to death, if you'll excuse the pun. The authorities agreed, but every time the subject

was mentioned the price went up. In the end the project had to be abandoned. So much for the much vaunted friendship between Australia and China. Once again Xian lived up to its reputation of 'Rip-off City'. Helene in fact had a pretty bad time of it there after I returned to work in Peking. Her hosts had originally agreed to a set price for filming, cars, hotels, meals and so on. When settling up time came they demanded a much higher figure and refused to return her passport until it was paid.

I was held to ransom in my hotel: my passport and plane ticket were confiscated until I paid over 50 per cent more than the agreed price.

Old Fan warned, 'If you don't pay, they'll keep you in Xian and it will cost more.'

In Toishan I felt genuine warmth. Honoured by toast after toast at a welcoming banquet, treated as a wealthy overseas Chinese, I was tempted to act like one. I felt so flattered that I glowed with the thought of making a donation to Toishan's modernisation. Only my less emotional, sceptical reporter's side kept my hand from my wallet.

As soon as I heard the Toishanese dialect, I was swept back to childhood. Sounds, such as *gnit, gnee, thlum, thlee* (one, two, three, four), *Gnum m gnum*? (Will it do or won't it?) and the exclamation *Aiyah!* (Wow!, or Watch out!, or Well, I never!) were familiar to me from when I was growing up. I'd not heard them anywhere else in China.

One lunch time, at the insistence of my hosts, I succumbed to the local delicacy, *gaorou*.

'You have to try it. It's special,' urged Chen, the tall, swarthy interpreter. 'Here, let me help you.'

I half-closed my eyes as he spooned some of the brownish casserole flecked with tofu onto my rice. Then, with everyone else wide-eyed, I raised the rice bowl to my lips and shovelled rice and casserole into my mouth with my chopsticks.

'Not bad.' I took another mouthful. 'You're right. Like sweet pork,' I agreed with Chen's description of dog meat.

In Toishan my favourite food was the simple stir-fried home dish of sweetened steak and tomato, which I loved as a child but had never before eaten in a restaurant. The couple of times I ate it in Toishan reminded me of Uncle Lester, a wonderful cook who produced everything from basic sweetened steak and tomato to his specialty of fresh pigeon casserole. *Aiyah!*

Meeting 112-year-old Lee Lee Chong, who had returned to China after seventy years as a market gardener in Western Australia, moved me. With only a few wisps of hair remaining on his head, he was helped by his daughter-in-law to hobble several steps from his darkened bedroom into the light of the alley. As his frail figure collapsed into a chair, I thought of Great-grandfather Gin, who had survived to live a few years with his wife and family in the village after his son found him a penniless opium addict and sent him home from the Tasmanian tin fields.

The Chinese who made me most aware of my ancestral links were octogenarian Mr Lui and his septuagenarian wife, seated in front of a wall plastered with photographs of their son and three generations of relatives thriving in Melbourne. Their sizeable village home, with its expensive blackwood furniture, was built on savings sent by Lui's father from California and maintained through remittances from Victoria, including proceeds from the *Wing Lok*, or Happiness Forever, restaurant. We filmed Lui striding through the village, drinking tea, gossiping with his lifelong friends and devouring *dim sum* in a cafe. Scoffing glutinous rice buns stuffed with peanuts and sugar and covered with coconut, the men seemed unperturbed by the myriad flies that settled on their faces.

When we returned to Mrs Lui, dressed in black silk and seated in her living room, Lui told me he'd like to join their son in Australia but Mrs Lui shook her head. She trembled slightly; her hands fluttered: 'I don't have my husband's energy. I'm too feeble for the journey.'

The longer I spent with the Luis, the more I wished I'd tried to find my own links to Toishan. Back in Peking, when planning the

Guangdong trip and proposing to my bosses in Sydney a story on Chinese who had lived in Australia or who had relatives there, I used knowledge of my own family in Tasmania as a guide to what I might find. But having begun journalism in the era of objective reporting – 'Never use "I" in a report', an ABC style sheet instructed – I would never have dreamt of using taxpayer funds to finance my own family history. Only on rare occasions, when directed by a producer, had I been the subject of my own story. As a rule, I covered other people's stories and in China, where my Singapore-based cameraman and I had no producer, I followed routine.

To ease my way through the labyrinth of negotiations by telex, long-delayed post and shouting over the chronic hiss and crackle of China's telephone lines, I did mention to the Cantonese official arranging my visit, Lu Jian, that my ancestors came from Toishan, from Dragon Field Village – *Loong Hen Lee*. I had no idea what trouble the name of that village would cause.

When Lu Jian, cameraman Willi Phua and I reached Toishan, interpreter Chen blurted: 'We've found forty Dragon Field Villages and fourteen that include the clan name Chung. But so far, none with any established links overseas, let alone Australia.'

'Chung?' I said. 'Oh, I'm sorry.' I felt remorse for wasting Chen's time.

Turning to Lu Jian, I explained, 'When I said my family comes from Toishan, I meant my mother's family, the Henrys, whose original name was Gin, not my father's family, the Chungs.'

As Lu interpreted for Chen, his face lengthened.

'I didn't mean to send you on a wild goose chase. I didn't know you were looking for my family links.'

'Never mind,' he shrugged. 'I suppose we should have checked. But we wanted to surprise you.'

That he did. Determined to find my roots, despite lack of evidence, Chen had organised a family of Chungs in a Dragon Field Village in the remote south of Toishan to expect the visit of a very distant relative from *Aozhou*. I had to play the part.

As we bumped along in a minivan in sweltering heat, the varied nineteenth- and twentieth-century architecture and paved roads of the county centre gave way to crude, dilapidated structures and mud tracks. Rice paddies stretched into the distance and labourers wearing conical hats and harnessed to buffaloes ploughed the soil. Cyclists bore loads of bok choy, piled to the sky. They balanced cages of birds, whose feathers fluttered around from behind bamboo bars. Slaughtered pigs slumped over rear wheels. We stopped at various points as we continued on to the impecunious south until, finally, at *Sam Ging* (Deep Well District), our van skidded to a halt in the dirt.

In front of a row of grimy brick dwellings, the entire village of 400 men, women and children stood waiting to welcome me. None had ever ventured beyond a mile or so from the village or ever been in a motorcar. They had no television and had never seen a cameraman with his tripod, lights and other equipment, or anyone as exotic as me: not quite of the East nor of the West. At a time when blue Mao suits prevailed and cosmetics were reserved for the stage, I was wearing casual Western clothes: my face made-up with eyeliner, shadow and lipstick and my black hair blow-waved over the shoulders. My fingernails were painted red, as were my toenails, which peeped out from under the straps of my high-heeled sandals. As I stepped from the van, I felt a wave of awe sweep from the crowd.

Surrounded by gawking locals, I shook hands with the oldest member of the village, Mrs Chung, a dignified 84-year-old woman. Wearing loose-fitting black trousers and a top with a Mandarin collar, she shuffled with the aid of a walking stick as high as her bosom. Her face was crumpled and dark, her hair limp and grey. Pushed by the crowd, we were both swept up the lane and into her home, a hovel begrimed by the years. We were seated on plastic chairs and served steaming hot tea. As beads of perspiration spread over my face, a teenage girl with a wide smile stood fanning me with a large palm frond.

While Chen translated the words of the matriarch, the others crushed through the door, edging as close to me as they could.

'Long before I was born,' Mrs Chung recalled, her speech hissing through gaps in her teeth, 'my father went off to the red-haired devil land. After he left, my mother gave birth to my brother. After my father returned I was born. Then he went back and settled in the red-haired devil land.'

'But which foreign land?' I asked. '*Aozhou, Yinguo, Meiguo* [Australia, England, America] or somewhere else?'

'I don't know,' she shook her head. Then, pointing in the direction of the South China Sea, 'All I know is he went off to the red-haired devil land.'

Outside again, I stood for a group photograph, my right arm intertwined with that of Mrs Chung senior, supported by her stick, and my left arm intertwined with that of Mrs Chung junior, a babe in her other arm and a toddler at her feet, and with all the other Chungs, not one of whom was related to me, though neither they nor I were so impolite as to mention this. And why would they? I'd broken the daily monotony in this Dragon Field Village.

As light faded, we bounced from one Dragon Field Village to another. Intent on finding a family named Gin, the undaunted Chen took us to the soggy south of Toishan to *Man Chun* (Man Family District), over 50 miles from the centre, a rundown pigsty of a village where we were not expected. No synthetic table, no set of plastic chairs and no steaming pot of tea awaited us. Amid the grunting of pigs and their droppings in the rice straw, I no more than they knew where sty ended and homes began. Anchored in slush, I stood surrounded by open-mouthed villagers, while Chen rushed about in search of an elder.

Suddenly, with elder in tow and full of enthusiasm, Chen reappeared. 'He's heard of some Gins in an adjoining Dragon Field Village.'

With trepidation and a gaggle of village youngsters, Willi Phua, Lu Jian, other officials, Chen and I tagged the Pied Piper, as he led us down a squalid track and across a bridge. In near darkness, the elder halted to point to a stone inscribed, Dragon Field. We trailed him through the remains of an abandoned village while he recalled: 'An elaborate house was built here. A house built on remittances from overseas. But this is a low-lying area, close to the South China Sea. From time to time it's flooded.'

He stopped, searching with his eyes as we searched him. 'The house has been destroyed. I think it was owned by a family called Gin.'

The elder knew of no specific overseas or Australian link.

Defeated, disappointed and tired, we drove off, without lights, a practice designed to preserve the weak batteries of Chinese-made vehicles, but blasting our horn into the blackness of night.

Only after I returned to Australia did I learn that my mother's Dragon Field Village is in *San Fou* (Three Unities District), close to Toishan City. My Chung family village is in another of the Four Counties, the adjoining county of Sunwei, although my father was born in the Chung house in Sunwei City.

Now, twenty years on, it seems absurd that I didn't use the opportunity to visit both my mother's ancestral village and my father's ancestral city. My objective was to film families with strong Australian links and, in my mind, my family were the Henrys or Gins as I had no contact with the Chungs and I knew that we, the Henrys, had lost close association with relatives in China and had nothing like the link of the Toishan-Melbourne Lui family. Also, apart from the professional need to keep myself out of the story and the ethical need not to use ABC funds for private research, perhaps, at a very deep level, I felt ambivalent after all those childhood years trying to assimilate to escape my Ching Chong roots.

Be all that as it may, I came to realise that just as I had lived in the motherland ignorant of my Chinese origins, I had grown up in Tasmania ignorant of my island origins. I had to find out. If I didn't, how could I ever again toast to my Australian–Chinese links: sweet or strong?

27

Puzzling the Tin Trail

'Tassie preserves its Chinese past' heralded a double-page spread of the *Sunday Tasmanian* in May 2003. 'Tourism lure for dragon economy' speculated another story in the same edition. The discovery near Moorina in the island's northeast of Chinese artefacts, including rice bowls and spoons, frying pans, bottles, coins, opium tins and a miner's hut, had excited archaeologists, researchers, curators and councillors.

I too was excited. A century after my ancestors toiled in the tin mines came the promise of additional light on the life they had led. A heritage trail of the district's mining history was planned and, by late 2007 was scheduled to open in early 2008.

Far bolder was the proposal to lure Chinese tourists to Tasmania. Academics postulated that thousands of descendants of Chinese miners who returned to Guangdong might be interested in their Tasmanian links. Ever since the southerners set off for Gold Mountain and then New Gold Mountain in the nineteenth century, investments in Guangdong, remittances to families and travel there by their American, Australian and other overseas sons helped sustain the province and make it one of the wealthiest in China.

Australia already featured as a holiday destination for the burgeoning middle class of new capitalist China and analysts forecast one million Chinese tourists Down Under annually by 2012. Could a fresh generation of Cantonese, even remote clan members of mine from Toishan, help stimulate Tasmania's economy as did my forebears and their compatriots before them?

As I contemplated this, I thought of the decades that passed before I began to explore my island birthplace.

In Melbourne in late May 1987, I received an envelope that had been forwarded to me from ABC Hobart. The cream stationery of St Helens History Room bore a sepia photograph of sailing boats moored in a tranquil harbour against a background of forest. The caption read, 'The St Helens and Georges Bay 1879'. I found St Helens on the map of northeast Tasmania but knew little more about Weldborough than did Great-grandfather Gin when he ventured there from Toishan in the period of the photograph.

But why was the history room asking me about Maa Mon Chin? I was baffled. I had never heard the name. Intrigued, I examined the brochure enclosed with the letter, 'Early days in Weldborough'. The text of the brochure was written by a European woman, Mrs Bill Grose:

> Mr Chin brought his two sons with him to Tasmania and when they arrived in 1875 at Weldborough there was only a partly settled township. Indeed Mr Maa Mon's father had been found dead on a bush track on his way to bank money at Derby or Moorina. He had been robbed and murdered. Maa Mon Chin became the mandarin of the Camp at Weldborough which had a population of over 800 Chinese. I have seen Mr Chin in his fine silk Mandarin clothes and cap. The Chins ran a trading centre in the camp.

I noticed that this central figure of Weldborough's mining days is referred to as both Mr Chin and Mr Maa Mon. His family or clan name is unclear. Chinese names can be confusing because the traditional order of family name, followed by given name or names, is often reversed to accord with Western practice. On reading Gin Kee

Chin, no one can be sure of my great-grandfather's surname until I refer to him as Gin or Mr Gin. More confusion can arise from the romanisation used: Chinese write their names in Chinese characters and how the sounds are rendered in English can vary.

Great-grandfather's name could just as well be romanised as Jin Gee Chin, which is how it appeared in the Hobart *Mercury* in the opening paragraph of an article headed, 'Helene finds an alien life in land of her ancestors':

> Jin Gee Chin left China in the 1880s, lured by Tasmania's tin mines. A hundred years later, his great granddaughter, Helene Chung, went to China as an ABC correspondent. Jin Gee Chin was an alien in Tasmania – Miss Chung felt alien in China.

This report, written by Margaretta Pos after I gave a public lecture on China at the University of Tasmania, had prompted co-curators Kathleen and Peter Burns to contact me. I read their letter again:

> The article in the *Mercury* of the 16/5/87 regarding yourself and your past has interested us very greatly in the St Helens History Room.
> The town of Weldborough is in our Municipality and therefore a part of our presentation of history. We have always referred to the head Chinese man at Weldborough as Maa Mon Chin. Can you tell us where or why the name was different?

It dawned on me that the Burnses thought my great-grandfather's surname was Chin and that he had been 'the head Chinese' at Weldborough. Just as in Toishan when I had been wrongly linked with Chungs in Dragon Field Village, once again I became the subject of mistaken identity.

On the Monday before Christmas, John and I bided our time at Port Melbourne queuing in our Mazda to board the *Abel Tasman*. Next morning, when the ferry docked at Devonport, we drove down the ramp under a clear Tasmanian sky. After Devonshire tea in a Georgian house at Carrick and a swim for me at Windmill Hill in Launceston, we headed for the Queen Victoria Museum.

An elaborate Chinese temple, which had originally belonged to Weldborough, had been rearranged to hold the remaining contents of the Garibaldi and other joss houses of the district. As my eyes fixed on the ornate figures robed in red, gold and green, the intricate carving, scrolls and plaques, I thought of my ancestors out on the tin fields paying tribute. I imagined each man prostrate himself in turn, place sticks of joss before the altar, smell the incense as it burnt and see the smoke rise to the heavens.

Frail and muttering, Great-grandfather would have knelt and implored the gods, 'Please let me return to the motherland.'

Young and determined, Grandfather would have sought spiritual guidance, 'Please teach me how to succeed.'

Back in the car, we had to accelerate down to motor our way through the steep hills of Scottsdale, along the winding wooded country roads to Weldborough. When we switched off the engine we could almost hear ourselves breathe. I found it hard to conceive of this little hollow of only fifty-nine souls as a thriving Chinese village, the site of my Tasmanian roots. Sentimentally, I had dressed in the pair of Toishan-made sneakers I bought in my ancestral county. Now, in the emptiness that was Weldborough, almost my only link to Toishan seemed to be the red, blue and white footwear laced to my feet.

The original pub, said to have slept three shifts to a bed while miners worked around the clock, had vanished. At a bend in the bitumen, a stone's throw from where the pub once stood, we parked by the verandah of the off-white All Nations Hotel and checked in. We laughed at the menu, chalked on a blackboard and printed on the pub's postcards, but weren't disappointed to find all the dishes off: Tasmanian Devil $7.50, Stewed Rat $3.00, Possum Pie $3.00, Maggot Mornay $2.00, Leeches + Cream 5¢, Blow Fly Sponge $1.50, Ant Rissoles 10¢. On the hotel walls, sepia photographs testified to the tin-mining days.

'I wonder if my great-grandfather is here.'

'What did he look like?' asked John.

'I don't know. I've never seen a photograph of him.'

'Then we'll never know.'

'Well, my grandfather, then. Let's look for him.'

We were familiar with him: his photo resided under glass on the camphorwood chest that served as a coffee table for Mama at Lambert Avenue. His deep-set eyes, intelligent high forehead and oval face, his heavy head of hair parted to the left, looked out from a formal portrait; he is wearing a jacket and stiff-collared shirt. Once he wore a pigtail, or queue, which was imposed by the invading Manchus after they conquered the Ming empire in 1644. The new rulers forced Chinese men, who had previously worn their hair long and loose, to shave their foreheads and plait their hair like their foreign masters. When Sun Yat-sen's Republican Revolution overthrew the last emperor in 1911, it ended Chinese imperial rule and freed Chinese men to cut off their queues. By the 1930s, when the photograph was taken, Grandfather had long since shed his pigtail.

'Come and look at this,' John called to me. He was in front of a porcelain statue of the Chinese god of war, Kwan Ti, known for his righteousness, justice and guardianship. The colourful deity, about 20 centimetres high, looked fierce with his upturned eyebrows and straggly beard.

'A bit frightening and gaudy,' I said, 'but I think it's the statue Uncle Gordon was asked to present on behalf of the Chinese.'

We couldn't find Grandfather, let alone Great-grandfather, but unmistakeable in an elegant silk robe and Chinese cap was the man who was, for a brief moment, thought to be my great-grandfather, community leader Maa Mon Chin. As a storekeeper, he organised workers at Weldborough and gave them loans. He helped them with their problems and interceded in English for them with the foreign devils, much as my grandfather would do in Hobart in the 1920s and 1930s and later Uncle Gordon. Unlike most early overseas Chinese, who were separated for endless years from their loved ones, Maa Mon

Chin was joined by his wife and children. She made an impact on Mrs Bill Grose:

> Mrs Chin lived in a nice house overlooking the joss house and was a very gracious lady. Her home and children were kept very clean and smart. It was a pleasure to see her serve her friends and visitors afternoon tea in fine tiny Chinese cups, using Hang Mee tea, often wearing her Chinese robes and tiny, pretty slippers on her tiny feet. Having been born within the walls of China, her feet were bound so that her feet would be becoming to a Chinese lady. Her children attended the Weldborough school and we spent many happy evenings in her home.

Waking up in out-of-the way Weldborough was surreal. Was this barren space really where my Tasmanian heritage began? I lay pondering. Why had I never been here before? Why did I not remember any mention of Weldborough when I was growing up? Was the family too busy with the present to worry about the past? Yet I'd known of Toishan for as long as I could remember. If I hadn't gone to China, would I ever have bothered with Weldborough?

As John and I buttered toast and sipped tea, we wondered about Great-grandfather and Grandfather, spooning bowls of steaming Chinese rice porridge, which they prepared by the fire in their stringy bark hut.

'What do you think they had with their *jook*?' I asked. 'Pickled vegetables?'

'Yes, with hundred-year-old eggs. And chilli sauce from China carted here by horse.'

John, though no devotee of *jook*, was a convert to both chilli sauce and the so-called 100-year-old preserved duck eggs that acquired their brownish glazed texture and indigo yokes over months – rather than years – of being clad in a mixture made of rice straw blended with clay, salt, ash and lime.

I was spreading marmalade when Peter Burns pulled up. In a cheerful mood and dressed in an open-necked pink shirt, the St Helens curator was keen to show us around, to introduce us to the locals, even though I wasn't a descendant of Maa Mon Chin.

Peter led us up onto a grassy rise by the deserted Tasman Highway where we shook hands with 74-year-old poet and oral historian Bill Butt. Tall, with a head of silver waves, Bill exuded avuncular warmth. In the morning sun I readied for my first onsite account of life in the tin fields.

'These low-lying areas where the scrub is still growing,' Bill pointed with authority to the empty plain, 'they've all been mined. The ground was shallow and there was plenty of water.' This reminded me of my grandfather whose job it was to turn on the taps. 'If you had a pick and a shovel back then you were in business.'

'How did they work?' I asked, Spirax and Parker poised. Unlike the elder in Toishan, who had been unable to help us find the Gins' Dragon Field Village, Weldborough's upright, steady-voiced elder inspired confidence.

'You'd almost always find two Chinamen working together,' Bill explained in a schoolmasterly way. 'It didn't cost them anything. In deeper areas it meant pumps and things that were out of the question. There were a thousand Chinese here at one time.' He paused, surveying the empty plain as though he were gazing at the pigtailed miners. 'They used to congregate here at this camp. It was always called the Chinese camp.' Then, his tempo quickened. 'They had a sort of gambling place.'

This remark conjured up my childhood memory of Uncle Lester and his cronies, sitting in a foursome around a mahogany mah-jong table, their arms spread out as they clattered and shuffled the tiles marked with Chinese characters I didn't understand. From the pieces in the centre, each player selected enough to build a wall of ivory. Suddenly, Uncle Lester seized a crucial block, slammed it into the middle of the table and cried out '*Aiyah!*'

That, multiplied a hundredfold, must have been what Weldborough's gambling house was like. Miners could risk all on the round counters of fan tan or make a killing on mah-jong. No need for a roulette wheel or the cards of blackjack.

'They ran a lottery in the early days. One of the Chinese taking the proceeds to bank at Moorina was murdered on the way.'

'Did they ever find out who did that?' John asked.

'No, I don't think so.' Bill shook his head, his rugged, broad-nosed face solemn.

'The Chinese offered a reward of £200, but the police still didn't find out who did it,' Peter chipped in.

I felt relieved that my family escaped such brutality, and only later realised that this murder was probably the same one that Mrs Bill Grosse wrote about in the brochure that enticed us to Weldborough. I imagined Great-grandfather gambling on the lottery and his horror at murder.

'Your great-grandfather would have been here when the opera came to Weldborough.' Bill, seeming to sense my thoughts, changed the subject. 'A Chinese opera company, in 1893.'

'Yes, Great-grandfather was here then. He must have seen that.' I pictured him holding his cap over his knees, among the eager crowd under the tent. He sat transfixed, unlike the ageing Mao-suited comrades John and I sat alongside in Peking in the 1980s, who talked out loud, cracked peanut shells and walked in and out of the opera they obviously enjoyed and knew by heart. For Great-grandfather, coming from his village in Toishan, the Weldborough performance was perhaps his first and only exposure to opera: the clash of Chinese cymbals and high-pitched singing that sometimes sounded like screeching. Confronted by such novelty, his eyes darted with the swift sword-play, the movement of jewel-encrusted headdresses, the heavily painted faces and the costumes embroidered with swirling dragons and beautiful butterflies.

While Peter, John and I stood occupied with Bill, his reclusive neighbour, 76-year-old Ron Chintock, was quietly keeping tabs on us.

'Come on up,' Bill called with a wave of his arm. But Weldborough's last surviving part-Chinese stayed out of earshot, in the shadow cast by his timber cottage, close to where he had been raised.

Eventually, overcome by curiosity, Ron, in an open-necked shirt and pullover, emerged into the light. He paced up the slope, his black hair and figure gleaming as he moved towards us.

'Ron, this is Helene and John,' Peter introduced us to a man who radiated suspicion.

'Hello, Ron.' I offered my hand, feeling him size me up from behind thick glasses. 'You were brought up here in Weldborough?'

'Oh, yes.'

'And when did your father come out here, Ron? Did he come out or your grandfather?'

'He came out in 1870 or something.' He hesitated. 'I don't know,' he muttered, agitated.

Bill tried to calm him. 'Around 1877 towards 1878 according to Mark Ireland's book, that's when your grandfather came out, Ron. That's what we've settled on. You've been here all your life. She'll ask you what she wants to know.'

I took my cue. 'So your grandfather came out and then your father came out and joined him?'

'I don't know all these things.' He looked around, as though seeking escape. 'What's the big reason for all this? That's what I want to know.' He flashed daggers at Bill.

'My great-grandfather also came out here, in the 1880s.'

'There's a lot came out but there's a lot you don't want to know.'

That puzzled me. 'Why wouldn't you want to know?' I stared at him.

'I don't know. Forget these things, will you.' He turned away.

Bill, his lifelong mate with whom he had batted and kicked a ball when they were among only eighty-seven kiddies at their school, leapt to Ron's defence: 'The Chinese were engaged in mining and different things like that.'

'Did your dad die here, Ron, or did he go back to China?' I persisted.

'Died here as far as I know.' Then, sweeping angry eyes from his old school pal to Peter, 'Who's idea is this?'

'What about your grandfather? Where's he buried?'

'Up in the cemetery,' he dismissed my question. 'Why do you want to know all these things?' he demanded of me.

'It's very interesting, Ron. I'm very interested in the fact you don't think we should remember. You see, you're one of the few people left who can remember these things, you and Bill. And it's very interesting for the record. And now I'm interested in the fact that you think no one should know. Did you have a pretty rough time? Is that why you think people shouldn't know?'

'It might be. But why's it the business of anyone else?' He lashed like a caged animal. 'That's what I want to know.'

'It's just a matter of historical record.' I didn't run in fright.

'It's just the way people are today.' He scowled, kicking at a tuft of grass. 'They want to know this and they want to know that and they want to know something else.'

'Why do you think it should all be forgotten?' I stayed locked on him.

'Well, a lot of it should be forgotten. You've only got one life to live, girl. You've only got one life to live.'

'You think it was not very nice. Is that why –?'

'No,' he rounded on me. 'I'm proud of being here and everything else and living here all my life.'

'But that's why we want to have a record.'

'Why do you want a record?'

'Because it's part of Australia's heritage.'

'Aaah, bull!' Ron spat the words.

That must have given him some relief, for after a silence he gradually began to open a little. 'I've had to work for a living and mess around and work hard.' Then, turning to Peter, 'Is this the lady you said was the great-granddaughter of the storekeeper, Maa Mon Chin?'

'I thought she was, but she's the great-granddaughter of someone else.'

'Gin,' I said.

A cloud fell from Ron's face. 'That's what I was trying to think of. I knew the family but couldn't place –'

'Just explain to him the relationship,' Peter prompted me.

'My great-grandfather on my mother's side came here in the 1880s. Then he went back to China and he died.'

'Came here to Weldborough?' Ron leant towards me.

'Yes, then his son came at the turn of the century and mined in Weldborough. His name was Gin. My grandfather went down to Hobart. He had five, six children. One was my mother. She was born in Hobart and I was born in Hobart. And I've been to Toishan and around China but arranged to come here –'

'That's quite all right but when they told me your name and told me you were Maa Mon Chin's granddaughter, well, I couldn't make it out.'

'I'd never heard of Maa Mon Chin until Peter wrote to me.'

'I've got something I'd like you to see.' Ron nipped down to a room off his verandah and reappeared with several pieces of ebony. 'They're the dominoes the gamblers used to play with here. You don't get them like that now.'

'Beautiful.' I turned one over in my hand. It felt as smooth as silk.

'They definitely came from China.' His face shone with pride.

'Yes,' Bill fingered a piece. 'When we were kids it was quite common to find them lying around under the old buildings they pulled down.'

'Thousands of pounds wagered on them,' said Ron. 'They used tokens.'

'Yes.' I thought again of Uncle Lester playing mah-jong. Coloured discs, the sizes of threepenny, sixpenny and shilling pieces, sat in grooves at the edges of all four sides of the table. 'In mah-jong they used tokens and then counted the real money afterwards.'

'It was illegal, gambling,' said Ron. 'They were raided a few times.' He stared down at a column of ants, then looked up, beaming. 'They say they'd be delighted to see you at the museum and show you around the joss house.'

John assured him, 'The Launceston museum would be delighted to see anyone from Weldborough and show them around the joss house.'

'Where was the joss house?' I asked.

'See where that white gravel is?' Ron extended his right arm. 'You go along not quite to where it dips over there.' I followed the direction of his index finger to a depression in the ground. 'Just past there. It covered that area there within about half a chain of that pole.'

I saw the telegraph pole against blue sky and tried to imagine the joss house. 'They came from all over the area to worship?'

'Yes. And they came into the stores.' Bill waved a fly from his cheek, directing his gaze towards a clump of weeds. 'Down there was a store for many years. A chap named Ah Lin Chinaman had it then. To give you an idea of how many were here in the early days, you could see an unbroken line of Chinamen coming up on the brow of the hill to visit the shops.'

'Good business for Mr Maa Mon Chin,' I quipped. Then Peter broke the bonhomie.

'How many were there in your family?' he asked of Ron.

Ron tightened his jaw.

Bill came to his rescue. 'Ron is like me. You would have to do a lot of counting up.'

'It's quite normal for Chinese to have several wives and there could be several parts of a family,' I jumped in with my own background.

'No, they didn't here,' Ron unclamped himself. 'There were families of different –'

'Oh! Well, they didn't here,' Bill backed his mate. 'I don't think that was ever a practice, apart from in China. I don't think it was ever a practice in Tasmania.'

'I know my great-grandfather on my mother's side, my grandmother, Mary Lum Lee's father, had three wives. He could afford to house each of them in a separate home. My grandmother was the first daughter of wife number one.'

Bill interjected with an anecdote from America: 'There was a Chinaman worked for a rancher for twenty years. And one day he came out all smiles and showed his boss two photographs. "These be my son; him twenty and him nineteen." But the boss said, "That can't be right because you've been with me twenty years and you haven't once been back to China." The Chinaman said, "No, boss. But I got velly good friend back in China."'

We all laughed.

We drifted with Ron down to his cottage, then Peter, John and I began strolling towards the car when Bill sidled up to me. 'Excuse me for sort of reprimanding you. I mean he's a bit sensitive and Ron's mother was concerned with this Merle Oberon, you see.'

I stopped on the gravel. 'What's the link with him and Merle Oberon?' I couldn't imagine a link between Ron and the Hollywood beauty of the 1930s and 1940s.

'Well, Ron's mother was Lottie Chintock,' Bill weighed every word. 'She was the daughter of a Chinese miner and a European woman. And,' he sneaked a look over his shoulder towards Ron's cottage, 'a lot of people seem to think she was also the mother of Merle Oberon.'

'Really?'

'Lottie was a maid at St Helens Hotel,' Peter explained, 'and she fell pregnant to the publican, John W. Thompson.'

'So people believe Ron Chintock is Merle Oberon's half-brother,' said Bill. 'The questions about his family made Ron a little bit touchy because –'

'He thought I might be leading to questions about Merle Oberon.' I finished his sentence, chuckling at having been an unwitting stirrer of controversy. 'I didn't know anything about Merle Oberon's link here until what you just said.'

Only after we left Weldborough and spent a night at St Helens Hotel (which would be burnt down in an accident in 2005), did casual conversation in Hobart and elsewhere confirm me as Tasmania's ignoramus on Merle Oberon, the glamorous star who reached her zenith in 1939 as Cathy to Laurence Olivier's Heathcliff in the film of *Wuthering Heights*. Folklore has it that young Lottie gave birth to a baby named Merle O'Brien who grew up and left Tasmania to become a screen legend. Among the many tales about Merle Oberon, one is that, as a child at St Helens, Merle was adopted by her father's cousin, a visiting Indian army officer who had her raised on the subcontinent; another is that, as a young beauty in Hobart, she was inveigled to India by a company of travelling players. Whether born in St Helens or at Battery Point, Hobart, she is always part-Chinese in these tales and, to an extraordinary number of Tasmanians, specifically the daughter of Lottie Chintock.

So sensitive was the subject in 1987 that when Peter Burns sent me a twenty-page transcript of our conversation, he withheld the section relating to the woman reputed to be Ron's half-sister. 'The balance of the conversation is confidential while Bill Butt or Ronnie Chintock are alive,' he typed on page 17. On a blank sheet, he wrote in black ballpoint, 'Page 18 has been excluded for confidential reasons.'

Thirteen years later, when I asked for the missing page, it had disappeared. St Helens History Room could supply only a photograph of Merle Oberon in passionate though decorous embrace with Laurence Olivier in the Bronte classic. Both Peter and Ron had died, too soon to see the 2002 television revelation that Merle was an Anglo-Indian, not Tassie's most celebrated female export and not the most famous person of Chinese ancestry Down Under.

Australian filmmaker Maree Delofski's documentary, *The Trouble with Merle*, is based on Charles Higham's biography, *Princess Merle*, in which he tracks down a retired Captain Harry Selby, who shows him a birth certificate confirming Merle as his mother's half-sister. Born on 19 February 1911 at St George's Hospital, Bombay, Estelle Merle O'Brien Thompson had an English father employed on India's railways and a mother of mixed blood. It's alleged that Oberon's husband, British film producer Alexander Korda and his publicist fabricated a pure white British-Tasmanian pedigree for her to triumph over the prevailing racial prejudice. Ironically, the remote island of her reputed birth foisted on her the half-caste status her promoters had sought to negate.

Delofski's program at first convinced me that Merle was Indian; then I wondered whether it was merely another claim. A birth certificate can be forged. But whatever Merle's origins, Delofski shattered a myth.

'Rubbish,' my mother dismissed Deloski's film. Like so many on the island, she clung to the Tasmanian truth. 'Of course Merle Oberon was born in Tasmania. I remember a Chintock who worked for us in the store.'

I had only the vaguest impressions of such a man, but I do remember Uncle Gordon talking about Old Chintock.

'He was an uncle or a cousin of Merle Oberon,' Mama insisted. 'He knew her as a child, when she was Merle O'Brien. She later changed her name from O'Brien to Oberon.' And, with vehemence in her voice, 'If she wasn't a Tasmanian, why did she come back in 1978? There was a reception for her in the Hobart Town Hall. Why did she go and visit her mother's grave?' Then, as a challenge, 'Of course she was Tasmanian. If she wasn't, what happened to the little Chintock girl?'

Fellow Tasmanian, author and historian Cassandra Pybus, published her own take on 'Lottie's Little Girl' in her memoir *Till Apples Grow on an Orange Tree*. When she was a girl Pybus kept the Fantales wrappers that chronicled the 'delicious fact' of Merle's Tasmanian birth. I remember Fantales, the gooey mixture of firm caramel and chocolate, sticking to my teeth in the picture theatre, just as I remember the blue boxes of Fantales we sold in the shop. Fantales, which I could have off the shelf at any time, didn't appeal to me the way cobbers did, but I had to buy them from the corner shop opposite school. Nor, as a child, was I fascinated, as was Pybus, by the movie queen. My curiosity was not roused until my encounter with Ron Chintock.

Pybus and Nicholas Shakespeare, another author, see the Merle Oberon story in the context of Tasmania's search for identity. According to Pybus, it's a story that reassures Tasmanians 'we have not slipped unnoticed over the rim of the world'. As Shakespeare puts it: 'Not many proofs of Tasmania's remoteness and of the tendency of Tasmanians to deny their history, can surpass the case of Merle Oberon who overnight found herself billed as "a true daughter of Tasmania".'

It took not a Tasmanian, nor a mainlander from Melbourne or Sydney, but this British sleuth with an illustrious name who has embraced Tasmania as home, to inspect the grave Lottie Chintock shares with her son and to detect that Ron was born on 6 October 1911 – seven and a half months after Merle.

Or so it is claimed. With so many sworn submissions and competing truths, not even Sherlock Holmes could be sure. Ron, suspicious of me and my motives, seemed to be harbouring his family secret of an illegitimate half-sister. Whether the mother of Merle Oberon or only of Ron rests at Weldborough remains a puzzle.

Back in 1987 when John and I bade farewell to Bill, our first destination with Peter was Weldborough cemetery. In the warmth of summer, we wandered knee-high through weeds, with no reason to search for Ron's or any mother's sepulchre. Dislodged, weather-beaten tombstones surrounded by collapsing barriers gave meaning to the expression, 'pushing up daisies'. All Chinese had hoped to succeed and then return to Guangdong. Some individuals, such as my grandfather, stayed on and settled in Tasmania, building assets to enjoy in retirement in Toishan. Yet derelict graves inscribed with Chinese names show that some, like my grandparents in Hobart, died far from home: most of them, unlike my grandparents, still heathens buried beside Christians. I wondered how many were remembered by descendants in their native land or in the land that claimed them.

At nearby Moorina cemetery the grass was mown. A worn path led to a stone monument, erected in honour of deceased Chinese, that stood in a well-maintained enclosure and featured a tall, triangular-shaped stove in which to burn offerings to the spirits.

We ploughed on northeast of Weldborough through the Blue Tier, known as Mountain of Tin in Great-grandfather's day because its granite is the rock from which tin is derived, in search of the former mining village of Garibaldi. When we eventually found it, it looked indistinguishable from the surrounding bush of blackwood, myrtle and casuarinas. Only closer inspection revealed its past. Fossicking through a mass of shards, I picked up a curved and rusted piece of metal about the size of a dinner plate.

'What's this?'

'Maybe part of a large cooking pot.' Peter's remark triggered an image of simmering sweet pork and chicken broth.

I handed the piece of metal to John, along with some bits of broken china. We ferried them back to Melbourne and put them by the camellias in our courtyard garden, a reminder of Toishan in Tasmania.

Peter motioned to a circular, hollowed-out area in an embankment of rocks, grass and ferns. 'A pig oven, but not the only one.' He kept poking about in the growth.

We eventually found the remains of three ceremonial ovens in which pigs had been roasted for Lunar New Year, celebrated by foreign devils and Chinese alike. I thought of the pork crackling and the hissing and spluttering of fireworks as they exploded into the night.

'The pigs for Weldborough's festivities were fetched from Pyengana,' said Peter. John and I had stopped by the roadside in Pyengana, hungry for the local cheddar. 'The Chinamen used to walk in front of the pigs dropping wheat and the pigs followed them along the 5-mile trail.'

'The pigs followed the Chinese home like a paper chase,' John summed up.

A black-and-white photograph captures Garibaldi's main street in 1914: its crude pitch-roofed timber shopfronts and a straggle of a dozen Chinamen posing in their Sunday best for posterity. With one exception they look directly to camera, all motionless as they hold their poses.

At St Helens History Room we bought a mounted photograph of three of the miners after they'd been repositioned across the road onto the verandah of the Garibaldi joss house. A ravaged character known as Sharkey stands to the right, wearing an open jacket over his shirt and baggy trousers, a boater on his head and a wild white beard sweeping his chin from ear to ear. A hint of a smile exposes the gaps in his teeth. To camera left two younger, clean-shaven men sport cloth caps, the buttoned vests of their three-piece suits bearing fob chains; on their feet are soft black cotton Chinese shoes. The temple doorway is framed by banners bearing Chinese inscriptions and the altar is visible with the tapestry we saw displayed at the Queen Victoria Museum.

Sometimes, when I have that photograph hung on the wall at home, friends point to Sharkey: 'Is that your grandfather?'

No. My grandfather left the district a decade before Harold King arrived with his cumbersome camera, tripod and black cloth. Gin junior left for Launceston in 1904 and two years later began business in Hobart, where, in a different era, I would be born to retrace his route and puzzle over my origins.

28

A Chinese Cupid's Arrow

Fresh from Weldborough and exploring my Gin or Henry links, John and I cruised into Hobart for a family Christmas with our mothers. Nothing could have been further from my mind than my Chung family links. Despite my surname, I had grown up a Henry and, like the Montagues and the Capulets, the Henrys and the Chungs weren't on speaking terms. Nonetheless, given Hobart's small population of 100 000 in the 1950s – fewer than 100 of them Chinese – the two leading Chinese families inevitably had some contact, yet so minimal that I could recall almost every sortie I made into the enemy camp.

When we were very young, Lehene and I popped by ourselves into W. Chung Sing & Co., which was a few doors down from Henry & Co., past the Pekin Gift Store. We went to see Aunty Ivy, who ran the shop started by our parents after they were married. From Queenstown on the west coast, where Ivy's Chinese parents had a general store for the mining community, she had married our father's older brother Sim. They lived over the shop with their two little boys, Michael and David. Uncle Sim also had another, much older son, Peter, older than Lehene and me, who worked at the original Chung shop, Ah Ham & Co. He had been born in China, the son of Uncle Sim's first wife who lived in China.

Aunty Ivy was full of kindness. She and Mama had been friends before the divorce. She even held a birthday party for Lehene with party hats and a big cake with candles. She arranged for the Parker pen salesman to turn up and juggle from his case of tricks. Lehene's eyes lit up with glee at the sight of all the pens and nibs. She chose a fine blue fountain pen. The gift of an expensive pen proved that Aunty Ivy valued her.

When the rep closed his case and was about to leave, Lehene looked up at him and asked, 'How much did it cost?'

Though shy, Lehene could behave in a more direct, more open manner than I.

'It doesn't matter,' Aunty Ivy brushed her aside.

I felt embarrassed. As a child I knew it was impolite to ask the cost of a gift. Only when I grew up did I realise that Lehene, as the elder, was more conscious of the big question looming over us – who would pay the bills? Lehene would carry her insecurity about money throughout her life.

After I began school, I hardly saw Aunty Ivy, except for a trip to her home at her market garden at Lenah Valley. Apart from that and being sent on an errand to my father with a bill, I only dared onto Chung territory twice: when we painted the weatherboards and when we held a party at his house at Tranmere Road.

Not long after the party we heard Tranmere Road had a new occupant. Our father had been to Hong Kong and returned with a new wife. I spotted her when I happened to be walking through the Cat and Fiddle Arcade. Serving in the latest Charles Fruit Store, she was slim and attractive and seemed not much older than Lehene.

Later, when I was a uni student, I noticed a pretty little girl capering about in the shop. She lacked the serious demeanour I'd seen on the other four children; this one had the frills and airs of a spoilt child.

Rumour spread across to the Henry camp.

'Ah, she's got him under her thumb, number four. She's the boss.'

Although Lehene and I knew nothing else about our father's children, we did know their names: Phillip, Spencer, Kathleen and

Maple of wife number three and the toddler, Anne, of wife number four. As I was to learn, they knew even less about us.

One evening in 1975 my cousin Peter Chung, who knew Lehene and me from our visits as children to Aunty Ivy and his father, Sim, found himself in the company of his much younger cousin Phillip, an accountant in his mid twenties. A big Chung family function at one of their homes had drawn together several generations and branches of the clan, who all milled through the house, eating, drinking, laughing, gossiping and catching up. Peter and Phillip chanced to be by themselves next to a television set. It was 7.30. The ABC weather forecast had just finished when the theme tune of *This Day Tonight* flooded the room. Peter glanced at Phillip but discerned no change in his expression as presenter David Flatman appeared, 'Good evening and welcome. In tonight's program –'

Against the background hum of other voices, the two cousins continued to chat, half talking to each other with half an ear and half an eye to the box. Peter had just caught the words 'woodchip industry on Tasmania's east coast' when he heard, 'This report from Helene Chung.'

Peter watched Phillip for any sign of recognition. Not a flicker. Then, from a forest of pines a Chinese reporter walked into view.

'Do you know who she is? Peter asked as Australia's only non-white reporter filled more of the screen.

'No.'

'She's your half-sister.'

Phillip stared at the screen. Turning to his cousin, he spoke slowly over the modulated tones of the reporter: 'So, it's true. Dad does have other children.'

'You knew?' Peter grinned.

'Well, not really, but sort of. Something Mum said a long time ago made me think that Dad had been married before.'

Phillip and I would not meet for another thirteen years. Much later, when he revealed how he'd first heard of me, I imagined the off-screen drama.

*

Meanwhile, shocking news reached me about Phillip. In 1977, not long after I'd transferred to *TDT* Melbourne and settled into Queens Road my mother phoned: 'Gordon's beside himself! His little Debbie! My little Yum Yum!'

Uncle Gordon and Aunty Monica, model Catholics, had raised a family of nine children, including seven daughters. Deborah, their fourth, became Mama's favourite, her little Yum Yum. When her parents went overseas – Deborah was about two – she stayed with us at Longley. Deborah sat on the end of my bed as Mama dressed her in a red woollen tunic. Rex knelt down, slipped on her socks and buckled her feet into a pair of little red shoes.

In 1960, once Mama had banished herself to Luxor in the land of the pharaohs with Leslie, she began to pine for home:

> I think I would feel almost better if little Deborah was here – she is such a little pet – my Apple Dumpling, little ball of wool – soft fluffy kind – something delicious that you want to take a bite from.

Seventeen years later, at the time of the Henry family consternation – 'Gordon's beside himself' – Deborah had blossomed into an arts and music student. She had smitten a young accountant named Phillip. They wanted to take delicious bites of each other.

Decades after my parents' divorce scandalised Hobart and pitted two Chinese clans against each other, another young Henry and another young Chung formed another pair of star-crossed lovers. Their romance sent the heads of both houses into apoplexy. But once the lovers exchanged their vows, the two Chinese elders – former friends turned foes – Uncle Gordon and my father, Charles, put aside their ancient grudge to toast to a joint grandson.

In January 1988, after John and I had rambled through the mining relics of northeast Tasmania and were replete with Christmas and

New Year cheer in Hobart, the telephone rang at Lambert Avenue. The young couple surprised us with an invitation to afternoon tea.

Their home rang with the play and zest of tiny tots, the table groaned with culinary delights, enough to fuel any Heart Foundation campaign. Dotted between bemused foreign devil spouses and romping offspring sat the five adult children of my father's wives, number three and number four. My cousin Debbie and my half-brother Phillip brought their son over to me.

'This is Adrian,' smiled Debbie.

'Hello Adrian.' I bent down to my second cousin.

'Say hello to Aunty,' said Phillip.

'Aunty?' I queried.

Around the sitting room beamed one uncle, Phillip's brother Spencer, a cartographic draughtsman, and three aunts: Phillip's sisters Kathleen, a nursing sister, and Maple, a future librarian, and Anne, daughter of wife number four and a future businesswoman.

'Phillip looks like you,' John remarked.

Enmity in Verona between the Montagues and the Capulets wreaked tragedy for Romeo and Juliet. In Hobart, after sporadic forays and prolonged silence, settlement had finally been achieved. A Chinese Cupid's arrow ended combat between the Henrys and the Chungs.

29

The Mystery of the Red Envelope

One evening in 1979, the year *Nationwide* replaced *TDT* and after the rapprochement between the Henrys and the Chungs, but long before it impinged on me and before I worked in China or thought of Weldborough, I ended another long day's filming. I bolted from Ripponlea to the lights of St Kilda Road, headed towards town and soon turned into the grounds of 30 Queens Road. Up on the third floor, John had laid the table, prepared the salad and had two chicken thighs poised for the grill.

'There's a red envelope waiting for you. It's on the desk.'

I slit it open and scanned the gold lettering. 'We've been asked to a wedding reception but I've never heard of the couple. Take a look.'

'Well, the groom's Christopher Chung, so presumably he's some relative of yours.'

'Must be very distant.'

I couldn't think who Christopher Chung was. I knew the names of the principal Chungs related to me but why would any Chung invite me anywhere, let alone to a wedding?

After scratching around I uncovered the first layer of the mystery. I was dumbfounded. Christopher Chung was not so distant a relative after all. Raised in China, he was my half-brother, the son of my father's first wife.

As a child I'd heard mention of a Chinese wife and so understood my mother was my father's second wife. But China was a distant, unknown entity and the notion of a Chinese wife faint. When Mollance appeared in Hobart and I heard her talking secret women's business in Mama's room over the shop, I realised she was the third wife. Later, after Lehene and I had the party at our father's house, the new young wife, Susan, became the fourth. But, like everything else about the Chungs, that was their business.

Now, suddenly, at thirty-four, I learnt of a half-brother, an electrical engineer I didn't know existed. Christopher lived and worked in Melbourne. Filled with curiosity, John and I met Christopher and his Chinese bride, Lai Yoke, in October as we mingled among 200 guests at the Rickshaw Inn. Speaking English with an accent that made him seem Chinese to me, he welcomed us. In Hong Kong style, each table for ten was laden with its own supply of whisky, brandy and gin, while waiters also served wine, soft drinks and tea throughout course after course of the banquet. Along with everyone else, John and I enjoyed ourselves as we raised glass after glass to wish happiness to the newlyweds who had asked us, two strangers to them, to their lavish night of nights.

I meant to contact Christopher but weeks, months and years slid by. Only after I'd returned from Peking and begun to write *Shouting from China* in late 1986, did I put pen to paper. If I were to place my wild goose chase in Toishan in perspective, if I were to comment on my Chinese ancestry, I couldn't entirely omit my Chung background. My father was as remote as the man on the moon and had declined to see me, even as I departed for Peking. Christopher, by contrast, had extended a brotherly hand. What's more, he'd not long since left China and he spoke Cantonese and read Chinese characters.

To check a few points I sent him a brief note. He replied promptly in a clear, neatly written hand on a sheet of A4. I didn't need all the information, nor to take up his offer to provide more, but I filed the details away, where they stayed until I began work on this memoir and I needed to touch base with him again. Then he unfolded all the layers behind the mysterious red envelope.

'So you must be the oldest,' I put it to him, 'older than Lehene and me, because your mother was the first wife and ours the second.'

'No,' said Chris. 'I'm younger. I was born in 1948.'

'What?' Surely I'd misheard. 'I turned three in '48. My parents divorced in '46. Yet you were born after the divorce but before wife number three?'

'You have to understand,' he said.

With my Western blinkers, I needed Chris to shed light.

From the first glint of California's Gold Mountain in the nineteenth century, Chinese village elders married off their fortune-seeking sons, sometimes in group ceremonies to total strangers. Fireworks crackled and lit up the sky as the entire village joined in celebrations and feasting. Each newlywed couple enjoyed a night together before being parted as the husband set forth in hope of finding riches in a foreign land. Marriage preserved the man's link with the village and, ideally, provided a son to continue the family line. The same practice prevailed with New Gold Mountain.

Like their American counterparts, Australian Chinese journeyed back to their wives in the village, where they might also acquire more wives. Although a female had one option in life, to take one husband, Chinese custom allowed wealthy men to take multiple wives. Each additional wife improved a man's status. The adage ran: the first wife has status, the others – all concubines – have love.

Some Chinese settled and married overseas, where they followed a mixture of Eastern and Western code. Many sent remittances to their wives in China while living apparently monogamous lives in the West. My father followed a version of this Chinese tradition.

'Come on, son, we're going back home,' Grandfather told Charles when he was in his mid-teens. 'It's time for you to get married.'

They left Hobart and sailed to Hong Kong, from where they made their way through the Pearl River delta, not to their village home in *Ping Kong* – Undulating Land – from where Grandfather had set forth as an impoverished twenty-three year old, but to the double-storey brick house he had built in Sunwei City on the fruit of his overseas toil.

'I've consulted a matchmaker,' Charles's mother welcomed him. 'I've found a wife for you.'

Charles played his role in the ceremony and the new bride joined the household. Then, with his father, the new husband set off again for Tasmania, leaving his wife behind with his mother and the wives and children of his brothers.

Back in Hobart, Charles resumed life as a young Australian. Years passed and he married Dorothy.

In 1947, a year after the divorce and sixty years after Grandfather first ventured to New Gold Mountain, boarded a train from Launceston and began market gardening in Hobart, father and son returned to Sunwei, the father to retire on his wealth. In Grandfather and Grandmother's comfortable extended family home, where the Chinese wives and children of Charles's two brothers still in Hobart also lived, Charles's first wife gave birth to Chris. Chris's sister, conceived immediately after the marriage, died during the Japanese invasion, when she was a baby, so Chris grew up an only child.

Chris grew up knowing about Lehene and me. He surprised me by producing photographs of us as infants that had made their way to the Chung household in Sunwei. Lehene, at twelve months, is at the piano in Hobart and I, at six months, am in Brisbane in my mother's lap with cousin Anne, five days younger but half my size.

No wonder Aunty Joyce had laughed when she told me, 'Oh, I was so proud of you. So plump. I had to take you to the butcher. I had to show you off. I walked along the road and almost collapsed with the weight.'

'Now, look at this.' Chris had the air of a conjurer.

I stared at my mother and father, young and radiant with love, photographed on a wintry day at the Botanic Gardens in Hobart. Both are wearing the fashionable coats with wide lapels of the forties. He is jaunty in his check wool scarf and narrow-brimmed trilby, she fresh-faced with her hair styled in a Victory Roll.

'And this.' From the envelope slipped a bombshell.

Their wedding day: my mother with a flower in her hair and my father next to Grandfather, seated behind a three-tier cake, an image I had never seen.

I could hardly believe that while I passed through Sunwei in 1984, bound for neighbouring Toishan, these relics were sitting in the Chung home. I recalled how the Luis' home and their pictures of three generations of their family in Melbourne made me wish to know about my family links. How could I have guessed that, within close range, a similar collection of photos showed three generations of my family in Hobart?

'I went back in 1989, ten years after I met you and they were still there,' Chris revealed. 'Some cousins had lived in the rooms upstairs but left the photos intact. There's also this one of the house, this studio portrait of the whole family in 1950 and this one of us in 1955 when our cousin Peter Chung came to visit. I brought them all back to Melbourne.'

Then, jolting me anew, he said, 'Do you know what Charles did in Sunwei?'

'No.' I didn't know what to expect.

'He opened a cafe called Hawaii that sold icecreams and cool drinks. That was new. Nothing like it before.'

'Really?' I pictured the Green Gate on the corner opposite Henry & Co. I pictured the cityscape in Toishan with its triple-storey stone terraces and colonnaded shopfronts. From that I cobbled together an image of my father's Hawaii Cafe in Sunwei City. 'Chinese have traditionally shunned dairy products. It must have been quite an innovation. Like KFC in the 1980s.'

'He didn't stay though because of the Chinese Civil War.'

As Chiang Kai-shek and his Nationalists desperately defended their shrinking territory against the Soviet-backed Communists, Mao's Red China threatened. Encouraged by his father, Charles left his wife and son Chris with his parents and the other wives in Sunwei and rejoined his brothers at Ah Ham in Hobart.

By the early 1950s, after the Communist victory and Grandfather's death, funds grew scarce. Grandmother died and the other wives and children fled to Hong Kong or Australia; Chris and his mother alone remained.

'The government took control and moved in other people,' he recalled. 'Mum and I lived upstairs but we had to sell whatever we could to buy food.'

By the late 1950s, the economic insanity of Mao's Great Leap Forward unleashed death through starvation to tens of millions of Chinese. In 1960 Chris, a determined twelve year old, escaped with his mother to Macao, then braved an overnight journey through shark-infested waters.

'It was awful. We were all squashed into the boat. People vomiting. Children screaming. Then, in the middle of the night, we were told to stay completely still. Not a sound. The Hong Kong water police were on patrol, searching with machine guns.'

Mother and son washed up in Hong Kong. She slaved in a garment factory while he assembled plastic toys and flowers. An illegal, with no identification papers, he managed to put himself through night school, proved to be skilled in electronics and graduated in electrical engineering from the Hong Kong Polytechnic; it was to be his ticket out. Mother and son went to Singapore, where Chris landed a job: he worked and saved for four years. From the island republic he applied to study at the Royal Melbourne Institute of Technology in Melbourne. He and his mother moved again.

'It was expensive living in Melbourne, so I went over to Hobart to the TCAE. I took Mum. We lived at Ah Ham and I worked there for Ivy and Sim.'

An image found its way into my memory; I remembered hearing about an 'original Chinese wife' being at Ah Ham. I remembered passing by that shop and glancing through the window and seeing an older Chinese woman in an office or some recess at the rear. Perhaps she was Chris's mother.

'Was that about 1976?'

'Yes, I was there in '76.'

So, around the same time that I interviewed John on the Tasmanian College of Advanced Education and fell in love, my half-brother from China, unknown to me, was studying there.

Late on Monday, 23 October 2006, John's birthday, I closed the book I was reading and switched off the lamp. I was asleep when the phone rang at around midnight. I assumed it was Chris.

'Chris,' he confirmed.

'Thanks for calling back. I just wanted to tell you about La Trobe University's online article on the Chungs in Tasmania. I learnt about it today.'

'Really? Who wrote it?'

'A China academic in Hobart and a visiting scholar from Canton. The same one, it seems, who translated Grandfather's record of his travels. The translation you gave me. It's central to the piece.

'There's also a reference to the Chungs not getting on with the Henrys in the first decades of the twentieth century, wrongly attributed to me. Not the first time I've been wrongly named as a source or misquoted. The feud didn't begin until the divorce in 1946. And I need to check something with you, Chris. When you returned to Sunwei in 1989 and brought back those photos, was the house still standing?'

'Yes, it was still there in 1989, was still there into the 1990s. But it's not there now.'

'The article says the house has been replaced by a new Overseas Chinese Building.'

'That's wrong. I've just been to Sunwei. The house and some adjoining property were taken over by a developer. He had everything demolished for a large block of apartments. After a lot of haggling with the government the Chungs got allocated four of them. When did you last speak to Phillip?'

'Not since his trip to China.'

'Well, I saw him there. With Charles. I arranged my business to be in Sunwei at the same time so I could show them Grandfather's grave and Grandmother's too, side by side, so Charles could pay his last respects. Otherwise, they wouldn't have found the site. Grandfather's shops, including the one where Charles opened the Hawaii Cafe, they were all pulled down for the Overseas Chinese Building back in the 1950s. That's where Phillip and the Old Man stayed.' His voice rippled with irony.

'And where'd you stay?'

'At one of the apartments, the one I recently had done up, to make it liveable. Apartments in China aren't like in Australia. All you get is a concrete floor. Not even windows. Just open spaces for the rain and dirt and everything to fly in. So I had this one fixed so at least there's water, a bathroom, kitchen and you can stay there.'

'What about the other ones?'

'Uncle Sim installed a caretaker in one and insisted on putting Grandfather's image in another, so a picture of Willi is sitting there. It's his memorial. After Uncle Sim passed away, those two became Peter's. The third unit belongs to Alfie, Uncle George's son. And Charles owns the one that I've fixed up. You can stay there too if you're ever over there.'

In the dimness I tried to picture Grandfather Chung's shrine in Sunwei. Then I recalled the words of Uncle Gordon, 'Oh, I had to fight those commies.'

After cutting through miles of red tape, he eventually retrieved Grandfather Gin's properties in Toishan and Canton.

'Here, Doff. If Big Girl's to get the property we all have to sign.'

I last ran into Ah Thlaw during the oppressive summer of 1984 when I was on leave from Peking and shepherding Mama around the rackety Chinese sections of Hong Kong.

A tropical downpour almost drowned out her greeting. 'Ah Dor-lor-thee.'

'Ah Thlaw.'

'Ah, Wo Wo.'

I tried to duck for cover as the clouds spilt asunder.

Big Girl, who stood bedraggled in the rain, her teeth glinting, lived across the border in Canton, like the Chungs, a Gin–Henry preserving her links with the motherland.

30

Double Ninth

John and I stood under a line of plane trees bursting with fresh spring growth. Two years after the end of our China adventure and not defeated in our Herculean struggle with architects, builders, lawyers and Melbourne city councillors and planners, we were about to begin life in our new inner city home. Filled with excitement, happiness and hope, we looked with pride at the renovated double-fronted Victorian house. Carriers had unloaded the effects from our Queens Road flat as well as boxes of books and chests of forgotten treasures, some of them stored for up to five years.

'This will be home until I'm carried out through the picket fence,' John boldly declared.

It was a sun-filled Friday, 9 September 1988.

Three years earlier, on Monday, 9 September 1985, smog from Peking's coal-fired furnaces blotted out the diplomatic missions that stretch north of the ABC office on the twelfth floor of the building. Glancing up from my desk into the dreary grey through the window, I answered the phone.

'Neil Davis has been killed.' I heard the mid-Atlantic accent of Peking Associated Press bureau chief Jeff Bradley. 'News has just come on the wire from Bangkok.'

I was incredulous. The invincible Neil Davis? Dead?

After two years in China, I'd recently been back to Australia on ABC business and to see Mama and John. John had returned to work there having exhausted a year's leave during his initial stint in China. I now typed away, writing a family circular to my mother in Hobart, Lehene in London and John in Melbourne:

> Today learned that Neil Davis killed in the Bangkok coup. He was working for NBC [National Broadcasting Company] and when the coup took place he went to the radio station – where new power mongers usually announce control. Details are still sketchy, but presumably this – including Neil's death, as Australia's most noted Vietnam War cameraman and as a Tasmanian, will also be on the News. There is the film from [David Bradbury's documentary on Neil] *Frontline* which will be used no doubt.
>
> I feel quite stunned by the news, because although I've not seen him for years – and not that many times in my life, it doesn't seem ten years ago since we last had dinner, at the Mona Lisa … Hobart … I remember [when] I was 14 years old and waiting for the Longley school bus outside St David's park when a Tasmanian film centre van pulled up and Neil gave me a lift home, through the snow of Fern Tree to Longley.
>
> Many of the correspondents here, not only Bud Pratt from NBC, but Jim Pringle from *Time* – know Neil well from the Indo-China War. He was the last Western cameraman to pull out of Saigon and got that much used shot of the tank … crashing into and through the gate … He was always at the 'frontline', that's why he has such graphic footage of the Vietnam War – shooting it with the soldiers fighting, not from a distance.
>
> He had a brief spell in Angola – during the war and then went back to Asia. He felt uncomfortable in the West and intimated in Australia … that he wouldn't be coming back. I think he was one

of those newsmen who thrive on the 'frontline', who need that flow of adrenalin that comes with the action. I believe that his death was quick and hopefully not too painful. If anyone I know was going to die 'in action', it was Neil. In a way, if it was not too painful, it was a fitting death.

It was in fact a most unfitting death. Tasmania's famed survivor of action in Indo-China died during a military coup in Thailand, where the regularity of these usually bloodless events made them tedious. Neil had been killed in tank and machinegun fire aimed at the radio station behind him. He and his soundman Bill Latch, joined together by a cord linking their equipment, had sought shelter with another camera crew behind a metal junction box. Bill Latch was fatally wounded; Neil died within seconds. He had been dragged by his friend Gary Burns, the other cameraman, along the road away from further fire. Meanwhile, Neil's blood kept spilling out of his shattered body and leaving behind a terrible trail. Because his camera was attached to him and rolling when he was hit, he inadvertently filmed his own death.

The bloke I shall always associate with the white snow of Fern Tree, the Tasmanian who introduced me to Asia, the newsman who influenced my decision to move on from Hong Kong, the cameraman who wrote to me on 'the very latest action film of blood & guts', had himself become news.

On Thursday, 9 September 1993, precisely five years after we moved into our house, John and I stepped onto the wisteria-entwined verandah, then down the bluestone steps onto the tiled square set between the garden of camellias, azaleas, anemones, hydrangeas and hellebores, walked through the cream gate and got into the car. For twenty minutes we crawled through peak hour traffic until, by 5 o'clock, we were through the door and waiting on the blue carpeted entrance of Freemasons Hospital opposite Fitzroy Gardens in East Melbourne.

Two years earlier, on a balmy evening in May, I'd joined John at a reception he helped organise for Chinese, Japanese and French international teaching fellows, who were in Melbourne as part of the exchange program on which John worked for the Victorian Ministry of Education. Held in the lush Lansell Road Gardens of the Toorak Professional Development Centre, it went well. John was pleased. We retreated with friends to the nearby Kingdon Restaurant and then came home. John popped into the bathroom, then emerged, frightened. He'd just passed blood.

'It could mean cancer,' he said.

John was admitted to Cabrini in Malvern and underwent what we believed was successful surgery on his bowel — just a small section had to be removed — and he soon returned to work. He immersed himself in the details of the renegotiation of the educational agreement between Victoria and its sister state Jiangsu. Some mornings he disappeared at dawn to meet Chinese landing at Tullamarine airport. He entertained them at home, led them to various campuses around the state and escorted one delegation on a packed itinerary to Canberra and Sydney.

We grew so confident of John's health that, within a year, we finalised plans to holiday overseas together for three months in England, France, Holland and Russia. I would set off before John and meet him in London. But first, I would take up an invitation from the United States Information Agency to be briefed on foreign affairs, especially American views on North Asia, to help me in my work as presenter of Radio Australia's *International Report*, which was broadcast daily on ABC Radio National. Then, weeks before we were due to leave, John began to feel unwell and we wondered whether we should cancel our trip. A colonoscopy had cleared John of cancer. The surgeon and the GP assured him that it was just a matter of fine tuning his bowel by trying different medications. Although still not absolutely sure I should go, in mid May 1992 I flew out, three weeks ahead of John:

Dearest Wo Wo,

You have only been gone a few days and I miss you terribly. How I must take you for granted. It was wonderful hearing from you on Saturday. Of course I would have liked to have heard more detail about your interviewing all the top military brass in Honolulu ...

Please take very good care of yourself my love and have a wonderful time – Stateside.

Much love *John* xxxxxx

In that American presidential election year few predicted that Democrat Bill Clinton would win over incumbent Republican George Bush senior (who had opened the US liaison office in China). The odds of a Bush victory seemed so high that in my twelve-city tour. I gave Clinton's home state, Arkansas, a miss.

Meanwhile John was having less than a wonderful time in Melbourne. The best he felt was flat. Yet, assured that he was fit to travel, he boarded his plane for Thailand but not feeling excited, armed as he was with boxes and bottles of pills.

In his hotel in Bangkok John experienced his first violent attack of shivering: he felt frozen with cold and his teeth chattered uncontrollably. He pressed on to Amsterdam, feeling ghastly, still trying to fine tune his bowel through a combination of suppositories, tablets and fibre and arrived in London hot, exhausted and suffering from abdominal pain. When Lehene saw him at the airport she couldn't believe he'd travelled alone halfway around the world. Next day, Saturday, David called their GP to their home. The doctor had no doubt that John should be in hospital and arranged for a surgeon to visit on Sunday and he, in turn, ordered a CAT scan. As John wrote in his diary:

Monday, 15 June: My worst day. Have CAT scan ... Radiologist
says it's most probably a recurrence of the bowel cancer ...
Surgeon confirms this. Says it's inoperable but may be treated with chemotherapy.

While John, accompanied by Lehene, was having a biopsy, I telephoned from San Francisco and heard David say, 'The surgeon thinks it's most likely incurable cancer.' I stopped breathing. 'But there's a chance, although slight, that it's only a pelvic abscess.' I cursed myself for not being with John. I wished we'd stayed at home.

> *Tuesday, 16 June*: Wo Wo phones while I'm away and David breaks news to her. I am grateful. Radiologist phones and last of all Wo Wo phones that night.

John spent what he called 'a very depressing' Wednesday. While Lehene was at her part-time work at the library, David, by now an honorary part-time magistrate, tried to comfort him. John's concern wasn't for himself. He told David I would be devastated. He sat on the off-white settee, staring into space.

My overnight plane touched down early next morning and we were reunited.

> *Thursday, 18 June*: Lehene and I drive to Gatwick where we meet my darling Wo Wo. Helene stays up but retires early.

That night, locked in each other's arms in bed, still anxiously awaiting the result of the biopsy, the telephone rang.

> *Thursday, 18 June*: Surgeon phones about 10.00 pm to say he has good news. Biopsy shows no sign of cancer cells. I get up and tell David and Lehene.

We felt so relieved that, despite John's condition, we enjoyed a little of London. We walked the streets hand in hand, happy to be alive and feeling so optimistic that we bought a new dinner set in Regent Street. We browsed through the shelves at Hatchards and picked up the latest title, Andrew Morton's *Diana: Her True Story*. At a sale in a menswear shop high on the hill in Hampstead, John chose two cotton shirts, two silk ties and a wool and silk sportscoat. The future lay before us.

According to the surgeon, the pain in John's abdomen was caused by a large pelvic abscess that could only be relieved by surgery. The surgeon offered to perform the procedure there, in London, and we thought about it: John would take only a few weeks to recover and then we could resume our travel and holiday with friends in Moscow. Then we thought that recuperating in the familiar surrounds of our own home seemed preferable to recuperating in unfamiliar surrounds abroad. And so it was that only a week after I'd landed in London I was airborne again, this time with John, flying back to Melbourne.

We no longer had confidence in the original surgeon, who had misdiagnosed John, so within three days of arriving home John was wheeled into the operating theatre of a hospital new to him to go under the knife of a new surgeon.

That Wednesday, 1 July 1992, my world began to fall apart. I was seated at my desk in the study when the surgeon telephoned to say 'I've got bad news. I've found a tumour in John's pelvis, a huge lump. It's inaccessible but I dissected a bit and sent it to the pathologist. It unequivocally shows cancer cells.'

I asked what he could do and was shocked to hear the answer was nothing. 'I wouldn't recommend any treatment. Radiation won't work. It only slows the cancer while producing more hazards. Only a very brave radiotherapist would risk treating him. And I suspect chemotherapy wouldn't help either. It only makes you feel worse. I think it's best just to keep him comfortable and treat symptoms as they come.'

'Does that mean John won't be coming home, that he's simply waiting to die?' I asked, horrified by my own words.

'Yes.'

'How long do you expect John to live?'

'It's hard to put a time on it but of patients who aren't cured by surgery, 80 per cent die of liver failure within six to eighteen months.

I wouldn't give him more than that. The tumour will inevitably destroy some vital structure. There's no cancer in the liver and no sign of threat to the kidney, but the tumour will ultimately block an organ. He'll always feel below par. His working days are over. I'm 99 per cent sure he won't last two years.'

With this dreadful scenario before me, I drove to the Richmond-based Epworth Hospital's cancer ward near the Treasury Gardens and the Fitzroy Gardens in East Melbourne (now the Peter MacCallum Cancer Centre), and found John in a fourth-floor room looking out onto the spire of what he called the 'gloomy' St Patrick's Cathedral. He was calm and determined to fight his cancer. 'It may be operable,' he said, 'but surely it can be treated by chemotherapy?'

With the surgeon's ominous words in my ears, I was dumb. How could I tell John that treatment would be useless? Why should I dampen his spirit? I sat beside him, tried to comfort and support him, but felt in my heart that the end was near.

The following evening brought hope. Our friend Sally Brodie phoned to ask about John. I unburdened myself to her and, with tears running down my face, repeated what the surgeon had said.

'I'll put Graham on the line,' she said.

Sally and her husband, an oncologist, had been friends of ours for years but it hadn't occurred to us to ask him to intervene in John's treatment. After all, we'd been told that no further treatment was needed after the first operation because the cancer had been removed.

With Graham's encouragement, as soon as John was fit enough he began treatment from which he experienced hardly any side effects. As he wrote to his former colleague Robbie Howell at the Australian Embassy in Beijing and her husband, historian Stanley Campbell, long since settled back in Texas:

> I'm now having a five week course of radiotherapy and chemotherapy combined. My oncologist, who is an old friend of ours, is confident the problem can be managed successfully. Anyway I'm feeling fine and Helene and I are both out and about

seeing shows and visiting people and I'm told I can go back to work in October or November.

A fortnight later, he told Lehene and David that,

> Despite the warning from the doctors of all sorts of dire side effects I have felt reasonably well and apart from having to visit the bathroom a little more frequently and to have a rest in the afternoon I have lived a happy normal life. Oh! I must admit to having lost, temporarily, some of my pubic hair but hardly anyone has noticed that and no-one has commented on it.

And a month later he wrote:

> Since leaving hospital and undergoing therapy I have had no energy for gardening at all. However one day last week I started pulling out a few weeds and ended up working until sundown pruning trees and ripping out vines and creating huge piles of garden waste to be disposed of. I decided I must really be a lot better.
> 'Wuthering Heights' is being serialised on T.V. here and Wo Wo and I have not missed an episode. I am even rereading the novel. It is remarkable that the Bronte sisters living such an isolated life could have had such powerful imaginations.
> Wo Wo is preparing the evening meal as I write – a scene of domestic bliss.

And then:

> My main news is that I am back at work. I returned early last week; and apart from feeling tired at the end of the first day it is now almost as if I had not been away …
> Perhaps Wo Wo has told you of the results of my five weeks of radio & chemotherapy. I had to wait a month after the end of the treatment before having a C.A.T. scan. We were pleased that the

result was above average for such treatment. The tumour had shrunk considerably and I am not having any further treatment, for the time being. My doctor will no doubt want to monitor it from time to time, but for the present the prognosis is good.

We were so elated that we decided to celebrate by getting married. Until now we had felt no need for formalities. My mother had always cautioned me against marriage and urged me to maintain my independence. On John's part, his former marriage also made him wary of legal ties. Yet before going to China we signed an affidavit declaring that we regarded our relationship as permanent, which was not only required by the ABC in order to recognise John as my spouse, it also reflected our state of mind.

In Melbourne, on Saturday, 20 December 1992, in the presence of eight friends, we exchanged vows in an elegant room of the former Royal Mint, which now housed the Registry Office. After the ceremony, we lunched well and drank vintage wines for five hours. The next day we flew to Hobart and settled ourselves into a suite in the Wrest Point tower, overlooking the yachts on the Derwent.

> Yes it is true. Helene and I were married on last Saturday – a very quiet wedding. Just a handful of friends as witnesses followed by lunch at a restaurant in Carlton. We all fitted at one round table and Con O'Donohue provided wines from his vast collection.

John became quite sentimental about our wedding and made a point of introducing me as 'my wife, Helene'. When I introduced him as 'my partner, John', he took me to task: 'You should refer to me as "my husband, John".'

Wistfully, he felt the plain gold band he'd slipped onto my finger, looked at me and sighed, 'We should have done this years ago.'

We were exhilarated, filled with hope for our life together.

*

In March 1993 John's cancer count rose. The oncologist who until then had administered his treatment shrugged at the idea of any more. That left us flat. 'It's a strange feeling being told that nothing can be done. You'd think they could do something,' John mused.

After the initial shock, even as he gradually weakened over the following months, we remained positive and continued a normal life, seeing friends, exhibitions, films and theatre, going for walks and driving to the countryside. What we treasured most was our time alone. Now, when I reflect on that period, I especially remember the deep sense of intimacy we developed, our moments of heightened joy – some of our happiest times.

On Thursday, 9 September, John felt abdominal pain. Over dinner the night before he told me his bowel was troubling him. I gave him an extra serve of salad and encouraged him to eat more fruit. Only then did I learn that he'd been constipated for three days. Now that he felt more constipated and in pain I telephoned the doctor, who suggested that John have tests in hospital. The doctor could arrange John's admittance to the Freemasons, a block from the Epworth in East Melbourne. We imagined his stay would be a temporary setback, similar to what we'd twice experienced before. Once, after his first operation, John, fully dressed in corduroys and tweed jacket, was hunched in agony on his hands and knees on the bed. In that emergency, we rushed back to Cabrini hospital where in a couple of days, his bowel righted itself. Expecting much the same outcome this time, I packed his overnight bag, including the book he was reading, *Beijing Jeep*, by our former China colleague Jim Mann, and threaded my way through the traffic.

Over the next twenty-four hours John underwent various tests and was wheeled in and out of his room for x-rays; he stayed calm and patient. We were relaxed enough to be watching the SBS television news when the doctor appeared. I switched off the set and we exchanged pleasantries. John and I listened intently as he explained that, because the surgeon from the previous year was abroad, we could expect a visit from another surgeon. At that moment, a stranger walked into the room.

'He's here already,' the doctor said and vanished on his busy hospital rounds.

Dressed in a dark business suit, the stranger introduced himself as a colorectal surgeon. He was to be the final of three surgeons to operate on John in three different hospitals in little more than two years. He said that John's x-rays showed a bowel obstruction. He slipped his hands into a pair of rubber gloves, took some equipment from his bag, bent over John and pumped water into his bowel to try to make it work. To no avail.

Upright again, the surgeon said, 'Well, Mr Martin, you've already had two major operations and now you've got a bowel obstruction. Unless it moves, you can't survive. I can operate but I don't know what I'll find. It might be an adhesion, it might be the effects of the radiation, or it might be another tumour. I don't know. With surgery you still may not survive. Now, you don't have to have surgery. It's your choice. But as the person who'll have to perform the operation, I want you to know what's involved if you do decide on surgery.'

The surgeon had no sooner left than I burst into tears. I climbed onto John's bed and we hugged each other for all we were worth. 'Yes, you can cry now,' John tried to soothe. 'Let it all hang out.'

I was still sobbing, my arms wrapped around him, when he said, 'What a way to die, with a blocked bowel.' Then he added, 'I didn't think we'd ever see another colorectal surgeon.'

Around 10 o'clock I eventually left John. I stepped from the hospital onto the footpath and began to howl. I pierced the night with my cries for the loss of the only man I had ever loved. As I rounded the corner on my way to the carpark, a phrase kept repeating itself in my mind, words from *The Last of the Knucklemen*, a play by John Powers set in a mining camp in northwestern Australia, that depicts the rough life of men on the run, riff-raff and shady characters who go by names such as Mad Dog, Horse, Pansy, Monk and Tarzan. The crude sentence now haunting me was 'If you don't eat, you don't shit and if you don't shit, you die.'

*

On Saturday night, at around 6.30, when John was wheeled out of his room on a stretcher on his way to theatre, he seemed as composed as a healthy man about to have his temperature taken. 'I'll be all right,' he tried to assure me.

In his room I climbed onto his bed, stretched out, closed my eyes and tried to collect myself. If the operation was over soon it would be bad news, a sign that the obstruction couldn't be freed. Equally, if the operation continued for a long time, it would mean complications had occurred. I was still lying down when the surgeon appeared. I immediately sat up.

Looking relaxed, he said, 'I'm pleased with what I've done. It was only a kink.'

I sighed with relief. John's bowel had simply adhered to the tumour and become kinked, like a kink in a garden hose, and now that it had been straightened it could function normally.

'It was a simple procedure but because of John's weakened state before the operation,' the surgeon cautioned, 'we just have to wait and see how he recovers.'

I had to wait until 9 o'clock before I was allowed to see John in the recovery room. Lying with a Perspex oxygen mask over his face, he was still under the effect of the anaesthetic. I sat looking at him, as he breathed heavily, and I felt a weight lifting off me. The operation had been a success. We had been saved.

In the days after surgery John responded normally and my fears about his untimely death in hospital vanished. When he complained that he was being starved and was hungry and thirsty, I had to explain that his body couldn't yet tolerate food. The surgeon saw this as a healthy sign and allowed him to have small spoonfuls of crushed ice. Next, he began to sip water and on Wednesday, three days after his operation, he drank his first cup of tea. However, when told he could eat and drink whatever he wished, he didn't advance much beyond small servings of soup.

Sitting up in bed in a reflective mood one day, John said, 'I'm a wreck.' When I told him he showed strength and courage, he said, 'In this situation you have to or you're gone.' Then he squeezed my hand, 'Don't worry, we're on top of this.'

By the Saturday afternoon John was strong enough to receive his first visitor, his brother-in-law John Gregory, who was passing through Melbourne. The visit tired John and he soon fell asleep; but afterwards he said he felt so pleased he'd like to have more visitors: 'Perhaps they'll help me get better.'

From the outset I kept family, close friends and colleagues up to date with John's progress: Mama in Hobart and Lehene in London, John's mother, Marcia, and half-sister, Gillian, both in Hobart. His room was filled with their flowers and cards sending their love and wishing him well. But his fragile condition had ruled out visits. Now, one week after his operation he seemed to have turned the corner.

Next morning, Sunday, as I made my way to John's room, the surgeon stopped me in the corridor. John's condition had changed. Overnight, he had become feverish and had a temperature of 38° Celsius. He had also developed a lung infection and was now being treated with antibiotics through an intravenous drip. Importantly, the surgeon repeated his conversation with John's doctor who had agreed that if John's condition worsened, 'putting him on a life support system wouldn't be appropriate'.

My heart sank as I realised that John still might not come home.

Nonetheless, in the succeeding days as he enjoyed visits from friends and family, I clung to hope. As John told his cousin Paul Watkins, who had asked him about his operation: 'The surgeon said if I didn't have the operation, I'd die, but even if I did have the operation, I still might die. But my operation's been very successful. I'm not going to be out of here in a hurry. What I need is lots of rest and then I'll be all right.'

Yet a fortnight after the operation, John barely had strength to sip from a straw. On the Saturday afternoon when John's sister,

Gillian, had arrived to visit, I leant over his head on the pillow, saw his eyes closed contentedly and asked, 'Is there anything you want, my love?'

'No thank you, darling,' he replied ever so softly.

They were to be his last words before he drowsed off into his final sleep.

For the next four days and nights I stayed with John as he lay unconscious in his room. I slept on a fold-up bed at the end of his. I ushered visitors in and out and followed the example of the nurses and spoke to John as though he could still hear and understand. I wanted the present to continue and couldn't bear any thought of the future. While he continued his distinctive, deep, rhythmic breathing, his strong heart and his will to live kept us together in our shrinking world.

On Wednesday, shortly after midday, I had a light lunch of soup, salad and bread roll, which I ate while flicking through the *Age* yet still keeping an eye on John. Then I rose, went over and kissed him and told him I was going to lie down on the floor on my exercise mat. I was stretched out, my body beginning to loosen and relax, when I heard a nurse enter the room. I stayed on the floor, my eyes closed, but aware of John and the nurse. Then I heard her whisper, 'Helene.'

I was instantly on my feet, leaning over John, whose head faced me as he lay on his right side. I kissed him and said, 'Darling, I love you' as the blood rushed from his face and he breathed no more. I began to cry uncontrollably. With my arms around him and tears running down my face, I repeatedly pressed my lips all over his now ashen face and sunken cheeks. My sweetheart was dead.

I lingered for almost eight hours over John's still, silent body, shifting from disbelief to despair to calm acceptance. I sat staring into the blank nothingness of life. Then I kissed him one last time and dragged myself away, leaving him, in Byron's words, in 'the silence of that dreamless sleep'.

MARTIN, *John Winton* –
Lover, adviser and husband
of Helene Dorothy Chung,
died peacefully, at 1.30 pm,
Wednesday, 29 September 1993,
in Melbourne, aged 59.
A perfect union. Together always.

After John's funeral on the Monday, our home overflowed with family and friends and the fragrance of fresh spring blooms. With Mama, Lehene, Gillian and others there to pamper and support me, I had never felt so alone; with more people than ever before milling around, the house had never seemed so empty. I longed for John. He would have enjoyed himself. I expected him there, to open the door and greet the guests, to stand and uncork the wine on the bench, to pour the drinks and pass around the savouries. It was such an eerie experience to feel John's presence in every room but to know that he wasn't and could never be there again.

I had been to seven funerals in my life for relatives, friends or colleagues but until now, I had no understanding of the grief that death entails. I envied former ABC chairman Ken Myer and his wife Yasuko who had died together in a plane crash over Alaska in 1992, with neither left to mourn. With John's death I had forever lost a part of myself.

I felt as though I'd been plunged into an abyss, condemned to survive in darkness. For what seemed an interminable time, I functioned purely like a machine, telling myself each morning to get up, get dressed and get on with the day. I had no enthusiasm or any sense of purpose. I developed such distaste for material things that in Hobart I refused to accept a Christmas present from Mama. When I relented, it was only to suggest she give me Mal McKissock's *Coping with Grief*.

I became absorbed in my own internal world and relived my life with John. I examined his hospital records and visited the first and second surgeons to try to understand what had gone so disastrously wrong. I gave most of his clothes to his friends but kept several of his shirts and had them resized to fit me. I had photographs of John blown up and displayed throughout the house. I sifted through his private papers, reread the letters we wrote to each other, read the entries in his diaries and tried to enter his mind.

On the first anniversary of John's death, I realised that I'd survived the worst year of my life. Now, nothing that might befall me could be worse than that year. At the same time, I realised that I had gradually been drawn upwards, involuntarily and imperceptibly, and that I would eventually emerge into light.

In April 1994, seven months after John died, ABC colleague Peter Couchman had telephoned to ask me onto his lunchtime radio program. He planned to interview the Queensland-based counsellor Doris Zadanski on her new book, *Stuck for Words: What to Say to Someone Who is Grieving*. Suddenly, I found myself in a studio from where I had for three years presented an objective, impartial view of public affairs, including disasters in remote parts of the world. Now, I was subjective, revealing my interior world, my intimate feelings about John and the personal disaster of his death. As I answered questions from Peter and Doris, I sat alone in Melbourne not believing what was happening. Until John died, I'd always kept my feelings to myself, yet here was I – live on air – opening up to anyone who happened to be tuning in.

The response surprised me. I received more letters from listeners to that program than from listeners to any other broadcast I'd made. Although I thought myself incoherent and inarticulate, crying throughout, I seemed to have reached a number of people: 'I am writing because I was so moved by what you said and by your courage to speak publicly and because you are the only person who has put into words exactly what I have been experiencing since my husband died three years ago.'

Just after John died, I'd made a record for myself of our last days together. The words poured out of me onto the screen. Now, I took what was meant as a private memoir to the publisher of *Stuck for Words*, Hill of Content, and hours later Michelle Anderson phoned to say she would like to publish it. When *Gentle John My Love My Loss* appeared in 1995, the response it received renewed my sense of purpose.

September 1997. Diana and John. Worlds apart. Together now in that mysterious forever. A beautiful, sad calm. Resting, resting always. Gone, but only in the flesh. The spirit lives on. Triumphant.

A Sunday night. Time, in one of those patterns you set yourself, for Alistair Cooke, to listen to his *Letter from America* over soup and toast. But let's catch the first ten minutes of television news before switching to radio. What? She's dead? Diana? How come? Impossible. With Dodi, in Paris, a terrible car crash. One minute smiling, laughing, kissing, in love, bobbing in the water in her bathers in the south of France. Next minute, pffff, gone.

My pain, my memories, my loss.

Thank God we didn't split up. We almost did, in China, when I sent you off after that traumatic session with us both on our knees, crying, hugging but parting nonetheless. You did go – but hurt, crushed, perplexed. I know, I read your diary. But you came back. You weren't too proud. Cautious, yes, not wanting to be hurt again, but not so proud as to reject my pleas for you to return after I'd got rid of him, or at least after he made it clear he wasn't meant for me. He was right. You were the only one for me. I'm sorry for those weeks of insanity.

Along with millions of others I watched the funeral cortege but I was alone, alone with you. Just you and me. As her cortege reached the Wellington Memorial, I thought of us in the Citroën, with Lehene giving us a guided tour. 'You're going too fast,' you said. 'I can't see.' The bus was better, the upper deck of a London bus. There was also that night in the rear of the Rolls, up Regent Street on New Year's Eve, past Liberty's, the roof open and you standing up, excited, taking pictures of all the lights of Regent Street. They do that now in Melbourne, you know, and not just in Collins Street at the Paris end of town, but also elsewhere. Along St Kilda Road, where strings of fairy lights glitter, not just for the Arts Festival but also for every night of the year.

I read the story over breakfast, the same as the breakfast we used to have together, only now I have to squeeze the juice. I looked up from the newspaper, out to the courtyard, through the magnolia now in bloom and over to the apple tree. Your ashes, under the apple tree and covered with your own Madame Grégoire Staechelin roses. There's another camellia there now and a dwarf lilac and Lesley's mourning widow with its delicate sprigs of deep purple and black. Both look dead in winter, but burst into life in spring, in time for your anniversary.

In China I knew that John wrote copious letters, his 'ill-formed impressions', to friends and family but I didn't read them. It didn't occur to me to do so and I was too busy churning out my own ill-formed impressions for the ABC. Now that I read them I laughed and I cried. I'd not seen China with his clarity and wit. His letters also reminded me how, in the rush of adrenalin that drove me in those difficult and exhilarating years, I let my work jeopardise my relationship with John.

With his death I'd lost any interest in my job. Also, I'd been assigned to another program that neither inspired nor challenged me. For most of my life I'd worked around the clock for a modest sum at something that I loved. Now, I dragged myself to the office, switched on to automatic, got the job done, got my pay and I loathed it. It wasn't my style and it wasn't me. After the Liberal Party came to power in 1996 and Prime Minister John Howard slashed the ABC budget, I took the opportunity, as did half the Radio Australia staff, and left. As I pondered at a farewell function in the newsroom in November 1997:

> To leave, or not to leave, that is the question:
> Whether 'tis wiser in the mind to suffer
> The slings and arrows of outrageous cuts
> Or to take flight from a sea of trouble
> And by the package end them.

My formal departure took effect after the summer break, in January 1998, on my fifty-third birthday. Three decades after I rode on the back of the Tasmanian tiger, the career I began as a paff (public affairs) rejectee ended as a caff (current affairs) sackee.

Ever since I'd begun to read John's China letters, I'd thought of taking leave without pay. Now I was paid to leave. As ABC supremo Brian Johns presided over this mass dumping of staff, the former Penguin publisher who had accepted *Shouting from China*, my account of life as a foreign correspondent in Beijing, gave me another chance to write.

As soon as I began working on John's letters, my interest in life revived. I began to feel more, though never completely, myself again. After numerous drafts and changes of title, I was, in 2004, thrilled to see *Lazy Man in China* published by Pandanus with ninety colour photographs taken by John and me intertwined between the text of John's letters and my commentary. To update the story of China's transition from old communism to new capitalism, I'd returned to Beijing and Shanghai and stayed on Shanghai's famous waterfront, the Bund, at the Peace Hotel, where I'd also stayed with John and it seemed the most natural thing in the world to pen a postcard to him. Back in Melbourne I'd forgotten about it by the time it arrived in the post. Sad yet pleased, I read it, then I pinned it, as John would have done, on the noticeboard beside my desk. When I came to write the closing chapter, I happened to glance up and there it was, so I unpinned it and placed it on the last page:

Tue 11/6/02
10.45 pm

Darling John

I have walked my feet off in this fabulous city, trying to absorb some of its excitement, romance, seediness and culture. It certainly makes Beijing staid and sedate. The new architecture here is extraordinary – an imaginative blend of East and West, The towers are inspirational, not heavy monumental and overbearing as in the capital. Shanghai seems to throb with life. All it needs is my Shanghai adventurer-at-large.

Love Wo Wo xxx

31

The Twelve Apostles

At the base of Mount Wellington. I'm rugged up in a long brown sheepskin coat and suede boots. In sombre mood I wend my way through a crowd of familiar and unfamiliar faces into the sandstone cathedral. People bend over to sign condolence books; Mama, Lehene and I add our names. It doesn't seem real. So many people, so many walks of life, so many Chinese pouring in through the portals, along with the Antarctic chill.

Here, where we used to assemble, row after row of girls in green school uniforms and felt hats facing straight ahead but with eyes to the right to catch a glimpse of the boys in their grey. This day, only some are children; most are grown ups. I suppose I'm one of them. I don't feel grown up. Uncle Gordon was grown up. We move from the porch into the nave, down the centre aisle towards him, the rock upon whom the family was built. It's long, this aisle with Uncle Gordon at the end. At the funeral parlour yesterday his face looked just as I remembered it for as long as I could remember.

'We'll sit here.' Mama moves to the right and Lehene and I follow her into a pew. How strange: I've never been in church with my mother and sister before. With Lehene, yes, when Uncle Gordon took us to Sunday Mass, but only once with my mother, when I made my First Communion, but I can't remember Lehene being there.

That was when we lived over the shop. I haven't been there for years. Not even sure what it's used for. Uncle Gordon let it out.

'Bo Co,' I hear his voice. 'Now you tell Uncle what you want it for.' I scamper off with a shilling.

It was a Friday, 21 July 1995. Through rows of heads I looked at Uncle Gordon's coffin but I saw John's casket. I was transported back to that crisp spring morning, a Monday, 4 October 1993. I followed four of John's friends whom I'd chosen as pallbearers, to carry him shoulder-high into the chapel that swelled with the music of Palestrina. At the base of the altar John's coffin rested, glowing a golden brown and covered by a sheath of spring blooms. I couldn't believe he was up there, centre stage, not seated as a spectator beside me. But how wonderful that Michael Kelly had turned up, a Jesuit priest we knew from China forums, who arranged everything for me and conducted a beautiful secular service.

I refocused on Uncle Gordon's coffin in its wheeled stand in the cathedral. Had almost two years ticked by? I still felt raw.

'Twelve,' whispered Lehene in my ear. 'The twelve apostles.'

I counted the priests, all in white vestments, advancing into the sanctuary. 'With Monsignor Green,' I whispered back. 'The twelve apostles. Uncle Gordon would like that.'

He's already in heaven, I thought to myself as I replayed the previous Friday night's scene in my mind.

'Uncle Gordon's collapsed at Mass. He's unconscious, in intensive care at the Royal Hobart Hospital,' my distraught mother told me over the phone. 'Aunty Monica's with him.'

'What happened?'

'He was at St Joseph's, reading from the pulpit. He stepped down and then collapsed in front of the altar.' I listened, shocked. 'They gave him extreme unction, there, at the altar.'

'When? When did it happen?'

'Just now, this evening.'

'What was he doing there? I thought he went to Mass in the morning.'

'He does, every morning. Been going every morning for years. This was another Mass.'

'His second one?'

'For McMinn. You remember John McMinn: he managed the supermarket for Gordon.'

'Yes, of course I remember McMinn.' I pictured the pale-faced, buff-haired manager checking all the shelves as I, aged 10, stacked the refrigerator with Duck River butter.

'Gordon was at his Memorial Mass.'

I stayed on the line to call my cousin Monica, also in Melbourne and her sister Carol, in Sydney, the eldest of Uncle Gordon's nine children. Then I dialled Lehene in London.

Next morning, Saturday, at 6.30, when I was still snuggled up in bed, I was awakened by Mama.

'Uncle Gordon passed away at 3.45. He collapsed and didn't regain consciousness. I telephoned Lehene an hour ago. She's on her way.'

'I had to come for Uncle Gordon,' Lehene said as Mama fussed over us both back at Lambert Avenue. 'There'll never be another family reunion like this one.'

Monsignor Philip Green in his vestments looked out from the pulpit:

> On December 3, 1940, Gordon Henry, with his brother Lester and sisters Dorothy and Marie, stood in this cathedral and sought from the Church – baptism. The exquisite colours in the stained glass window depicting Our Lady of China which Gordon organised for the church will glow always as a reminder of the significance of that event. From that moment Gordon, with his usual drive and enthusiasm, immersed himself in that love story and became a powerful and active witness to the Risen Christ in this community.

My eyes caught the side of Aunty Joyce's face, her devout expression, her silver hair, and I remembered her story of how she had introduced the faith to the family.

She first heard mention of Christianity and Christ's love as a schoolgirl in Tasmania, at Hobart Ladies' College and St Mary's College. But she found that there were lots of churches, they were all different and they all competed for souls. As there's only one God, she thought, there must be only one true Church. She prayed to Our Lord until she heard His call to the Holy Catholic Church.

When she asked her father for permission to be baptised, he refused. 'I'm sorry, Joyce,' he said, 'but no daughter of mine can be baptised.'

In China in the 1930s, like Gordon and Lester, Joyce too boarded in Canton. As a teenager without any Chinese schooling, she was too old for primary school so she enrolled in a Protestant boarding school designed for married ladies whose husbands wanted them to learn reading and writing. It was very strict and stressed the Bible. Joyce puzzled the teachers, whom she didn't like, with her knowledge of scripture. After a while, each fortnight on her free Sunday afternoon, she took herself off to the nuns at the Catholic convent school.

When she turned sixteen, the principal put it to her: 'Joyce, you've been visiting us for nine months. We didn't ask you to visit. But still you visit. You're old enough now to decide for yourself if you'd like to be baptised.'

'Oh, Reverend Mother,' she said, 'I so much want to be a Catholic.'

'But what would you do if your parents disowned you?'

'I'd come and stay here with you.'

'Still, I think you should tell your father. I think you should write to him.'

From Toishan Grandfather gave his permission. 'Now that you're becoming a Catholic,' he wrote, 'be a good one.'

Aunty Joyce was baptised in 1933 under the neo-Gothic twin towers of Canton cathedral.

*

I watched the altar boys. Adrian, grandson to my uncle and my father, wore a white alb and cincture; he was swinging the censor on its chain. Puffs of smoke rose and the acrid-sweet smell of incense assailed my nostrils. Once again I was back in my green school tunic and blazer and envious of boys. Why couldn't there be altar girls? Lehene knelt beside me. I remember her dressed as a bride. We're on the front verandah of her classmate Mary Imlach's home. Lehene is swathed in white lace, a full-length white lace dress and a white lace veil cascading almost to the floor. Holding a bouquet tied with white ribbon, she smiles sweetly to camera. To her left, a pace behind, Mary is in attendance, the bridesmaid in three-quarter-length frock and brimmed hat with floral trim. To camera right, I'm the priest in altar boy's black and white, the bible open in my hands. Two pigtails flap against the sides of my stiff, white collar as I gawk rather than smile, a middle tooth missing from my upper jaw. It's about 1952, when I'm seven.

Now, at fifty, my moment arrived. I passed through the altar rail into the sanctum for the first time. Nervous, I genuflected before the altar and mounted the steps into the pulpit. Before me sat Aunty Monica and my cousins. Stretched out on both sides behind them, from stained glass to stained glass, St Mary's Cathedral was full to overflowing with family, friends and associates. I glanced up to the choir in the loft and then down to Isaiah, chapter 25, verses 6 to 9:

> And in this mountain shall the Lord of hosts make unto all people a feast of fat things, a feast of wines on the lees, of fat things full of marrow, of wines on the lees well refined ...
>
> He will swallow up death in victory; and the Lord God will wipe away tears from off all faces ...
>
> And it shall be said on that day, Lo, this *is* our God; we have waited for him and he will save us: this *is* the Lord; we have waited for him, we will be glad and rejoice in his salvation.

I resumed my place, imagining Uncle Gordon's voice, 'Thank you, Bo Co.'

When it came time for Holy Communion people spilt down the aisles to the altar to receive the host, representing Our Lord, and drink of the wine, representing His blood. Mama, Lehene and I, as non-practising – or, as John would say, cultural – Catholics, stayed in our seats. As suited, jacketed and weatherproofed bodies of varying contour, colour, height and age drifted to our left, Lehene and I simultaneously elbowed each other like twelve year olds. A slim man in a brown tweed coat, his neatly combed black hair slightly greying at the sides, proceeded with other communicants down the aisle: our father, who we knew was of neither Catholic nor any other Christian persuasion. What would Mother Imelda say? I wasn't sure what Uncle Gordon made of it, but this is a postmodern, ecumenical era.

At the end of Requiem Mass, as I made my way out of the pew, I peered between mourners to see the stained glass window that commemorates Ah Gong and Ah Hool. Designed by Professor Lou of Beijing University, it's composed of three frames, with an inscription that runs across the base of the frames: 'In Loving Memory, Our Lady of China, Mary Lum & Gen Chung Henry'. Our Lady of China is willowy and reminded me of the holy cards I'd been given as a child by Father Wong, the Chinese priest who lived in Hobart for a time in the 1950s. I'd been struck by seeing Our Lady with Chinese features and especially struck by seeing such a slender Chinese face. Until then, most of the Chinese I'd seen in Hobart had the more rounded faces of southern, Cantonese Chinese. Now, as an adult, I realised that Professor Lou of northern China had given his Chinese lady, like the lady in the holy cards, the stature and figure of a northern lady. On the stained glass window, Our Lady of China has downcast almond eyes, flowing black hair falling onto her shoulders and her long flowing robes, and nestled in her left arm is the infant Jesus, who is supported by her slender right hand placed against his chest: he is clothed in red, the Chinese colour of good luck.

I stepped into the aisle and joined the others. We flowed down the aisle and out the heavy doors, just as we'd done in our school class groups all those years before.

Outside, the sun shone as all the mourners mingled with each other and with Aunty Monica cloaked in black: Carol down from Sydney with the twins, Chubby over from Melbourne and her two grown so tall, Debbie and Phil with their little Yum Yums, Madeleine so like Aunty Monica, Boodles a man about town, young Norm standing back for others, the Nucks Nucks whom I hadn't seen for a thousand years, Atum her hair gone completely grey, even Dickie over there, that stooped old Chinese whose name I'd never known, Peter Chung still fresh-faced and Aileen doing well, Aunty Marie with Butchy grown a beard, the two good-looking brothers we called Sydney and Melbourne, that politician whatsisname always in the papers, and a buxom woman with feathers in her hat chatting to the priest.

Mama, Lehene and I climbed into a grey limousine to go in procession to the Pontville cemetery.

'Why aren't we going to Cornelian Bay? Ah Hool and Ah Goong are buried there.' I remembered my childhood visits there with Lehene, when we played hide-and-seek amid the pines in a maze of granite and marble graves. At the time of Grandfather's death, when Mama was fifteen, she had helped Grandmother dress her father in his best suit and fit his feet into his best shoes. She couldn't believe what she was doing.

'He must have enough to look after himself in the afterlife.' Her mother wept as she folded crisp £1 notes and slipped them into his pockets.

The undertakers, dressed in morning suits, climbed upstairs and lifted his body into a special tin coffin that was designed to be disinterred to enable him to be returned to the motherland. They laid the tin coffin inside a solid blackwood coffin.

'He's worked hard all his life,' her mother sobbed. 'He's gone without. I want him to have the best coffin there is.'

Ah Goong never was returned to China.

*

'Cornelian Bay's full,' Mama, dressed in her grey woollen outfit and long grey scarf, explained as she disappeared into the grey interior of the vehicle. 'Gordon bought a double plot at Pontville when he came back from Melbourne. He must have known.'

I pondered on my uncle, when I last saw him, in Melbourne in May. He and my aunt had stayed the night and in the morning I dropped them off to see the doctor. 'He'd lost a little of his lustre,' I said, 'but he was active to the end. What a way to go: a heart attack and straight to heaven.'

'I want a Requiem Mass when I die,' Mama startled us both.

'What?' Lehene stared at her. 'When did you last go to Mass?'

'I don't know.'

'Well, you'd better start going if you want a Requiem Mass.'

'But you won't get the twelve apostles,' I added.

And we all laughed.

At Pontville Cemetery, which spreads out wide and open with unlimited space, so different from Cornelian Bay, Uncle Gordon received a Tasmanian burial with Chinese characteristics. Two ribbons in white – the Chinese colour of mourning – with black Chinese lettering adorned his coffin.

Bai, or white, means pure, plain or blank. In a remote part of Fujian, John and I chanced upon a funeral procession in which all the mourners, even little children, were dressed in white jackets and several wore tall white hats. On another occasion, in Guangdong Province, I wandered over a hillside, which Chinese regard as auspicious, to see the graves of Chinese who had returned from Australia to die. One was the grave of a market gardener who had worked for thirty years for the Sydney firm of Wing On & Co. which grew into one of the great department stores in Shanghai and Hong Kong. The inscription said that he died aged 89 in 1965, that his wife was buried beside him and that the site was also prepared for the concubine who had survived him. All the graves were marked by smooth white headstones, each inscribed with details of the deceased. All the headstones faced south, towards New Gold Mountain.

Later, my aunt would have white cards printed: each had a black ribbon and my uncle's name inscribed in black in Chinese characters and in English: Gordon Yian Henry OAM JP.

Meanwhile, at the Pontville Cemetery, a man went around and distributed $2 coins to everyone.

'What do I do with this?' Lehene asked.

I thought we might have been meant to drop the coins into the grave. But the man said, 'Keep it, for good luck.'

Paper money plays a role in the Ching Ming or Qing Ming festival (Clear and Bright festival) that honours the dead and is held in early April, the exact day determined by the date of the winter solstice. Ching Ming is a public holiday in Hong Kong but not on the mainland, where Mao abolished so-called feudal practices, although this and other traditions have now been revived. On this day Chinese families sweep the gravesides clean, young and old bow and pay their respects to their ancestors, place food, including roast pork, fruit and sweets, on the graves and burn incense sticks and paper money to provide for the afterlife of the deceased.

At Uncle Gordon's graveside our father wandered among the mourners. When we spotted him, Lehene seized the opportunity. 'Oh, let's get a photo. Mama, wait there.'

We approached him. 'Hello, Daddy. Could we have a photograph?' Lehene asked.

He didn't object.

'Now, you stand here next to Daddy.' She positioned me and dashed away, to reappear seconds later with our mother.

'Oh, no.' He skulked off.

'You just have one with Daddy,' Mama insisted.

Lehene persuaded him to come back. Click: Lehene, in her black rain cape, to his left; I, in my brown sheepskin, to his right. We flank our father at the cemetery. It's the only photograph of the three of us. Of the hundreds, probably thousands of photographs in our collection, not a single photograph exists of all four of us.

On that cold July day in Tasmania, the place of the dead was the only place that I almost found myself with my complete family. The one chance of a lifetime – lost.

32

Jekyll and Hyde on Harley

In the biting final weeks of December 2000, I made regular trips to 97 Harley Street.

Treading warily through the snow outside her front door, Lehene was wrapped in a red woollen coat, a red cashmere scarf, red sheepskin gloves and my black fox fur hat that I bought in Canada. From Hampstead Garden Suburb we taxied around the heath extension up to Highgate (not far from the work and company Lehene enjoyed as a part-time librarian in Haringey), down through St John's Wood, past Regent's Park and London Zoo and into Harley Street. Here, she trusted – and I hoped – that she would be cured.

After waiting while Lehene was treated with megadoses of vitamin C, pumped through veins of her arm, against cancer, I pulled on my mink hat.

'Go on, buy it,' Lehene had urged at a Liberty sale back in the 1970s. 'You'd be mad not to.'

I braced myself for the outside. David, who had been disabled by an accident at an early age and used a walking stick, who had regularly undergone surgery and been nursed by Lehene, was by this time in his mid seventies and in increasing need of care. Now that Lehene barely had strength to care for herself, she could no longer take care of him, so he had to hire home help and on this day had asked me to pick up something in the West End. I was glad to go; I also needed a bite to eat and to exercise in the open.

As I walked along Harley Street the row of Regency terraces took me back to my first visit to London, when, at twenty-six, I landed at the end of summer 1971 relatively unscathed by life's realities.

My sole encounter with 'time's winged chariot' had been Rex's death in 1966. Rex had fostered in me not only an interest in English literature, the stage and broadcasting, but also in England itself, in particular London. I pictured him very much alive and an integral – though spurned – part of the Old Country.

When Rex began living with Mama, I considered him to be an Englishman who had been transported as a baby to New Zealand. On their first meeting in Sydney, he regaled her with his life story before charming listeners in Hobart with his deep, rich voice.

I don't remember Harley Street on the Monopoly board, but long before my endless window shopping in London's West End and my exploration of Mayfair and Marylebone made my knees sag and my feet ache, I knew of Harley Street. It far surpassed Macquarie Street in Hobart and Collins Street in Melbourne. Harley Street epitomised the best of medical care. Any doctor, dentist or other medical consultant worth his fees aimed for a brass plaque in Harley Street.

When I made an appointment with a Harley Street dentist and mounted the few steps to his rooms, I believed I was receiving top treatment. As I opened my mouth uncomfortably wide to be prodded with fine steel instruments, I also knew – but didn't say and couldn't say – that I had a special connection to Harley Street.

I examined the white street signs – Harley Street W1 – and imagined Rex as a baby born into the de Walden family. His aunt, I'd been told, had owned the whole of Harley Street. At various points along the street, I noticed the name of Howard de Walden attached to the black cast iron railings of the terraces. I felt a pang of sorrow for Rex's mother, an unfortunate wretch who had fallen pregnant to his aristocratic father. In her baby's interests – and to avoid scandal – she had given him up, allowed him to be banished to his uncle and aunt in the antipodes. Reared as his father's brother's child, he grew up as plain Rex Walden. His uncle and aunt had a son of their own but he, the illegitimate one, was the favourite.

I remembered Rex in his gold-buttoned reefer jacket. I'd never seen or heard of such a garment until he appeared from the mainland resplendent in his. And I remembered his tale of visiting London during the Second World War: 'I was in the navy – served on the *Belfast* – and met my cousin at his club. He said to me, "I hear you married a native, old boy."'

He chortled – and so did we – at the upper crust condescension towards his Maori wife.

So I thought of Rex after his death. As I wrote on 20 December 1971:

Dear Mama

Quite an extraordinary thing. I've been looking forward to Canada for some time now. I simply adore travel. But as I sit here at Heathrow waiting for my flight call I feel flat and inert – doesn't seem to matter whether I go at all …

I've been thinking about Rex. I quite often do. And the more I hear the announcers in Britain on both radio and T.V. the more I realise he was world class. I sometimes think too that it's a loss to me personally that he's not here to give me a few clues on my sort of work. And I wonder to what extent in my radio field I'm following him?

Three decades on, in 2006, when I was seated at my computer in Melbourne with the jacaranda in view and the Burmese honeysuckle climbing outside the upper floor window, I called Rex's son Peter in Launceston.

In the course of the conversation he said, 'My grandmother –'

'You mean your mother, Noni's mother?'

'No, Rex's mother.'

'Rex's mother? In London?'

'No, in New Zealand.'

'Oh, you mean Rex's aunt?'

'No, Rex's mother.'

'In London.'

'In New Zealand.'

'New Zealand?'

'Listen, Wo Wo, I knew her when I was a little boy. She lived with us in Wellington.'

'Rex's own mother?'

'Yes. She was Jewish and his father was a travelling salesman. I've got my grandmother's birth certificate.'

I suddenly saw Rex's dark Jewish features, his prominent nose. I recalled those words of Shylock in *The Merchant of Venice* that I recited as a schoolgirl with Rex as my mentor:

Hath not a Jew eyes? hath not a Jew hands, organs, dimensions, senses, affections, passions? fed with the same food, hurt with the same weapons, subject to the same diseases, healed by the same means, warmed and cooled by the same winter and summer, as a Christian is? If you prick us, do we not bleed? if you tickle us, do we not laugh? if you poison us, do we not die? and if you wrong us, shall we not revenge?

'He was ashamed of being Jewish, Wo Wo. As for his cousin in London, he didn't exist. Dad never went near London. He wasn't in the navy. He'd suffered from rheumatic fever, which weakened his heart muscles and he had hammer toes. I've seen the discharge papers. He was called up but rejected as unfit for duty. I went through everything after Mum died. Dad was a Jekyll and Hyde character.'

I reeled.

Rex brought home a recording of the Robert Louis Stevenson story, *The Strange Case of Dr Jekyll and Mr Hyde*, which had intrigued me; I played it over and over again, frightened yet fascinated by the split personality of a man who could appear so good and yet be so evil. That's not to suggest any evil in Rex: he had no trace of evil. Nor was he a Walter Mitty character, fantasising a life that might have been. Rex didn't just fantasise – he lived his fantasies.

On Melbourne's 3AW he produced a regular radio feature, 'And So the Story Goes'. According to Peter, 'Dad used to tell a story, about Winston Churchill, Hitler, anyone. He was good at it.'

He had perfected the technique of storytelling. From his imagination, he created his own story of his life.

I phoned Mama in her Melbourne unit to tell her the truth of Rex's story.

'What! He made it all up? Told me a pack of lies? And I swallowed every word.' She laughed at her own gullibility.

When Peter set me straight about Rex, part of my childhood vanished, along with much of the meaning of Harley Street.

I wondered how Lehene would react.

33

Requiem: Saturday, 17 February 2001

St John's Church sits on a hill above the arts and crafts village of Richmond, twenty minutes' drive from Hobart. At 2 o'clock in the afternoon Monsignor Philip Green celebrated a Memorial Mass of Thanksgiving. At this Mass, where Mama and I received the Blessed Sacrament, I once again passed the altar rail and looked out onto the faces of the rows of mourners:

> It's been my painful privilege, since Lehene passed away in
> London in winter on New Year's day, to bring back to an Australia
> in summer some of her private papers. Among them is this
> treasure – a scroll to Lehene, beautifully scripted here in Hobart in
> the unmistakably flowing hand of Uncle Gordon.
>
> It's called 'Lehene':
>
> *To Lehene my niece as nice ever sweet.*
> *All praise admiration and regard should she reap.*
> *Of charm and delight with manners to please.*
> *Of friends and acquaintances she mixes with ease.*
> *Gentle of spirit with kindness imbued.*

Resplendent in dress and good taste pursued ...
Long years have passed ere she left these shores
Joy fills the air when homeward bound once more.

Lehene has now made her final journey home. There's little joy in the air. Mama and I have taken the saddest flight of our lives – with Lehene's ashes. Some of her ashes also remain with David in London.

The Australian ashes are destined for my courtyard garden in Melbourne, where, next to the Tasmanian Richmond rose and some new hellebores, they will rest with those of my darling John. Lehene was at John's ashes ceremony in 1993 and thought that burying his ashes in the garden, among his favourite plants, was a wonderful way to commemorate him. Just as I think of them both now, caring for each other in the spirit world, their physical remains will enrich the garden.

All of us have our own memories of Lehene – as family member, friend, or colleague. Let me share my memories of Lehene as my gentle, generous, kind, trusting and loving sister.

Lehene joined me in London in 1972. Together we went to Cairo and Luxor to be with Mama and Leslie. In that exceptionally bitter northern winter of 1972–73, Lehene, always fragile, caught pneumonia. She had already met David in London, so when she was well enough to travel she accepted his invitation to stay with him and London became home. But in twenty-eight years abroad Lehene never forgot the home of her birth and always sent presents for birthdays of family and friends in faraway Australia.

Lehene loved her husband's three children, her young cousins in Australia and all their children too. But the appearance of her own son in 1997, by then aged thirty-three, transformed Lehene.

In Hobart in her late teens Lehene fell in love with an engineering student, Brian Butler. A photograph taken at a Masonic Ball at the City Hall in 1962 shows the pair in formal attire: Lehene is wearing a long satin dress and matching stole and long gloves that reach to her elbows; Brian is wearing a dinner suit and bow tie. In another photograph, taken on a train to the National Park, he wears a suit and tie, his hair is neat and trim, his arms are around Lehene and both are smiling, not just to camera but to each other; they are in love.

Next year, in 1963, when she was nineteen, Lehene's worst fear was realised: she found that she was pregnant. The disgrace made her an outcast.

One evening, when I was staying with Uncle Gordon at Lenah Valley, I was on my way out the front door to an Old Nick rehearsal when Uncle Gordon said to me under his breath, so none of his children could hear, 'Oh, she's in the family way.'

'She said she only did it twice.'

'You only have to do it once.'

To fall pregnant in the 1960s was the worst fate that could befall a single girl. Some families disowned their fallen daughter; many banished her to a special institution behind closed walls to bear her shame out of sight.

The atmosphere at Longley was charged. I remember standing in front of the fireplace when I heard Leslie say, 'They could have the cottage. They could live there. I could move my things out and work up here.'

I was horrified. I could imagine nothing worse for Lehene than being condemned to living with a baby in the cottage at Longley. The cottage had no facilities to bring up a baby: a small bathroom, where the only basin was a metal bowl that sat on a bench across the bath, a narrow kitchen with a narrow kitchen bench and a blackened, old-fashioned stove, a shaded main room with nowhere to change a nappy. I wouldn't want Lehene to be stuck forever at Longley – the cottage or the house – with a baby. I stood, filled with fear for Lehene, but didn't voice a word.

Brian's parents, who lived in Burnie on Tasmania's northwest coast, drove down to Longley to discuss the predicament. Whatever was said that afternoon, the upshot was that Brian was given an ultimatum: marry

Lehene and forfeit his parents' financial support or abandon Lehene and stay on at university. Brian ditched Lehene. He broke her heart.

Would his parents have given him the same choice had he been careless with a fair-haired, blue-eyed girl named Lucy Jones? Had he defied them and stuck with Lehene, would his parents really have stopped paying his way? And, had the two married, would that have been in anyone's ultimate best interests?

Speculation aside, Lehene now had not only the turmoil of sin on her conscience, but also the dilemma of bearing an illegitimate baby. To a St Mary's College girl in early 1960s Hobart, sex outside of marriage damned her to hell, a conviction that could take years, if ever, to erase.

Long before the term 'Ms' existed, long before an unmarried woman dared admit to, let alone showed pride in, having a child, long before every child born received government support, illegitimacy carried a terrible stigma. Even if Lehene could bear for herself the upturned noses, the closed doors of nice homes, the sneers, the silences, the furtive looks as conversations ceased when she entered the room and the constant sensation of eyes peering at her, could she subject her own baby to even worse treatment by bullies and smarties and goody goodies on the school playground? She had experienced a childhood way outside the norm, so could she inflict upon her baby a life even further outside the norm?

Who would pay the bills? The rows we endured as children over who would pay for our upkeep made an indelible impression on Lehene. As she recalled as an adult: 'We had the best of everything, but what we had to go through to get it. No child should have to go through what we went through.'

With these thoughts churning in her mind, when Mama offered to look after the baby, Lehene was adamant, 'No, I don't want my baby being brought up at Longley.'

As it happened, Longley's distance from Hobart now proved useful as fewer people were likely to drop in there than to somewhere in town. Lehene took leave from the state library on the pretext that Mama was ill and needed Lehene to care for her. Wearing a loose grey-buttoned mohair cardigan that disguised her pregnancy, she regularly slipped in with Mama through the gynaecologist's back door, as the receptionist kept Lehene away from the stares of expectant married mothers, including anyone she knew. Then, on 13 December 1963 at Queen Alexandra Hospital in Battery Point, three months after her twentieth birthday Lehene gave birth to a baby boy.

> She followed the practice of the time and made the wrenching decision that her baby should be adopted.
> She wanted the best for her baby, opportunities afforded only by a stable married couple. To be a single mother in Hobart in 1963 was more unthinkable than it was to be Chinese.
> For thirty-three years Lehene kept her secret until, suddenly, at the age of fifty-three, she was reunited with her baby. By 1997 he had grown into a handsome young man, an engineer called Graham.

In 1982, ten years after she left Australia, Lehene returned for the first time, accompanying David who had a meeting in Melbourne at the headquarters of the International Wool Secretariat. While in Hobart introducing David around, she gave her address to the supervisor of adoptions at the Social Welfare Department in case her child should ever wish to contact her. As she lived abroad, she also gave Mama's and my contact details.

Fifteen years later, in January 1997, out of the blue, I received a letter from the department telling me it had recently heard from my nephew. I was so excited that I immediately telephoned the department and learnt that he was an engineer called Graham who lived in Melbourne. I quickly tracked him down over the phone, introduced myself and asked him to dinner. Over our meal I listened to Graham's story.

At the time he was born and his adoptive parents who lived interstate were notified to collect him, his adoptive mother, Jean, found there were no flights to Hobart available. Still, she somehow managed to get a seat on a special flight reserved for the governor-general so that on the return flight Graham began his life cradled in the arms of Australia's last British governor-general, Lord De L'Isle of the historic Penshurst Place and Gardens in Kent. As Jean and her husband, Andrew, an engineer, both much older than Lehene, were a loving, enlightened, professional Anglo-Saxon couple with means, they sent Graham to top private schools, took him overseas where he grew fluent in French, and enabled him to gain a doctorate in engineering that led him to a research position in Melbourne. He had grown up lavished with love but knowing that his real mother was Chinese. He decided to contact her.

Graham wanted to know everything about Lehene, so I said, 'Let's phone her.' In the thirty-three years Lehene had kept her secret, she had barely mentioned her baby. Now, not even thinking about how long a letter from Tasmania would take to reach London, I dialled Lehene's number and put Graham on the line. She was speechless.

Mama raced over from Hobart and embraced her grandson as the most wonderful young man in the world. Lehene and Graham exchanged letters, photographic portfolios and phone calls and, by Easter, they were about to meet in my living room. She waited, her chest tight with nerves while I opened the front door to Graham, shy and holding a bouquet of red roses. I led him down the corridor and left them alone.

> She experienced a mutual love such as she had never before experienced. A perfect bond, an intensity of love, an overwhelming joy, a completeness incomprehensible to the rest of us.
>
> All the maternal emotions she had repressed for thirty-three years exploded. A love like no other love. A love so powerful it changed Lehene. She put an acute accent on her name. She hoped to reduce the mispronunciation she had suffered all her life. She had her hair cut short – a completely new style. She projected a new, more confident image.

Graham flew to London, stayed with Lehene and David, and then mother and son drove south to Torquay for a holiday on the English coast just by themselves.

> My quiet, submissive sister suddenly found her voice. In response to an article on adoptions, Lehene wrote a letter to the *Times* of London and it was published. (She preferred the term 'natural mother', but the article referred to birth mother.)
>
> From Mrs Léhene Goodenday
>
> Sir, I am a so-called birth mother who has recently been reunited with my son who was adopted 34 years ago in Australia, where birth mothers and adoptees have equal access to each other.
>
> It took him several years to respond to a letter from the adoption agency informing him that I was available to be contacted. Like Michael Gove, he did not want to risk hurting his adoptive parents. He tells me he now feels "complete", much happier and far more confident because he knows his origins.
>
> The reunion has undoubtedly caused stress to both mothers as well as overwhelming joy for me, but surely the adoptee's interests are paramount? "Our" son is the only one in the adoption triangle who had no choice in being adopted.
>
> Yours faithfully,
> LÉHENE GOODENDAY,
> Bunkers Dip,
> Neville Drive, N2 0QR
> July 24.

Two months later, Lehene took the opportunity of Graham's presence in London to introduce him to her friends. With full support from David, who had always shared Lehene's secret, she held a reception at home for him and, to my surprise, my sister suddenly stepped onto a platform, called for attention and delivered a spell-binding speech. I had never before heard her speak before a crowd. Articulate and confident, she grew determined to develop aspects of her individuality long denied.

Back in Melbourne Graham kept in close touch with Lehene as well as with me, while on the phone from London Lehene talked about him incessantly to Mama in Hobart and to me in Melbourne. Lehene became obsessed with her baby, as she called him, just as he called her Mummy. She regretted the lost years. She yearned for those years of his childhood that she hadn't shared with him and that she could never share.

She seethed with contradictions. She was grateful that I had befriended him but also she berated me. Why did I have to take things into my own hands? Why did I have to meet him first? Why did Mama have to meet him first? We should have waited and let her meet him first. And what's more, Mama should have insisted that Lehene keep the baby, no matter what Lehene had said. Mama should have known better. But wasn't it wonderful that he had turned out the way he had: she had made the right decision; she had given him a chance. Lehene was thrilled, yet jealous, when he moved into my street. She wanted the details of every second that I spent with him, but with every detail that I gave her I jabbed her in the heart.

Meanwhile, Graham met and fell in love with a demure young Chinese girl. Lehene felt happy for him. When he got engaged, she was thrilled for him. At the same time she felt that she had only just found him and that now she had lost him again. She felt a knife go through her heart.

In mid June 1998 Lehene phoned to say she had a lump in her left breast and was to have surgery next day. Mama, who by now, like David, used a walking stick, was wheeled onto the next flight and seated beside me. Lehene's prognosis was good. A small lump was removed and her doctors gave her every chance of recovery if she undertook chemotherapy and radiotherapy. After her first chemo, Lehene stretched out on her yoga mat on the floor for a long while, then sat up and said, 'I can't take it. I'm not having any more.' She opted for complementary treatment and I stayed on in London to help her to recover.

Lehene flew to Australia for the wedding in 1999, Graham and his bride flew to London in 2000, and in August that year Lehene and David took their annual vacation in the south of France. They watched the fireworks at San Tropez, where, on 2 September, Lehene celebrated her 57th birthday. A week later, back in London, she felt a shortening of breath, a sign of a recurrence of her cancer. Again she felt unable to withstand conventional treatment and so opted for megadoses of vitamin C, administered in Harley Street. And, as the weeks went by, she gradually deteriorated.

> In the final five weeks of her illness, as her body weakened, her spirit and resolve strengthened. When Mama entered the hospital room and put her hands on her, Lehene felt as if she was being healed. She told me that Mama, by staying with her in her room, was helping her to get better.
>
> Yet that would be her last week, a week in which she looked out onto a sweeping view of Hampstead Heath and the historic house and garden of Kenwood where she enjoyed so many walks and open air concerts over the years.
>
> Despite orthodox medical opinion, Lehene was convinced to the end that she would recover. She sought to improve her immune system with the aid of complementary medicine. I wanted to believe it too and so kept on hoping. She believed she would live to help others who had experienced the pain of relinquishing their babies.
>
> On her final night, a Monday, shortly before 11.30, Lehene was assisted back from the bathroom and was sitting up in bed. She told me precisely how she wanted me to spread out her mohair blanket. Then I slipped out of the way as she adjusted the foot and head positions of her electronic bed with a remote

control pad. One nurse stood to her left, another to her right, reading her pulse.

I heard a low gasp and leapt to the foot of the bed. Lehene looked up at me, ever so intently, as though straining for something just out of reach. Was it for a bit more breath? A tear rolled from the outer edge of her left eye and was wiped away by the nurse to her right. Then, she closed Lehene's eyelids and lowered the head of the bed so Lehene lay flat. As I kissed my sister I don't think I realised – perhaps I didn't want to realise – that in that lightning time she had breathed her last. The sensation, I'm told, was probably like that of fainting. She was on no medication, not even aspirin, and in no pain. Her death was swift, painless, peaceful. In the hours that Dorothy sat praying beside Lehene until the new dawn, Mama believes she saw her daughter smile. In death, Lehene's spirit and her selfless love endure.

Now cracks a fragile heart. Goodnight, sweet Princess,
And flights of angels sing thee to thy rest.

Epilogue

Much of the account of my reaction to John's death in 'Double Ninth' is adapted from *Gentle John* and *Lazy Man in China*. Because I'd already written these two books, I didn't intend to dwell on John's death and my grief in *Ching Chong China Girl*, which I conceived purely as a memoir of my childhood and experience of being an Australian Chinese. But the manuscript developed way beyond that into advanced adulthood.

Similarly, though I knew I had to write about Lehene's death, I'd been reluctant to deal with the last period of her life, her private life, because I considered it too difficult and, perhaps, still forbidden territory. Graham's sudden appearance in 1997 and Lehene's joy in their reunion prompted me to write a 3000-word fictional account, 'My Sister's Secret', for the *Age* short story competition, something I'd never before attempted. I saw it as a loving tribute to Lehene, but she was furious. 'Don't you write about me again,' she warned. However, as a decade has passed since Lehene issued that injunction, and as she fervently wished to live to help others who have experienced the pain of relinquishing their babies, I'm now sharing Lehene's secret.

My extended family, Graham and Mama knew about this memoir from its inception. Many read drafts of chapters or listened to me read sections, and, although I've included nothing Mama expressly ruled out about her or the family, I've not checked everything with her. I'm anticipating a bit of 'Why did you have to include *that*?', or 'That's not how I remember it'.

I hope that, despite her advanced macular degeneration, and her type 2 diabetes, Mama manages to magnify and make out most of the text in between checking her blood-sugar levels. Alas, my mother has lost the figure that won her the title of Miss China 1942; she now belongs to the brigade of overweight Australians. I tell her that her weight is partly due to her healthy appetite (and, I suspect, to some of her diabetes medication).

In 1991 at Lambert Avenue she suffered a fall (possibly caused by her childhood rickets and leg irons that made her walk on her shins for years). She can no longer exercise as she used to, or garden or perform the headstands and other yoga postures she used to do daily to keep fit. When at her worst, she's had to be hoisted into an aircraft, wheeled on and off the tarmac, and has had to use a walking frame, but in her Melbourne unit she usually copes fine and gets around the crowded city by walking very slowly with the aid of her stick.

Mama takes herself out to lunch each day – she hasn't the space or energy to cook, she says – and insists that her spiritual healers keep her alive. When I speak to her about her weight, she accuses me of being only skin and bone. At such moments, I remember John's advice – 'Just listen to your mother and don't get into an argument' – and try to heed it, just as he heeded it himself.

Almost seven years after Lehene's death, on an urge to escape work on *Ching Chong China Girl* I suddenly find myself in India.

My travels begin in rain-sodden Calcutta, a city that oozes with incense, spices, poverty and rotting rubbish. In a Hindu temple, where mangy dogs anticipate fresh blood on the bespattered compound, I watch the ritual slaughter of a terrified goat, conducted to the beat of drums. At the gate to the arched and domed Victoria Memorial, a monkey performs. I wander into the grounds, gaze up at the statue of the seated Empress of India, and then pace through corridors and galleries that showcase life at the time when Calcutta ruled the raj. I wish that John were by my side.

I squash into an overnight train, assailed by whiffs of curry, body odours and the pong of the lavatory. In an open, eight-berth cabin, I score the middle of three tiers for a night filled with snoring, snorting and the chiming of a mobile phone, which reminds me of another rumbling overnight ride. The closed, four-bunk cabin John and I shared from Beijing to Datong seems luxurious by comparison, despite its incessant loud speaker extolling us with martial music and socialist propaganda in high-pitched Mandarin. This morning, the vendor swaying in with his pot of sweetened hot spiced chai is welcome.

In Varanasi, the holiest of Hindu cities, I'm wary of the wet road and try to avoid holy cowpats and pestering boys. Hindus believe that Varanasi is a propitious place in which to die, because death here frees a being from the cycle of birth and death and sends the soul straight to heaven. To bathe in the Ganges at Varanasi is to Hindus what the pilgrimage to Mecca is to Muslims.

Beggars line the steep *ghat* (steps) I descend to edge my way down to the river, where I board the bobbing boat. As light dawns, two oarsmen row us out from shore; other parties paddle by, and all around us candles flicker. The spectacle of the west bank gradually widens to reveal a series of *ghats* onto the Ganges, a mass of Hindu temples and spires of intricate Asian baroque jostling with Buddhist stupas, domed mosques, Christian bell towers, colonnaded buildings, arched rooftops of figurines, images of the auspicious one, Lord Shiva, and a multitude of the faithful. Bangled and bejewelled women in colourful saris, and men naked except for cloths around their loins, immerse their bodies in the river. Oblivious to its pollution from untreated sewage, they wash their clothes, shampoo their hair, brush their teeth, and fill brass pots with the blessed water, in the hope of spiritual cleansing.

The sun burns orange over the eastern bank. Smoke begins to rise from fires lit along the western bank.

The mourners – all of them men, many of whom are wearing white kurthas – gather around as smoke billows from the funeral pyre and the smell of sandalwood drifts across the water. The body of their loved one has been borne by the city's lowest caste Indians through the grimy streets and lanes of Varanasi. The ashes will be scattered, like those of the other 250 cremated each day; most are destined to fall into the waters of the City of Life.

Why do families choose strangers to bear the bodies of their loved ones? I wonder as we are rowed to shore. John's male friends carried his casket aloft into the chapel; otherwise, there seems to be no essential difference between an Indian funeral pyre and a Western cremation, which I chose for John and David chose for Lehene. Neither had expressed any preference, whereas Mama has always instructed, 'Whatever you do, don't put me in a home and don't cremate me.' Now, she not only insists on a Requiem Mass but also wants to be buried in the grounds of St John's Church in Richmond.

On the fourteenth anniversary of John's death, I fly into the sprawling cosmopolitan capital of Delhi to join the other 250 Australian delegates attending an Asialink conference on India. In my hotel room I relive the eight hours I stayed with John as he lay, silent, on his bed; the moment I kissed him for the last time and then tore myself away, wanting to stay and to die with him. Yet, here I am, in a strange and fascinating country with strangers whose company I enjoy. If John were with me, we would have so much fun together. Yet even though that's not the way it is, it's still fun. Life is worth living.

By the time the anniversary of John's funeral falls, the conference has moved to Agra, site of the Taj Mahal, mausoleum, symbol of love and death. I'm up early to see the Taj, bathed in the rising sun, from across the river, and return, missing John, in the afternoon crowds. As the reflection of white marble domes shimmers in the lake, more beautiful than in any image, I picture John at St Mark's Square by the Doge's Palace, transfixed by its pink façade that shimmers on the Venetian Lagoon.

After two weeks of heat and humidity, I journey overnight by train, then by bus, along a slow, winding track through steep wooded valleys into the foothills of the Himalayas, and on to Dharamsala, headquarters of the Dalai Lama.

Among wandering monks and worshippers, I enter the temple where His Holiness is said to worship before a gilt-painted statue of Buddha; the smoke of incense is all around. Guarded locked gates beneath a yellow hip roof lead to the Dalai Lama's home. In the Tibetan library complex that serves as Tibet's parliament in exile I examine cabinets of sacred texts. I mount pagoda-roofed monasteries, nestled in tiers among forests of pine, pass countless strings of orange, blue, yellow, emerald and white prayer flags, file through recreations of the Potala Palace and life in old Tibet. I watch a legion of robed monks follow the drumbeat to prayer and assemble in rows to chant as they sit cross-legged under layers of vermilion and saffron. I peep at sleeping babies and watch youngsters at play, all of them separated from their Tibetan parents, who want their children brought up freely in their own culture and religion, which China limits in Tibet. I visit the top-floor apartment where the Dalai Lama once stayed the night and enjoyed the views, the bed on which he slept, the modern bathroom that he used. Yet no one tells me where the Dalai Lama is or even if he's in residence here in Little Tibet.

'It's a question of security,' explains our guide, Sunil. 'No one can say.'

Which takes me back to the god-king's first visit to Australia in 1982. On that occasion, Mama and John joined me and the television crew as we filmed His Holiness at the airport and interviewed him in the private North Fitzroy house where he stayed. No security guards – robed or suited – stopped John from using his camera at close range, or me from introducing Mama and John to the smiling, self-styled 'simple Buddhist monk', who shook their hands and bestowed his blessing.

Another time and another place.

In India, as I begin each day, invigorated anew, the past imbues and enriches the present.

*

After nineteen days, I return to Melbourne and realise I didn't ask any Indian about Merle Oberon or her origins. My dip into the subcontinent has made me more aware of its massive contradictions, the gulf between rich and poor, the often violent tension between its religious and ethnic mix, and how the competing demands of democracy stifle Delhi's attempts to solve problems. I think of how Beijing's authoritarian regime can impose policies on the people and, while I detest China's widespread denial of human rights, I wish India could use such tenacity to clean the Ganges. Meanwhile, I have hundreds of images to download, hundreds of emails to scroll through, a stack of snail mail to sort. And then, a heavy bundle containing page proofs lands on the front verandah. It's back to the Ching Chong girl.

I've barely put away my two new *salwar kameez* (long, loose pants, tunic and shawl), longing to post one off to Lehene, when I collect Mama from her apartment and bring her home to my house for an evening with Gabrielle, Lehene's tireless 4-year-old granddaughter. Another little Ching Chong girl, Gabrielle lives and travels abroad with her parents. She speaks English and French but hardly any Chinese.

Acknowledgements

To my parents, Dorothy and Charles, not for my birth but for their divorce that catapulted me into the challenging childhood that, for better or worse, made me what I am. To my sister, Lehene, for putting up with me, though I wish she'd stood up to me. And to John, for so much happiness though I didn't expect him – or Lehene – to depart so soon.

To Monash Asia Institute for an honorary research fellowship that pays nothing but sounds better than nothing.

To family members, friends, colleagues, teachers (in habit or not), superiors, inferiors, rogues, bullies and others who inhabit these pages, thank you.

I am indebted to Australian Broadcasting Corporation, including its archives and Guy Tranter; Baillieu Library, the University of Melbourne; Monash University, especially Monash Asia Institute director Professor Marika Vicziany and Chinese studies librarian Dennis Kishere; Special Broadcasting Service; State Library of Victoria, St Helens History Room; St Mary's College; Archives Office of Tasmania, especially Margaret Glover; Tasmanian Parks and Wildlife Service; Queen Victoria Museum, especially Keeper of the Temple David Barratt; and the Victorian Writers' Centre.

To Chou Ping (Julie) Davis, widow of Neil Davis, for permission to quote from the letters Neil wrote to me; to editor in chief of the *Herald Sun*, Bruce Guthrie, for permission to use a substantial part of my *Herald* report on interviewing HRH The Princess Anne; and to Adrian Tame for permission to reproduce his article on me in the now defunct *Truth*.

To Maurice Alexander, Michael Anderson, Max Angus, David Balderstone, Tim Bowden, Pamela Caldwell, Charles Calvert, Emily Cheng, Marita Crothers, Professor Richard Cullen, Joan Faulkner, Professor Antonia Finnane, Andrew Fisher, Dr John Fitzgerald, Diana Giese, Pauline Hook, Dr Paul Jones, Sue Jones, Dr Robert Kamener, Michael Kelly SJ, Jill Kitson, Maurice Leong, Paul Macgregor, Geoffrey Millar, Marie Morrisby née Henry, Kate Ritchie, Dr Paul Rule, Dr Pauline Rule, Dr Norman Sanders, Mary and William Smith, John Thorpe, Garry Woodard and others for various forms of assistance.

To teachers and fellow students in creative writing at RMIT University for guidance and/or workshopping parts of my material, especially in the classes of Laurie Clancy, Penny Johnson, Olga Lorenzo, Di Websdale-Morrissey and Judy Womersley.

To Christine Niven and Nigel Sinnott for their suggestions after reading drafts.

And to ABC Books, especially the manager Stuart Neal for his decision to publish this, commissioning editor Jody Lee for her friendly efficient manner in coordinating all the elements of the production, Darian Causby for his imaginative design, and my editor, Sandra Goldbloom Zurbo, who has at times rescued me – and you – from my mistakes, and whose experience and expertise have greatly enhanced this memoir.

One or two individuals have undergone a slight change of identity while one or two nuns are composite characters.

In 'Foreign Devils' I embroider the account of my first taste of plum pudding with my adult experience of having it brought flaming to the table. Much of 'Alien in the Motherland' is condensed from a section of the same title in *Shouting from China*. And although 'What My Sister Might Say' draws on conversations with Lehene over the years, the final sentiment would fall outside the bounds of her modesty.

Helene Chung Martin
Melbourne, 2008

Sources

Conversations, consultations and correspondence over decades and recorded interviews with Dorothy Henry Greener in Hobart (on 22 and 24 December 1996) and Melbourne (on 5, 6 and 7 March 1998); consultations over years and a recorded interview with Joyce Lee née Henry in Hobart (on 27 December 1996); consultations and correspondence with Christopher Chung and Gordon Henry; conversations and correspondence with Lehene Goodenday née Chung, Neil Davis, Leslie Greener and John Martin; consultations and emails with Maple Chung, Phillip Chung, Guy Greener and Deborah Chung née Henry; consultations with Ivy Chung, Sim Chung, Robert Chung Gon, Bernard Lee and Peter Walden; and a recorded interview with Bill Butt and Ron Chintock in the presence of Peter Burns of the St Helens History Room and John Martin in Weldborough (on 23 December 1987).

References

This list of titles is not exhaustive, rather, it is a guide to the main works used in research for this book.

The opening words are adapted from Shakespeare's *King Lear* and the quotation from my farewell speech at the ABC in 'Double Ninth' is adapted from *Hamlet*, as are the final words of my eulogy to Lehene, in 'Requiem: Saturday, 17 February 2001, adapted from Horatio on the death of Hamlet.

Age, including 'The legend of Merle', 21 August 2002.
Cyril Aldred, *Egypt to the End of the Old Kingdom*, Thames and Hudson, London, 1965.
W. H. Auden & Christopher Isherwood, *Journey to a War*, Faber and Faber, London, 1973.
Tim Bowden, *One Crowded Hour*, Imprint, Sydney, 1990.
——, *Spooling Through: An Irreverent Memoir*, Allen & Unwin, Sydney, 2003.
Lord Byron, *The Poetical Works of Lord Byron*, Oxford University Press, London, 1945.
Jung Chang & Jon Halliday, *Mao: The Unknown Story*, Jonathan Cape, London, 2005.

Helene Chung, 'Middle Kingdom Downunder' and 'Ancestral Village', in H. Chung, *Shouting from China*, Penguin, Ringwood, 1988 (expanded edn, 1989).

——, '1985 Sunday October 6, Peking P.R.C.' in Jennifer Campbell (ed.), *Letters from Our Heart*, Hardie Grant, Melbourne, 2002.

Helene Chung Martin, 'Death and Ritual: An Australian–Chinese perspective', in 'Multicultural Aspects of Funerals', symposium papers, Australian Funeral Directors Association, Melbourne, 1996.

——, *Gentle John My Love My Loss*, Hill of Content, Melbourne, 1995.

——, *Lazy Man in China*, Pandanus, Canberra, 2004.

——, 'Tasmanian Tin Miners, Addicts and Merchants', Chinese Heritage of Australian Federation, <www.chaf.lib.latrobe.edu.au/stories/henry.htm>

——, 'The Reception is over', *Meanjin* Australasian, vol. 63. no. 2, 2004, pp. 108–118.

Willi Chung Sing, 'Record of Overseas Travel, 1950', *Journal of Chinese Australia*, 2 October 2006, <www.chaf.lib.latrobe.edu.au/jca/issue02/14Englishtrans.html>

Bill Cranfield (ed.), *All-Asia Guide*, The Far Eastern Economic Review Ltd, Hong Kong, 1984.

Christiane Desroches-Noblecourt, *Tutankhamen*, Penguin, Harmondsworth, 1965.

Fifteen Poets, Oxford University Press, London, 1941.

John Fitzgerald, *Big White Lie: Chinese Australians in White Australia*, UNSW Press, Sydney, 2007.

Diana Giese, 'Interview with Helene Chung Martin', Melbourne, 29 May 2000, TRC 4578, National Library of Australia.

——, 'Interview with Dorothy Henry Greener', Melbourne, 29 May 2000, TRC 4579, National Library of Australia.

Jean Gittins, *The Diggers from China*, Quartet Books, Melbourne, 1981.

Leslie Greener, 'A man may hate another but should not hate a whole nation', *Life Australia*, 15 May 1967, pp. 14–15.

——, *High Dam Over Nubia*, Cassell, London, 1962.

Charles Higham & Roy Moseley, *Princess Merle: The Romantic Life of Merle Oberon*, Coward McCann Inc., New York, 1983.

Maxine Hong Kingston, *China Men*, Picador, London, 1981.

——, *The Woman Warrior: Memoirs of a Girlhood Among Ghosts*, Allen Lane, London, 1977.

P. H. M. Jones, *Golden Guide to Hongkong and Macao*, The Far Eastern Economic Review Ltd, Hong Kong, 1969.

Christopher J. Koch, *Highways to a War*, Minerva, Melbourne, 1996.

Gregory Kratzmann, *A Steady Storm of Correspondence: Selected Letters of Gwen Harwood, 1943–1995*, University of Queensland Press, St Lucia, 2001.

Jeanie Lang, *Stories from Shakespeare*, Thomas Nelson, London, c. 1950.

John Le Carré, *The Honourable Schoolboy*, Hodder & Stoughton, London, 1977.

Colin Mackerras, *Modern China: A Chronology from 1842 to the present*, Thames and Hudson, London, 1982.

Andrew Marvell, *The Poems of Andrew Marvell*, Routledge & Kegan Paul, London, 1963.

Mercury, various issues, including Margaretta Pos, 'Bitter-sweet story in death of last Chinese', 24 December 1994.

Jan Morris, *Hong Kong*, Viking, London, 1988.

Mustafa Munir (ed.) *Prism: A Cultural Report and Record*, Egyptian Ministry of Culture and Information, vol. IV, issues 12–13, 1972.

David Noakes (producer), Maree Delofski (director), *The Trouble with Merle*, ABC TV, 29 August 2002.

Margaret Olds (ed.), *Australia Through Time*, Random House, Sydney 1998.

Cassandra Pybus, 'Lottie's Little Girl', in C. Pybus, *Till Apples Grow on an Orange Tree*, University of Queensland Press, St Lucia, 1998.

Lloyd Robson, *A History of Tasmania, vol. II Colony and State from 1856 to the 1980s*, Oxford University Press, Melbourne, 1991.

Joan Scott, *Celestial Sojourn: The Chinese on the Tinfields of North East Tasmania*, St Helens History Room, Tasmania, 1997.

Nicholas Shakespeare, 'Daughter of Tasmania', in N. Shakespeare, *In Tasmania*, Knopf, Sydney, 2004.

William Shakespeare, *The Complete Works of William Shakespeare*, Oxford University Press, London, 1905.

Ray Winfield Smith, 'Computer Helps Scholars Re-create an Egyptian Temple', *National Geographic*, vol. 138, no. 5, November 1970, pp. 634–55.

Jonathan D. Spence, *The Search for Modern China*, Hutchinson, London, 1990.

Tch sellst Myself Moi-même, Children's Self-portraits, International Children's Library, Munich, 1952.

Sunday Tasmanian, various issues.

Helen Vivian, 'Tasmania's Chinese Heritage: An Historical Record of Chinese Sites in North East Tasmania', Australian Heritage Commission and the Queen Victoria Museum, Launceston, 1985.

Oscar Wilde, *The Works of Oscar Wilde*, Collins, London, 1948.

Wu Qianlong & Mobo Gao, 'Decoding historical scripts in Chinese: The Tasmanian Chungs from Xinhui', *Journal of Chinese Australia*, La Trobe University, issue 2, October 2006, <www.chaf.lib.latrobe.edu.au/jca/issue02/14WuGao.html>

<www.trailofthetindragon.com>

Herman Ziock, *Guide to Egypt*, Lehnert & Landrock, Cairo, 1965.

Quotations

36 'children and fools speak true', John Lyly, *Endimion* (Bergen Evans, *Dictionary of Quotations*, Avenel Books, New York, 1968)

120 'I live in terror … ', Oscar Wilde, *Intentions*

184 'World's largest jigsaw puzzle', Ray Winfield Smith

293 'The silence of that dreamless sleep', Lord Byron, 'And Thou Art Dead'

311 'Time's winged chariot', Andrew Marvell, 'To his Coy Mistress'

Chinese names

This story begins in the 1880s when English speakers knew Chinese cities as Peking, Nanking, Amoy, Canton and so forth, using the conventional Wade-Giles romanisation that persisted into the 1980s. The ABC appointed me as Peking representative, switching to the Pinyin romanisation, Beijing, only in the last week of my posting, in July 1986.

When living in China I found most Chinese outside the capital used the traditional forms and preferred their own dialects; they resisted the central government's attempt to impose Mandarin throughout the nation. In Fujian, for example, only officials travelling with us from the north spoke of Xiamen. The locals called their provincial capital Amoy.

Similarly, in my ancestral county of Toishan, only a few government representatives referred to Taishan, a Mandarin term that, even today, Australian Chinese from the Four Counties don't seem to use as much as they use their dialect name, Toishan.

For consistency, therefore, I mostly adhere to the traditional names, especially in early sections of the book, while using Peking or Beijing as appropriate in later, especially contemporary, sections.

Conventional	Contemporary
Amoy	Xiamen (Shar-men)
Canton	Guangzhou (Gwong-jo)
Chin (first) dynasty	Qin
Ching (Manchu and last) dynasty	Qing
Nanking	Nanjing (Nan-jing)
Peking	Beijing (Bay-jing)
Sunwei (Sun-way) County or Sunwoi (Sun-woy County)	Xinhui (Shin-hway)
Toishan (Toy-shun) County	Taishan (Tye-shun)

TASMANIAN-CHINESE HOMELAND

CANTON (Guangzhou)

FOUR COUNTIES
SEE YUP (Si Yi)

HOPING (Kaiping)

YANPING (Enping)

TOISHAN (Taishan)

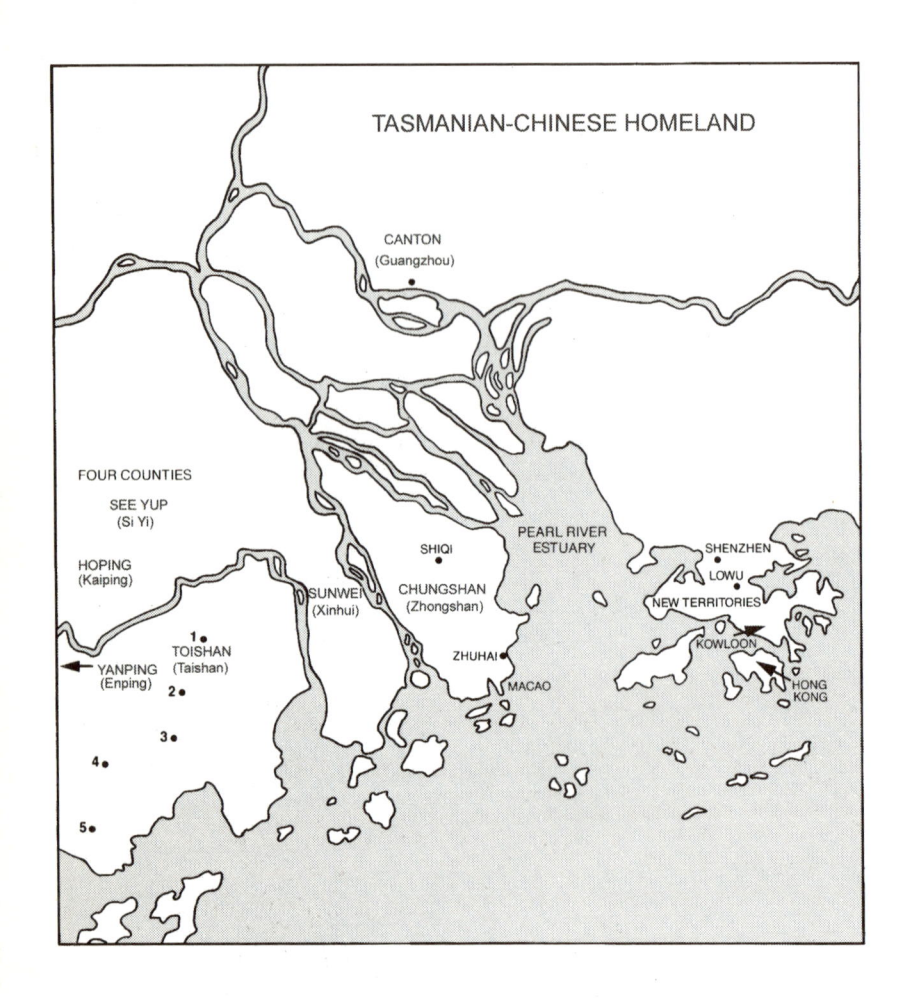

SUNWEI (Xinhui)

SHIQI

CHUNGSHAN (Zhongshan)

PEARL RIVER ESTUARY

ZHUHAI

MACAO

SHENZHEN
LOWU
NEW TERRITORIES
KOWLOON
HONG KONG

KEY

1 • TOISHAN (Taishan) - COUNTY CENTRE
2 • SAN FOU (Sanhe) - THREE UNITIES DISTRICT
3 • TAILONGDONG RESERVOIR
4 • SAM GING (Shenjing) - DEEP WELL DISTRICT
5 • MAN CHUN (Wencun) - MAN FAMILY DISTRICT

EAST AND CENTRAL CHINA

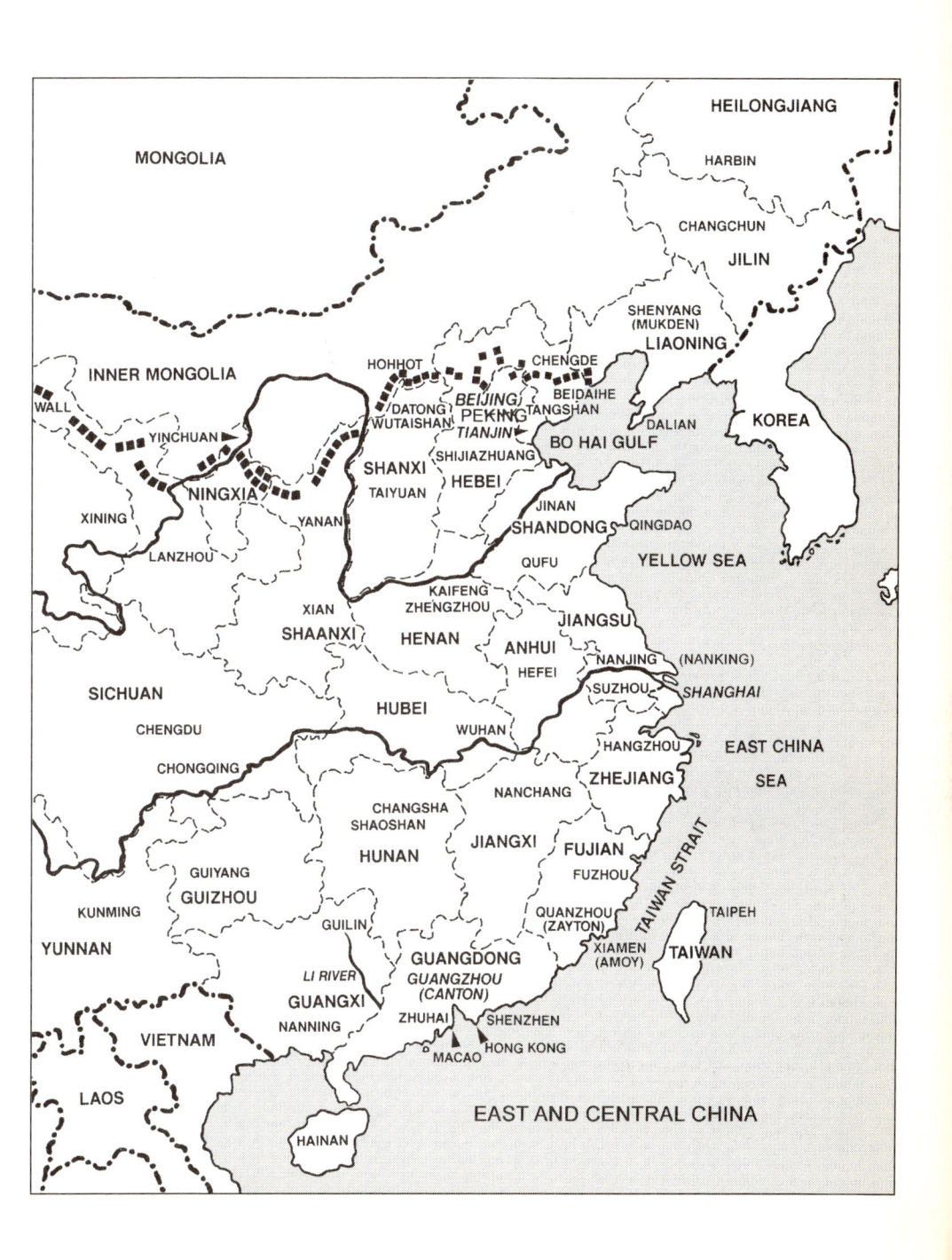

HENRY Family

originally **GIN/JIN** (Toishanese) or **GEN/YAN/YIAN** (Cantonese)

Maternal Great-grandfather **GIN Kee Chin** b Toishan County, tin miner

s Chung* (pron: *Jung* as in *Jungle*, GIN Chung/Gen Chung HENRY, Ah Goong) tin miner and fruit merchant 1885–1941

m Mary Lum Lee* (Ah Hool) 1891–1947

s Chung* (Jung) children	d Marie 1927 m Mervyn Press
s Gordon 1919–95 m Monica	d DOROTHY 1925 m Charles Chung*
s Lester 1921–86 m Eva* (Atum)	d LEHENE 1943–2001 (s Graham) m David Goodenday 1924
	d HELENE 1945 m John Martin 1933–93

d **Joyce*** 1916–2008   adpt 1916 s **Fon*** (Moonshine) 1913–88   s **Lester** 1921–86   d **DOROTHY** 1925   d **Marie** 1927
m **Timothy Lee**   m **Big Girl***   m **Eva*** (Atum)   m **Charles Chung***   m **Mervyn Press**

d Marie d Anne   s* d Laraine* dd Nuck Nucks   d d s d **Deborah** d d s d   d **LEHENE** 1943–2001   d **HELENE** 1945
                                                         m **Phillip Chung**   (s Graham)   m **John Martin** 1933–93
                                                         adpt s Michael   m David Goodenday 1924

Dorothy lives with **Rex Walden** 1920–66 (s Michael s Peter)
Dorothy m **Leslie Greener** 1900–74 (s Guy '**Pot**')

* Chinese-born

CHUNG Family

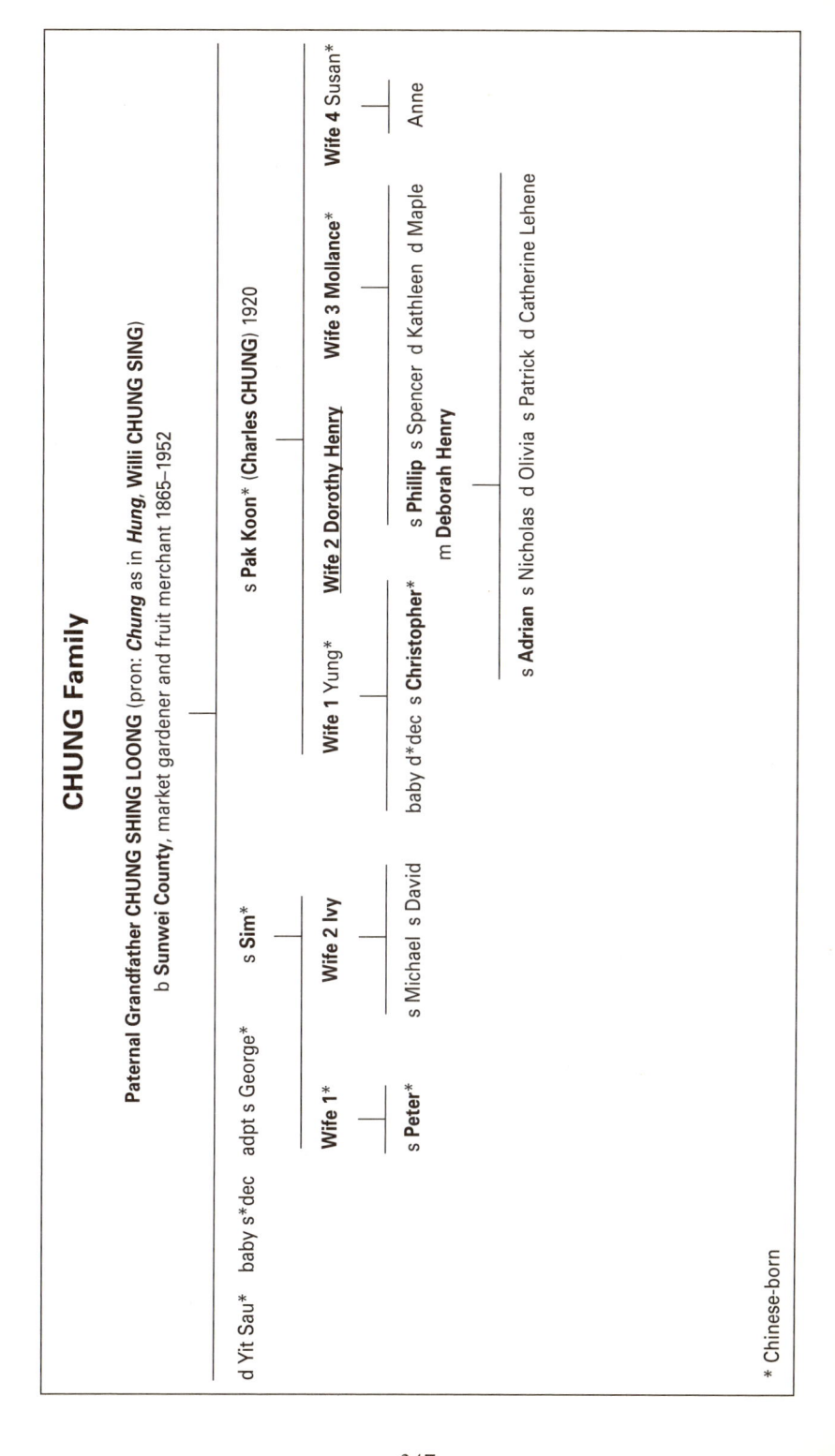

Paternal Grandfather CHUNG SHING LOONG (pron: *Chung* as in *Hung*, Willi CHUNG SING)
b **Sunwei County**, market gardener and fruit merchant 1865–1952

s **Sim***

s **Pak Koon*** (Charles CHUNG) 1920

Wife 1* / **Wife 2 Ivy** / **Wife 1** Yung* / **Wife 2 Dorothy Henry** / **Wife 3 Mollance*** / **Wife 4 Susan***

d Yit Sau* baby s*dec adpt s George*

s **Peter*** s Michael s David baby d*dec s **Christopher*** s **Phillip** s Spencer d Kathleen d Maple Anne
m **Deborah Henry**

s **Adrian** s Nicholas d Olivia s Patrick d Catherine Lehene

* Chinese-born

Index

ABC (Australian Broadcasting Corporation) *see also* Radio Australia
Argonauts Club 18, 37
chairman Myer on Mandarin course 229
electronic news gathering 230
HC fails to enter front door 120–1, 122, 199–200, 220–1, 222–3
HC farewells 297–8
HC interviewed on grief 295
Hobart radio 79, 121–3, 166
Hobart TV and culture 121, 200–5, 206, 210, 267
Howard budget cuts 297
London bureau 167, 168, 176, 180, 182, 190, 199–200
Melbourne TV 211, 212–7, 219–20, 222, 226, 329
Peking bureau 198, 220, 227, 230–1, 236–7, 279
race row over Chinese face 211, 213–7
radio drama 66, 84
Radio National 282
reference library 127
reporting guide 243, 246
schools' broadcasts 66, 79, 84
sexist policy 122, 200, 208, 221, 226

Singapore bureau 121, 132, 143, 227
Sydney radio and culture 122, 197–200, 201, 202, 221
television car crash 212–3
Tokyo bureau 220–1, 226
TV arts forum satirised 102
Visnews 126
war footage censored 132
Wran's libel suit 234
ABCs (Australian-born Chinese) ix, 148, 231
Aborigines 77, 118
Acropolis 135
ACT (Australian Capital Territory) Senate seat 204
Adelaide 124
   Arts Festival 106, 124
adoption 70, 319–22, 323, 325
Adult Education, Tas. 84, 198
Afghanistan 223
Africa 92, 167, 171
Age 198, 214, 216, 293, 325
Agilka Island, Egypt 195
Agra, India 328
Ah Foo, Jack 81
Ah Ham & Co. 12, 33, 275–6
Ah Louey 138
Akhenaten Temple Project 183–4, 191
Akhenaten, King 184, 185, 186
Akhetaten (Tell el Armarna) 184
Al Fayad, Dodo 296

Al Gomhuria 195
Al-Ahram 190
Alaska, Canada 294
Albee, Edward 105
Aldrin, Buzz 142
Alexander VI, Pope 211
Alexandria 85
Allah 240
Allen, Woody 113
amahs (maids) 138, 153, 157
AM (radio program) 122, 198, 201
AMEB (Australian Music Examinations Board) 74, 77, 100
Amenhotep III, King 185
Amenhotep IV, King 185
America's Cup 79–80
American Dream, The 105
American President Lines 144
Americans 144, 147, 159
Amoy (Xiamen), Fujian 239, 342
Amsterdam 283
ancestors 8, 23, 150, 219, 236, 243, 247, 249, 250, 271, 308
Angkor Wat 130
Angola 280
Angus, Max 45
Anne, HRH The Princess 164–5, 171–81, pic
Anouilh, Jean 77
Ansett Airlines 137
anti-Semitism 119, 120, 123
Apple Isle 137, 169
Arabs 188, 189, 193
archaeology 85, 87, 183, 247

Are You Being Served (TV comedy) 171
Arena (journal) 223
Arendt, Hannah 120
Aristophanes 105–6, 162
Armidale, NSW 104
Armistice Day 7
Armstrong, Louis (Satchmo) 141
Armstrong, Neil 142
Ashton, Julian (art school) 43
Asia 126, 127, 129, 135, 239, 280, 281
Asialink 328
Asians 103, 141
assimilation, policy of 2, 81
Associated Press newsagency 279
Aswan, Egypt 193, 195
Aten, sun god 184, 185
Athens 135, 144, 153, 162
    Drama Company 106
atomic bomb 221
Auden, W.H. 154
Australia ix, 129, 156, 190, 197, 198
Australia Council literary award 201
Australia House, London 167
Australian Japan Foundation journalist award 220, 221
Australian
    Colleges of Advanced Education, Federation of the Staff Associations of 205
    Embassy, Cairo 190, Peking 234, 235, 237, 286
    Imperial Force 85
    Journalists' Association 214
    Labor Party ix, 105, 197
    National University 80, 220
Australian Chinese ix, 123, 153, 231, 232, 234, 272, 325, 333, 342
Australians 143–4, 187
Avalon (picture theatre) 20
Avengers, The (TV show) 171

B-52 bombers 130
Babington Macaulay, Thomas 149
Bach, Johann Sebastian 18
Badcock, Lidia 70
Baghdad 221
Baillieu Library 127
Baldwin, John 104
Balfe, John Donnellan 209
Bali, Indonesia 129
Ballarat, Victoria 119
Bangkok 143, 279, 280, 283

Bangladesh 143
Barcelona, Spain 208
Barnett, Peter 132, 221
Barre, Martin 182
Bass Strait 72, 103, 127
Battery Point, Hobart 58, 207, 260, 319
Bauhaus architecture 211
BBC (British Broadcasting Corporation) 126, 167, 171, 176, 177, 190, 220
    African Service 167
    Broadcasting House (home service) 167, 172, 180
    Bush House (overseas service) 164, 167
    freelance fees 168–9
Beardsley, Aubrey 119
Beckett, Samuel 104–5
Beethoven, Ludwig van 74
Beihai Park (pr. Bay-high), Peking 27
Beijing (pr. Bay-jing) 342 *see also* Peking
Beijing Jeep 289
Beilharz, Wolfgang 212, 213
Beirut 221
Belloc, Hilaire 77
Benenden school, England 172
Benghazi, Libya 188
Bennetto, Gail 12
Berlin 70
Berlin Stories 70
Bethlehem 41, 113, 205
Bible 302
Big Girl *see* Fon Henry
Biggles 86
bin Laden, Osama 223
Birch, Tim 135, 151
Birds, The (film) 54
Black September terrorists 189
Blackman, Charles 43
Blain, Ellis 78, 79
Blain, Virginia 78
Blake, William 77
Bleriot, Louis and Bleriot monoplane 168
Blue Ensign 190
Blue Peter (TV show) 171
Blue Tier, Tas. 262–3
Blyton, Enid 29, 35, 54, 57, 58, 59
boats and ships 8, 33, 37, 58, 127, 144, 145, 148, 162–3, 185, 187, 203, 233, 236, 288, 327,
    Abel Tasman (car ferry) 249
    Gretel (yacht) 79
    HMS *Belfast* (battle cruiser) 312
    Lady Nelson (ship) 118

Lake Illawarra (bulk carrier) 202
President Taylor (cargo ship) 144, 147
SS *Macao* (ship) 162
Star Ferry (passenger ferry) 147
Taipooshan (cruise ship) 144, 162–3
Wan Fu (brigantine) 156
Boer War 84
Bombay 260
bound feet 251
Bowden, Tim 129, 200
Boxall, Ronald 165, 171–2, 174, 178
Boy Scouts 54, 75
Bradbury, David 280
Bradley, Jeff 279
Brendan, Sister 3, 82
Brighton, England 177
Briginshaw, Sue 43
Brisbane 11, 79, 104, 108, 149, 273
Britain 77, 84, 92, 120, 133, 136, 147, 149, 154, 155, 160, 162, 175, 177, 180, 183, 189, 206, 218, 245, 282, 311
British
    Embassy, Nanking 232
    Forces Broadcasting Service 169
    Museum 186
    Rail 168
Brodie, Sally and Graham 286
Brontë sisters 287
Bronte, Emily 260
Brooker, Eileen 42, 43
Brooks, Donald 151
Broom Lynne, James 104
Brown, Richard 124
Brussels 223
Buckingham Palace 164, 171, 174–5, 177
Buckley, Vincent 102
Buddha, The Life of the 38
Buddhism 130, 145, 161, 239, 327, 329
Bulletin 101
Burnie, Tas. 317
Burns, Gary 281
Burns, Peter and Kathleen 249, 253–60, 262–4, pic
Burton, Richard 78
Burvill, Tom (OfBedlam) 106
Bush House *see* BBC
Bush senior, President George 283
Butler, Brian 316–8
Butt, Bill 253–9, 262
Byron, Lord 293

349

CAAC (Civil Aviation
    Administration of China)
    230–3
Cabaret 70
Cabrini hospital, Melbourne
    282, 289
Cadbury Chocolate Factory 77
Cairo 182, 183, 184, 187–9,
    191–2, 316
    Khan el-Kalili 193
    Museum 187
    Tahrir Square 188–9, 191
Calcutta 326–7
California 150, 242, 272
    University of 203
Calvary Hospital, Hobart 14,
    62–3
Calvert, Charles 119
Cambodia 130–2, 134, 136
    US bombing of 129,
    130
Cambridge, University of 119,
    123, 173
Camillagate 181
Camille's Bread 104
Cameron, Clyde 201
Campbell, Stanley 286
Canada and Canadians 153,
    155, 161, 176, 310, 312
Canberra 80, 119, 129, 153,
    220, 228, 282
cancer 282, 283–6, 289, 310,
    322–3
Canice, Sister 92
Canton (Guangzhou) 7, 154,
    155, 231, 233–4, 235, 276
    Catholic cathedral 303
    Henry family property 7,
    277–8
Cape Town 84
Carington Smith, Jack 43
Carter, Howard 184, 186
Carver, Jean 75–6
caste system 238
Cat and Fiddle Arcade,
    Hobart 266
Cathay films 162
Catholic Church principles
    and practice 3, 20–1, 53,
    55, 101, 127
    baptism 9, 302
    confession 59–60
    fires of hell 28, 59, 69
    Henrys' conversion to 9,
    56, 302–3
    Holy Communion 20–1,
    40, 305, 315
    marriage 4, 35, 68–9, 318
    meat on Fridays 67–8
    Memorial Mass 302, 315
    Our Lady of China 302,
    305

Requiem Mass 301, 302–3,
    304–5
    sin 21, 53, 58–60, 67–8,
    68–9, 318
    Ten Commandments 35
Catholics and stigma of
    broken home 4
Cave, Peter 221, 226
CBC (Canadian Broadcasting
    Corporation) 176
CBS (Columbia Broadcasting
    Service) 131, 176
Cecilia, Sister 39
censorship 131, 132, 180,
    189–90
Central Office of Information,
    London 168, 169
Champs Elysées 209
Changi prison 85, 225
Channel 0–10 (10) 212, 216
Charles Davis hardware store,
    Hobart 44
Charles Fruit Stores 32, 266
Charles, HRH The Prince of
    Wales 181
Charlton, Michael 89
Chaucer, Geoffrey 19
Checker, Chubby 96
Chelsea, London 177
Chen Junyuan 231–3
Chiang Kai-shek 24, 232, 275
Chicago House, Luxor 93, 183
Chicago, University of 87
Chick's Own (comic) 46
childhood 44, 46–8, 53–66, 87,
    93, 109–10, 119, 125–6,
    154–5, 181, 265–7, 300,
    302, 304, 314, 318, 331
Children's Hour (radio
    program) 18
Chin, Emperor 27
Chin, Lee Lin 217
Chin, Maa Mon 248–9,
    251–2, 253, 256–7, 258
China Daily 230
China International Travel
    Service 153
China, imperial (221 BC–
    1911) 14, 27, 251
China, People's Republic of
    (PRC, 1949–) 97, 157,
    193, 229, 230–1271, 277,
    288, 289, 298–9, 301, 329
    and Australia 150–1,
    155–6, 198, 226, 247–8
    and United States 155,
    156, 283
    defence against Taiwan
    238
    Mao's Communist victory
    24, 238
    visas 153–4, 200, 228, 234

China, Republic of (ROC,
    1911–, Taiwan) 2, 12, 16,
    23, 24, 25, 32, 65, 136,
    150, 155, 238, 306
Chinatown 139, 141
Chinese
    acrobats 198
    artefacts 247
    in Hong Kong 136,
    149–50, 152–3, 157–8
    international teaching
    fellows 223, 282
    marriage customs 258,
    272–3
    motherland 7, 153–4, 229,
    236, 238, 239, 246,
    250, 278, 306, 333
    motor vehicles 232, 246
    names within families 24,
    46
    names, romanisation and
    confusion 248–9
    names, Wade-Giles and
    Pinyin romanisation
    342
    New Year 157–8, 234, 263
    opera 161, 231–2, 254
    physical features 305
    queues (pigtails) 235, 251
    refugees 154
    students 151, 239
    sweeping of graves 308
    temples 250, 257–8, 264
    tin miners 6, 235, 236,
    247–64
    tourists 239, 247–8
Chinese Australians ix *see also*
    Australian Chinese
Chinese Civil War 16, 24, 232,
    274–5
Chinese Foreign Affairs and
    officials 230, 233–4,
    237–41
Chinese god of war 251
Chinese language ix, 24, 25,
    46, 49, 80–1, 128, 139,
    147, 149–51, 161, 198,
    218, 224, 226–9, 241, 271,
    327, 342
Chinese Nationalist Party
    (Kuomintang) 10,
    24, 232
Ching Ming festival 308
Chintock, Lottie 259–62
Chintock, Old 261
Chintock, Ron 254–62
Chong, Lee Lee 242
Chopin, Frederic 18, 74
Christeller, Christian 177, 183,
    184, 185–7, 191, 208–9
Christie, Agatha 195
Christie, Bert 220

350

Christie's auction house 167–8
Chung family, Toishan (not related to HC) 244–5
Chung Gon, Teddy 11
Chung Goodenday, Lehene (sister, pr. Lay-heen) 1–5,13–6,18–9, 21–3, 26, 30–4,36, 41–5 passim, 44, 46, 48, 49, 51, 54–5, 57–8, 61–5, 67–9, 70, 72, 74, 78, 79–80, 81, 82, 83, 85, 86, 88, 90–8, 100, 102–3, 105–9 passim, 110–4, 118, 119, 120, 123, 127–9, 131, 135, 141, 153–5, 156, 165, 170, 173, 182, 183, 191–2, 191, 201, 209, 219–20, 218–9, 265–7, 272, 273, 280, 283–4, 284, 292–6 passim, 287, 302, 304, 305, 316–23, 308–9, 310–1, 314–5, 316, 318, 319, 320, 321, 322–4, 321, 321, 323, 325, 328
Chung Martin, Helene (pr. He-lane, Chung as in hung) see also Lehene Chung, Neil Davis, Leslie Greener, John Martin, Rex Walden ix, 1, 3, 4, 14, 15, 16, 18–21, 32–5, 34–8, 41–5, 49–52, 54, 66, 68–9, 70–2, 74, 79–5, 88–91, 93, 96–9, 102, 108–10, 113, 114, 116–7, 122, 123, 141, 152, 161, 162, 164, 165, 171, 172, 177, 182, 183, 184, 186, 199, 201, 202, 206, 208, 211–3, 216, 217, 218, 219, 195, 208, 209, 225, 226, 236–46, 248–9, 265–7, 271, 273, 277–8, 280, 288, 292, 294, 298, 300–2, 305–7, 308–9, 312, 314, 315, 316, 319–322, 323, 324–6, 330, 331, 342
Gentle John: My Love My Loss 296, 325
Lazy Man in China 298–9, 325
Shouting from China 271, 298, 333
Chung Sing & Co. 13, 265
Chung Sing, Willi (paternal grandfather) 12, 13, 14, 272–3, 274, 276, 277
Chung, Adrian (second cousin and half-nephew) 269, 304
Chung, Anne (half-sister) 266, 269

Chung, Charles (Pak Koon, father, pr. Chung as in hung) 12–3, 15, 32, 34–5, 49–52, 96, 109–10, 274, 266, 268, 304, 276, 308, 266, 96, 267, 271–3, 275–6
Chung, Christopher (half-brother) born and raised in China 270–8
Chung, Kathleen (half-sister) 266–7, 269
Chung, Maple (half-sister) 34, 266–7, 269
Chung, Peter (cousin) 265, 267, 274, 306
Chung, Phillip (half-brother) marries HC's cousin Deborah 266–9, 277, 306
Chung, Sim (uncle) and Ivy 365–6, 267, 275, 277
Chung, Spencer (half-brother) 266–7, 269
Chungking (pr. Choong-king, Chongqing) 232
Churchill, Sir Winston 314
Claremont, Tas. 77
Cleese, John 168
Cleopatra's Needle 193
Clinton, President Bill 283
Coleridge, Samuel Taylor 21, 27
Colombo Plan students 103
Colossi of Memnon 185
colours, significance of
  red 305
  white 307
Commercial Bank of Australia 9
Commercial High School, Hobart 10
Como, Perry 22
Confucian classics 27
Cooper, Lorraine 93
Coping with Grief 294
Copts 183
Cornelian Bay Cemetery 9, 16, 306, 307
Correspondents Report (radio program) 200
Couchman, Peter 295
County Court, Melbourne 127
Crawcour, Sydney 220
Crean, Frank 201
Crisp & Gunn 7
Cubbage, Robert 79
Cultural Revolution 234

Dabrowski, Anthony 2
Dacca 143
Daily Express 180
Daily Telegraph 167, 180

Dalai Lama 329
Dali, Salvador 116
D'Arcy, Archbishop Eric 1
Dargie, Sir William 43
Dateline London (radio program) 164
Datong, Shanxi 327
Dattilo Rubbo Art School, Antonio 43
Davies, Derek 135, 136, 151
Davis, George 121
Davis, Neil
  and Asia 126, 129
  and Cambodia 130–2, 134, 136
  changes course of HC's career 127, 136, 143–4, 162, 281
  dies filming attempted Bangkok coup 279–81
  generous 127, 134
  on Hong Kong 135–6, 143–4
  Indo-China War cameraman 126, 130–2, 133, 134, 136, 143
  and Singapore 126, 134, 136
  relationship with HC 124–7, 129–38 passim, 143–4, 147, 209
de Chardin, Pierre Teilhard 107
De L'Isle, Viscount William Sidney 320
de Walden family 311–2
Deakin University 205, 223
death 1, 5, 9, 16, 85, 107, 108, 188, 203, 228, 262, 275, 281–2, 285, 293, 294, 296, 301–2, 311, 324, 327
Death on the Nile 195
Delhi 328, 330
Delofski, Maree 260–1
democracy 236, 330
Dench, Judi 124
Deng Xiaoping (Chinese leader, pr. Derng Shiow-ping) 97
Depression, the Great 9
Derby, Tas. 248
Deveson, Anne 78, 79
Devlin, Bernadette 177
Devonport, Tas. 72, 249
Dharamsala, India 329
Diana, Princess of Wales 296
Diana: Her True Story 284
Die Fledermaus 161–2
dim sum see food and beverages
Dinky toys 86

Diplomatic Services Bureau, China 237
diplomats ix, 190, 226, 228
divorce 2, 4, 15, 35, 68–9, 88, 205, 268, 272, 276, 331
Doge's Palace 328
Donikian, George 217
Dover, Tas. 209
Downing, Malcolm 168
Dragon Field Village 8, 24, 25, 243–6, 249, 253
drug addiction 168, 176
Duckmanton, Talbot 216
Dunn, Marney 229
Dymphna, Mother 14

East Pakistan 143
East Sydney Technical College 43
Easter 70, 320
Egypt 85, 87, 88, 89, 110, 116, 130, 177, 182–96, 200, 208, 221
electronic news gathering (ENG) 220
Elizabeth Street State School, Hobart 7, 8, 9, 58, 79
Ellis, Havelock 107
Emma 174
Empire Day 8
Encounter (journal) 89
Encyclopaedia Britannica 114
England *see* Britain
English, spoken 77, 81, 93, 100, 201, 222, 232, 238, 271, 342
entombed warriors 240–1
Epworth Hospital, Melbourne 286
Euripides 162
Europe 77, 132, 135, 144, 162, 187, 192, 204
Europeans 138, 140, 183, 212, 248
    in Hong Kong 147–8, 149, 153, 157
Eurovision 132
Exit the King 104

Fan, Old (interpreter, pr. Fun) 231, 234, 241, pic
Fang Fei (pr. Fung Fay) 231, 232–3
Far Eastern Economic Review 135, 151
Fehlberg, Tas 45
Female Eunuch, The 173
Fern Tree, Tas. 82, 115, 125, 126, 209, 280, 281
Fifth Formers of St Clare's 58
Fire on the Snow, The 18
FitzGerald, Stephen 198, 226

Fitzgerald's department store, Hobart 99
Flatman, David 267
Flynn, Errol 131
Flynn, Sean 130, 131
food and beverages
    boarders 40, 114
    breakfast 63, 86, 107, 138, 148, 179, 221, 297
    buttered-up Hong Kong press 156
    CAAC 230
    Cantonese 30, 133, 150
    chicken's blood 55, 173
    Chinese 25, 30, 150
    Chinese wedding 271, 274
    Coca-Cola 238
    Continental (wog) 173–40
    couscous 209
    cream cakes 55, 67
    dairy products 30, 77, 84, 193, 274
    Devonshire tea 83, 84, 85, 250
    dim sum (touch the heart) 141, 158, 242
    Egyptian 193
    Fantales 261
    fish and chips 58, 68
    fish-head curry 227
    gaorou (dog meat) 241
    health 164, 172, 173–4, 179–80
    hamburgers 166
    hundred-year-old eggs 252
    Indian 327
    jook (porridge) 20, 252
    lamb, southern Chinese repelled by 30
    Lane's emulsion 63
    lup cheong (sausage) 48, 139
    lychees 25, 161
    maggot mornay 250
    mango management 160–1
    Mateus Rosé 154
    milk 25, 26, 28, 36, 50, 63–4, 77, 90, 93, 154, 261
    Peking Duck 159
    pet 90
    plum pudding 29–30, 332–3
    pre-multicultural 133
    school lunch 67–8
    seaweed 47–8
    Singaporean 139–41
    toasting sweet and strong 232–3
    toffee apples 159, 160
    vegetarian 167
    Western 22, 23, 25, 28
    yoghurt 36, 173, 174, 179, 180

foreign correspondents *see also* journalists 129, 130, 131, 133, 148, 190, 280, 298
    killed 130, 131, 279–81
Foreign Correspondents' Club, Hong Kong 148, 151
foreign devils (*fangwei*, pr. fung-gweer) 7, 23, 29, 83, 159, 229, 245, 251, 269
    features of 28, 31, 235
    Grandfather Gin's reaction to 235
Forsyte Saga, The 77
Four Corners (TV program) 234
Four Counties (See Yup) 150, 246, 342
France 12, 177, 208, 282, 296, 323
Franco, General Francisco 208
Freemasons Hospital, Melbourne 281, 289
French language 3, 36, 82, 85, 128, 173, 177, 208, 320
French Riviera 177
Frenchmen 36, 209
Friends' School, The, Hobart 85–6
Friendship with Foreign Countries, Association for 233
Frontline (film) 280
Fujian Province (Tasmania's sister province) 237–40, 342
    Australian trees 238, 239
funerals 9–10, 16, 107, 108, 139, 188–9, 294, 300, 301, 302–3, 304–8, 327–8
Fuzhou (pr. Foo-jo), Fujian 238, 239
Furlonger, Brian 221, 222

gambling 253–4, 257
Gang of Four 234
Ganges River, India 327, 330
Garibaldi, Tas. 250, 263–4
Gaza Strip 187
Geelong, Victoria 119, 205, 207, 211
Gent, Maurice 190
Gentle John: My Love My Loss see Helene Chung
Georges department store, Melbourne 43
Ghurkhas 152
Gilmore, Mary 78
Gin Jee Chin (maternal great-grandfather) 6–7, 27, 144, 233, 235–6, 242, 248–9, 250–63
Giza Strip, Egypt 187
God Save the Queen 77

Golden Fleece 37
Gold Mountain 150, 247, 272
Golders Green, London 123
Goodenday, David *see* Lehene Chung
Goons, The (radio comedy) 86
Gordon Institute of Technology 119, 205
Gordon, Murray 122
Government House 33, 124
Graham, Keith 80
Grassby, Al 216
Great Hall of the People 97, 236
Great Mosque, Xian 240
Great Leap Forward 275
Great Wall of China 27, 155–6, 237, pic
Greece 12, 135, 144, 194
Green, Monsignor Philip 1, 301, 301, 315
Greener, Guy (Pot, step-brother) 84, 85–6, 90, 115–116
Greener, Leslie (step-father) 74, 83–90, 110, 121, 129, 165, 182, 183–184, 186, 194, 201–202, 225–226
Greer, Germaine 173
Gregory, Gillian (half sister-in-law) and John 292, 294
Griffiths, Doris 22
Gropius, Walter 211
Grose, Mrs Bill 248–9, 252, 254
Guangdong Province (pr. Gwong-doong, NSW's sister province) 24, 150, 240–8 passim, 262, 307–8
Guangzhou (pr. Gwong-jo) *see* Canton
Guardian 180
Guy Fawkes 8

Hakkas 139, 154, 158
Haley, Bill 96
Hall, Lesley 297
Hampstead, London 218, 285, 323
Hansard's Parliamentary Debates 118, 120, 123
Haringey, London 310
Harley Street, London 167, 310–2, 314, 323
Harrison, Daryl 36–8
Harrison, Rowland 37, 105, pic
Harwood, Gwen 101–2, 108
Hastings Caves, Tas. 209
Haszard, Rhona see Leslie Greener
Hatshepsut, Queen 185

Hawke, Prime Minister Robert 151
Hawthorn Dene, Longley, Tas. 82–7, 88–91, 114, 115–6, 209, pic
Heath, Prime Minister Edward 177
Hegazi, Selwa (Mama) 188–9
Helsinki 132
Henri, René 46
Henry & Co. 9–28, 57, 135, 261, 265, 274
Henry Chung, Deborah (cousin and half sister-in-law) marries HC's half-brother Phillip 268–9, 306
Henry Greener, Dorothy (mother) *see also* Helene Chung and Lehene Chung, *see also* Rex Walden 2, 4, 7, 8, 10–15, 18, 20–4, 34–8, 40–7, 49–50, 56, 61, 64, 68–9, 79–80, 84, 90, 93–5, 98–9, 109–10, 117, 153–5, 173, 192, 219, 261, 268, 271, 273–4, 307–9, 320, 322, 324, 326, 329,
Henry Press, Marie (aunt), first Henry to marry a foreign devil 8, 28, 29, 56, 302, 306
Henry, Carol (cousin) 302, 306
Henry, Fon (Moonshine, adopted uncle) and Big Girl 23–7, 81, 116, 277–8
Henry, Gen Chung (maternal grandfather, pr. Jin Jung) 6–10, 16, 22–4, 250–8, 262–4, 277, 300–6, 308–9,
Henry, Gordon (uncle) 11, 19, 22, 23, 26, 35–8, 44–5, 48–50, 56, 61–2, 75, 88–9, 92, 100, 103, 109–10, 116, 135, 225, 251, 268, 277, 300–8, 315–317,
Henry, Laraine (cousin) 26
Henry, Lester (uncle) 7, 8, 15–24, 30–1, 36, 46–7, 49–50, 54, 56, 57, 61–2, 67, 70, 75, 89–90, 92–3, 96, 110, 124, 143, 149, 172, 175–6, 189, 212–3, 221, 225, 242, 253, 257, 258, 260, 296, 302, 306, 327–9
Hobart 7, 12, 15, 40, 43, 68, 79, 103, 104–5, 108, 133, 138, 141, 146, 173–4, 261, 265, 316, 319,
Hodge, Errol 222
Hodgkinson, Brian 133

Hodgman, Roger 105
Holland 282
Hollinshead, Peter 227
Hollywood 15, 259
Homfray, Peter 128
Hong Kong 97, 135, 145–63, 165, 166, 171–6 passim, 198, 218, 221, 226, 226, 227, 228, 230, 231, 235, 266, 275, 281, 307, 308
Hongkong Standard 180
Honi Soit (uni. newspaper) 106
Honolulu 283
Honourable Schoolboy, The 148
Horemheb, King 184
hotels 1, 46, 87, 94, 103, 108, 109, 131, 133, 138, 146, 147, 148, 152, 154, 156, 157, 160, 161, 184, 185, 191, 192, 194, 195, 196, 227, 228, 232, 233, 237, 250, 259, 288, 298, 299
Howard, Prime Minister John 297
Howe, Sir Geoffrey 97
Howell, Robbie 286
Howrah, Hobart 33
human rights 330
Humphries, Barry 214
Humphries, Kevin 234
Huon Valley, Tas. 82, 115, 169, 209
Huonville, Tas. 83, 209
Hutchins School, The, Hobart 169

I am a Camera 70
I Love Lucy (TV show) 89
illegitimacy 5, 262, 312, 318
Ilyushin 230
Imelda, Mother 3, 41, 52, 59, 101, 114, 161, 178, 305
immigration 2, 77, 123, 217,
India 143, 192, 260–1, 326–30
Indians 123, 138, 141, 142
Indo-China War 126, 130–2, 133, 136, 280, 281
Indo-Chinese refugees 123
Indonesia 133, 130, 138
Industrial Revolution 113
International Report (radio program) 282
International Wool Secretariat 192, 218, 319
Intervarsity Drama Festival 103, 104, 108
Ionesco, Eugene 104
Ireland 165, 167, 177, 206
Ireland, Mark 255
Irish immigrants 123
Irish Times 181
Isherwood, Christopher 70, 154

353

Israel 187, 188, 189
Israeli phantom rockets 188
Ivanoff, Peter 168

Jack and the Beanstalk (pantomime) 75–6
Jackson's newsagency 46
Jaguar Mk II 90–1, 110
Jakarta 129
Jamaica 44
Japan 155, 220–2, 223–6
 Airlines 223–4
 bullet train 221, 224, 229
 Edo era exhibition 219
 invades China 24, 232, 273
Japanese attack on foreigners 224–5
Japanese language 128, 220–1, 221–2, 224, 228, 229
Jesuits 127, 301
Jews 119–20, 123, 189, 313
 and homeland 189
Jiang Qing (Mao's wife, pr. Jiung Ching) 234
Jiangsu Province (pr. Jiung-su, Victoria's sister province) 231, 282
Johns, Brian 298
Jones, Geraldine 2
Jones, Margaret 198
jook see food and beverages
joss house *see* Chinese temples
journalism 78, 120, 235, 243
journalists 3, 78, 143–4, 152–6 passim, 161, 176, 177, 189, 190, 195, 196, 237, 238 *see also* foreign correspondents

Kahan, Louis 43
Karnak temple complex 184
Keeler, Christine 89
Kelly SJ, Fr Michael 301
Kenya 177, 191
Kent, England 168, 172, 320
Kenwood, London 323
Khan, Genghis 27
Khan, Kublai 14, 27
Khmer Rouge 130
Khmer kingdom 130
Khrushchev, Mrs Nikita 92
Kindergarten of the Air (radio program) 18
King, Brian 102
King, Harold 264
King's Hussars 172
Kingsley, Ian 152
Kingston Beach, Tas. 13, 15, 109, 110, 159, pic
Kissinger, Henry 130, 155
Koch, Philip 129–30
Kompong Speu 132
Korda, Alexanda 260

Kriesler radio 80, 114, 126
Krishnamurti, Jiddu 36
Kuala Lumpur 142, 148
Kuhn, Miss 64
Kuomintang *see* Chinese Nationalist Party
Kupa, Miles 190
Kyoto 221, 224
Kyoto Shimbun 224

Labor Party conference 177
La Grande Bouffe (film) 209
La Trobe University 276
Lachal, John 127, 182
Lacy, Sally 2
Lady Franklin Museum 42
Laing, Marcia (mother-in-law) 237, 265, 292
Lake District, England 86
Lake Nakuru, Kenya 191
Lake Peddar, Tas. 129
Lambert Avenue, Hobart 108–9, 110, 114, 116–7, 124, 130, 206–7, 302, 326
Lamers, Cornelius 212, 213
Last of the Knucklemen, The 290
Latch, Bill 281
Launceston, Tas. 7, 80, 250, 264, 273, 312
Lawrence of Arabia 190
Lawrence, Sister 40–1, 42
Lazy Man in China see Helene Chung
Le Carré, John 148
Lebanon 189
Lee Kwan Yew, Prime Minister 141, 146
Lee Lee Chong 242
Lee, Anne (cousin) 53, 54, 55, 57–8, 61, 69, 273
Lee, Joyce (aunt) 7, 9, 11, 23, 55–7, 59, 273, 303,
Lee, Marie (cousin) 54, 57–8, 61
Lee, Mary (China correspondent) 239–40
Lee, Timothy (uncle by marriage) 53, 54, 57
Letter from America (radio program) 296
Lewis, Jamie 104
Liberal Party 297
Liberty department store, London 297, 310
Libyan Boeing shot down 188
Life (magazine) 89
Lippi, Julian 225
Lipton, Sir Thomas 79–80
Lisbon 208
Literary Society 108
Little Red Book 168

Little Richard 96
Lohrey, Amanda 104
London 4, 123, 164, 165–7, 166–71, 171–180, 181, 182, 186, 187, 283–5, 296–7
Longley, Tas. 70, 73, 82–91, 107, 108, 114–6, 125, 169, 170, 209, 126, 268, , 280, 317, 318
Lowe, Douglas 97
Lowu, Guangdong 154
Lu Jian (pr. Lu Ji-arn) 243–6 passim
Lucy, Sister 35, 67, 68–9, 94, 190
Lui family, Hong Kong (pr. Louey) 158
Lunar New Year *see* Chinese New Year
Luxor 85, 87, 93, 183, 184–7, 268, 316, pic
Lymburner, Francis 43, 56
Lysistrata 105–6, 133, 157

Ma Liangji, Imam 240, pic
Macao 145, 154, 155, 188, 234, 275
Madrid 28
Mafeking, siege of 84
mah-jong 253–4, 257
Mainichi Shimbun 224
Malachy, Sister 3, 39–40, 55
Malays and Malaysia 133, 137, 138, 139, 141, 142
Manchus 251
Mann, Jim 289
Mao Zedong, Chairman (pr. Mao as in now, Dzay-doong) 24, 168, 234, 275, 308
 badges 158
 Great Helmsman statue 238
 meets Nixon 156
 news of death 210
Maoris 87, 321
Marceau, Marcel 76
Marshall, Ric 76
Martin, Alan 213
Martin, John Winton (husband) 1, 4, 31, 59, 100–1, 129–30, 100–1, 108, 113, 119, 130, 205–10, 211, 214, 216, 219, 220, 223, 224, 225, 229, 234–41, 249–59, 262–3, 265, 268–71, 276, 279, 281–8, 289–93, 294–9, 301, 316, 325, 326, 327, 328, 329, 331
McAuley, James 101

McCulloch, Rosamund 43
McKissock, Mal 294
McLeod, Dugald 115
McMinn, John 302
Mecca 145, 327
media ethics 3, 181
Mediterranean Sea 187
Melbourne 79, 103–4, 105, 127–8, 127, 129, 133, 141, 146, 211–27 passim, 263, 279–89, 294–8, 297, 307, 312, 316, 320, 330,
Meltzer, Lynn 224–5
ménage á trois 82, 88
Mentone Grammar, Melbourne 89
Menzies, Prime Minister Robert 92
Merchant of Venice, The 119–20, 313
Mercury 9, 10, 11–12, 77, 84, 92, 104, 105, 107, 120, 121, 249, pics
Mexican 65
Middle East 95, 123, 183, 187, 189, 192, 199–200
Middle Kingdom 31, 217, 219
Midsummer Night's Dream, A 75
MG TF1500 2, 4, 66–73 passim
MiG fighters 188, 238
Millar, John 63–4
Miller, Glenn 22, 93
Ming Dynasty 232, 251
Miro, Joan 19
Mitchell, Claire 76, 77–8, 100, 105
Mohammed 240
Mokhtar, Dr Gamel 193–4, 195–6
Mongolia and Mongolians 14, 27
Mongolian spot on Chinese babies 14
Montagues and Capulets 19, 46, 265, 269
Monty Python's Big Red Book 168
Moore's Variety store, Hobart 62, 212–3
Moorina, Tas. 247, 254, 262
Morton, Andrew 284
Moscow 142, 189
Moses 187
Mount Everest 124
    Faber 138
    Menthosa 142
    Vesuvius 77
    Wellington 82, 109, 115, 125, 126, 203, 300
multiculturalism 2, 133, 197, 216–7

Muslims 183, 327
Mustafa, Awad 188
Mutianyu section of Great Wall pic
Myer, Ken and Yasuko 229, 294

Nagasaki 221, 224
Nagra tape recorder 121, 142, 198
Nairobi 183, 191
Nakasone, Prime Minister Yasuhiro 221
Nanking (Nanjing), Jiangsu 231–3, 234
Nanyang University, Sin. 142
National Gallery Art School, Melbourne. 43
National Geographic (journal) 89
Nationwide (TV program) 213, 217, 222, 224, 225, 270
Nazism 70
NBC (National Broadcasting Company) 280
Nefertiti, Queen 184
Nefetari, Queen 186
Nepalese 152
Nesbit, Tania 225
New Australians 77
New China (Xinhua, pr. Shinhwa) newsagency 228
New Gold Mountain 30, 150, 233, 247, 272, 273, 308
New South Wales (Guangdong's sister state) 104, 231, 234, 150
New Year's Day 5, 148, 191, 208, 315
New Year's Eve 145, 147–8
New York 223
New Zealand and New Zealanders 12, 43, 65, 66, 84, 151, 206, 234, 311, 313
Newman Society 101, 205
news
    high-tech instant 189
    Northcliffe's definition of 181
Newsweek (magazine) 89
NIDA (National Institute of Dramatic Art) 80
Nineteen Eighty-Four 103
Nixon, President Richard 130, 155, 156
No Time to Look Back 225
Nobel Prize for literature 202
Northcliffe, Lord 181
Novello, Ivor 22
Nubians 192, 195
Nunn, Trevor 124

Oberon, Merle 259–62, 330
O'Donohue, Con 288
Odyssey, The 144
Old Nick Company 101–6, 107, 108, 129, 133, 167, 203
Old Vic Theatre 101
Olivier, Sir Laurence 259, 260
Olsen, John 206
Olympic Games 92, 175
Open University 4, 218
opium 6, 27, 162, 247
Opium Wars 149, 239
Orban, Desiderius 43, 84
Oriental Institute of Chicago 87, 183
Origins of Totalitarianism, The 120
Orr, Sydney Sparkes 92
Orwell, George 103
Outlook (radio program) 164
Overseas Chinese 237, 238–40, 241, 251

Packer, Sir Frank 79
Pakistanis 123, 143
Palestinians 189
Palestrina, Giovanni Pierluigi da 301
Pandanus Books 298
Pang Hick Loong 142
Paris 85, 177, 183, 191, 208, 209, 223, 296
Parker Bowles, Camilla 181
Peach, Robert 199
Pearce & Son 47
Pearce Pickering's Ragtime Five 94
Pearl River, Guangdong 233, 235, 236, 273, 276
Pei, I.M. 237
Pekin Gift Store, Hobart 154–5, 265
Peking (Beijing) 2, 27, 97, 154, 155, 161, 210, 226, 230–42 passim, 254, 271, 277, 298, 299, 327, 342,
    Language Institute 226, 227, 228–9
    University 305
Peking Duck *see* food and beverages
Peking Opera 231–2, 254
Penguin Books 18, 298
Penn, Patricia 221
Pennsylvania, University of 183
Pension Newbury House, Cairo 191, 192
Pépin, Jean-Luc 155
Petersen, Neville 182, 190
Petronas Twin Towers 142

Phenomenon of Man, The 107
Philae Island, Egypt 193, 194–5
Philippine band 141
Phnom Penh 130, 131–2, 136, 138, 143
Phua, Willi 240, 293–6 passim
Pickwick Papers, The 77
pig ovens 263
pigtails *see* Chinese queues
ping-pong diplomacy 155–6
Pioneer buses 83, 90
Pix (magazine) 85
Playhouse, Hobart 75, 77, 141
PM (radio program) 198, 202
pogroms 189
Pollock, Jackson 41
Pompeii, Italy 77
Pontville Cemetery 306, 307, 308
Portugal and Portuguese 154, 188, 208, 221
Pos, Margaretta 249
Powers, John 290
Pratt, Bud 289
Presentation Convent 304, 64, 202
Presley, Elvis 43
Press, Mervyn (uncle by marriage) 28–9
Prince (picture theatre) 135
Princess Merle 260
Pringle, Jim 280
prisoners and imprisonment 27, 115, 223
prisoners of war 85, 133, 225
Proctor, Thea 43
Profumo, John 89
Psychology of Sex 107
Punch (magazine) 119, 120
Pybus, Cassandra 261–2
Pyengana, Tas. 263

Qantas 135
Qin, Emperor (pr. Chin) 27
Qing Dynasty (pr. Ching) 343 *see also* Manchus
Quadrant (journal) 89
Queen
    Alexandra Hospital, Hobart 319
    Elizabeth II 32, 33, 77, 102–3, 176, 216
    Victoria Memorial, London 175
    Victoria Museum, Launceston 250, 257–8, 264
Queen's Domain, Hobart 33, 57, 204
Queensland 108, 295
Queenstown, Tas. 265

racism 2, 10, 81, 123, 152–3, 141–2, 214–6, 217
Radio 2UE 66
    3AW 66, 212, 314
    7H0 80
    7HT 66, 78, 90
    Australia 80, 124, 128, 133, 143, 167, 176, 214, 217, 222, 282, 297–8
    Hong Kong 135, 136, 151–3, 155, 156, 162–78 passim, 180, 236
    Television Singapore 142
Raffaele, Paul 197–8
raj, the 152
Ramadan 240
Ramses II, King 186
Randall, Kenneth 155
Ransom, David 255
Red Bandits 198
Red China 155, 188, 275
Red Flag 24
Redemptorist monastery 55, 58
Rediffusion TV channel 142
refugees 123, 143, 154, 275
Regent Street, London 284, 297
René Henri salon 47
Republican Revolution 251
Reuters newsagency 126, 143, 182, 190, 191
Rice Burroughs, Edgar 203
Rice-Davies, Mandy 89
Richardson's building, Hobart 50, 51
Richmond, Oliffe 42
rickshaws 146, 149, 235–6
Rigg, Diana 171
Rimmer, Gordon 113, 119
Ripponlea, Melbourne 211, 221, 270
Risdon Cove, Tas. 118
Risdon Gaol 115
Rita, Sister 2, 74
Rite of Spring 128
Riviera, the 177
River Derwent, Hobart 33, 58, 93, 109, 203, 288
River Nile, Egypt 93, 184, 185, 190, 194–5, 196
Roe, Michael 119
Rogers, Father Bernard 59–60
romantic poets 86
Romberg, Frederick 211
Rome 80, 132, 183
Rooke, Warren 151
Ross Bridge and the Sculpture of Daniel Herbert 201

Royal
    Academy of Arts 219, 220
    Hobart Hospital 72, 301
    Hobart Show 70
    Hong Kong Yacht Club 148
    Melbourne Institute of Technology 275
    Shakespeare Company 124
    Welsh Fusiliers 160
RSL (Returned Services League) 106, 217
Russia 12, 189, 282
Rudd, Prime Minister Kevin ix
Ruxton, Bruce 217
Ryan, Damien 214, 222, 224, 225

Sadat, President Anwar 189
Saigon 131, 133, 134, 138, 143, 280
Saint-Saëns, Camille 57
Salamanca Place, Hobart 58
Sales, Julie 2, 75
Sahm, Bernard 43
San Francisco 150, 284
San Tropez 323
Sanders, Norman 105, 203–4
Sandhurst Royal Military Academy 84
Sansom, Clive 201–2
Santa Barbara oil spill 203
Santa Claus 29, 34
Santa Maria (school magazine) 1, 26, 75
Sartre, Jean-Paul 36
Saturday Evening Mercury 105, 106, 107
Saturday Evening Post 19
Save the Children Fund 172
Savio College, Hobart 87
SBS (Special Broadcasting Service) 216–7, 289
Scales, Prunella 104
Schubert, Franz 18
Scott, Peter 111
Scottsdale, Tas. 250
Selby, Harry 260
Sendai, Japan 221, 225
Seven Mile Beach, Tas. 15
Seven Wonders of the World 27
Sewell, Bill 43
Sexton, John 168
Shakespeare, Nicholas 261–2
Shakespeare, William 19, 75, 101, 119–20, 124
Shamian Island, Canton 233
Shanghai 232, 233, 298–99, 307
Shaw Brothers films 162
Shaw Neilson, John 77

Shaw, George Bernard 77
Shelley, Percy Bysshe 185
Shenzhen, Guangdong 236
Shouting from China see Helene Chung
Sikhs 137
Simonds, Archbishop Justin 9
Simpson department store, London 171
Singapore 85, 121, 126–45 passim, 146, 150, 162, 183, 192, 217
Sin-Til-Eight (uni. revue) 101–2
Sitmar Line 135
Six-Day War 187
Sleeping Fire, The 77
Smart, Jeffrey 37
Smith, Vivian 102
Snow, Brigid 147
Snugglepot and Cuddlepie 18
Social Welfare Department 319
Society of Realist Artists 43
Sony audio equipment 126, 176
Sorbonne 149, 208
South Australia 124
South China Morning Post 148, 180, 235
South China Sea 144, 148, 245, 246
South Vietnam 133
South Vietnamese 130, 131, 133
Southampton 135
Spain 168, 208, 209
Spanish Civil War 167
Speed, Clive 202
St Catherine 39
St Cecilia 39
St Columba's School, Hobart 10
St David's Day ball 160
St David's Park, Hobart 125, 280
St Helen's Hospital, Hobart 72
St Helens, Tas. 260
  History Room 43, 248–9, 263
St John's Church, Richmond, Tas. 315, 328
St Joseph's Orphanage, Hobart 21
St Joseph's Church, Hobart 21, 301
St Mary's Cathedral, Hobart 20, 300, 301, 302–3, 304–6
St Mary's College, Hobart 1–4, 26, 39–44, 52, 59–69, 74–82, 92–4, 100–1, 103–4, 201, 303, 318

St Paul's Church, Macao 154
St Peter's Hall, Hobart 78, 94
St Stephen's Hospital, Hobart 13
St Virgil's College, Hobart 12, 37, 94, 167, 207
stage and theatre 3, 70–1, 75–81, 101–6, 107, 108, 122, 129, 133, 161–2, 166, 167
Stanfield, Ann 4
Stanfield, Robert 155
Star of the Sea College, Melbourne 173
Stary, Frank 108
Stevenson, Robert Louis 314
Stewart, Douglas 78
Stoner, Dorothy 43
Stork Club 93, 94
Straits Times 138
Strand (picture theatre) 57
Strange Case of Dr Jekyll and Mr Hyde, The 78, 314
Strine 77
Stuck for Words: What to say to someone who is Grieving 295
Students' World 111–3, 114
Sudan 189
Suez Canal 92, 187, 189
Sukarno, President Achmed 133
Sun Yat-sen 251
Sun 103–4, 216
Sunday Tasmanian 247
Sunwei County (pr. Sunhway) 273, 274, 275, 276–7
  Chung city home 273, 276–7
  Chung village home 273
  Chung photographs 273–4
Sutton, Rory 203, 204, 205
Sydney 7, 43, 197, 198, 199
  University of 106
Sydney Morning Herald 198
Syria 189

TAA (Trans Australia Airlines) 137, 210
Taipei 101, 142, 156
Taishan County (pr. Tye-shun) *see* Toishan
Taiwan 150, 226, 228, 238
  Strait 238
Taj Mahal 328
Talking Point (radio program) 128
Tame, Adrian 215
Tanzania and Tanzanians 167, 234
Tarzan and Jane 203–4
Tasman Bridge 202

Tasmania (Fujian's sister state) 77, 103, 169,
  State Library of 78, 90, 104, 108
  Tasmania House, London 167
  University of 92, 100–1, 103, 109, 118–9, 120, 185, 205
Tasmanian
  College of Advanced Education 205, 276
  Government Film Unit 125, 280
  National Parks and Wildlife Service 210
  Tasmanian devil 25, 28, 31, 118
  Tasmanian tiger 118, 121, 122, 198, 208, 298
Taylor, Brian 202, 203
Taylor, Sister 13
Tchaikovsky, Piotr Ilyich 107
Tea for a Stranger 201
television 66, 92, 189, 216–7, 220
Tell Me I'm Here 79
Terai, Jesuke 225–6
Texas and Texans 234, 286
Thailand 281, 283
Theatre Royal, Hobart 70, 75, 76, 102, 141
Thebes, Egypt 183, 184
Thiessen, Jeremy 94–5
This Day Tonight (TV program) 201, 202, 203, 204, 210, 211, 213, 215, 267, 270
Thomas, Dylan 78, 177
Three Unities District (San Fou) 256
Thwaites, Richard 227, 230
Tiananmen massacre 150–1
Tiananmen Square 221, 236
Tibet and Tibetans 329
Till Apples Grow on an Orange Tree 261
Time (magazine) 89, 280
Times 180, 182, 239, 321
tin fields 10, 242, 247–64, 268
Togatus (uni. newspaper) 105, 106
Toishan County (pr. Toy-shun; Taishan) 7, 8, 16, 24, 25, 26, 233, 235, 241–6, 248, 271, 274–58, 262–4, 277, 303
Tokyo 219, 224
Toorak Professional Development Centre 282
Toorak Village, Melbourne 237

Tora Tora Tora (film) 162
Torquay, England 321
tourism 83, 140, 145, 175, 185, 224, 238–9, 247
Träumerei (Robert Schumann) 32
Trigon, The 104
Tristan and Isolde 107
Trouble with Merle, The (film) 260
Truth 15, 214–6
Tull, Jethro 182
Tulloh, John 147
Tutankhamen, King 184, 186
Tuthmosis III, King 185

Uher tape recorder 142, 166, 167, 171, 176, 178
United Nations 187, 193, 194–5, 196
United Arab Airlines 183
United Kingdom 127
United States of America 62, 123, 187, 203, 239, 245, 258, 283
   and China (PRC) 155, 156, 283
   and Indo-China War 129, 130
   Information Agency 282

Valley of the Kings, Egypt 93, 185–6
Valley of the Queens, Egypt 186–7
Van Diemen's Land 201, 209
Vandenbeld, John 213
Vanity Fair 174
Varanasi (Benares), India 327–8
Vatican II 3
Venice 119
Vermey, Bill 135
Vernon's delicatessen 35
Victoria (Jiangsu's sister state) 119, 150, 231, 242, 282
   State Library of 120, 223
Victoria Memorial, Calcutta 326
Victorian Artists' Society 43
Victorian Education Department/Ministry of Education 223, 234

Vietnam War 129, 130–2, 133, 136, 143, 159, 280
Vietnamese 103, 219–20
Visnews (TV news service) 126, 143, 147
Vote No (uni. revue) 102

Wagner, Richard 107
Wags (comic) 25
Waiting for Godot 104–5, 203
Wailing Wall 221
Walden, Michael (de facto step-brother) 89, 105
Walden, Peter (de facto step-brother) 89, 105, 212–4
Walden, Rex (de facto step-father) 66, 67, 68, 79–81, 82, 87–8, 89, 90, 91, 92, 105, 107–8, 125, 268, 311–4
Wales, UK 177
Walker, Stephen 45
Walt Disney comics 33, 46
Walters, Gordon 35, 43
Wandsworth, London 165, 167
Wang, Mabel 11
Warner, Russell 199, 200, 201
Warrane, Hobart 111–2
Warwick, University of 173
Washington 133, 223
Watchorn, Geoffrey 169–70, 182
Waterloo (film) 162
Waterworth, David 102
Watkins, Paul 292
Watts, Granville 182, 190
Weldborough, Tas. 6–7, 248–9, 250–62, 264, 265, 270, pics
Wellington, New Zealand 313
Wells, Tony 221
West Indians 123
Western Australia 242
White Australia policy 6
White, Derek 213–6, 217
White, John 105, 165
White, Patrick 202
White, Paul 166–7
Whitlam, Prime Minister Gough 155–6, 197, 198, 201, 226
Wilde, Oscar 119, 120
William the Conqueror 77

Willman, Diane 221
Willmore, Bertram 165, 167, 170
Wilson, David 121, 122
Wilson, Prime Minister Harold 177
Wing Dan family, Melbourne 11
Wing On & Co. department store, Hong Kong, Shanghai 307
Winter, Arthur 121, 201
Winter's Tale, A 124
Woman's Session (radio program) 143
Women's liberation 172–3, 178, 179–80
Women's Electoral Lobby 197
Woolfrey, Josephine 224–5
World this Weekend, The (radio program) 180
World War I 17
World War II 1, 12, 14, 85, 225, 312
Wran, Premier Neville 234
Wuthering Heights 259, 287

Xiamen (pr. Sheea-men) *see* Amoy
Xian (pr. Shee-arn), Shaanxi 240–1
Xinhui County (pr. Shin-hway) *see* Sunwei

YMCA International House, Hong Kong 147, 151
yoga 174, 177, 178, 179, 180, 221, 323, 326
Yom Kippur War 189
Yomiuri Shimbun 224
Youth Speaks for Tasmania 79–80
yum cha see food and beverages dim sum

Zadanski, Doris 295
Zhang Yi, Deputy Governor 238
Zhou Enlai, Prime Minister 155
Zhuhai (pr. Jew-hi), Guangdong 236